Recreation and Risk

Recreation and Risk

William Gordon Childs
Adjunct Professor of Law
Western New England University School of Law &
Mitchell Hamline School of Law

CAROLINA ACADEMIC PRESS
Durham, North Carolina

Library of Congress Cataloging-in-Publication Data

Names: Childs, William G., author.
Title: Recreation and risk / William Gordon Childs.
Description: Durham, North Carolina : Carolina Academic Press, 2024. | Includes bibliographical references and index.
Identifiers: LCCN 2024006549 | ISBN 9781531026325 (paperback) | ISBN 9781531026332 (ebook)
Subjects: LCSH: Recreation areas—Law and legislation—United States. | Recreation—Law and legislation—United States. | Parks—Law and legislation—United States. | Respondeat superior—United States. | Risk management—Law and legislation—United States. | Exemplary damages—United States.
Classification: LCC KF5638 .C45 2024 | DDC 344.73/099—dc23/eng/20240214
LC record available at https://lccn.loc.gov/2024006549

Carolina Academic Press
700 Kent Street
Durham, North Carolina 27701
(919) 489-7486
www.cap-press.com
Printed in the United States of America

Contents

Table of Principal Cases

Author's Note

> "Do you know what that means, to be in the amusement business?"
>
> "No, sir, not exactly."
>
> His eyes were solemn, but there was a ghost of a grin on his mouth. "It means the rubes have to leave with smiles on their faces.... [T]he place turns 'em into rubes with their mouths hung open. If it doesn't, it's not doing its job.... [They] have to leave happy, or this place dries up and blows away. I've seen it happen, and when it does, it happens fast."
>
> Stephen King, *Joyland* (2013)

Most rides and attractions are designed to make you feel like you're in danger—that's why you get that adrenaline rush—without, you usually assume, actually endangering you. Get on a roller coaster, go into a haunted house, or board a drop ride: Do any of these, and you probably expect to get through the experience with a thrill and nothing else more unpleasant than maybe a bump or a mild bruise.

ATTENTION

NO INSURANCE

RIDE AT YOUR OWN RISK

A sign with this text hung for years at the coasters at Mount Olympus at Wisconsin Dells.

This book is about the case law, statutory provisions, and regulatory structures related to that core idea and what happens when those expectations are not met in various recreational contexts.

Amusement parks and carnivals, which are central to the book, sit at intersections that make them particularly interesting legally. Fixed-site parks' rides aren't regulated by the federal government, leaving them to a patchwork of state regulations; carnivals are—kind of—federally regulated, but also fall under some state rules. Questions of assumption of risk and comparative fault are complicated when the idea of the attraction is to make you feel simultaneously in danger but also in a bubble of assumed safety. The contractual questions raised by waivers purporting to limit liability are complex. And so on.

This book grew out of a course I created. That course was originally framed by New Jersey's Action Park, and Action Park will appear throughout the book. Action Park upended or defied most of the assumptions about amusement parks. It generated thousands of stories (many of them true), countless injuries, a number of deaths—and at least 100 lawsuits. At its peak in the 1980s and 1990s, it was wildly popular with kids on the East Coast for many of the reasons it was also far more dangerous than more conventional parks—the guests had a great deal of control over their experiences, and, thus, their risks. The risks that were illusions in most other places were, at Action Park, the genuinely dangerous, and, by most accounts, very fun, reality.

My premise is that we can sometimes learn the most about the development of various areas of law by exploring situations in which someone pushes those areas' boundaries. Accordingly, the book spends a lot of time on tort law, but also touches on administrative law, criminal law, the interplay of federal and state law and regulations, and insurance law.

The goal here is for you to better understand the various ways that tort and other doctrinal law evaluates (and affects?) the conduct of actors—both plaintiffs and defendants—and to be better prepared to make arguments related to such topics, recognizing that conduct often falls within more than one doctrinal approach.

Given the topic, the book includes some upsetting fact patterns. They are included not for shock value, but because they represent an opportunity to explore important issues. Keep in mind—as I do—that these are real people and real injuries with real consequences. That said, I hope you find the course as much fun to take as I have found it to teach. I *love* amusement parks (my roller coaster count is around 200) and I *love* thinking about these issues.

In focusing primarily on one broadly defined industry rather than a doctrinal area, this book is unusual. In doing so, it seeks to help you think about the range of legal issues that affect people and businesses. In practice, lawsuits don't come in your door labeled with just one doctrine ("Hello, my name is Products Liability—Warnings Defect"), and so we're spending a course thinking about an area of life rather than an area of law. Whether you're advising or defending a business or suing it, it's necessary to recognize those cross-doctrine questions. (It also, I understand from students, is a pretty good way to review material you've heard before.)

Notwithstanding the somewhat uncommon subject matter, the book is broadly conventional in structure. However, because of the range of issues addressed, the chapters necessarily often touch on more than one topic, notwithstanding their relatively narrow titles—so a chapter about waivers of negligence claims might meander into intentional tort stuff for a while. I have attempted to keep the notes focused and less voluminous than in some books. I've also included a chapter with extensive (largely primary) materials from one (real and tragic) incident from the fall of 2021, to provide the opportunity for you to do an in-depth case study.

More than many other books you've used, you'll see a lot of primary source materials (like investigation reports) and pleadings (as opposed to opinions). In the same way cases don't come in the door labeled with a doctrine, they also don't come in with all of the issues identified, and a lot of being a litigator in particular involves getting good at analyzing things like investigation reports. You'll get some practice doing so.

Some of the book will feel like a refresher from other classes you've taken. From time to time, it may feel like it's at odds with some of those classes. As you have no doubt already figured out, there's more than one way to approach some key issues in the law, and certain subjects here are, I think, easier to understand with a particular approach. For example, I think primary assumption of risk is best thought of as a no-duty rule (as opposed to the more mundane defense some treat it as). Each approach has support in various cases and I won't fuss about which approach is "right"—but for our purposes, the no-duty rule makes the most sense. Because not every Torts professor uses that approach, the book takes a bit of time to establish it.

Thank yous, academic division: Professor Erin Buzuvis (for taking my idle "I could make this a class" as an offer to create and teach it at Western New England University School of Law); my former colleague Eric Gouvin (also at Western New England) for always being interested in what I'm up to; all the nice folks at Mitchell Hamline School of Law for making me feel welcome as an adjunct; South Carolina's Professor emeritus David Owen (for pointing out that this would make a good book); Professor David Anderson and the late Professor David Robertson, both of the University of Texas School of Law (for helping me as a baby professor and for co-authoring my favorite Torts casebook). I am also grateful to Christopher Churilla and Greg Van Gompel from the National Amusement Park Historical Association for their patience as we scrolled through hundreds of wonderful amusement park photos for the cover. On that note, I should add that the pictured coaster, the Lakeside Cyclone, has not had any significant accidents of which I am aware, and is on the cover because it's beautiful, not because it's risky. Thanks also to Ana Marie Cox for her assistance in the editing process and helpful comments on the text. Thanks to all the great folks who have visited my class, sharing their wisdom and ideas, including Prof. Serena King; Judge Colette Routel; Zamperla Rides' Adam Sandy; Ride Training International's Erik Beard; Prof. Kathryn Woodcock; author Andy Mulvihill; activist Kathy Fackler; and attorney Elijah Watkins. And thanks, as always, to my students (especially Maggie Solis and Jasmine Campbell), both recent and in the distant past, for enjoying, or at least putting up with, my ramblings about this stuff, and for asking great questions.

Thank yous, personal division: My family—my wife Dena and our kids, Joss and Liam—for riding the rides with me and putting up with my ramblings about this stuff. Joss, despite being a scholar of early Christianity, is also obsessed with the National Transportation Safety Board Go Team and loves lengthy conversations about the appropriate model for regulations and investigations. Liam goes to enough hardcore shows that he can get me up to date on the unwritten rules of the mosh pit, since I'm a few years out from my time up front at shows. Thanks also to my mom and late dad—Holly and Ves—for encouraging deep dives into obscure topics, even if they never really liked riding the rides, as far as I know.

Thank yous, other division: Andy Mulvhill, co-author of a book about his dad's Action Park, and Seth Porges, director of the documentary film about the same place. Both sources were useful and both people generous with their time, and both kindly visited my class multiple times.

Dedication: To the memory of Mount Holyoke College Professor Jon Western, who kept gently nudging me back towards teaching.

As I reference from time to time in the book, many materials related to this subject are available at RecreationAndRisk.com. I will try to post there from time to time as events warrant.

I hope you enjoy the book, and the course. Get in touch with any ideas. One of the weird delights of my specialty is former students reaching out every time something goes awry in an amusement park, and I'd be glad to add readers of this book to that list of correspondents. If you find yourself in Minnesota, get in touch and we'll go ride some rides at Valleyfair or, if the time is right, the greatest state fair in the country.

Bill Childs
Saint Paul, Minnesota
bill.childs@me.com
(he/him/his)

P.S. I should note that none of this is legal advice and none of this is necessarily representative of the view of any of my various employers.

Acknowledgments

Excerpts from ACTION PARK: FAST TIMES, WILD RIDES, AND THE UNTOLD STORY OF AMERICA'S MOST DANGEROUS AMUSEMENT PARK by Andy Mulvihill with Jake Rossen, copyright © 2020 by Andrew J. Mulvihill. Used by permission of Penguin Books, an imprint of Penguin Publishing Group, a division of Penguin Random House LLC. All rights reserved. Cover photo courtesy of the National Amusement Park Historical Association Archives, John M. Caruthers Collection.

Recreation and Risk

CHAPTER 1

Introduction

The traditional approach to the Introduction for a doctrinal casebook would be to provide an overview of what's to come—the history of the doctrine, some basic language, and the policies being pursued. Since this casebook is about amusing people as a business, the materials in this chapter introduce some of the issues that attach to that business, including the psychology of people encountering recreational activities, assumption of risk, design defect claims, and claims that amusement operators have put profits over safety.

We start, as all good conversations about amusements do (or at least should), at Coney Island in Brooklyn, New York.

> "A ride on [the Coney Island] Cyclone is a greater thrill than flying across the Atlantic at top speed."
>
> —Charles Lindbergh, supposedly

> "Bump, bump, bump your ass off."
>
> —Coney Island's El Dorado Bumper Cars
> (open as of this writing, home of, so far as I know,
> the greatest bumper cars in the world)

Murphy v. Steeplechase Amusement Co.

Jury instructions, given by Judge John M. Tierney
Quoted in Rabin & Sugarman, *Torts Stories*
(Foundation Press 2003) 179

This young lad, with his sweetheart and some friends ... came down to this park that night to be amused ... providing as it does, all kinds of entertainment, liquid, solid, things that make life more enjoyable, especially to those whose conditions of life were like this lad's was. He was a truck driver—he probably could not come to the Ritz-Carlton to a dance or anything of that kind, but he could go to Coney Island if he wanted to, and dance or do whatever else attracted him in the way of pleasure, and he could give the girl who was then his sweetheart, and now his wife, such delights as she could find in his companionship.... [H]e finally landed upon this moving plane preceded by his friends, including his sweetheart, and when he got on there, he says a sudden jerk occurred and they were all thrown down, he striking his knee and getting this injury.

After a jury verdict for the plaintiff awarding damages, the defendant appealed. The intermediate appellate court affirmed, and the case then landed with the Court of Appeals of New York and Chief Justice Cardozo.

Murphy v. Steeplechase Amusement Co.

250 N.Y. 479, 166 N.E. 173 (N.Y. 1929)

Cardozo, Ch. J.

The defendant, Steeplechase Amusement Company, maintains an amusement park at Coney Island, New York.

One of the supposed attractions is known as "The Flopper." It is a moving belt, running upward on an inclined plane, on which passengers sit or stand. Many of them are unable to keep their feet because of the movement of the belt, and are thrown backward or aside. The belt runs in a groove, with padded walls on either side to a height of four feet, and with padded flooring beyond the walls at the same angle as the belt. An electric motor, driven by current furnished by the Brooklyn Edison Company, supplies the needed power.

Plaintiff, a vigorous young man, visited the park with friends. One of them, a young woman, now his wife, stepped upon the moving belt. Plaintiff followed and stepped behind her. As he did so, he felt what he describes as a sudden jerk, and was thrown to the floor. His wife in front and also friends behind him were thrown at the same time. Something more was here, as every one understood, than the slowly-moving escalator that is common in shops and public places. A fall was foreseen as one of the risks of the adventure. There would have been no point to the whole thing, no adventure about it, if the risk had not been there. The very name above the gate, the Flopper, was warning to the timid. If the name was not enough, there was warning more distinct in the experience of others. We are told by the plaintiff's wife that the members of her party stood looking at the sport before joining in it themselves. Some aboard the belt were able, as she viewed them, to sit down with decorum or even to stand and keep their footing; others jumped or fell. The tumbling bodies and the screams and laughter supplied the merriment and fun. "I took a chance," she said when asked whether she thought that a fall might be expected.

Plaintiff took the chance with her, but, less lucky than his companions, suffered a fracture of a knee cap. He states in his complaint that the belt was dangerous to life and limb in that it stopped and started violently and suddenly and was not properly equipped to prevent injuries to persons who were using it without knowledge of its dangers, and in a bill of particulars he adds that it was operated at a fast and dangerous rate of speed and was not supplied with a proper railing, guard or other device to prevent a fall therefrom. No other negligence is charged.

We see no adequate basis for a finding that the belt was out of order. It was already in motion when the plaintiff put his foot on it. He cannot help himself to a verdict in such circumstances by the addition of the facile comment that it threw him with a jerk. One who steps upon a moving belt and finds his heels above his head is in no position to discriminate with nicety between the successive stages of the shock, between the jerk which is a cause and the jerk, accompanying the fall, as an instantaneous effect. There is evidence for the defendant that power was transmitted smoothly, and could not be transmitted otherwise. If the movement was spasmodic, it was an unexplained and, it seems, an inexplicable departure from the normal workings of the mechanism. An aberration so extraordinary, if it is to lay the basis for a verdict, should rest on something firmer than a mere descriptive epithet, a summary of the sensations of a tense and crowded moment (*Matter of Case*, 214 N.Y. 199; *Dochtermann v. Brooklyn Heights R.R. Co.*, 32 App. Div. 13, 15; 164 N.Y. 586; *Foley v. Boston Maine R.R. Co.*, 193 Mass. 332, 335; *Work v. Boston El. Ry. Co.*, 207 Mass. 447, 448; *N. W. Ry. Co. v. Birchett*, 252 Fed. Rep. 512, 515). But the jerk, if it were established, would add little to the case. Whether the movement of the belt was uniform or irregular, the risk at greatest was a fall. This was the very hazard that was invited and foreseen (*Lumsden v. Thompson Scenic Ry. Co.*, 130 App. Div. 209, 212, 213).

Volenti non fit injuria. One who takes part in such a sport accepts the dangers that inhere in it so far as they are obvious and necessary, just as a fencer accepts the risk of a thrust by his antagonist or a spectator at a ball game the chance of contact with the ball (Pollock, Torts [11th ed.], p. 171; *Lumsden v. Thompson Scenic Ry. Co., supra; Godfrey v. Conn. Co.*, 98 Conn. 63; *Johnson v. City of N.Y.*, 186 N.Y. 139, 148; *McFarlane v. City of Niagara Falls*, 247 N.Y. 340, 349; cf. 1 Beven, Negligence, 787; Bohlen, Studies in the Law of Torts, p. 443). The antics of the clown are not the paces of the cloistered cleric. The rough and boisterous joke, the horseplay of the crowd, evokes its own guffaws, but they are not the pleasures of tranquillity. The plaintiff was not seeking a retreat for meditation. Visitors were tumbling about the belt to the merriment of onlookers when he made his choice to join them. He took the chance of a like fate, with whatever damage to his body might ensue from such a fall. The timorous may stay at home.

A different case would be here if the dangers inherent in the sport were obscure or unobserved (*Godfrey v. Conn. Co., supra; Tantillo v. Goldstein Bros. Amusement Co.*, 248 N.Y. 286), or so serious as to justify the belief that precautions of some kind must have been taken to avert them (cf. *O'Callaghan v. Dellwood Park Co.*, 242 Ill. 336). Nothing happened to the plaintiff except what common experience tells us may happen at any time as the consequence of a sudden fall. Many a skater or a horseman can rehearse a tale of equal woe. A different case there would also be if the accidents had been so many as to show that the game in its inherent nature was too dangerous to be continued without change. The president of the amusement company says that there had never been such an accident before. A nurse employed at an emergency hospital maintained in connection with the park contradicts him to some extent. She says that on other occasions she had attended patrons of the park who had been injured at the Flopper, how many she could not say. None, however, had been badly injured or had suffered broken bones. Such testimony is not enough to show that the game was a trap for the unwary, too perilous to be endured. According to the defendant's estimate, two hundred and fifty thousand visitors were at the Flopper in a year. Some quota of accidents was to be looked for in so great a mass. One might as well say that a skating rink should be abandoned because skaters sometimes fall.

There is testimony by the plaintiff that he fell upon wood, and not upon a canvas padding. He is strongly contradicted by the photographs and by the witnesses for the defendant, and is without corroboration in the testimony of his companions who were witnesses in his behalf. If his observation was correct, there was a defect in the equipment, and one not obvious or known. The padding should have been kept in repair to break the force of any fall. The case did not go to the jury, however, upon any such theory of the defendant's liability, nor is the defect fairly suggested by the plaintiff's bill of particulars, which limits his complaint. The case went to the jury upon the theory that negligence was dependent upon a sharp and sudden jerk.

The judgment of the Appellate Division and that of the Trial Term should be reversed, and a new trial granted, with costs to abide the event.

NOTES AND QUESTIONS

1. We will return to the doctrine reflected in this famous case in more detail in future chapters. While not always followed, it remains, nearly a century after its writing, foundational to many cases involving amusements and recreational activities. Indeed, you'll see it cited in a very recent case from California addressing the same questions as to bumper cars.
2. What was your reaction to Justice Cardozo's evaluation of the facts involved as evidently found by the jury? Did the appellate court answer legal questions or factual questions—or some combination? What *should* an appellate court be doing with an appeal like this one?
3. In this case's era, Coney Island was less like an amusement park of today and more like a series of funhouses, many of which were designed to end up with patrons bumping ("inadvertently" or not) into

each other. Consider the Human Roulette Wheel, photographed in 1908 in a calmer moment:

As you can probably guess, this ride would spin around, faster and faster, until patrons were flung to the edges. What risks are inherent in this? What risks aren't?

The defense in the *Murphy* case included this next photograph in its case filings (obtained by Professor Kenneth Simons, author of the excellent *Torts Stories* essay excerpted above):

How does this photograph (which, as noted, comes from the court file and is therefore not the greatest quality) compare to what you pictured when reading the case? How do you think this compares to what Mr. Murphy experienced?

4. Cardozo writes: "One might as well say that a skating rink should be abandoned because skaters sometimes fall." His clear assumption is that skating rinks ought not be closed due to the accompanying injuries, at least not due to tort liabilities. Do you agree? Why? What dangers to skaters, if any, should be subject to potential tort liabilities?
5. Is it possible that The Flopper in fact malfunctioned, either jerking more than designed or going faster than designed? If so, would that make a difference to Justice Cardozo? Would it make a difference to you? If the injury that occurred was of the same kind as had been classified as an "inherent risk," should it matter if it occurred in a different way than one would have expected?
6. If a complaint, identical to the one in this case, were filed against a park operating The Flopper today, should a judge grant a motion to dismiss under Rule 12(b)(6)? If the same facts were established during discovery and the facts are established as described, should the judge grant the park's motion for summary judgment under Rule 56? If the matter proceeded to trial and you were on the jury, would you support a finding of liability? If it proceeded to trial and a jury awarded damages, should the judge grant a motion for judgment notwithstanding the verdict? If judgment were entered on a jury's verdict for the plaintiff and an appeal is presented with the same record as in this case, should the jury verdict be reversed?

Let's fast forward seventy years and head southwest to San Antonio. When the Fiesta Texas amusement park (now known, after an acquisition, as Six Flags Fiesta Texas) opened in 1992 in a former quarry, the flagship attraction was a massive wooden roller coaster named The Rattler—with a drop of 166 feet, considerably longer than originally proposed. The prior year, Cedar Point, in Sandusky Ohio, had opened the Mean Streak roller coaster, with a first drop of 155 feet.

Documents produced in later litigation related to injuries on The Rattler noted that the owner of Fiesta Texas was concerned that The Rattler "remain the record holder in all the intended categories, for at least the season it opened: height of drop, steepness of angle, height of structure above the ground, highest continuous wood bent member, and speed."

At that time, amusement parks were particularly focused on records, and it appears that Fiesta Texas wanted to beat Mean Streak's record for the longest first drop on a wooden roller coaster.

John Tedesco,
Heated competition: biggest always best for amusement parks; Experts blame Rattler's bite on rush to be faster

San Antonio Express-News
Dec. 19, 1999

The Rattler's troubled history—a legacy of injuries, lawsuits and bankruptcy—stemmed from problems that afflict the amusement industry today.

In the competitive business of building scary attractions, theme parks sometimes rush to open a new ride and shorten crucial test runs, industry experts say.

Staking a claim to a record, such as the world's tallest wooden coaster, becomes a major selling point for a theme park.

* * *

Documents that emerged from litigation reveal the Rattler underwent design changes to make it the tallest wooden coaster, but a steeper drop had the unintentional effect of making a harsher ride.

For two years after its opening, Fiesta Texas was still adjusting the Rattler's design and brake system, trying to tone it down.

* * *

Gary Thompson, an engineer based in Scottsdale, Ariz., who testified during the Rattler litigation, said some riders couldn't handle the stress of the thrill attraction.

"(Fiesta Texas) wanted the highest, fastest ride," Thompson said. "In doing so, they overstepped the bounds of human tolerance."

Excerpts from Letter from D. H. Morgan Mfg. Inc. to Roller Coaster Corporation of America

March 25, 1992

The decision to increase the height of the lift hill last August in an effort to obtain better 'statistics' than other recently completed rides has adversely affected the overall quality and ride ability. As I understand it, the increased lift height resulted in a tighter radius at the bottom of the first drop and higher velocities, thus increasing the pull out forces from the original design of 3 g's to 5 g's at a 1:38 running time. These forces are probably much higher at 1:35 and well beyond safe limits for the equipment or the guests when times dip below 1:30.

* * *

We agree ... that people can withstand 5 g's in most cases: however, it must be recognized that the possibility of injury, particularly to guests with pre-existing conditions is much higher at 5 g's than at 3 g's. It should also be noted that the 5 g readings were obtained after very little [time running] and are possibly higher at this time.

* * *

NOTES AND QUESTIONS

1. According to the *San Antonio Express-News*, another internal memorandum analyzed over 100 injuries reported on the Rattler. Half occurred during the first drop; about a third reported bloody noses, head wounds, or mouth injuries. Slightly fewer reported neck injuries, and about one in five involved back injuries. Assume these 100 injuries occurred over the course of a five-month season. How concerning are these counts?
2. For the 1994 season, Fiesta Texas shortened the first drop from the original 166 feet to 124 feet. I rode the coaster both before and after the reprofiling, and it was definitely more fun *and* more probably dangerous (in terms of the physical forces) before. The park recently used much of the same structure for a new steel roller coaster, Iron Rattler, which, in my view, is more fun (and less concerningly forceful) than either of the earlier versions.

Richard Stephens, *The Psychology of Roller Coasters*

Scientific American, The Conversation, July 11, 2018
https://theconversation.com/the-psychology-of-roller-coasters-99166

What is it about roller coasters that some love so much, and is it an experience we tend to like less as we get older?

* * *

We know that a roller coaster ride is likely to trigger [the "fight or flight"] response thanks to researchers who measured the heart rates of riders on the double-corkscrew Coca Cola Roller in 1980s Glasgow. Heart beats per minute more than doubled from an average 70 beforehand to 153 shortly after the ride had begun.

* * *

[N]ot all stress is bad. Eustress—from the Greek "eu", meaning good, as in euphoria—is a positive kind of stress that people actively seek out.

We know that a roller coaster ride can be experienced as a "eustressful" experience thanks to an intriguing study carried out by two Dutch psychologists.... [S]ome asthmatic student volunteers were transported to a theme park and rode a roller coaster while their respiratory function was checked. The research findings were remarkable. While lung function predictably reduced from the screaming and general upheaval, so did the feeling of shortness of breath. This suggests that thrill seekers riding roller coasters perceive the experience as stressful in a positive way.

* * *

[E]njoyment of intense physical experiences such as riding on roller coasters may reflect individual differences in brain chemistry. People who have higher levels of dopamine may be more prone to a number of sensation seeking behaviours, ranging from harmless roller coaster rides to taking drugs or even shoplifting.

NOTES AND QUESTIONS

1. Stephens notes elsewhere in this *Scientific American* article that the specific question of whether people lose interest in riding roller coasters as they age has not been directly answered. Research on other thrill-seeking behaviors suggests that it may; he notes, "Perhaps

experiencing one's heart rate spiking dangerously close to medically accepted risk levels is not such a draw for the over 50s." As we will see, warning signs for amusement rides routinely advise those with heart conditions not to ride; ponder whether, in litigation, the risks (assumed or otherwise) to "over 50s" should be treated any differently from the risks to younger riders. Although a small sample size, as I noted in the Author's Note: I still ride coasters (into my 50s); my wife does not.

2. Though this article was about roller coasters, similar considerations likely apply to all of the contexts we'll be addressing in the book—other amusement rides, skiing, water parks, haunted houses, and the like.
3. Is there anything about the psychology of those who might want to ride roller coasters (or engage in other recreational thrill-seeking behavior) that should inform how we think about the law or regulations related to those activities?
4. Throughout the casebook, we'll grapple with a core question: How should we think about risk in contexts where patrons are paying to experience the *perception* (the eustress) of risk but—presumably—do not believe that they are in fact experiencing *actual* risk, at least not as much as their bodies would tell them.

I'd suggest that there are a handful of themes that will come up throughout the casebook, expressly or implicitly. It might help you to think about them some up front:

- **Choice:** You've already seen this when Justice Cardozo famously writes, "The timorous may stay at home." Essentially every event you'll read about in this book is fundamentally voluntary and, in some sense, frivolous. So we aren't talking about risks that are attendant to, say, basic transportation or surgery or the like. One could argue that the inessential nature of the attractions should mean they should have fewer risks—but, likewise, some might say for entirely voluntary (and fun) things, people should get to choose to accept whatever risks they wish.

- **Perceived Risk:** As noted just above, at most parks and similar attractions, the foundation is the *illusion* of risk, with the business model being the creation of eustress. But, to varying degrees, those perceived risks do come with some (usually fewer and less extreme) risks. The disjunction between those—and what happens when the risks are greater than a patron might expect—will be a recurring theme.
- **The "Bubble" Effect:** I am not sure this is the best term, but I haven't come up with a better one yet. Judging from some patrons' conduct, at least sometimes, people recognize that mostly the risks are illusions, and from that basis, conclude, wrongly, that they are protected from harm more generally, and can behave in ways that exacerbate risk because of this illusory bubble of protection. Put in more legal terms, it is at least plausible that for some patrons, the breadth of "misuse" is enormous indeed. If that's the case, what might it mean for the obligation of operators, ride owners, and the like?
- **Regulatory Scope:** As alluded to in the Author's Note, the extent of regulation of all of these attractions varies considerably. The main example we'll talk about is rides, where fixed-site parks are mostly regulated, if at all, by state or local authorities, while traveling carnivals also have some degree of federal oversight.
- **Employee Responsibility:** The question of employees' duties is not unique to this area, of course, but given the young and seasonal nature of the employees, and the extent of forces that are sometimes at play, the questions can be more complicated here than in some settings.
- **Societal Changes:** The casebook doesn't touch on this as explicitly as some other subjects, but I hope you'll think about and discuss it some. When I talk to my friends and colleagues about this course (and especially about Action Park, described briefly in the Author's Note and which will return in subsequent chapters), those who are around my age (that is, Generation X) are much less shocked by what I tell them about the risks and freedoms that kids encountered/enjoyed in the 1980s, while younger people are often shocked.

I will not be that guy who talks nostalgically about kids riding around without bike helmets and playing with knives or whatever, because that really did often end up with concussions and puncture wounds. At the same time, when we get to the point (in Chapter 10 on Insurance) where we'll discuss City Museum in St. Louis, Missouri, you'll see that, as a parent, I've probably been less risk-averse in terms of our kids' experiences. How all of that plays out in the law is a different and as yet unanswered question. But there are certainly some attractions (Action Park among them) that couldn't exist today.

CHAPTER 2

Tort Law & Background Literature

You have presumably taken Torts, but it may have been a while. And, as you no doubt have figured out, different states, courts, professors, and, yes, casebook authors have different ways of thinking about and framing various issues and elements of claims and defenses.

This chapter is designed in part to establish some basics about how this casebook approaches torts, both intentional and negligence, as well as to provide a brief look at some of the psychology of evaluating risk, especially among adolescents and young adults, that being the core audience of most businesses we're discussing.

We start in a haunted house, in a case we will return to in considerably more detail in Chapter 12.

Molenda v. Universal City Studios LLC

Case No. 2:20-cv-02554
(C.D. Cal. June 8, 2020)

The Honorable R. GARY KLAUSNER, United States District Judge

Plaintiffs Melinda Molenda, Lisa Molenda, and Josiah Steele (collectively, "Plaintiffs") filed a Complaint in state court against Defendants Universal City Studios LLC and Universal Studios Hollywood (collectively, "Defendants" or "Universal"). [The Complaint includes allegations of assault and battery, among other things. This motion to dismiss followed removal to federal court.]

* * *

II. FACTUAL BACKGROUND

Plaintiffs' Complaint alleges the following:

Plaintiffs were actors at the Universal Studios Hollywood theme park who played zombies in a haunted house-like maze attraction based on the hit show The Walking Dead. While they were in character in the maze, Plaintiffs were physically assaulted and sexually harassed by park guests. For example, Plaintiff Melinda Molenda ("Plaintiff Melinda") was groped several times during her employment. On one occasion, a guest spat in her eye. Plaintiff Lisa Molenda was also groped by park guests. On one occasion, a guest threw soda in her eye, causing a severe eye infection. Plaintiff Josiah Steele was punched so hard by a park guest that he went to the hospital.

Plaintiffs reported many incidents of physical assault and sexual harassment to their supervisors. However, little action was taken in response. In fact, Universal contributes to the volatile situation in the maze. Indeed, [per the complaint,] Universal's website promotes the Walking Dead attraction by telling guests to "[p]repare to *fight* for survival in a fully immersive journey ... as you *battle* your way through nightmarish iconic landscapes."

III. JUDICIAL STANDARD

To survive a motion under Rule 12(b)(6), a complaint must contain "sufficient factual matter, accepted as true, to 'state a claim to relief that is plausible on its face.'" *Ashcroft v. Iqbal*, 556 U.S. 662, 678 (2009) (quoting *Bell Atl. Corp. v. Twombly*, 550 U.S. 544, 570 (2007)). A claim is facially plausible if the plaintiff alleges enough facts to permit a reasonable inference that the defendant is liable for the alleged misconduct. *Id.* A plaintiff need not provide "detailed factual allegations" but must provide more than mere legal conclusions. *Twombly*, 550 U.S. at 555. "Threadbare recitals of the elements of a cause of action, supported by mere conclusory statements, do not suffice." *Iqbal*, 556 U.S. at 678.

* * *

IV. DISCUSSION

Defendants move to dismiss Plaintiffs' Complaint in its entirety. The Court first considers Plaintiffs' assault and battery claim....

A. Assault and Battery (Claim 1)

Plaintiffs' first claim is for assault and battery. Defendants argue that this claim must be dismissed because ... Plaintiffs cannot state a claim for assault and battery against Defendants for actions taken by third parties (*i.e.*, park guests).

1. Failure to State a Claim

Plaintiffs purport to state one claim for assault and battery. However, assault and battery are two distinct claims, each of which has its own elements. To state a claim for assault, a plaintiff must allege that: "(1) defendant acted with intent to cause harmful or offensive contact, or threatened to touch plaintiff in a harmful or offensive manner; (2) plaintiff reasonably believed she was about to be touched in a harmful or offensive manner or it reasonably appeared to plaintiff that defendant was about to carry out the threat; (3) plaintiff did not consent to defendant's conduct; (4) plaintiff was harmed; and (5) defendant's conduct was a substantial factor in causing plaintiff's harm." *So v. Shin*, 212 Cal. App. 4th 652, 668–69 (2013), *as modified on denial of reh'g* (Jan. 28, 2013). To state a claim for battery, the plaintiff must allege that: "(1) defendant touched plaintiff, or caused plaintiff to be touched, with the intent to harm or offend plaintiff; (2) plaintiff did not consent to the touching; (3) plaintiff was harmed or offended by defendant's conduct; and (4) a reasonable person in plaintiff's position would have been offended by the touching." *Id.* at 669. Assault and battery are both intentional torts. *Bartosh v. Banning*, 251 Cal. App. 2d 378, 385 (1967).

There are several theories of liability that a plaintiff can pursue when suing for assault and battery. Relevant here, the plaintiff can sue on (1) a direct theory of liability, (2) a *respondeat superior* theory of liability, and (3) an aiding and abetting theory of liability. In this case, Plaintiffs specifically disclaim that they bring their assault and battery claim on a *respondeat superior* theory.... Instead, Plaintiffs aver that they bring this claim on a direct theory and an aiding and abetting theory....

* * *

Here, Defendants argue, among other things, that Plaintiffs have not stated a claim for aiding and abetting assault and battery because they have not satisfied the "knowledge" requirement. The Court agrees. Plaintiffs allege that Universal had "knowledge of many violent assaults[.]" (Compl. ¶ 13.) However, at most, the Complaint plausibly alleges that

Defendants knew about the assaults and batteries upon Plaintiffs *after the fact—i.e.*, after Plaintiffs reported these incidents to their supervisors. The Complaint does not allege enough facts to permit a reasonable inference that Universal knew about these incidents before they took place, let alone that they knew the "specific primary wrong" that they were assisting. The Court therefore dismisses Plaintiffs' assault and battery claim.

NOTES AND QUESTIONS

1. The court, in a separate part of the order, permitted the plaintiffs' claims for sexual harassment and failure to prevent sexual harassment to get past the Rule 12(b)(6) stage, concluding that those claims were not necessarily preempted by the Labor Management Relations Act and that they were adequately pleaded. The complaint alleged that the park's human resources department failed to investigate reports of harassment by guests and that, after reporting an assault, one plaintiff's manager told her that there were things she "could have done to better protect herself."
2. Notice that damages are not an element of either assault or battery ("harm" is required for the latter, but it need not be something as concrete as what is required in a negligence claim). These are "dignity" torts—the invasion of personal dignity is what is being protected, and so, unlike negligence claims, a plaintiff need not show actual damages.
3. We will return to this case in considerably more detail in Chapter 12.

Overall v. Kadella

361 N.W.2d 352 (Mich. Ct. App. 1985)

Per Curiam.

On April 17, 1975, two amateur hockey teams, the Waterford Lakers and the Clarkston Flyers, played each other in a hockey game. After the game had ended, a fight broke out between defendant, who played for the Flyers, and a member of the opposing team. This fight soon became general, with players leaving the benches to join the melee. During the fight, defendant struck plaintiff, knocking him unconscious and fracturing the bones around plaintiff's right eye.

At trial, defendant stated that he had gone to shake hands with the opposing team after the game when he was struck from behind. Both benches cleared and a scuffle ensued, during which defendant stated he saw a hockey stick coming toward his head. Defendant testified that he was hit several times before he turned around and hit the person swinging the stick. He did not know plaintiff had been injured by the blow and, in fact, did not know whom he had struck until much later. Three witnesses testifying on behalf of defendant stated that plaintiff remained on the bench during the fight, but poked or hit defendant with a hockey stick during the fight. They all saw defendant retaliate by turning and throwing one punch.

Plaintiff's testimony and that of two spectators at the game differed from this testimony in significant respects. According to these witnesses, plaintiff remained on the bench even after all other players had joined the fray. The bench was well removed from the fighting and plaintiff did not poke or hit anyone with a hockey stick. Defendant skated over to the bench and struck plaintiff who had done nothing to provoke the attack. Defendant then skated away.

The hockey referees at the game testified that defendant had engaged in at least three separate fights after the game was over. He was given three game misconducts because fighting is against the rules of the Michigan Amateur Hockey Association. These rules are designed to stop violence. The bench is considered part of the playing field. One of the referees saw plaintiff poke defendant with a hockey stick to get defendant's attention and then saw defendant attack plaintiff by striking him.

At the conclusion of the bench trial, the district court found that "without provocation the Defendant in the heat of his battles swung his hockey stick at the Plaintiff who was off the field of play and not engaged in the fight and struck him on the right side resulting in the injuries of which he complained". The court also found that plaintiff had suffered damages of $21,000 for out-of-pocket expenses, pain and suffering, and permanent injury, and awarded an additional $25,000 as exemplary damages because defendant's act had been "intentional and malicious".

* * *

Defendant ... argues both that the trial court did not properly disclose the basis of its findings of fact and that those findings were clearly erroneous....

Defendant objects to three findings.... He first objects to the court's finding that defendant's attack was not provoked by plaintiff. We find that the trial court amply provided this Court with the factual basis for this conclusion and further find that the court's conclusion was not clearly erroneous. The court concluded that plaintiff's witnesses were more credible than defendant's witnesses, including defendant himself, especially in light of the fact that defendant would not have been able to see a hockey stick swung at him while he was "actively engaged in fighting". Defendant next objects to the court's finding that plaintiff was not in the "field of play" when he was struck. As there was no dispute over the "fact" that plaintiff was seated on the bench throughout the brawl, the only dispute was over whether or not the bench was part of the "field of play". We find that the court correctly concluded that the bench is not part of the area in which the game is actually played. Although the referee may still have jurisdiction over the players while they are seated on the bench, this does not convert the bench to part of the playing surface.

Defendant's last objection is to the court's finding that defendant struck plaintiff with a hockey stick. We find, and plaintiff concedes, that this statement is clearly erroneous as there was no evidence that defendant used anything but his fist in striking plaintiff. However, this erroneous finding is harmless as it is clear that the court properly found that a battery was committed.

Defendant's next contention is that plaintiff may not sue for an injury incurred while plaintiff was voluntarily participating in a hockey game. This argument is expressed in the phrase, "*volenti non fit injuria*", or "he who consents cannot receive an injury".

Participation in a game involves a manifestation of consent to those bodily contacts which are permitted by the rules of the game. Restatement of Torts, 2d, § 50, comment b. However, there is general agreement that an intentional act causing injury, which goes beyond what is ordinarily permissible, is an assault and battery for which recovery may be had. 4 Am.Jur.2d, Amusements and Exhibitions, § 86, p. 211.

In *Nabozny v. Barnhill,* 31 Ill.App.3d 212, 334 N.E.2d 258 (1975), a player in an amateur soccer match kicked the opposing goalkeeper in the head while the goalkeeper was in possession of the ball in the penalty area. This act directly violated the safety rules of the game. In deciding whether or not the goalkeeper could bring a tort action against the soccer player, the *Nabozny* Court held that a player is charged with a legal duty to every other player to refrain from conduct proscribed by a safety rule. The Court then rejected the defendant's contention that there should be tort immunity for any injury to another player that occurs during the course of a game:

> This court believes that the law should not place unreasonable burdens on the free and vigorous participation in sports by our youth. However, we also believe that organized, athletic competition does not exist in a vacuum. Rather, some of the restraints of civilization must accompany every athlete onto the playing field. * * *
>
> It is our opinion that a player is liable for injury in a tort action if his conduct is such that it is either deliberate, wilful or with a reckless disregard for the safety of the other player so as to cause injury to that player, the same being a question of fact to be decided by a jury.

334 N.E.2d 260, 261.

Other cases have also held that the violation of safety rules during a game gives rise to tort liability. In *Griggas v. Clauson*, 6 Ill.App.2d 412, 128 N.E.2d 363 (1955), a player who intentionally struck an opposing player during a basketball game was found liable, and, in *Bourque v. Duplechin*, 331 So.2d 40 (La.App., 1976), liability was found where a baserunner in a softball game dove into the second baseman five feet from the base and struck him with his forearm in order to break up a double play. We agree with these Courts that liability may be found on such facts. In this case, defendant's own witness testified that the rule against fighting in hockey is designed to stop violence. Defendant's intentional battery certainly violated this rule. In addition, under the facts found by the trial court, it is arguable that the battery did not even occur during the hockey game. It is therefore doubtful whether consent to a battery during a game would constitute consent to a battery after the game.

* * *

Affirmed.

NOTES AND QUESTIONS

1. The court also rejected a claim of self-defense.
2. Let's again consider the haunted house scenario. If you're advising the management of such a place, and you think the employees are likely to occasionally make some physical contact with a patron (even if it's a haunt where the goal is to avoid such contact), what would you recommend to reduce the likelihood of successful battery claims based on employee conduct? Would signs outside the attraction discussing the "rules of the haunt" help? If so, what should those signs say? In later cases, you'll read about haunted houses that use pre-recorded spiels describing what's to come.
3. In a different haunted house case in Chapter 12, we'll see one court blur the lines between assumption of inherent risks and consent, concluding that a finding of the former can to some extent override the absence of the latter. Here, the court doesn't do so.
4. What are the various interests that the *Overall* court is balancing in drawing the lines around what contact is and isn't consented to? Do you agree with how the court draws those lines? Does this case provide sufficient guidance to people navigating these issues?

Nichols v. Land Transport Corp.

223 F.3d 21 (1st Cir. 2000)

LIPEZ, Circuit Judge.

Robert Nichols brought this diversity action in the district court for the District of Maine to recover for personal injuries he suffered in a "road rage" attack by Oscar Gonzalez, a truck driver employed by Land Transport Corp. The [magistrate judge] granted Land Transport's motion for summary judgment, concluding that under Maine law Gonzalez was not acting within the scope of employment when he attacked Nichols.... We agree with the magistrate judge and affirm the judgment.

On November 11, 1996, Nichols, driving his pickup truck, and Gonzalez, driving a tractor-trailer for Land Transport, were traveling westbound on Route 9 in eastern Maine. Driving recklessly behind Nichols, Gonzalez made multiple attempts to pass Nichols in no-passing zones, nearly causing a collision, and followed Nichols at an unsafe distance.

Nichols responded twice with the predictable obscene gesture. When both drivers stopped at a red light in Brewer, Gonzalez exited his truck, confronted Nichols, and attacked him with a rubber-coated metal cable. In the ensuing struggle, Nichols briefly subdued Gonzalez, but then fell to the ground, and Gonzalez stabbed him in the thigh with a knife. Gonzalez was later convicted of aggravated assault.

Nichols seeks to hold Land Transport vicariously liable for Gonzalez's actions, alleging that Gonzalez was acting within the scope of employment. Maine courts apply the test of Restatement (Second) of Agency § 228 (1958) in determining whether conduct is within the scope of employment.... The Restatement test provides:

> Conduct of a servant is within the scope of employment if, but only if:
>
> (a) it is of the kind he is employed to perform;
>
> (b) it occurs substantially within the authorized time and space limits;
>
> (c) it is actuated, at least in part, by a purpose to serve the master, and
>
> (d) if force is intentionally used by the servant against another, the use of force is not unexpectable by the master.

Restatement (Second) of Agency § 228(1).

We confine our discussion to the third prong of the test because we conclude as a matter of law that Nichols has not satisfied that prong. There is no evidence in the record that Gonzalez was in any way motivated by a purpose to serve Land Transport when he fought and stabbed Nichols. Indeed, Nichols does not seriously contend otherwise. Instead, he argues that "an employer may be held liable for an assault by its employee when the assault arises out of an employment-related dispute and the assault occurs within work-related limits of time and place," regardless of whether the employee had a purpose to serve the employer.

Nichols's argument is plainly incompatible with the Restatement rule. This is obvious enough from the text of § 228. The Restatement commentary is even clearer, stating that a master is not liable

> if the servant has no intent to act on his master's behalf, although the events from which the tortious act follows arise while the servant is acting in the employment and the servant

> becomes angry because of them. The fact that the servant acts in an outrageous manner or inflicts a punishment out of all proportion to the necessities of his master's business is evidence indicating that the servant has departed from the scope of employment in performing the act.

Restatement § 245, comment f.

There is, nevertheless, a split of authority on the issue of whether a purpose to serve the master is a requirement for *respondeat superior* liability. Nichols cites cases from a number of jurisdictions holding that an assault can be within the scope of employment if it arises out of an employment-related dispute, even if in committing the assault the servant lacked a purpose to serve the master.... We, however, are applying Maine law, which follows the Restatement. The cases from other jurisdictions that support Nichols's position represent a rejection, rather than an application, of Restatement § 228(1)(c).

For example, in a case heavily relied on by Nichols, *Weinberg v. Johnson,* 518 A.2d 985 (D.C. 1986), the court purported to apply the Restatement in holding that it was a jury issue whether a laundromat employee acted in the scope of employment in shooting a customer who was leaving the laundromat after an argument with the employee concerning the customer's missing shirts. In reaching this conclusion, the court held that District of Columbia law had so evolved that the requirement of a purpose to serve the master "has become broad enough to embrace an intentional tort arising out of any dispute that was originally undertaken on the employer's behalf." *Id.* at 991 (internal quotation marks omitted)....

* * *

Because Gonzalez's attack on Nichols was not actuated by a purpose to serve Land Transport, it was not within the scope of Gonzalez's employment, and Land Transport may not be held vicariously liable. The magistrate judge did not err in entering summary judgment for Land Transport.

Affirmed.

NOTES AND QUESTIONS

1. The scope of vicarious liability (also called *respondeat superior*) varies, as this opinion notes. The overall trend has been to broaden its reach (generally by relaxing the requirement that the conduct be "actuated by a purpose to serve the master"), but this case is not out of the mainstream.

2. In the Washington, D.C., case cited, it was, we can safely assume, against the employer's wishes and rules that the employee shot a patron. Why not have the job's rules be the boundaries of vicarious liability?

Standard Fruit & Vegetable Co. v. Johnson

985 S.W.2d 62 (Tex. 1998)

PHILLIPS, Chief Justice.

In this case, we again explore the parameters of the tort of intentional infliction of emotional distress. A truck driver drove a tractor-trailer rig into a parade, killing one participant and injuring two others. Another participant, Rueben C. Johnson, was not himself struck, but witnessed the accident. Johnson brought this suit for emotional distress against the truck driver, the driver's employer, and the lessor of the rig (the "Defendants"). The trial court granted summary judgment for all Defendants. The court of appeals reversed, however, holding that Defendants failed to establish as a matter of law that: (1) the truck driver had not intentionally or recklessly inflicted emotional distress on Johnson; and (2) his conduct was not "extreme and outrageous." 984 S.W.2d 633.

We hold that intentional infliction of emotional distress is not available as an independent cause of action unless the actor intends to cause severe emotional distress or severe emotional distress is the primary risk created by the actor's reckless conduct. Johnson does not allege that the truck driver intentionally caused the accident. Instead, he argues that the truck driver recklessly caused his emotional distress. Because the primary risk of reckless driving is physical injury rather than emotional distress, we reverse the judgment of the court of appeals and render judgment that Johnson take nothing....

The march, which Johnson organized to bring attention to issues regarding Vietnam veterans, was about five car-lengths long and included both vehicles and pedestrians. It began in Cleveland, Texas, and proceeded along U.S. Highway 59 to Houston. During the march, Johnson, who has used a wheelchair since losing both legs in a landmine explosion in Vietnam, was positioned immediately behind three flag bearers who led the parade. Johnson in turn was followed by about twenty pedestrians marching two-by-two, a mule-drawn wagon, and two pick-up trucks. A trooper from the Liberty County Sheriff's Department followed the procession, flashing the emergency lights of his squad car.

Shortly after the march began, a tractor-trailer rig driven by James W. Marshall, an employee of Standard Fruit and Vegetable Company, Inc., rear-ended the trooper's vehicle. On impact, Marshall's rig became airborne, landing on the bed of the pick-up truck at the back of the parade. The trooper was killed, while the pick-up driver and her passenger suffered physical injuries. Johnson did not see the initial impact with the trooper's car, but he turned around in time to see the tractor-trailer rig land on the pick-up truck. The tractor-trailer finally stopped about two car lengths from Johnson. When impact occurred, Marshall was traveling 5 to 15 miles per hour above the 55 miles per hour speed limit, and he may have fallen asleep at the wheel.

Although Johnson suffered no physical impact, the accident aggravated a pre-existing post-traumatic stress disorder (PTSD) that arose from his war experiences. Johnson's PTSD symptoms, which first appeared several years after his combat injury, included trembling, twitching, feeling shaky, tense or achy muscles, restlessness, fatigue, shortness of breath with anxiety, heart pounding and racing, frequent sweating, dryness in the mouth, gastro-intestinal distress, hot flashes, frequent urination, a sense of being "keyed up" or "on edge," startle phenomena, difficulty concentrating, marked irritability, and sleep disturbances. Although his condition had gradually improved, the accident aggravated and exacerbated all the symptoms.

Johnson sued the Defendants in Harris County district court, alleging five grounds for recovery: (1) "[n]egligent infliction of physical injury [by mental shock] ... as recognized and defined in *Boyles* [*v. Kerr*, 855 S.W.2d 593 (Tex.1993)];" (2) intentional infliction of emotional distress based on reckless driving; (3) negligent infliction of physical and emotional injuries based on a "special relationship" between the Defendants and the driving public created by state and federal safety regulations; (4) infliction of physical and mental injuries by "egregious conduct"; and (5) "grossly negligent" infliction of mental anguish and physical injuries.

After discovery, Defendants moved for summary judgment on all claims, asserting that Johnson had failed to state a cause of action under Texas law because he sustained no physical injury in the accident, was not a statutory beneficiary under the wrongful death statute, and did not qualify for bystander recovery. Furthermore, Defendants maintained that, as a matter of law, Marshall had not engaged in willful, wanton, or extreme and outrageous conduct, and Defendants had no special relationship with travelers on public highways. Finally, Defendants argued that Johnson's claims for emotional distress based on egregious or grossly negligent conduct were simply not recognized under Texas law. The trial court granted summary judgment on all claims.

Johnson appealed on only two claims, intentional infliction of emotional distress and negligent infliction of emotional distress based on breach of the duty Defendants allegedly owed to highway users under state and federal traffic laws. The court of appeals affirmed summary judgment on Johnson's negligent infliction of emotional distress claim, concluding that traffic laws do not create a "special relationship" giving rise to compensable mental anguish damages. 684 S.W.2d at 635. It reversed summary judgment on the intentional infliction of emotional distress claim, however, holding that Defendants failed to establish as a matter of law that Marshall's conduct was not extreme and outrageous and that Johnson was not a "direct victim" of Marshall's reckless driving. 684 S.W.2d at 638–639....

We now consider Defendants' claim that they were entitled to summary judgment on Johnson's claim for intentional infliction of emotional distress. In 1993, we recognized the independent tort of intentional infliction of emotional distress.... To recover under this tort, a plaintiff must prove that 1) the defendant acted intentionally or recklessly, 2) the conduct was "extreme and outrageous," 3) the actions of the defendant caused the plaintiff emotional distress, and 4) the resulting emotional distress was severe.... Only the first two elements are at issue in this case.

Johnson does not claim that Marshall intentionally caused the accident, but he does argue that Marshall recklessly caused his emotional distress.... However, until today we have not examined an intentional infliction of emotional distress claim based solely on reckless conduct.

Defendants argue that Johnson cannot prevail on his intentional infliction of emotional distress claim for two reasons. First, they contend that the Restatement contemplates separate standards for plaintiffs who are "direct victims" of intentionally or recklessly inflicted emotional distress and "bystanders" who suffer emotional distress from conduct "directed at" some other person. Johnson makes no claim as a "bystander," and Defendants argue that, as a matter of law, Marshall's conduct could not have been "directed at" Johnson because there is no evidence that Marshall was aware that either Johnson or the marchers were on the highway....

Second, Defendants argue that because [the tort] is directed solely to conduct that was intended or likely to produce emotional distress, an actor is not "reckless" for [these] purposes unless the defendant consciously disregards a high probability of *severe emotional distress*, ... not merely a high probability of *physical harm* to which emotional distress may be causally linked. Defendants maintain that although Johnson's conduct created a significant risk of physical injury, the incidental risk that someone else would suffer severe emotional distress was not "highly probable" as a matter of law.

Johnson counters that reckless conduct is sufficiently "directed at" the plaintiff if the plaintiff is directly imperiled by the defendant's conduct. Furthermore, Johnson contends that the risk of physical injury and the risk of emotional distress are co-extensive. Thus, a defendant who acts in conscious disregard of a high probability of *any harm* is responsible for emotional distress resulting to people who are within the area made dangerous by the defendant's conduct or who may rightfully come within that area....

We do not decide whether and to what extent conduct must be directed at a particular individual to give rise to liability under an intentional infliction of emotional distress theory. Instead, we hold only that Johnson is not entitled to recover because the tort of intentional infliction of emotional distress is available only in those situations in which severe emotional distress is the intended consequence or primary risk of the actor's conduct.... [W]e hold that a claim for intentional infliction of emotional distress cannot be maintained when the risk that emotional distress will result is merely incidental to the commission of some other tort. In the present case, Marshall's conduct, even if reckless, involved a primary risk of physical injury or death. To the extent it also involved a risk that others would suffer only emotional distress, Texas permits recovery under the limitations imposed by courts for public policy reasons, such as bystander recovery.... We, therefore, hold that Johnson may not recover under an intentional infliction of emotional distress theory because emotional distress was not the intended or primary consequence of Marshall's conduct.

NOTES AND QUESTIONS

1. The premise of countless rides and attractions is specifically to terrify a patron—as noted in the *Scientific American* excerpt in the prior chapter, riding a roller coaster creates a "fight or flight" physiological response. For some unwitting patrons getting on a coaster, the experience may well result in severe distress. Or consider the haunted attractions described earlier in the book, or the more "extreme" ones we'll discuss in later chapters—many such attractions are specifically created to offer conduct that would unquestionably be considered outrageous in other settings. As we'll see later, such attractions presumably rely on consent, sometimes express, sometimes implied. Spend some time thinking about how the emotional distress doctrines (whether under negligence or intentional torts) should or shouldn't apply to such attractions.
2. While it doesn't come up terribly often, consent *is* a defense to intentional infliction of emotional distress claims. *See, e.g.*, *Rzayeva v. Foster*, 134 F. Supp. 2d 239 (D. Conn. 2001). You should consider whether—and how—consent can and should be subject to withdrawal by the patron. The parallel concept for negligent infliction of emotional distress (and negligence claims more generally) is, roughly, the idea of primary assumption of risk, a no-duty doctrine relating to inherent risks. We will spend a lot of time on that, including addressing a situation where a court seems to get them confused.
3. Why do courts have higher standards when the damages claimed are purely emotional distress? Consider, for example, the implication of the constraints on negligence claims for emotional distress: the court in many such cases is necessarily concluding that the defendant (a)

acted negligently, (b) that negligence was the factual cause of harm to plaintiff, (c) that negligence was also the legal cause of harm to plaintiff, and (d) that harm could be assigned a dollar value. Other than the nature of the damages, that would usually satisfy the elements of a negligence claim. But most state courts have concluded that defendants don't have a duty to avoid that sort of purely emotional harm *except* when the plaintiff was closely related to someone who *was* physically injured. Given (a) through (d), does that make sense? What's the policy goal being achieved here? (We'll spend more time on this in Chapter 4, so don't worry about it too much yet.)

Risk Taking

> It is ... the case that adolescents engage in more risky behavior than adults, although the magnitude of age differences in risk-taking vary as a function of the specific risk in question and the age of the "adolescents" and "adults" used as comparison groups; rates of risk-taking are high among 18- to 21-year-olds, for instance, some of whom may be classified as adolescents and some who may be classified as adults. Nonetheless, as a general rule, adolescents and young adults are more likely than adults over 25 to binge drink, smoke cigarettes, have casual sex partners, engage in violent and other criminal behavior, and have fatal or serious automobile accidents, the majority of which are caused by risky driving or driving under the influence of alcohol. Because many forms of risk behavior initiated in adolescence elevate the risk for the behavior in adulthood (e.g., drug use), and because some forms of risk-taking by adolescents put individuals of other ages at risk (e.g., reckless driving, criminal behavior), public health experts agree that reducing the rate risk-taking by young people would make a substantial improvement in the overall well-being of the population.
>
> — L. Steinberg, *A Social Neuroscience Perspective on Adolescent Risk-Taking,* Dev Rev. 2008 Mar; 28(1):78-106. doi: 10.1016/j.dr.2007.08.002. PMID: 18509515; PMCID: PMC2396566.

In Six Flags's 2021 Annual Report (a document produced by publicly-traded companies), the park chain noted this:

> As part of the seasonal employment program, we employ a significant number of teenagers....

Elsewhere in the same document:

> There is a risk of accidents occurring at our parks or competing parks which may reduce attendance and negatively impact our operations.
>
> Our brand and our reputation are among our most important assets. Our ability to attract and retain customers depends, in part, upon the external perceptions of the Company, the quality and safety of our parks, services and rides, and our corporate and management integrity. While we carefully maintain the safety of our rides, there are inherent risks involved with these attractions. An accident or an injury (including water- or air-borne illnesses) at any of our parks or at parks operated by competitors, particularly an accident or injury involving the safety of guests and employees, that receives media attention, could negatively impact our brand or reputation, cause loss of consumer confidence in the Company, reduce attendance at our parks, and negatively impact our results of operations. For example, in September 2019, a coaster accident at La Feria, a competing park in Mexico, resulted in two fatalities. We believe that the publicity surrounding this accident had a significant negative impact on attendance at our park in Mexico during that period. The considerable expansion in the use of social media over recent years has compounded the impact of negative publicity. If any such incident occurs during a time of high seasonal demand, the effect could disproportionately impact our results of operations for the year.

Cedar Fair is another publicly-traded large amusement park operator (though it is structured as a partnership). In its 2021 Annual Report, it notes: "The demographic groups that are most important to our business are families and young people ages 12 through 24. Families are believed to be attracted by a combination of rides, live entertainment and the clean, wholesome atmosphere. Young people are believed to be attracted by the action-packed rides."

Burnett v. Family Kingdom, Inc.

691 S.E.2d 170 (S.C. Ct. App. 2010)

Tracy Burnett (Wife) appeals the trial court's decision granting Family Kingdom, Inc.'s (the Amusement Park) motion for a directed verdict in her negligence action. We reverse.

FACTS

Wife; her husband, Douglas Burnett (Husband); Wife's brother, Clyde Adams; and Adams' friend, Patricia Smith, were vacationing in Myrtle Beach, South Carolina. While there, the party visited the Amusement Park, which operates a go-cart attraction. After purchasing two tickets, Husband and Adams proceeded to get in line to ride the go-carts. Wife testified that while Husband and Adams were waiting in line, three young men came behind them and began acting boisterously. According to Wife, the three young men stated they were going to bump or collide with the go-carts during the upcoming ride. Upon hearing this, Husband warned the young men not to collide with him.

The ride operators put Husband, Adams, and the three young men in the go-carts after they took the tickets from the riders. The operators belted in and gave instructions to the drivers. They were warned not to bump or collide with the other go-carts and not to drive recklessly.

The go-cart ride had a controller box that contained a device with which the ride operators could deactivate the ride. When pressed, the "All Stop" button would stop all of the go-carts. The Amusement Park's manager, Donald Sipes, testified that after the second warning not to bump, the ride operators were required to push the "All Stop" button and stop the ride. Sipes also stated a collision that resulted in a go-cart being turned around required the ride operators to stop the ride.

Before Adams' go-cart reached the first turn of the first lap, one of the three young men hit his go-cart and caused Adams' go-cart to spin around 180 degrees. Subsequent to this collision, for the next few laps the three young men continued to repeatedly bump or collide with Husband and Adams. Wife, Husband, Adams, and Smith repeatedly asked the ride operators for assistance because the three young men were driving in a reckless and dangerous manner. Wife testified that rather than providing help to Adams and Husband, the ride operators encouraged the three young men and cheered them on.

After the second lap, Husband drove his cart off of the track and into the pit area, where his cart was hit from behind by one of the young men's cart. The collision caused the go-cart, with Husband inside, to be lifted off the ground. Shortly thereafter, another young man collided with Husband's go-cart. Only after these collisions did the ride operators press the "All Stop" button to deactivate all the go-carts.

Husband brought a negligence action against the Amusement Park. [Husband died during the pendency of this action, not due to injuries sustained during the ride; Wife was appointed as his personal representative.] At the close of Wife's case, the Amusement Park moved for a directed verdict, arguing Wife had failed to prove the Amusement Park acted negligently. The trial court granted the motion. This appeal followed.

* * *

Wife argues the trial court improperly granted the Amusement Park's motion for a directed verdict in her negligence action. Specifically, Wife contends the trial court erred by holding she failed to show the Amusement Park owed a duty of due care. We agree.

In order to succeed in a negligence cause of action, the plaintiff must establish (1) the defendant owed a duty of care to the plaintiff; (2) the defendant breached the duty by a negligent act or omission; (3) the defendant's breach was the actual and proximate cause of the plaintiff's injury; and (4) the plaintiff suffered an injury or damages. *Moore v. Weinberg*, 373 S.C. 209, 220–21, 644 S.E.2d 740, 746 (Ct.App.2007). A crucial element in a cause of action for negligence is the existence of a legal duty of care owed by the defendant to the plaintiff. Absent a duty, there is no actionable negligence. *Id.*

The question of negligence is a mixed question of law and fact. *Id.* First, the court must resolve, as a matter of law, whether the law recognizes a particular duty. *Id.* If the court determines there is no duty, the defendant is entitled to a judgment as a matter of law. *Id.* However, if a duty does exist, the jury then determines whether a breach of the duty that resulted in damages occurred. *Id.* Thus, we must first determine if the Amusement Park owed a duty to Husband.

At common law, a person ordinarily has no duty to protect another from a harm inflicted by a third party. *Burns v. S.C. Comm'n for the Blind,* 323 S.C. 77, 79, 448 S.E.2d 589, 590–91 (Ct.App.1994). Usually, a person incurs no liability for failure to take steps to benefit others or protect them from harm not created by his or her own wrongful conduct. *Id.* However, an affirmative legal duty can be created by a statute, among other things, and thus, the statute can be a source of a duty owed in a negligence case. *Id.*

The existence of such a statutorily imposed duty is determined by applying a two-prong test. *Id.* Both of the following elements must be satisfied to find a statute imposes a duty sufficient to support a cause of action in negligence. *Id.* First, it must be established that the essential purpose of the statute is to protect the plaintiff from the kind of harm suffered. *Id.* Second, the plaintiff must be a constituent of the class of persons the statute seeks to protect. *Id.*

As to the first element, the South Carolina Amusement Rides Safety Code (the Act) was passed to prevent injuries to visitors and employees at amusement parks and fairs. S.C.Code Ann. §§ 41-18-20 et seq. (Supp. 2008); *see Steinke v. S.C. Dep't of Labor, Licensing & Regulation, 336 S.C. 373, 391, 520 S.E.2d 142, 151 (1999)* ("The Act's purpose is to prevent injuries to visitors and employees at amusement parks and fairs."). Section 41-18-20(A) of the South Carolina Code (Supp.2008), entitled "Legislative intent," states, "The purpose of this chapter is to guard against personal injuries in the ... use of amusement devices at ... amusement parks to persons employed at or attending ... amusement parks...." Subsection (B) of this section states, "It is the intent of this chapter that amusement devices must be ... maintained, and operated so as to prevent injuries." § 41-18-20(B).

The first element is satisfied because the purpose of the Act is to prevent personal injuries that result from the use of amusement devices. In the present case, Husband was visiting the Amusement Park and suffered the type of personal injury the Act seeks to avoid as a result of the use of the go-cart ride.

As to the second element, that the plaintiff must be a constituent of the class of persons the statute seeks to protect, section 41-18-20 states the purpose of the Act is to guard against personal injuries to persons attending amusement parks. This section also states, "[t]he purpose of this chapter is to ... ensure to the injured party the possibility of financial recovery as against the owner of the carnival, fair, or amusement park where the injury occurred." *Id.* Husband qualifies because he was attending the Amusement Park at the time of the injury. Additionally, the statute allows Husband as an injured party to seek financial retribution against the owner of the Amusement Park.

Wife meets both elements for establishing a statutorily imposed duty. Thus, the Act creates an affirmative legal duty on part of the Amusement Park, and the trial court erred in concluding Wife failed to show a duty existed.

The Amusement Park argues there are three additional grounds on which to affirm the trial court. The Amusement Park contends (1) the trial court found that even if there was a duty, it did not breach this duty; (2) there was no proximate cause; and (3) Husband's negligence outweighed any negligence on its part. We disagree.

As to the first contention, as explained above, the question of negligence is a mixed question of law and fact. *Moore,* 373 S.C. at 221, 644 S.E.2d at 746. If a duty does exist, the jury then determines whether a breach of the duty that resulted in damages occurred. *Id.* Thus, the Amusement Park's argument that it did not breach a duty fails because that determination rests with the jury.

Amusement Park's argument that it did not proximately cause Husband's injuries also fails. Only on the rarest occasion should the trial court determine the issue of proximate cause as a matter of law. *Bailey v. Segars,* 346 S.C. 359, 367, 550 S.E.2d 910, 914 (Ct.App.2001)....

Proximate cause requires proof of causation in fact and legal cause. *Hurd v. Williamsburg County,* 363 S.C. 421, 428, 611 S.E.2d 488, 492 (2005). Causation in fact is demonstrated by establishing the plaintiff's injury would not have occurred "but for" the defendant's negligence. *Id.* Legal cause is shown by establishing foreseeability. *Id.* An injury is considered foreseeable if it is the natural and probable consequence of a breach of duty. *Id.*

In the present case, viewing the evidence and all reasonable inferences in the light most favorable to Wife, we conclude the trial court erred in not submitting the proximate cause issue to the jury. A jury could reasonably conclude Husband's injuries would not have occurred but for the ride operators' failure to stop the go-carts after Wife, Husband, Adams, and Smith repeatedly asked the ride operators for assistance because the three young men were driving in a reckless and dangerous manner. If the ride operators had stopped the ride by pushing the "All Stop" button, Husband would not have been injured when Husband drove his cart off of the track and into the pit area. While Husband was in the pit area, he was rear ended by one of the young men with such force that the collision caused the go-cart with the Husband inside to be lifted off the ground. Thereafter, another young man collided into Husband's go-cart.

With respect to foreseeability, a jury could conclude Husband's injuries were the natural and probable consequence of the breach of the duty by the Amusement Park. The evidence presented showed: (1) the ride operators ignored repeated requests for assistance by Wife, Husband, Adams, and Smith when the three young men were hitting and colliding with Husband and Adams; (2) as a natural and probable consequence of the ride operators' failure to stop the ride, the three young men continued to drive their go-carts in a reckless and dangerous manner by repeatedly hitting and colliding with Husband; and (3) Husband suffered injuries. Accordingly, Wife did present sufficient evidence of proximate cause to survive the directed verdict motion.

As to the comparative negligence argument, the Amusement Park argues Husband's two prior back surgeries and a knee surgery constituted comparative negligence because he went on the go-cart ride knowing the three young men would collide with his go-cart.

In South Carolina, a plaintiff may only recover damages if his or her own negligence is not greater than that of the defendant. [*Hurd*] at 429, 611 S.E.2d at 492. The determination of respective degrees of negligence attributable to the plaintiff and the defendant presents a question of fact for the jury, at least when conflicting inferences may be drawn from the evidence. *Id.* In a comparative negligence case, the trial court should grant a motion for directed verdict if the only reasonable inference from the evidence is that the non-moving party's negligence exceeded fifty percent. *Id.*

In regards to Husband's prior surgeries, a defendant takes the plaintiff as he or she is found, and the plaintiff is entitled to recover damages resulting from the aggravation of a pre-existing condition. *Waring v. Johnson,* 341 S.C. 248, 260, 533 S.E.2d 906, 913 (Ct.App.2000). As to Husband's knowledge that the three young men would collide with his go-cart, neither the trial court nor this court is in a position to determine whether Husband's knowledge outweighed the fact that the ride operators failed to stop the ride after repeated requests for assistance by Wife, Husband, Adams, and Smith.

The Amusement Park also argues Husband's negligence is [not] outweighed by its negligence because Husband disregarded a safety sign. The sign reads, in pertinent part, "PARTICIPATE AT YOUR OWN RISK. THIS RIDE IS NOT RECOMMENDED FOR INDIVIDUALS WHO ARE PREGNANT OR HAVE HEART, NECK, OR BACK PROBLEMS." The Amusement Park presented no evidence Husband saw this sign. Adams testified he did not see the sign prior to entering the go-cart ride. Additionally, the sign states the go-cart ride is not recommended for individuals with back problems and does not state the ride is prohibited to persons with back issues. Even assuming Husband saw the sign, neither this court nor the trial court is in a position to determine whether this outweighed the ride operators' failure to stop the ride after repeated requests for assistance.

[Reversed.]

NOTES AND QUESTIONS

1. This case is unusual in being one where the analysis leading to the court finding the existence of a duty is outside the common law—the duty was created, the court concludes, by a statute and regulatory scheme. When a statute does create a duty, it also usually creates the standards for breach under negligence *per se*.

   In other cases where there's no statutory duty (*i.e.*, most tort cases), the facts are usually such that a duty is not disputed: In general, if one is acting in a way that potentially creates a risk to others, there is a duty to act with reasonable care. It is only in exceptional and limited circumstances where that duty is either eliminated or modified. We will address certain of those no-duty or limited-duty situations in a lot of detail in Chapter 4. This case notes one of those situations, where an actor ordinarily does not have a duty to *prevent* harm to others. Later (in Chapter 7), we will discuss the concept of negligent infliction of emotional distress, which itself reflects a limited-duty rule—if the facts as alleged only involve emotional distress resulting from the defendant's alleged conduct, most courts have developed a limited duty rule, permitting the potential for liability (importantly, as a matter of law) only under limited scenarios. In some cases, courts require that a plaintiff must show that the emotional distress itself resulted in some form of physical harm.

2. This case organizes factual and legal cause into one element it calls "proximate cause." You may find it easier to consider those as separate elements. First of the two is *factual causation*; in this case and many states, it is evaluated as "but-for" causation, where the fact-finder evaluates what would have happened if the negligent conduct (*i.e.*, the breach) had not occurred. If the harm still would have come about in that situation, the breach is not the but-for cause. (Some jurisdictions use "substantial factor" or other standards for factual causation.)

   The second part of causation in this way of thinking about it, *legal causation*, is often summarized as involving "foreseeability," which is an exceedingly fuzzy term. One more concrete way to evaluate the question is to look at the breach alleged and think about why that conduct is considered negligent—what harms we seek to avoid by calling that conduct improper. If the harm that resulted is on that list of harms we're hoping to avoid, then we deem it foreseeable and conclude that legal cause is satisfied. If it is beyond that list, then it is unforeseeable.

3. To summarize the elements of a negligence tort (as it will be discussed in the rest of this book), a plaintiff must meet the burden to establish every element:
   - *Duty*: an issue of law for the judge, generally present if an actor is acting in a way that potentially increases the risk of harm to someone else unless there is some specific reason that courts or legislatures have taken it off the table
   - *Breach*: a factual issue (for the jury), based on whether one failed to comply with the standard of care (usually but not always the duty to act with reasonable care under the circumstances)
   - *Factual causation*: another factual issue; often but-for causation, but can vary

- *Legal causation*: factual issue, sometimes labeled as "foreseeability" but the type-of-harm analysis above might help you think about it more methodically
- *Damages*: Nominal damages are not available in negligence claims generally, but courts also are usually not too picky about your actual damages evidence if all the other elements have been established. (Punitive damages are a separate issue, addressed separately *infra*.)

Of course, factual issues can be decided by a judge on summary judgment if there is (everyone sing together here) no genuine issue of material fact and judgment can be entered as a matter of law. This doesn't just mean that the judge thinks one side or the other *should* win—the judge must conclude that there's simply no fight about the evidence supporting one element.

4. The defendant has the burden to establish true defenses (as opposed to the failure of a plaintiff to establish an element as to which they have the burden). This case briefly discusses comparative fault and assumption of the risk; we will discuss those in more detail in the next chapter and other defenses in other chapters.

CHAPTER 3

(Secondary) Assumption of Risk and Comparative Fault

The core of most claims relating to personal injuries is negligence law, the elements of which we discussed earlier. Cases involving recreational activities often involve defenses based on the conduct of the plaintiff—either a contention that the plaintiff assumed the risk of injury or that the plaintiff's conduct was itself negligent and a factual and legal cause of their own injuries. The former—assumption of risk—can be divided into *primary* assumption of risk (which is better considered a no-duty rule and will be treated in Chapter 4) and *secondary* assumption of risk (a true defense, addressed in this chapter). This chapter also discusses comparative fault; today, secondary assumption of risk is probably best considered a flavor of comparative fault.

I mentioned in the Author's Note that this casebook grew out of a course that itself came from reading a book (*Action Park: Fast Times, Wild Rides, and the Untold Story of America's Most Dangerous Amusement Park*) and watching a documentary about New Jersey's Action Park (*Class Action Park* on Max). The former was written by Action Park's owner's son, who undoubtedly has a specific perspective and agenda; the latter was directed by a documentary filmmaker with no direct connection to the park.

Both the book and the film are fascinating in different ways, and I recommend them both. Action Park was unlike any park with which I am familiar at any point in history. It had very few traditional amusement park or water park rides, instead having many homegrown attractions like its famous but rarely-operational looping waterslide. But the attractions were not just unique in general design—they also were largely made to give patrons an unusual amount of control over their experiences, whether an Alpine slide without speed governors or a wave pool with effectively no maximum number of swimmers (or flailers) or a "Tarzan" rope swing where anyone could swing and drop into a pool, even though the pool might be filled with other people. As the park's ubiquitous advertising put it, Action Park was "where you're the center of the action!" That centering of patron preferences also provided a lot of opportunities for patrons to contribute to their own risk and to create risks for others.

Andy Mulvihill with Jake Rossen, *Action Park: Fast Times, Wild Rides, and the Untold Story of America's Most Dangerous Amusement Park*

pages 5–6 (Penguin Books 2020)*

Unlike most theme parks, Action Park did not strap in patrons and let them passively experience the rides. A roller coaster, thrilling as it may be, asks nothing of its occupants, and each ride is the same as the last. My father seized upon the idea that we were all tired of being coddled, of society dictating our behaviors and lecturing us on our vices. He vowed that visitors to Action Park would be the authors of their own adventures, prompting its best-known slogan: "Where you're the center of the action!" Guests riding down an asbestos chute on a plastic cart could choose whether to adopt a leisurely pace or tear down at thirty miles per hour and risk hitting a sharp turn that would eject them into the woods. They decided when to dive off a cliff and whether to aim for open water or their friend's head. They could listen when the attendants told them to stay in the speedboats, or they could tumble into the marsh water and risk getting bit by a snapping turtle.

It was not long before our visitors reworked our advertising to better reflect their experiences: "Action Park: Where you're the center of the accident."

The risk did not keep people away. The risk is what drew them to us.

NOTES AND QUESTIONS

1. What is your reaction to the ethos of Action Park? Do you think patrons there subjectively expected the risks to be materially different than the risks at a traditional amusement park?
2. How do you think people approach getting on a roller coaster or other amusement ride with the same attitude about their own safety as opposed to when they, say, get into a car or go for a bike ride? Should they think they have a significant role in their own safety on a ride?
3. Recall the previous chapter's discussion of the demographics of risk-takers. How, if at all, should the law (or regulators, or operators) take into account the ability, or inability, of kids and young adults to evaluate risk realistically?
4. As promised earlier, we're going to look now at a number of primary source materials and pleadings from the trial court level from a sad case from 2003. It encompasses questions about comparative fault and assumption of the risk, while also including interesting bits of choice of law.

Final Prosecutor's Report

Spencer County (Indiana) Prosecutor, 2003

On May 31, 2003 Holiday World [an amusement park in Santa Claus, Indiana] hosted an event [for coaster enthusiasts] called "Stark Raven Mad 2003." Roller coaster enthusiasts from around the country, including Tamar Fellner and her fiancé, Robert Weitzner, of New York attended the event. Before the event, records show the Raven Roller Coaster was inspected on May 31, 2003 and the roller coaster ran all-day and evening without any problems or guest complaints. Holiday World warned participants in "Stark Raven Mad 2003" that any attempt to interfere with safety mechanisms on any ride would subject the violator to removal from the park. At approximately 8:00 p.m. Tamar Fellner and her fiancé, Robert Weitzer [*sic*, Weitzner] got into the rear seat of the rear car of the Raven Roller Coaster. A ride operator states she specifically recalls checking Tamar Fellner's seat belt and lap bar before the coaster left the station. The coaster returned to the station and Fellner and her fiancé, Weitzner, stayed in their seats and decided to ride the coaster again.

Another ride operator states she checked Fellner's seat belt and lap bar again before the coaster left the station. Fellner's fiancé, Robert Weitzner, also stated that he and Fellner were both restrained by the belts and lap bars at the beginning of the last ride and that both were checked by an operator prior to departure.

At the time the last ride was in progress, three individuals in the Holiday World parking lot observed an individual matching the description of Ms. Fellner in the last car of the Raven Roller Coaster virtually standing up during the ride. Two of the witnesses were visiting the park and one of the witnesses was a tram operator in the park. Authorities verified the individuals could see the Raven from their vantage points. At the mid-course drop (Hill #5) Weitzner states Fellner fell out of the car and onto the tracks. Other passengers seated in front of Fellner and Weitzner stated after the last decline Weitzner began yelling and when the coaster returned to the station Weitzner told them that Fellner had fallen out.

[The following photo is not from the report, but shows the view of the ride from the parking lot mentioned.]

Photo: Jeremy Thompson, CC by 2.0 DEED, https://creativecommons.org/licenses/by/2.0/

Weitzner, rider operators, and a passenger who was a doctor ran back along the tracks where they found Fellner lying under the wooden structure of the coaster at the last drop. The doctor and park medical personnel immediately began CPR until an ambulance arrived and Fellner was pronounced dead by Coroner Bob Duley en route to the hospital. Fellner's body was examined by a forensic pathologist at St. Joseph's Hospital in Huntingburg and his opinion as to the cause of death was exsanguination (blood loss) as the result of multiple injuries as the consequence of a forty-foot fall from the roller coaster. He further stated the injuries included multiple open and closed bone fractures to her body. Blood and urine toxicology results were negative.

When the coaster returned to the station without Fellner a ride operator noticed that Fellner's seatbelt was unfastened. The coaster was evacuated and then quickly secured by a Santa Claus Deputy Marshal. The car was examined and photographed. Fellner's seatbelt was found unfastened and each end was tucked between the cushion and the sidewall on both sides of her seat. The lap bar where she had been sitting was down.

The coaster car was then examined by an inspector from the Indiana Department of Fire and Building Services on June 1, 2003 and the lap bar and seatbelt where Fellner had been sitting was found to be free of defects and functioning properly. Afterwards, the car was also examined by an independent roller coaster inspector who also found the car and its restraining devices to be in proper working order. An engineer from an engineering firm also tested the coaster and car and concluded that the forces experienced on the Raven wooden roller coaster are well within industry accepted standards and if Ms. Fellner would have been properly seated in her seat, with either one of the restraining devices properly used, she would not have left the roller coaster vehicle. The independent coaster inspector also reviewed all documentation of the Raven including operator handbooks, training records, maintenance records, ride manuals, and verbal and written guest instructions and found them to be complete and consistent. His preliminary opinion based on the evidence he examined was that:

> Ms. Fellner engaged in conduct contrary to the rules of operation and in disregard of the verbal instructions and posted written warnings. These actions resulted in Ms. Fellner placing her body in a position that the ride was not designed to

> carry human passengers. Once in this un-designed riding position, the forces exerted on the body resulted in Ms. Fellner leaving the passenger carrying area of the car and falling down through the wooden structure to the ground. The injuries sustained resulted in the unfortunate loss of Ms. Fellner's life.

The independent coaster inspector also stated his preliminary opinion was that the ride structure and ride vehicles have been maintained, operated, and used in accordance with the design standards and industry accepted standards. He concluded the Raven Roller Coaster is fit for use by the general public and that the ride will provide an enjoyable, safe experience for all passengers who are riding in the designed manner.

We believe it is also significant that there were no problems with the Raven before the incident and that there have been no problems since the incident.

Unfortunately, other than his original statement, we were unable to obtain further information from Ms. Fellner's fiancé, Robert Weitzner. He failed to return our calls or cooperate in the investigation despite several requests to do so. We continue to extend our sympathies to the family of Tamar Fellner and again I have been pleased by the thorough work of the investigating officers as well as the full cooperation of Holiday World under these difficult circumstances.

/s/ Jon A. Dartt
Spencer County Prosecutor

Mark Healy, *Fatal Attraction*

GQ Magazine, June 2005

Rob and Tamar came to Santa Claus (riding coasters in Cincinnati and Louisville on the way) to ride the world-famous Raven at an annual event that attracted more than 800 coaster enthusiasts from a half-dozen fanatical groups. The Raven doesn't look like a world-famous anything.... It isn't very fast—its top speed is about fifty-five miles per hour—but according to Larry Bill, who helped design the coaster in 1994, it takes advantage of the site's natural topography and gives people "a feeling of weightlessness as they crest the hills." [It] climaxes in the coaster's legendary fifth hill, a surprising floater that peaks in the tops of the trees and plunges toward the forest floor with a stomach-tossing whoosh. The fifth hill is all about air, that ethereal moment of levity and negative g's that are euphoric succor for coaster fans.

* * *

Parks have discovered enthusiasts (both affiliated [with enthusiast groups like the American Coaster Enthusiasts] and not) unbuckling seat belts and positioning their legs to prevent the lap bars from being lowered too far. There are even rumors of riders who have devised ways to unlock the lap bars for extra air, whose quest for flight goes a few steps beyond.

But was that Tamar? Had she unbuckled herself for that last ride, trusting only the safety bar? What if she'd determined that seat belts were for chumps who could not or would not see that there was more air, more joy, to be had if you dared to take it? She understood the ride's strength and the hazards of its infamous uplift. Maybe she was too arrogant or greedy; maybe she trusted the ride too much. Rob [Weitzner] won't speculate about whether or not she'd unfastened her belt, and he would not be interviewed by authorities investigating the accident.

NOTES AND QUESTIONS

1. Ms. Fellner was 32 at the time of her death.
2. The GQ piece references enthusiasts unbuckling seatbelts or otherwise avoiding restraints to get more airtime. Do you think parks should be, say, monitoring social media or online forums to find out about patrons doing that? If they know it's happening, does it change their obligations in terms of ride operation, ride design, or anything else?

Complaint, *Fellner v. Philadelphia Toboggan Coasters, Inc. and Koch Development Corporation*

No. 2:05-cv-02052-BMS
(E.D. Pa. April 29, 2005)

Comes now the Plaintiff, Azriel C. Fellner, in his capacity as the Personal Representative of the Estate of Tamar Etana Fellner, Deceased, and for his Complaint against the Defendants herein states as follows:

Jurisdiction and Venue

* * *

The jurisdiction of this Court is based upon the complete diversity of citizenship (28 U.S.C. § 1332) as between the Plaintiff [Tamar Fellner's father and her estate's personal representative, Rabbi Azriel C. Fellner], a citizen of New Jersey, PTC, a citizen of Pennsylvania, and Koch Development, a citizen of Indiana.... Venue is conferred pursuant to 28 U.S.C. § 1391(a)(2) in that a substantial part of the events or omissions giving rise to this claim occurred within this judicial district [the Eastern District of Pennsylvania].

General Allegations

At all times relevant, [Defendant] PTC has been engaged in the design, manufacture and sale of cars and trains for wooden roller coasters.... At all times relevant, Koch development owned and operated an amusement park known as Holiday World [and] operated, among other things, a wooden roller coaster at Holiday World known as "The Raven".... PTC developed, designed, manufactured and sold to Koch Development the cars and trains for The Raven.... On May 31, 2003, Tamar Etana Fellner was killed while riding The Raven. She was ejected from the car in which she was riding and fell to her death.

Count I: Negligence as to PTC

PTC owed a duty to Tamar, and to all riders of The Raven for that matter, to design and manufacture "restraints" within the cars of The Raven in such a manner that ejection therefrom during the operation thereof would be impossible.... PTC breached that duty by ... failing to safely develop, design, manufacture, test, and/or inspect the "restraints" within the cars for The Raven to prevent Tamar's ejection therefrom while riding the Raven.... As a direct and proximate result thereof, Tamar was killed.... [T]he Plaintiff has suffered damages [including medical and funeral expenses, Tamar's pain and suffering, expectancy income, and the loss of Tamar's love and affection], in excess of [$75,000, the threshold for diversity jurisdiction].... Furthermore, the Plaintiff is entitled to recover punitive damages against PTC as PTC's above-described breach was done through wanton willfulness and/or reckless indifference and was not the result of an honest error or judgment, overzealousness, mere negligence or other known failure....

Count II: Negligence as to Koch Development

Koch Development owed Tamar, and all riders of The Raven for that matter, a duty to safely maintain, monitor and administer the operation of The Raven.... Koch Development breached that duty by ... failing to ensure that Tamar was safely and properly secured by the "restraints" within the car of The Raven in which she was riding; [] failing to properly hire, train, monitor and oversee the ride attendants; [] failing to properly test, inspect, and maintain the safety restraints within the car of The Raven; [and] failing to provide proper and adequate warnings regarding use of The Raven.... As a direct and proximate result thereof, Tamar was killed. [Plaintiff's damages are as alleged above, including punitive damages claimed.]

Count[s] III [and IV]: Strict Liability as to PTC [and Koch Development]

The Raven was developed, designed, manufactured, distributed, leased, sold, and supplied for public use in a condition unreasonably dangerous to perspective [*sic*, prospective] users and consumers. The aforementioned product was defective by virtue of PTC's [same failures as alleged in the negligence claim, *supra*, and Koch Development's same failures as alleged in the negligence claim, *supra*].

Count V: Breach of Implied Warranty as to PTC

PTC designed, manufactured and sold the cars and trains for The Raven. PTC impliedly warranted that the cars were reasonably fit for their purpose. The Raven's cars were not fit for the intended use as warranted, nor were they free from defects, but to the contrary they were in a dangerous and defective condition unreasonably dangerous to prospective users and consumers. [Plaintiff suffered damages as a result.]

Count VI: Breach of Implied Warranty as to Koch Development

Koch Development sold admission to The Raven. Koch Development impliedly warranted that The Raven was reasonably fit for its purpose. The Raven was not fit for its intended use as warranted, nor was it free from defects, but to the contrary it was in a dangerous and defective condition unreasonably dangerous to prospective users and consumers. [Plaintiff suffered damages as a result.]

[Counts VII and VIII were wrongful death and survival actions under Pennsylvania law.]

Memorandum and Order, *Fellner v. Philadelphia Toboggan Coasters, Inc. and Koch Development Corporation*

No. 2:05-cv-02052-BMS
(E.D. Pa. October 18, 2005)

SCHILLER, J.

This case arises out of the tragic death of Tamar Etana Fellner resulting from a roller coaster accident at an Indiana amusement park. Defendant Koch Development Corporation ("Koch") owns and operates the amusement park, and Defendant Philadelphia Toboggan Coasters, Inc. ("PTC") designed and manufactured the roller coaster cars. Plaintiff Rabbi Azriel C. Fellner ("Plaintiff"), as the Personal Representative of Ms. Fellner's Estate, brings negligence and strict product liability claims against Defendants. Presently before the Court are Defendants' motions to dismiss. For the reasons that follow, Defendants' motions are granted in part and denied in part, and this case is transferred to the Southern District of Indiana.

[The court summarized the facts and claims in the Complaint.] Defendants seek to dismiss this action based on improper venue, or in the alternative, seek to transfer the case to the Southern District of Indiana.... [The movant has the burden of demonstrating that venue is improper.]

A. Proper Venue in This District

[Because Koch had chosen not to contest that personal jurisdiction was proper over it in the Eastern District of Pennsylvania, the court concluded that, under 28 U.S.C. § 1391(c), venue was proper as well.]

B. Transfer of Venue to the Southern District of Indiana

Pursuant to 28 U.S.C. 1404(a), "[f]or the convenience of parties and witnesses, in the interest of justice, a district court may transfer any civil action to any other district or division where it might have been brought." 28 U.S.C. § 1404(a). An action may be transferred to another district even if venue is proper where initially brought, provided venue is also proper in the transferee district. *See Simon v. Ward*, 80 F. Supp. 2d 464, 470 (E.D. Pa. 2000). Here, venue would be proper in the Southern District of Indiana pursuant to § 1391(a)(2), because a substantial part of the events or omissions giving rise to Plaintiff's negligence claims occurred at Koch's amusement park in Indiana, the site of the accident. []

The venue transfer analysis adopted by the Third Circuit incorporates and elaborates upon the three factors—convenience of parties, convenience of witnesses, and interests of justice—explicitly mentioned in § 1404(a). *See Jumara v. State Farm Ins. Co.*, 55 F.3d 873, 879 (3d Cir. 1995). The Third Circuit has outlined various private and public interests that are also relevant to the transfer inquiry. *See id.* Private interests include: (1) plaintiff's forum preference; (2) defendant's preference; (3) whether the claim arose elsewhere; (4) convenience of the parties as indicated by their relative physical and financial condition; (5) convenience of the witnesses, but only to the extent that witnesses may be unavailable to testify in one forum; and (6) location of books and records, limited to the extent they cannot be produced at alternative forum. *See id.* Public interests include: (1) enforceability of the judgment; (2) practical considerations that could make the trial easy, expeditious, or inexpensive; (3) relative administrative difficulty related to court congestion; (4) local interest in deciding local controversies; (5) public policies of both forums; and (6) familiarity of trial judge with applicable state law in diversity case. *See id.* at 879–80.

Defendant must show the desirability of transferring venue, and must present evidence upon which the court may rely in justifying transfer. *See Plum Tree, Inc. v. Stockment*, 488 F.2d 754, 756–57 (3d Cir. 1973).... In this case, the *Jumara* factors weigh strongly in favor of transfer, and Defendants' supplemental submissions support the Court's decision to transfer.

1. Plaintiff's Choice of Forum

Generally, "plaintiff's choice of a proper forum is a paramount consideration in any determination of a transfer request," and while "[t]he decision to transfer is in the court's discretion, [] a transfer is not to be liberally granted." *Shutte v. Armco Steel Corp.*, 431 F.2d 22, 25 (3d Cir. 1970).... However, when plaintiff brings suit in a district other than his home state, his venue choice is entitled to less deference. *See Piper Aircraft Co. v. Reyno*, 454 U.S. 235, 255 (1981) ("[P]laintiff's choice of forum is entitled to greater deference when the plaintiff has chosen the home forum...."). ... Here, Plaintiff's choice is entitled to less deference because Pennsylvania is not Plaintiff's home forum: Decedent Tamar Fellner resided in New York, and her Estate is domiciled in New York. [] Accordingly, although Plaintiff's choice of forum weighs against transfer, less significance is accorded to this preference than if Plaintiff's home forum were Pennsylvania.

2. Defendants' Forum Preference

Defendants' forum preference weighs in favor of transfer, as both Koch and PTC desire to litigate this case in Indiana. [] The issue of where this claim arose weighs slightly in favor of transfer as well. Despite the fact that the design and manufacture of the roller coaster cars in Pennsylvania support a finding of proper venue in this District, [], the accident itself occurred in Indiana, where the primary witnesses of Ms. Fellner's fatal ride are located....

3. Convenience of the Parties

The convenience of the parties, as indicated by their relative physical and financial condition, and the location of books and records, to the extent they cannot be produced at an alternative forum, are neutral here. Records and documents may be produced in either forum, and the inconvenience and expense of traveling to an alternate forum for discovery and trial exists for all parties. [The court cited evidence that travel to Indiana would be inconvenient for Plaintiff and that the park might have to shut down temporarily if members of the family were required to travel to Pennsylvania for trial.]

4. Public Interests

The public interests in this case are neutral as well and thus do not significantly impact the transfer analysis. Plaintiff and Defendants both validly claim that each forum has a strong policy interest in the outcome of the case; Indiana as the site of the accident has an interest based in promoting and monitoring safety in amusement parks within its state, and Pennsylvania as the site of the manufacture of potentially defective products has an interest in monitoring the design, manufacture, and sale of such products. []

5. Convenience of Witnesses

The factor which most strongly supports transfer in this case is the convenience of witnesses, to the extent they would be unavailable to testify at Plaintiff's chosen forum. This District has noted that "[t]he convenience of witnesses weighs heavily in making a decision regarding a motion to transfer venue," and "[t]o show inconvenience to witnesses, the moving party needs to provide the type of documents set forth in *Plum Tree.*" *Gonzalez v. Elec. Control Sys., Inc.*, Civ. A. No. 93- 3107, 1993 WL 372217, at *4 (E.D. Pa. Sept. 17, 1993)....

In support of their motions, Defendants have submitted appropriate supplemental documentation in the form of affidavits and written and recorded statements, indicating the materiality of testimony by witnesses who would be unavailable if this case proceeded to trial in this District. [] Defendants present at least twelve non-party witnesses who can provide material testimony regarding Ms. Fellner's accident, including:

> (1) Two guests in the parking lot of the amusement park and one summer Koch employee within the park who viewed a woman matching Ms. Fellner's description on the fatal ride prior to her death;
>
> (2) Three guests who were seated directly in front of Ms. Fellner on the fatal ride, one of whom gave medical care to Ms. Fellner after her fall;
>
> (3) A former Koch employee responsible for roller coaster maintenance;
>
> (4) A summer Koch employee who checked Ms. Fellner's coaster seat restraints on the ride Ms. Fellner took immediately prior to the fatal ride;
>
> (5) A former Koch employee who checked Ms. Fellner's coaster seat restraints on the fatal ride;
>
> (6) A summer Koch employee who viewed Ms. Fellner's coaster car and seat restraints upon the ride's return to the station after Ms. Fellner's fall;
>
> (7) An amusement ride inspector from the Division of Fire and Building Safety of the State of Indiana, who inspected Ms. Fellner's roller coaster car after the accident and prepared a report of his findings; and
>
> (8) The former Marshall of the Santa Claus Police Department, who performed an inspection after the accident, including observations of the roller coaster.

[] Seven of these witnesses completed affidavits indicating that they would not voluntarily appear in this District to testify in this case. [] Indeed, two of these primary witnesses indicated to Counsel for PTC via telephone that they did not intend to voluntarily give any further statement regarding the incident they observed. (Suppl. Docs. of Def. Koch Ex. 6.)

With the exception of one witness in Illinois and one in Kentucky, all of these witnesses reside in Indiana [] and thus the Court could not compel their attendance in this District. *See* Fed. R. Civ. P. 45(b)(2) (federal court's subpoena power over non-party witnesses only extends to persons within judicial district or within a 100-mile radius of courthouse). These witnesses would, however, be subject to the subpoena power of the district court in the Southern District of Indiana. *See id.* As important questions of liability will be addressed by the testimony of these non-party witnesses, the interests of justice require their live testimony, which can only be compelled in Indiana. *See, e.g., Ryer v. Harrisburg Kohl Bros.*, Inc., 307 F. Supp. 276, 280 (S.D.N.Y. 1969) (noting the importance of the location of material witnesses, especially when live testimony is preferable to assess difficult questions of liability).

Plaintiff essentially pursues two distinct theories in this case—a product liability claim against PTC for its design and manufacture of the roller coaster cars and a negligence claim against Koch for its operation of the roller coaster. [] The former could be successfully litigated as easily in Indiana as in Pennsylvania, with experts and relatively few PTC principals/employees testifying regarding the design and manufacture of the roller coaster cars. [] On the other hand, the latter must be litigated in Indiana to ensure a fair and just outcome of the negligence claim against Koch. The material testimony of numerous non-party witnesses, as documented in Defendants' supporting submissions to the Court, will be crucial to a jury's assessment of Defendant Koch's liability for this tragic accident. In weighing the Jumara factors and considering the interests of justice, the Court finds that transferring this case to the Southern District of Indiana is warranted. Thus, Defendants' motions to transfer this case are granted.

Entry on Defendant Philadelphia Toboggan Coaster's Motion to Dismiss, *Fellner v. Philadelphia Toboggan Coasters, Inc. and Koch Development Corporation*

No. 3:05-cv-00218-SEB-WGH
(S.D. Ind. Nov. 3, 2006)

[] PTC filed its Motion to Dismiss directed towards Counts I, III, V, VII, and VIII contending that Indiana (not Pennsylvania) law applies to PTC's causes of action. After careful consideration, we concur in PTC's analysis and hold that Counts I, III, V, VII and VIII against PTC must be DISMISSED....

Analysis

Because this case was transferred from the Eastern District of Pennsylvania, as we have previously noted,[] Pennsylvania's choice of law rules apply here in determining which state's laws govern the causes of action against PTC.

Under Pennsylvania law, the old rule of *lex loci delict* has been abandoned. *Griffith v. United Air Lines*, Inc., 203 A.2d 796 (Pa. 1964). Pennsylvania currently applies a more flexible approach which combines a "government interest analysis" with the "significant relationship" analysis consistent with Section 145 of the Restatement (Second) of Conflicts. *Normann v. Johns-Manville Corp.*, 593 A.2d 890, 893 (Pa. Super. Ct. 1991). If there is a conflict between the laws of the relevant states, (*Cipolla v. Shaposka*, 267 A.2d 854, 855 (Pa. 1970)), the Court must determine which state has the greater interest in the application of its substantive laws. As explained by the Pennsylvania Superior Court:

> In determining which state has the greater interest in the application of its law, one method is to see what contacts each state has with the accident, the contacts being relevant only if they relate to the policies and interests underlying the particular issue before the court. When doing this it must be remembered that a mere counting of the contacts is not what is involved. The weight of a particular state's contacts must be measured on a qualitative rather than quantitative scale.

Troxel v. A.I. duPont Inst., 636 A.2d 1179, 1181 (Pa. Super. Ct. 1994) (internal citations and quotations omitted). In a products liability context, Pennsylvania courts have clearly indicated that the fact that a product was designed and manufactured in a particular state does not automatically yield a finding that that state's laws apply. *See Apple v. Ford Motor Co.*, 2004 WL 3218425 (Pa. Ct. Comm. Pleas 2004); *Giovanetti v. Johns-Manville Corp.*, 539 A.2d 871, 873–74 (Pa. Super. Ct. 1988).

In the case at bar, the parties agree and the Court concurs that there is a clear conflict between the laws of Indiana and Pennsylvania in that Indiana products liability actions must be pled under the Indiana Products Liability Act, which includes defenses of misuse of a product and knowledge of a product's dangerousness, and recognizes the theory of comparative fault (Ind. Code § 34-20-6 & 8), whereas, Pennsylvania products liability actions are pled as separate causes of action sounding in negligence, strict liability, and breach of implied warranties. Additionally, Pennsylvania does not recognize comparative fault in strict products liability actions. Given this conflict between the laws of Pennsylvania and Indiana, we must determine which state has the greater interest in having its laws applied.

Pennsylvania's only contact with this case is that PTC was located in and manufactured the cars for "The Raven" there. Clearly, Pennsylvania has an interest in ensuring that products manufactured within its borders are safe for their intended use.

Significantly, Pennsylvania's consumer protection statutes (which, for example, foreclose comparative fault in strict products liability actions) are designed to protect Pennsylvania consumers. However, the injured consumer here was neither a Pennsylvania resident nor did her use of the product (*i.e.*, a patron on the roller coaster) occur in Pennsylvania.

Pennsylvania's interests are minimal compared to Indiana's far greater interests. The roller coaster cars manufactured by PTC were merely a component of The Raven roller coaster system which was constructed and operated in Indiana and, of course, the tragic accident which caused Ms. Fellner's death occurred in Indiana. The nexus of the relationships between and among all the parties centered in Indiana. If it is established that there was some misuse of the roller coaster by Ms. Fellner, it would have occurred in Indiana. Whatever warnings may have been given to Ms. Fellner concerning the dangerousness of The Raven would have been provided at the site of the ride in Indiana. Further, if other factors contributed to the accident, such as operational errors by Koch or its employees, they also would have occurred in Indiana.

Based on these contacts, Indiana has a substantial interest in having its products liability laws govern the resolution of this case. The availability of misuse and knowledge of dangerous conditions as defenses also impacts the standard of care applicable to patrons of amusement parks under Indiana law. Certainty and predictability in the results of tort litigation based on accidents at amusement parks in Indiana advance the goal of safe behavior by everyone involved. It can be assumed as well that Ms. Fellner purposefully availed herself of the laws of Indiana, including products liability statutes, when she came to Indiana to visit Holiday World and to ride The Raven. Neither her contact with Indiana nor PTC's contact with Indiana was fortuitous. Based on Indiana's strong interest in applying its products liability laws to the accident at issue in this case, especially in comparison to Pennsylvania's minimal interest, the resolution of this litigation against PTC shall be in accordance with Indiana law.

The Complaint alleges three separate causes of action: tort, strict liability, and breach of implied warranties. None of these causes of action comports with the Indiana Products Liability statutes. Further, because Plaintiff's wrongful death and survival actions were pled under Pennsylvania law, our previous ruling that Indiana law applies to this accident requires the dismissal as to PTC of Counts I, III, V, VII, and VIII.

Stipulation of Dismissal, *Fellner v. Philadelphia Toboggan Coasters, Inc. and Koch Development Corporation*

No. 3:05-cv-00218-SEB-WGH
(S.D. Ind. Oct. 15, 2007)

Comes now the Plaintiff, Azriel C. Fellner, in his capacity as the Personal Representative of the Estate of Tamar Etana Fellner, Deceased, by counsel, and comes now the Defendant, Philadelphia Toboggan Coasters, Inc., by counsel, and comes now the Defendant, Koch Development Corporation, by counsel, and advise the Court that the parties have executed a Confidential Settlement Agreement and General Release. Therefore, the parties have agreed to stipulate to the dismissal with prejudice of the within cause, each party bearing its own costs and attorney fees.

NOTES AND QUESTIONS

1. Why do you think Ms. Fellner's father, on behalf of her estate, filed this lawsuit in Pennsylvania? The decisions excerpted above give you some ideas, but think about other strategic reasons for the decision (and for why the park and the coaster manufacturer might prefer the Southern District of Indiana). Apart from the venue selected, why do you think that Ms. Fellner's father sought the application of Pennsylvania law, and why did the park argue for Indiana law?
2. It is not clear today that Holiday World (Koch) would be subject to personal jurisdiction in Pennsylvania, certainly not under general jurisdiction and maybe not under specific jurisdiction on these facts. *See Daimler AG v. Bauman*, 571 U.S. 117 (2014). Indeed, as the court notes, the park initially disputed that personal jurisdiction was satisfied, though it later made the decision to concede it. As far as I can tell, PTC did not dispute personal jurisdiction in Indiana, which was probably a sound decision.
3. Assume—and it's a good assumption—that the parties had good reason to have their preferences for venue and for applicable law. How do you feel about the remedies available being so dependent on where an incident happens to take place? What was your reaction when the court, in deciding which law would control, said, "It can be assumed as well that Ms. Fellner purposefully availed herself of the laws of Indiana, including products liability statutes, when she came to Indiana to visit Holiday World and to ride The Raven." Do you think Ms. Fellner thought at all about the laws of Indiana?
4. Why do you think the park settled this case? Why do you think Ms. Fellner's survivors did so? (The amount paid, if any, is confidential, so these are necessarily impossible questions to answer with certainty.) If you were representing the park, based on what you know, how confident would you feel in defending the case on the merits, and would you recommend seeking a resolution? What if you represented Ms. Fellner's survivors? Based on what you know here, how risky do you think it would be for the park to take this case to trial? What other factors do you think the park considered?
5. In the interest of full disclosure, I am a big fan of Holiday World and in fact appeared in a Discovery Channel special about the creation of

its Voyage roller coaster. (I was a member of the "Secret Committee" providing enthusiasts' views on various design features.) That coaster, Voyage, ended up being my elder child's first really big coaster, I believe. (They loved it.) That special, alas, never actually aired in the United States, for some reason (possibly my presence), but can be found from time to time on extremely sketchy websites and, if you go looking for it, you're assuming the risk of innumerable viruses and the like.

6. As noted, there are two distinct things crammed into the same box labeled "assumption of risk." The more modern way to look at the facts in the Holiday World case would be to simply classify Ms. Fellner's alleged conduct as comparative fault—that is, a jury could conclude that she didn't act reasonably under the circumstances and could conclude that her breach of the standard of care was the factual and legal cause of her harm, such that any recovery should be reduced or barred (depending on the state's law).

   But it could also be seen as secondary assumption of risk, where a jury could conclude that Ms. Fellner was aware of a negligently-created risk—in this case, perhaps, the park's failure to fully ensure that the lap bar was down and operating a coaster with a seat belt that could be removed by the patrons—and went ahead and encountered that risk voluntarily. In some states, applying an older approach, a conclusion that the plaintiff assumed the risk in this way serves as a complete bar to recovery, even if the state otherwise uses comparative fault. In the next chapter, we look at *primary* assumption of risk, which is quite different from the *secondary* version described here.

7. We'll return to the question of design in chapter 8, but consider briefly if you think it is plausible to argue that a seatbelt that can be undone by a patron is necessarily defectively designed.

8. Many states have adopted "Rider Responsibility" statutes, providing specific rules for patrons and, in Pennsylvania for example, providing that "proof that a rider sustained an injury in the course of knowingly acting contrary to [the law] shall be evidence of comparative negligence in a suit against an operator by that rider." Amusement Rider Safety and Liability Act, 4 P.S. § 504. If such a statute doesn't provide for that expressly but makes the failure to comply a crime, it could be used to support negligence *per se*.

CHAPTER 4

No-Duty and Limited-Duty Doctrines, Including Primary Assumption of Risk; Statutory Immunities

As briefly noted in Chapter 2 (and, presumably, in your first-year Torts class), the default duty of care owed in common law tort schemes is reasonable care—that is, if you're engaging in conduct that could create risk to others, you are obligated to act as a reasonable person would under the circumstances. In most cases, there's no question about the presence of a duty, or what that duty is by which conduct will be measured, and the court doesn't have to reach a conclusion about it.

In this Chapter, we'll dive more deeply into when and whether courts should modify or even eliminate a duty of care for specific situations, and we'll also look at situations where legislatures have done so statutorily.

We'll start not in a recreational context but with an early mass shooting.

McCarthy v. Olin Corp.

119 F.3d 148 (2d Cir. 1997)

MESKILL, Circuit Judge:

Plaintiffs include two surviving victims and the estate of one deceased victim of the December 7, 1993 assault on the 5:33 p.m. Long Island Railroad commuter train. The bullets used in the shootings were Winchester "Black Talon" hollowpoint bullets, designed to enhance the injuries of their victims. This action was brought in New York State Supreme Court against, *inter alios,* Olin Corporation, the manufacturer of the bullets. The complaint asserted causes of action in the negligent manufacture, advertising and marketing of a product that was unreasonably designed and ultrahazardous, the making of an unreasonably dangerous product and strict liability in tort.... Olin moved to dismiss the complaint in its entirety pursuant to Fed.R.Civ.P. 12(b)(6). The district court, Baer, J., granted the motion, finding that the complaint failed to state any claim under New York law upon which relief could be granted. *McCarthy v. Sturm, Ruger and Co.*, 916 F.Supp. 366 (S.D.N.Y.1996). Plaintiffs appeal from the order dismissing their suit, or in the alternative ask us to certify the question of ammunition manufacturer liability to the New York Court of Appeals. Finding sufficient precedents in New York law to evaluate the merits of plaintiffs' claims, we decline to grant certification and affirm the judgment of the district court.

BACKGROUND

On December 7, 1993, Colin Ferguson boarded the Long Island Railroad's 5:33 p.m. commuter train departing from New York City and opened fire on the passengers. Six people, including Dennis McCarthy, were killed and nineteen others, including Kevin McCarthy and Maryanne Phillips, were wounded in the vicious attack. Ferguson was armed with a 9mm semiautomatic handgun, which was loaded with Winchester "Black Talon" bullets (Black Talons). The injuries to Dennis and Kevin McCarthy and Maryanne Phillips were enhanced by the ripping and tearing action of the Black Talons because, unfortunately, the bullets performed as designed.

The Black Talon is a hollowpoint bullet designed to bend upon impact into six ninety-degree angle razor-sharp petals or "talons" that increase the wounding power of the bullet by stretching, cutting and tearing tissue and bone as it travels through the victim. The Black Talon bullet was designed and manufactured by Olin Corporation (Olin) through its Winchester division and went on the market in 1992. Although the bullet was originally developed for law enforcement agencies, it was marketed and available to the general public. In November 1993, following public outcry, Olin pulled the Black Talon from the public market and restricted its sales to law enforcement personnel. Colin Ferguson allegedly purchased the ammunition in 1993, before it was withdrawn from the market.

Plaintiffs brought this action against Olin, Sturm, Ruger & Company Inc., the manufacturer of the handgun used by Ferguson, and Ram-Line Inc., the manufacturer of the fifteen round capacity magazine used with the handgun....

The district court granted the motion [to dismiss]. First addressing the issue of negligence, the court held that plaintiffs' negligence theories must fail because Olin owed no duty to plaintiffs to protect them from criminal misuse of the Black Talon ammunition. *McCarthy,* 916 F.Supp. at 368–70. [The district court also granted the motion based on a conclusion that the complaint failed to allege a design defect, because "the ammunition must by its very nature be dangerous to be functional," and due to a conclusion that plaintiff failed to allege facts sufficient to support a finding of causation, because the shooting was an extraordinary act that broke the chain of causation.]

* * *

Negligence

The crux of appellants' negligence theory is that Olin negligently marketed and placed the Black Talon ammunition for sale to the general public. Appellants argue that because of the severe wounding power of the bullets, Olin should have restricted sales to law enforcement agencies, for whom the bullet was originally designed. They also argue that Olin should have known that their advertising, which highlighted the ripping and tearing characteristics of the bullet, would attract "many types of sadistic, unstable and criminal personalities," such as Ferguson.

To state a cause of action for negligence, the plaintiffs must show: (1) that Olin owed them a "duty, or obligation, recognized by law", (2) a breach of the duty, (3) a "reasonably close causal connection between [defendant's] conduct and the resulting injury" and (4) loss or damage resulting from the breach.... "In the absence of a duty, as a matter of law, no liability can ensue." *Gonzalez v. Pius,* 138 A.D.2d 453, 454, 525 N.Y.S.2d 868, 869 (2d Dep't 1988). "Thus it may be said that the defendant was negligent, but is not liable because he was under no duty to the plaintiff not to be." Prosser & Keeton, § 30 at 164.

In tort cases, foreseeability is often confused with duty. Foreseeability "is applicable to determine the scope of duty—only after it has been determined that there is a duty." *Pulka v. Edelman,* 40 N.Y.2d 781, 785, 390 N.Y.S.2d 393, 396, 358 N.E.2d 1019, 1022 (1976). "The mere fact that a consequence might foreseeably result from an action or condition does not serve to establish a duty owing from a defendant to a plaintiff." *Gonzalez,* 138 A.D.2d at 454, 525 N.Y.S.2d at 869. The existence of a duty is a question of law to be decided by the court. New York courts are reluctant to impose a duty of care where there is little expectation that the defendant could prevent the actions of a third party....

New York courts do not impose a legal duty on manufacturers to control the distribution of potentially dangerous products such as ammunition. Accordingly, although it may have been foreseeable by Olin that criminal misuse of the Black Talon bullets could occur, Olin is not legally liable for such misuse. As the district court pointed out, appellants have not alleged that any special relationship existed between Olin and Ferguson. Here, Olin could not control the actions of Ferguson. "[I]t is unreasonable to impose [a] duty where the realities of every day experience show us that, regardless of the measures taken, there is little expectation that the one made responsible could prevent the ... conduct [of another]." *Pulka,* 40 N.Y.2d at 785, 390 N.Y.S.2d at 396, 358 N.E.2d at 1022; *see also Forni* [*v. Ferguson*], 648 N.Y.S.2d at 74 ("Plaintiffs did not, nor could they, show that defendants-manufacturers owed plaintiffs a duty of care.... New York does not impose a duty upon a manufacturer to refrain from the lawful distribution of a non-defective product.").

It is "the responsibility of courts in fixing the orbit of duty, to limit the legal consequences of wrongs to a controllable degree and to protect against crushing exposure to liability." *Strauss v. Belle Realty Co.,* 65 N.Y.2d 399, 402, 492 N.Y.S.2d 555, 557, 482 N.E.2d 34, 36 (1985) (internal quotation marks and citations omitted). To impose a duty on ammunition manufacturers to protect against criminal misuse of its product would likely force ammunition products—which legislatures have not proscribed, and which concededly are not defectively designed or manufactured and have some socially valuable uses—off the market due to the threat of limitless liability. Because Olin did not owe a legal duty to plaintiffs to protect against Colin Ferguson's horrible action, appellants' complaint does not state a cause of action for negligence and the claim was properly dismissed.

NOTES AND QUESTIONS

1. This opinion does not reference the Second Amendment and any discussion would be well beyond the scope of this casebook. But it is worth considering if the *potential* Constitutional issues had any influence on the court.

2. The court does not go into detail about when courts modify or limit a duty of care, but we can infer some of the standards and pitfalls. Such actions should be taken as to a *category* of cases (here, we could term the category the sale of otherwise legal products that have the potential for misuse); and they should be based on a special problem of policy (here, the next-to-last paragraph summarizes it—essentially the court seeks to avoid tort liability wiping out businesses that it has concluded have some value). Is it necessarily the job of courts to "protect [defendants] against crushing exposure to liability"? Does this usurp the role of the jury?

3. A real danger in these cases is courts conflating duty and breach. This occurred in a 2023 case involving the tragic deaths by suicide of two teenagers who purchased sodium nitrite from a third party, Loudwolf, on the Amazon platform. *McCarthy v. Amazon.com*, No. C23-0263JLR, 2023 U.S. Dist. LEXIS 110801 (W.D. Wash. June 27, 2023). Sodium nitrite, based on the record in the case, has various practical purposes; it is used primarily to inhibit corrosion, as an antidote to cyanide poisoning, and as a microbial. But it is also used, when not diluted, to cause death—and that its purchase from Loudwolf and Amazon, and its use, had been promoted on a website aimed at people seeking to cause self-harm.

   The teenagers' families sued (among others) Amazon for selling the pure product, despite having received multiple reports of purchasers using it for suicide. Amazon and Loudwolf moved to dismiss under Rule 12(b)(6) of the Federal Rules of Civil Procedure, contending that the complaint failed to state a claim upon which relief could be granted. That context is important, since it means the court was obligated to take all plausibly alleged facts as true. The court dismissed the families' claims, concluding first that the product was not defective, "and that Amazon thus did not owe a duty to warn." *Id.* at *15.

The first part of that conclusion is arguably questionable, since defect is ordinarily an issue of fact and the court provides little to no analysis to reach the conclusion, but the second part is more interesting for our purposes. In concluding that there was no duty to warn, the court repeatedly focuses on the decedents' knowledge. "Plaintiffs do not allege any facts that contradict the clear implications that Ethan and Kristine were well aware of the dangers of ingesting Sodium Nitrite and intentionally purchased the chemical because of those known and obvious dangers." *Id.* at *18. That is, I'd suggest, a factual conclusion as to breach (or perhaps causation), but *not* a question of duty. A question of duty would not be so focused on what happened *here* but instead would focus on a class of cases and would more explicitly discussion the policy issues (as in the ammunition case above).

This Amazon *McCarthy* case (as opposed to the ammunition *McCarthy* case) would present a fine opportunity to establish or explore a no- or limited-duty rule, if the court so chose. It tracks the *McCarthy v. Olin* case issues rather neatly, involving the sale of an otherwise-legal and sometimes useful product that can, when misused, cause tragic outcomes. One could imagine an opinion stating that tort law ought not be used to effectively outlaw products that have social value based on their ability to be used for ill. But that's not the opinion as issued—instead of finding no duty as to a class of cases, the court found no liability in a single case.

4. It is important to note what the *McCarthy v. Olin* court makes plain—in some situations (including this one), it presumes that a reasonable jury *could* conclude that (a) Olin failed to act as a reasonably prudent ammunition manufacturer by making available to the general public this type of ammunition; (b) Olin's failure to act reasonably was the factual cause of the injuries and deaths of plaintiffs' decedents; (c) those injuries and deaths were foreseeable results of Olin's negligence; and (d) plaintiffs were damaged by Olin's negligence. In most cases (where duty is present), that's all one needs for a plaintiff's verdict.

   Not so here. The conclusion about duty is necessarily a conclusion that *even though* all of those other elements were satisfied under usual standards, the possibility of liability is to be taken off the table for some *other* reason—in particular, a reason of policy. Another way to contrast the *McCarthy v. Olin* case with the *McCarthy v. Amazon* case to illuminate the duty versus breach distinction is this: the former court doesn't say that these facts could never support a finding that Olin acted negligently and caused harm as a result (but excludes the possibility of liability on policy grounds); the latter court does say that as to Amazon and Loudwolf, without ever letting a factfinder answer the question (and without discussing the policy issue). It's better to expressly discuss the policy being advanced.

That's also the case in the Flopper case back in the Introduction—a jury presumably could have found that the ride maker acted negligently and that the negligence was the factual and legal cause of damages. But, though he didn't use the "duty" terminology, Justice Cardozo effectively concluded that the park had no duty to that patron.

5. It's also important to see when in both the *Olin* and *Amazon* cases the subject motions were brought—as motions to dismiss under Rule 12(b)(6) of the Federal Rules of Civil Procedure, brought at the outset of the case. So this is before any discovery has taken place; all we know is what's alleged in the Complaint. This is appropriate, at least in the former case—duty is a legal issue to be decided by the court, after all—but it also means expenses have been relatively minimal. That is one of the reasons to address this sort of question via the legal issue of duty—to try to avoid the expenses that might deter conduct the courts do not want to deter.

6. At least in the tort law context, deciding issues of duty is probably the time when courts act most like legislatures—they act in a way that affects swaths of cases (as opposed to just the case in front of them). Not coincidentally, statutory impositions of what are effectively no-duty or limited-duty rules also come into play by actual legislatures, as we will see now, in two instances where Congress considered excluding certain categories of conduct from potential tort liability. The first passed and is law today. (I promise we will get to recreational examples soon.)

Public Law 109-92

109th Congress

An Act

To prohibit civil liability actions from being brought or continued against manufacturers, distributors, dealers, or importers of firearms or ammunition for damages, injunctive or other relief resulting from the misuse of their products by others.

Be it enacted by the Senate and House of Representatives of the United States of America in Congress assembled,

SECTION 1. SHORT TITLE.

This Act may be cited as the "Protection of Lawful Commerce in Arms Act".

SEC. 2. FINDINGS; PURPOSES.

(a) Findings.—Congress finds the following:

(1) The Second Amendment to the United States Constitution provides that the right of the people to keep and bear arms shall not be infringed.

(2) The Second Amendment to the United States Constitution protects the rights of individuals, including those who are not members of a militia or engaged in military service or training, to keep and bear arms.

(3) Lawsuits have been commenced against manufacturers, distributors, dealers, and importers of firearms that operate as designed and intended, which seek money damages and other relief for the harm caused by the misuse of firearms by third parties, including criminals.

(4) The manufacture, importation, possession, sale, and use of firearms and ammunition in the United States are heavily regulated by Federal, State, and local laws....

(5) Businesses in the United States that are engaged in interstate and foreign commerce through the lawful design, manufacture, marketing, distribution, importation, or sale to the public of firearms or ammunition products that have been shipped or transported in interstate or foreign commerce are not, and should not, be liable for the harm caused by those who criminally or unlawfully misuse firearm products or ammunition products that function as designed and intended.

(6) The possibility of imposing liability on an entire industry for harm that is solely caused by others is an abuse of the legal system, erodes public confidence in our Nation's laws, threatens the diminution of a basic constitutional right and civil liberty, invites the disassembly and destabilization of other industries and economic sectors lawfully competing in the free enterprise system of the United States, and constitutes an unreasonable burden on interstate and foreign commerce of the United States.

(7) The liability actions commenced or contemplated by the Federal Government, States, municipalities, and private interest groups and others are based on theories without foundation in hundreds of years of the common law and jurisprudence of the United States and do not represent a bona fide expansion of the common law. The possible sustaining of these actions by a maverick judicial officer or petit jury would expand civil liability in a manner never contemplated by the framers of the Constitution, by Congress, or by the legislatures of the several States. Such an expansion of liability would constitute a deprivation of the rights, privileges, and immunities guaranteed to a citizen of the United States under the Fourteenth Amendment to the United States Constitution.

(8) The liability actions commenced or contemplated by the Federal Government, States, municipalities, private interest groups and others attempt to use the judicial branch to circumvent the Legislative branch of government to regulate interstate and foreign commerce through judgments and judicial decrees thereby threatening the Separation of Powers doctrine and weakening and undermining important principles of federalism, State sovereignty and comity between the sister States.

(b) Purposes.—The purposes of this Act are as follows:

(1) To prohibit causes of action against manufacturers, distributors, dealers, and importers of firearms or ammunition products, and their trade associations, for the harm solely caused by the criminal or unlawful misuse of firearm products or ammunition products by others when the product functioned as designed and intended.

(2) To preserve a citizen's access to a supply of firearms and ammunition for all lawful purposes, including hunting, self-defense, collecting, and competitive or recreational shooting.

(3) To guarantee a citizen's rights, privileges, and immunities, as applied to the States, under the Fourteenth Amendment to the United States Constitution, pursuant to section 5 of that Amendment.

(4) To prevent the use of such lawsuits to impose unreasonable burdens on interstate and foreign commerce.

(5) To protect the right, under the First Amendment to the Constitution, of manufacturers, distributors, dealers, and importers of firearms or ammunition products, and trade associations, to speak freely, to assemble peaceably, and to petition the Government for a redress of their grievances.

(6) To preserve and protect the Separation of Powers doctrine and important principles of federalism, State sovereignty and comity between sister States.

(7) To exercise congressional power under article IV, section 1 (the Full Faith and Credit Clause) of the United States Constitution.

SEC. 3. PROHIBITION ON BRINGING OF QUALIFIED CIVIL LIABILITY ACTIONS IN FEDERAL OR STATE COURT.

(a) In General.—A qualified civil liability action may not be brought in any Federal or State court.

(b) Dismissal of Pending Actions.—A qualified civil liability action that is pending on the date of enactment of this Act shall be immediately dismissed by the court in which the action was brought or is currently pending.

SEC. 4. DEFINITIONS.

In this Act:

(1) Engaged in the business.—The term "engaged in the Business" has the meaning given that term in section 921(a)(21) of title 18, United States Code, and, as applied to a seller of ammunition, means a person who devotes time, attention, and labor to the sale of ammunition as a regular course of trade or business with the principal objective of livelihood and profit through the sale or distribution of ammunition....

(4) Qualified product.—The term "qualified product" means a firearm (as defined in subparagraph (A) or (B) of section 921(a)(3) of title 18, United States Code), including any antique firearm (as defined in section 921(a)(16) of such title), or ammunition (as defined in section 921(a)(17)(A) of such title), or a component part of a fire-

arm or ammunition, that has been shipped or transported in interstate or foreign commerce.

(5) Qualified civil liability action.—

(A) In general.—The term "qualified civil liability action" means a civil action or proceeding or an administrative proceeding brought by any person against a manufacturer or seller of a qualified product, or a trade association, for damages, punitive damages, injunctive or declaratory relief, abatement, restitution, fines, or penalties, or other relief, resulting from the criminal or unlawful misuse of a qualified product by the person or a third party, but shall not include—

(i) an action brought against a transferor convicted under section 924(h) of title 18, United States Code, or a comparable or identical State felony law, by a party directly harmed by the conduct of which the transferee is so convicted;

(ii) an action brought against a seller for negligent entrustment or negligence per se;

(iii) an action in which a manufacturer or seller of a qualified product knowingly violated a State or Federal statute applicable to the sale or marketing of the product, and the violation was a proximate cause of the harm for which relief is sought, including—

(I) any case in which the manufacturer or seller knowingly made any false entry in, or failed to make appropriate entry in, any record required to be kept under Federal or State law with respect to the qualified product, or aided, abetted, or conspired with any person in making any false or fictitious oral or written statement with respect to any fact material to the lawfulness of the sale or other disposition of a qualified product; or

(II) any case in which the manufacturer or seller aided, abetted, or conspired with any other person to sell or otherwise dispose of a qualified product, knowing, or having reasonable cause to believe, that the actual buyer of the qualified product was prohibited from possessing or receiving a firearm or ammunition under subsection (g) or (n) of section 922 of title 18, United States Code;

(iv) an action for breach of contract or warranty in connection with the purchase of the product;

(v) an action for death, physical injuries or property damage resulting directly from a defect in design or manufacture of the product, when used as intended or in a reasonably foreseeable manner, except that where the discharge of the product was caused by a volitional act that constituted a criminal offense, then such act shall be considered the sole proximate cause of any resulting death, personal injuries or property damage; or

(vi) an action or proceeding commenced by the Attorney General to enforce the provisions of chapter 44 of title 18 or chapter 53 of title 26, United States Code.

* * *

(8) Trade association.—The term "trade association" means—

(A) any corporation, unincorporated association, federation, business league, professional or business organization not organized or operated for profit and no part of the net earnings of which inures to the benefit of any private shareholder or individual;

(B) that is an organization described in section 501(c)(6) of the Internal Revenue Code of 1986 and exempt from tax under section 501(a) of such Code; and

(C) 2 or more members of which are manufacturers or sellers of a qualified product.

(9) Unlawful misuse.—The term "unlawful misuse" means conduct that violates a statute, ordinance, or regulation as it relates to the use of a qualified product.

NOTES AND QUESTIONS

1. Unlike the opinion preceding it, this statute is explicit in its discussion of the Second Amendment. Do you agree with the implication that the failure to protect gun manufacturers, dealers, and others (including, interestingly, trade associations) from potential liability for crimes committed with their products would undercut the Second Amendment?
2. Legislation like this presumes that a court would permit the subject claims to proceed and also that a jury might find manufacturers (and others) liable for the conduct described. This, of course, means that

Congress (like the court in *McCarthy v. Olin* as to ammunition makers) presumed that a jury might find that, in at least some cases, a jury would conclude that a gun manufacturer had (a) failed to act with reasonable care under the circumstances (breach), (b) the manufacturer's breach was the factual cause of harm to a plaintiff (factual cause), (c) the manufacturer's breach was "foreseeable" (*i.e.*, the harm that resulted was the type of harm we'd seek to prevent by calling the conduct negligent—legal cause), and (d) the plaintiff was damaged as a result.

Do you agree with Congress that a court permitting such a case to proceed, and a jury finding for plaintiff, is properly considered "maverick"—*i.e.*, that such a conclusion finding a manufacturer liable would *always* be wrong and therefore it is appropriate to prevent such cases from proceeding in the first place?

3. Again, keep in mind that for legislation like this (or its common law analogues, no-duty findings), the issue to be decided is at least designed to be a purely legal issue and courts decide it based on Rule 12(b)(6) of the Federal Rules of Civil Procedure (or its state equivalents). This is important, among other reasons, because it means that in most cases, the litigation will end before any discovery takes place, resulting in far lower litigation costs. (And, if the statute is successful in its goals, lawsuits mostly won't get filed in the first place.) As we will see later, sometimes even when the statutes attempt to define the categories of cases cleanly, courts will conclude that there is a factual issue to be addressed by a jury, arguably eliminating much of the value of such statutes.

4. In *Soto v. Bushmaster Firearms International, LLC*, 331 Conn. 53 (Conn. 2019), the Connecticut Supreme Court, evaluating a lawsuit relating to the Sandy Hook Elementary School mass shooting in Newtown, Connecticut, concluded that the Protection of Lawful Commerce in Arms Act did *not* prevent a portion of a lawsuit brought by the survivors of some of the child victims from proceeding:

> The plaintiffs have offered one narrow legal theory, however, that is recognized under established Connecticut law. Specifically, they allege that the defendants knowingly marketed, advertised, and promoted the XM15-E2S for civilians to use to carry out offensive, military style combat

> missions against their perceived enemies. Such use of the XM15-E2S, or any weapon for that matter, would be illegal, and Connecticut law does not permit advertisements that promote or encourage violent, criminal behavior. Following a scrupulous review of the text and legislative history of PLCAA, we also conclude that Congress has not clearly manifested an intent to extinguish the traditional authority of our legislature and our courts to protect the people of Connecticut from the pernicious practices alleged in the present case.

Id. at 65–66. The U.S. Supreme Court denied *certiorari* and the matter settled.

5. The prior legislation was adopted and remains law today. The next example has never become law.

H. R. 339 (2004)

AN ACT

To prevent legislative and regulatory functions from being usurped by civil liability actions brought or continued against food manufacturers, marketers, distributors, advertisers, sellers, and trade associations for claims of injury relating to a person's weight gain, obesity, or any health condition associated with weight gain or obesity.

Be it enacted by the Senate and House of Representatives of the United States of America in Congress assembled,

SECTION 1. SHORT TITLE.

This Act may be cited as the "Personal Responsibility in Food Consumption Act".

SEC. 2. PURPOSE.

The purpose of this Act is to allow Congress, State legislatures, and regulatory agencies to determine appropriate laws, rules, and regulations to address the problems of weight gain, obesity, and health conditions associated with weight gain or obesity.

SEC. 3. PRESERVATION OF SEPARATION OF POWERS.

(a) In General.—A qualified civil liability action may not be brought in any Federal or State court.

(b) Dismissal of Pending Actions.—A qualified civil liability action that is pending on the date of the enactment of this Act shall be dismissed immediately by the court in which the action was brought or is currently pending.

* * *

(d) Pleadings.—In any action of the type described in section (5)(B)(i), the complaint initiating such action shall state with particularity the Federal and State statutes that were allegedly violated and the facts that are alleged to have proximately caused the injury claimed.

SEC. 4. DEFINITIONS.

In this Act:

(1) Engaged in the business.—The term "engaged in the business" means a person who manufactures, markets, distributes, advertises, or sells a qualified product in the person's regular course of trade or business.

* * *

(4) Qualified product.—The term "qualified product" means a food (as defined in section 201(f) of the Federal Food, Drug, and Cosmetic Act (21 U.S.C. 321(f))).

(5) Qualified civil liability action.—(A) Subject to subparagraphs (B) and (C), the term "qualified civil liability action" means a civil action brought by any person against a manufacturer or seller of a qualified product, or a trade association, for damages, penalties, declaratory judgment, injunctive or declaratory relief, restitution, or other relief arising out of, related to, or resulting in injury or potential injury resulting from a person's consumption of a qualified product and weight gain, obesity, or any health condition that is associated with a person's weight gain or obesity, including an action brought by a person other than the person on whose weight gain, obesity, or health condition the action is based, and any derivative action brought by or on behalf of any person or any representative, spouse, parent, child, or other relative of any person.

(B) Such term shall not include—

(i) an action in which a manufacturer or seller of a qualified product knowingly and willfully violated a Federal or State statute applicable to the manufacturing, marketing, distribution, advertisement, labeling, or sale of the product, and the violation was a proximate cause of injury related to a person's weight gain, obesity, or any health condition associated with a person's weight gain or obesity; or

(ii) an action for breach of express contract or express warranty in connection with the purchase of a qualified product.

(C) Such term shall not be construed to include an action brought under the Federal Trade Commission Act (15 U.S.C. 41 et seq.) or the Federal Food, Drug, and Cosmetic Act (21 U.S.C. 301 et seq.).

* * *

(8) Trade association.—The term "trade association" means any association or business organization (whether or not incorporated under Federal or State law) that is not operated for profit, and 2 or more members of which are manufacturers, marketers, distributors, advertisers, or sellers of a qualified product.

Passed the House of Representatives March 10, 2004.

NOTES AND QUESTIONS

1. As noted, the food-oriented statute has not become law, having never made it past the Senate. Litigation alleging the kinds of harmed described in it has not become prevalent in the decades since it was first proposed. Fast food places continue to sell fast food, apparently undeterred by whatever litigation is taking place or by the risk of such litigation.
2. Do you think the arguments for a statutory exemption like this are stronger or weaker in the context of food than firearms?
3. The proposed findings in the food-related statute are not as extensive as in the firearm-related statute, but we can assume that those in support of it would look askance at any jury that found for a plaintiff in a lawsuit on the basis addressed in the bill. They would, perhaps, call that jury "maverick" along the lines of the firearms-related statutes. Do you agree? Can you imagine any set of facts (under either statute) where you would be uncomfortable taking the *possibility* of civil liability off the table?
4. Both statutes are, at least in part, premised on the notion that an appropriate legislative goal is to maintain the viability of otherwise

legal businesses that might have challenges remaining viable due to litigation. As you will see, courts sometimes reach similar conclusions relating to the proper role of civil litigation when it might threaten otherwise legal businesses. Do you respond differently to the argument when advanced by legislators versus judges?

Now—"Finally," you may be muttering—we turn to a clearly recreational context, in a case that relies on a statute that, like those above, defines the extent of duty.

Dunbar v. Jackson Hole Mountain Resort Corp.

392 F.3d 1145 (10th Cir. 2004)

Before Seymour, Henry, and Lucero, Circuit Judges.

Opinion

Lucero, Circuit Judge.

While skiing at the Jackson Hole Mountain Ski Resort, Camie Dunbar fell approximately twelve feet into a snowboard half-pipe, suffering severe injuries for which she alleges negligence on the part of Jackson Hole. At the time of her accident, Dunbar was attempting to exit a specially designated ski and snowboard terrain park. Finding that Jackson Hole did not owe Dunbar a duty of care for risks inherent to her chosen recreational activity under the Wyoming Recreational Safety Act, the district court granted summary judgment for the resort. Dunbar now appeals, arguing that the risks inherent to alpine skiing do not include the risk of falling into the side of a snowboard half-pipe when following a Jackson Hole employee's instructions on how to exit the terrain park. We exercise jurisdiction under 28 U.S.C. § 1291 and **REVERSE.**

I

In March 2001, Camie Dunbar suffered the stated injuries when she skied off a snow ledge in a specially designed "terrain park" at the Jackson Hole Mountain Resort in Jackson Hole, Wyoming. A 33-year-old self-described intermediate skier from South Florida, Dunbar skied into the terrain park area with other members of her group who were part of a promotional ski trip sponsored by her employer Clear Channel Communications.

Containing various man made features such as a table top jump and a snowboard half-pipe, the Jackson Hole terrain park is designed for advanced skiers and snowboarders who choose to recreate in a very challenging risk-filled environment. The terrain park is separated by a fence and a boundary rope from an intermediate ski run. To enter the terrain park, skiers must pass through a gate marked with a warning sign, alerting them that they are entering an advanced ski area where "serious injuries, death, and equipment damage can occur." At the time of the accident, the terrain park had been relocated to its position in an intermediate ski run, and did not appear on the Resort's trail maps.

On the last day of her trip, Dunbar, along with Dave Dresher and Mike Jennings, went up the mountain intending to "investigate" the terrain park. In proceeding down an intermediate ski run, they skied through an initial gate providing a warning sign that they were entering a double black diamond "terrain feature trail." After stopping adjacent to a red tram car which served as the office for the "pipe and park" crew who were responsible for maintenance of the terrain park, Dunbar observed other skiers and snowboarders maneuver various features in the terrain park.

Based on their observations, Dunbar and her companions decided that they did not want to try any of the features. In her deposition, Dunbar attested to thinking "this is my last day [and] I want to go home in one piece." She stated that she did not know that there was a snowboard half-pipe in the terrain park, and believed instead that the area included only the jumps she observed from the red gondola. There is no suggestion by either party that Dunbar intended to jump any of the terrain jumps or intended to try her hand at stunts as a skier in a snowboard half-pipe. Having decided that she did not want to ski any of the double-black diamond features, she asked a Jackson Hole employee how to exit that area "if you don't want to take this terrain park." She was told either to take off her skis and hike back to the gate through which she had entered or to proceed in the direction of a "catwalk" to which the employee pointed. Unbeknownst to Dunbar, the "catwalk" led to a side entrance to the snowboard half-pipe.

Ms. Dunbar along with her companions skied along the "catwalk." Although it is a matter of some dispute between the parties, in order to proceed down the catwalk, skiers had to pass warning signs indicating that they were approaching a snowboard half-pipe area. Both Dunbar and her companions claim not to have noticed the signs. Dunbar and Jennings went along the catwalk, up an incline, across a flat deck, and fell approximately twelve feet into the half-pipe. Jennings managed to maneuver his snowboard in such a way as to avoid injury. Dunbar was not so fortunate. As a consequence of her fall into the half-pipe, she suffered severe injuries to her pelvis and thigh requiring surgery and intensive physical therapy. Dunbar testified that she will neither be able to return to her pre-injury range of motion, nor will she be capable of having a natural childbirth as a result of the injury to her hip.

Asserting that Jackson Hole's negligence caused her injuries, Dunbar filed suit in district court. Jackson Hole filed a motion for summary judgment and a motion to strike portions of Dunbar's affidavits as attempts to create sham factual issues in order to survive summary judgment. The district court granted both motions for Jackson Hole on the basis that portions of Dunbar's affidavit were inconsistent with her deposition testimony. Dunbar now appeals.

II

We review a grant of summary judgment *de novo*, applying the same legal standards as the district court pursuant to Fed.R.Civ.P. 56(c). *Chickasaw Nation v. United States,* 208 F.3d 871, 875 (10th Cir.2000).

* * *

A

To protect providers of recreational sports and activities from liability for alpine skiing, equine activities, and other outdoor pursuits in the state, the Wyoming legislature limited their duty of care by enacting the Wyoming Recreation Safety Act. Wyo. Stat. Ann. § 1-1-121 et seq.; *see Sapone v. Grand Targhee, Inc.,* 308 F.3d 1096, 1101 (10th Cir.2002). As a matter of common law, in order to prevail in a negligence action, a plaintiff would first have to demonstrate that the defendant owed her a duty to act with reasonable care. *See, e.g., Erpelding v. Lisek,* 71 P.3d 754, 757 (Wyo.2003). The Safety Act is designed to limit the duty a provider of recreational sports and activities owes to participants.

Under the Safety Act, a provider of a recreational opportunity has no duty to protect participants from "inherent risks" of the particular sport or recreational opportunity. Wyo. Stat. Ann. § 1-1-123. In relevant part, the act provides:

> (a) Any person who takes part in any sport or recreational opportunity assumes the inherent risks in that sport or recreational opportunity, whether those risks are known or unknown, and is legally responsible for any and all damage, injury or death to himself or other persons or property that results from the inherent risks in that sport or recreational opportunity.
> (b) A provider of any sport or recreational opportunity is not required to eliminate, alter or control the inherent risks within the particular sport or recreational opportunity.

§ 1-1-123. Wyoming defines inherent risks as "those dangers or conditions which are characteristic of, intrinsic to, or an integral part of any sport or recreational opportunity." Wyo. Stat. Ann. § 1-1-122(a)(i). Wyoming further defines "Sport or recreational opportunity" as meaning "commonly understood sporting activities," which include "alpine skiing." § 1-1-122(a)(iii). Thus, for example, a provider of an alpine skiing opportunity will not be liable for a duty of care with regard to dangers that are "characteristic of" or "intrinsic to" or "an integral part" of the sport of alpine skiing. However, the act does provide for a cause of action based on the negligence of the recreational opportunity provider when the injury is not the result of an inherent risk of the sport or recreational opportunity:

"Actions based upon negligence of the provider wherein the damage, injury or death is not the result of an inherent risk of the sport or recreational opportunity shall be preserved...." § 1-1-123(c). Thus, whether a recreation provider owes its patrons a duty of care depends entirely on whether the specific risks can be characterized as inherent to the sport or activity.

What is inherent to a sport or activity, however, is far from self-evident. In *Sapone,* we defined "inherent" under the Wyoming Safety Act as either "'those risks which are essential characteristics of a sport and those which participants desire to confront,' or they are undesirable risks which are simply a collateral part of the recreation activity." *Sapone,* 308 F.3d at 1103 (citation omitted). We have further defined a risk that is not inherent as "a risk that was atypical, uncharacteristic, [and] not intrinsic to the recreational activity...." *Id.* at 1104. Although equine activities are among those the Wyoming legislature clearly meant to protect, and although horseback riding indubitably involves inherent risks, we have concluded, following the Wyoming Supreme Court, that not all risks of horseback riding are inherent risks. *Cooperman v. David,* 214 F.3d 1162, 1167 (10th Cir.2000); *Halpern v. Wheeldon,* 890 P.2d 562, 566 (Wyo.1995). Some risks may occur from the choices a recreation provider makes on behalf of the participant and from the conditions in which the recreational opportunity is provided. Thus, atypical or uncharacteristic risks can arise even in those specific sports the Wyoming legislature clearly intended to exempt from liability for inherent risks. Following the Wyoming Supreme Court in *Halpern,* we have held that "where genuine issues of material fact exist, the determination of whether something is or is not an inherent risk is a factual question that must be sent to the jury for determination." *Sapone,* 308 F.3d at 1102.

As a preliminary matter, what sport or activity characterizes Camie Dunbar's behavior is a matter of considerable dispute. Most generally, she was engaged in alpine skiing—a sport clearly covered by the Safety Act. If we were to analyze the risk at this level of generality, then it would certainly appear that falling twelve feet into a trench in the middle of an intermediate ski-run would decidedly *not* constitute an inherent risk of alpine skiing. Such a level of generality, however, is not appropriate. To determine what risk is inherent to Dunbar's activity, we must go beyond a broad characterization and inquire into the specific circumstances of both her actions and those of the recreation provider.

When the *Cooperman* court examined the risks of horseback riding in the context of the specific facts of that case, for example, it employed a different analytical framework than if it had merely asked the abstract question whether falling off a horse is an inherent risk of horseback riding. *Cooperman,* 214 F.3d at 1167. Because a determination of what risks are inherent to a sport or activity may change by descriptive differences, we have stated that "[w]hen attempting to determine whether a risk is inherent to a sport, we can not look at the risk in a vacuum, apart from the factual setting to which the [participant] was exposed." *Cooperman,* 214 F.3d at 1167. Instead, we must analyze the risk "at the greatest level of specificity permitted by the factual record." *Id.* As an example of this principle, we have explained:

> [I]f the only fact presented to the court is that the horse bucked while the rider was properly sitting on the horse, we would frame the duty question as whether a bucking horse is an inherent risk of horseback riding. However, if the facts established that the owner of the horse lit firecrackers next to the horse and the horse bucked, we would ask whether a horse bucking when firecrackers are lit next to the horse is an inherent risk of horseback riding.

Id.

For instance, in *Cooperman,* we determined that the risk of a slipping saddle, in light of the lack of scientific precision in hand cinching, is inherent to horseback riding. *Id.* at 1168. However, in *Sapone,* we concluded that a child sustaining injuries when falling from the saddle during a trail-riding lesson was not an inherent risk when there was evidence that the horse was too large, that the instructions were inadequate, that no headgear was provided, and that the route was too dangerous. *Sapone,* 308 F.3d at 1104. Similarly, in *Madsen v. Wyoming River Trips, Inc.,* 31 F.Supp.2d 1321, 1329 (D.Wyo.1999), the district court determined that the risks inherent to white-water rafting did not include risks of injury resulting from the recreation provider's overcrowding the boat. *See also Carden v. Kelly,* 175 F.Supp.2d. 1318, 1329 (2001) (finding a genuine issue of material fact whether, given the actions and inactions of the recreation provider, a horse's stumbling and falling was an inherent risk of horseback riding).

In the present case, the district court's order hinged on a determination of where Ms. Dunbar was located when she made her choice to proceed down the catwalk. Thus, not simply a question of alpine skiing, but of alpine skiing in a designated terrain park became the significant "factual setting" the district court used to examine the inherent risks to which Dunbar was exposed.

In its order granting Jackson Hole's motion for summary judgment, the district court stressed, and Jackson Hole urges on appeal, the need to focus on the choices that Dunbar made when entering the terrain park. Reasoning that an inherent risk analysis could not properly be conducted without considering Dunbar's choices, the district court focused on the facts of Dunbar's conduct as the recreational participant. Central to the district court's determination of inherent risk was the simple fact of Dunbar's choice to enter the terrain park. The court found that "a terrain feature such as a half-pipe located within a fenced terrain park is an inherent risk to a skier that voluntarily and knowingly enters that park." *Dunbar v. Jackson Hole,* No. 02-CV-123-D, slip op. at 14–15 (D. Wyo. June 16, 2003). Furthermore, the court concludes that having entered the terrain park, Dunbar "decided to enter the [metaphorical] 'rodeo' and thus assumed the risk associated with that activity." *Id.* at 15. We disagree.

First, we note that the plain language of the Safety Act focuses on "[a]ny person who takes part in any sport or recreational opportunity," Wyo. Stat. Ann. § 1-1-123, and does not mention the location of the sport or activity. We fail to see how simply being present in the terrain park redefines the sport or activity in which Dunbar is engaged, especially absent further choices to take part in any of the terrain park features. No doubt location may have a bearing on how to characterize a participant's activity, but it is not automatically determinative as the district court suggests. Indeed, from the record, it is not clear whether the double black diamond designation applied to the area of the intermediate ski run from the putative entrance to the terrain park to the red tram car and from the tram car to the catwalk. There seems to be no dispute that in the areas Dunbar traversed a skier would not confront any unusual risks or features that differed from those elsewhere on the intermediate ski run (at least until the point where Dunbar fell into the half-pipe). Thus it would seem to be an open question whether the warning signs and double black designation properly applied to the area that Dunbar actually traversed or if they were limited to the physical space containing the dangerous terrain features. If the double black diamond designation applies only to the specific terrain features and if the warnings apply only to those skiers and snowboarders who attempt to maneuver over and among the trail features down the fall line of the mountain, then it may be difficult to conclude that Dunbar assumed a double black diamond risk simply by skiing across the fall line on an intermediate slope to the tram car and then proceeding, as directed, by way of the catwalk. Proper resolution of these factual questions concerning the impact of Dunbar's specific location on Jackson Hole's duty, however, are for a jury, not for the court, to decide.

Second, we conclude that there is a difference between the consequences of conduct chosen by Dunbar, and risks that are inherent to that choice. It does not necessarily follow, as the district court finds, that having entered the terrain park, Dunbar also chose to confront all the features and conditions present within it. Although the district court emphasized the choices and conduct of the plaintiff in determining what risks she assumed, the court makes no distinction between the risks that are inherent to her actual choices—to ski into the terrain park area, but not to "take" any of the features—and risks that are inherent to choices one would make when actually intending to ski over the specific features.

Indeed, a reasonable person who entered the general area of the terrain park would stop first to view the features and decide whether or not to attempt to maneuver over or through any of them. In fact, Jackson Hole's warning signs, the presence of which figure prominently in this dispute, direct skiers and snowboarders to "please observe terrain features, their risks, and their degree of difficulty before using." That is precisely what Ms. Dunbar did. She chose to enter the area of the terrain park—if not the terrain park itself—but specifically chose not to "use" or "take" any of the terrain park features after doing exactly what Jackson Hole's signs advised her to do: "observe ... before using." Presumably, Jackson Hole does not wish to claim that it operates like the Hotel California—where you can check in any time you like but you can never leave. Accordingly, it was error for the district court to conclude that having followed Jackson Hole's instructions, having assessed the risks and decided not to use the terrain features, that there is no material issue of fact concerning whether a skier could leave without accruing those very risks. Having "entered" the terrain park, Dunbar did not "use" the terrain park as a terrain park—viz., she did not attempt to jump the table top jump nor did she attempt to do stunts in the snowboard half-pipe. She attempted to exit the terrain park without "taking" any of the features, and followed instructions from a Jackson Hole employee on how to exit the park. Given the specific factual setting of this case, what risks are associated with Dunbar's actual choices and what duty Jackson Hole owed her are properly questions for the jury.

Accordingly, we conclude that the district court erred when it found that the risk of falling twelve feet into a snowboard half-pipe was an inherent risk of Dunbar's alpine skiing when she had stopped and observed double diamond terrain features and had chosen not to "take" those features. When, as is here, genuine issues of material fact exist, it is properly a question for the jury to determine whether dangers that are "characteristic of" or "intrinsic to" or "an integral part" of the sport of alpine skiing evaluated under the specific factual circumstances of this case include those encountered by Dunbar in skiing from the main intermediate run to the tram car and from the tram car along the catwalk. *Sapone,* 308 F.3d at 1102 ("whether something is or is not an inherent risk is a factual question that must be sent to the jury for determination"); *see also, Dillworth v. Gambardella,* 970 F.2d 1113, 1123 (2d Cir.1992) (holding under a Vermont statute similar to Wyoming's, that determination of inherent danger "is a question of fact properly submitted to the jury").

B

As we have observed, inquiry into what dangers constitute an inherent risk under the Safety Act is inextricably intertwined with an inquiry into what duty the recreation provider owes to the participant, and whether that question is properly one for the judge or jury. If Dunbar's accident was not the product of an inherent risk of her recreational activity, then a question remains for the fact finder concerning what duty was owed her and whether Jackson Hole fulfilled that duty. We conclude that the district court improperly analyzed the issue of Jackson Hole's duty.

When the issue of duty involves questions of fact, as is the case with "inherent risks," the Wyoming Supreme Court has held that the question of a defendant's duty should be resolved by a jury. *Halpern,* 890 P.2d at 565. However, in certain instances where no material questions of fact exist—e.g., if the risk is clearly one inherent to the sport—the district court may decide as a matter of law that a provider does not owe a duty to the participant under the Safety Act. *Halpern,* 890 P.2d at 566 (noting that "[i]n appropriate cases where no genuine issues of material fact exist, the district court may decide as a matter of law that the provider does not owe a duty to the participant."). Such was not the case here.

How the district court framed the statement of Jackson Hole's duty is crucial to a proper disposition of this case. It has become something of a standard analysis in this line of cases for a district court to frame the question of duty, in addition to the question of inherent risk, in the form of a fact-specific inquiry. Indeed, as the district court noted in another Safety Act case, "[t]he Court cannot stress how important it is to frame the duty question correctly. If the duty question is framed incorrectly, the legislature's intent to allow a cause of action for negligence will be lost." *Madsen,* 31 F.Supp.2d. at 1329.

In the present case, the district court framed the question of duty as follows:

> [W]hether Camie Dunbar's injuries occurred as a result of the inherent risk of alpine skiing when this thirty-three year-old experienced skier knowingly entered a specially designated terrain park, skied past five warning signs, made the choice not to exit by way of the gate she entered understanding that she would encounter expert and double expert terrain features, skied up the visible half-pipe wall, and across a fourteen-foot platform.

Dunbar, slip op. at 14. We have already concluded that Dunbar's mere presence in the entrance area of the terrain park does not give rise as a matter of law to a heightened risk above what is normal to alpine skiing. We now conclude that the question of Jackson Hole's duty was improperly framed because it employs facts in dispute, and does not view the facts in the light most favorable to the non-moving party.

Specifically, the district court's finding that Dunbar chose not to exit the terrain park area via the gate by which she entered understanding that she would encounter expert and double expert terrain features is itself a fact open to dispute. Whether or not her choice was made with that understanding is a disputed fact, and read in the light most favorable to the plaintiff, the district court improperly incorporated a disputed fact in a light favoring the defendant. Second, the district court frames the duty question by stating that Dunbar "skied up the visible half-pipe wall." *Id.* Whether or not what she skied up was in fact visibly a half-pipe wall is itself a disputed fact, and inclusion of this fact in a light most favorable to the defendant was improper. Finally, the district court states that Dunbar "skied past five warning signs," which although perhaps true (though contested), shades the "duty question" in a way that ignores the factual issues of the content and import of each of those signs in the context of the Jackson Hole employee's instructions on how to exit the park. Given the fact that we have previously held that the question of a provider's duty is partially determined by a fact-specific framing of inherent risk, we conclude that the district court erred in making factual findings that are properly findings for a jury. *See Sapone*, 308 F.3d at 1102.

Finally, we note that whatever risks Dunbar assumed herself, it seems clear that she did not also assume the risk of needing to interpret the delphic statements of Jackson Hole's employees. Both Jackson Hole and the district court focus on the issue of choices that Dunbar made, ignoring the choice that Jackson Hole made for her in directing her to exit the terrain park area by either hiking out the main entrance or skiing along the catwalk. We have made clear that a duty of care may arise from choices made for the participant by the recreation provider. *Sapone*, 308 F.3d at 1104; *see also*, *Madsen*, 31 F.Supp.2d at 1328–29; *Carden*, 175 F. Supp.2d. at 1328–29. Absent from the district court's order is any recognition that once Dunbar asked a Jackson Hole employee how to exit the terrain park area without "taking" any of the features, Jackson Hole owed a duty to provide her with appropriate instructions, which might have included a specific warning to beware of the drop into the half-pipe at the end of the catwalk. Whether or not they fulfilled that duty is a question for the jury. Accordingly, the district court erred when it framed the question of Jackson Hole's duty by incorporating facts in dispute and when it failed to submit the question of duty to the fact finder pursuant to Wyoming Supreme Court precedent.

* * *

III

For the reasons set forth above, we **REVERSE** the district court and **REMAND** for further proceedings consistent with this opinion.

NOTES AND QUESTIONS

1. This court grapples with a common challenge in no-duty and limited-duty circumstances, whether statutory or not: what happens when the purely legal issue of duty has embedded in it a tricky factual question? Its answer—send it to the jury—is not particularly controversial. But it is worth noting the implication: in at least some cases where the legislature was hoping to exclude the possibility of litigation beyond the Rule 12(b)(6) stage (thus reducing costs), that litigation is still going to happen. There's nothing particularly wrong with that. It is just the consequence of the reality, however frustrating, that

a legislature (or a court) cannot anticipate every single factual scenario and provide a clear answer to whether it is in or out of the "inherent risk" bucket. So while the legislature was presumably trying to give ski resorts protection from lawsuits such that most would not even be brought and, if brought, would be dismissed at an early stage, this case shows how difficult it is to provide that kind of protection in all cases while still allowing some particularly strong cases to proceed.

Consider what kind of incentives this ruling provides for plaintiffs' attorneys seeking to sue a ski resort in Wyoming. How would you try to develop the facts in a case and how would you try to be creative in pleading?

2. My home state of Minnesota provides certain protections for people who organize "livestock activities" from lawsuits from participants (and spectators who go into off-limits areas). The statute requires public postings to take advantage of its protections, so these signs are all over the greatest state fair in the country (that is, the Minnesota State Fair):

ATTENTION VISITORS
PLEASE NOTE:

Under Minn. Stat. 604A.12
The Minnesota State Fair
is not liable for the injury,
death or sickness of a
participant, or a spectator
in an unauthorized area,
arising from the inherent risk of livestock activities.

INHERENT RISK:
The dangers arising from the propensity of livestock to behave in unpredictable ways including kicking, biting, or spooking in response to sound, sudden movement, unfamiliar objects, person, or other animals.

ATTENTION

3. The sign above is, as noted, required under the statute, but consider how it might be useful to the Fair in any lawsuits that arise from the listed risks, even if for some reason the statute does not provide immunity.
4. I observe, mostly as an aside, that in 2021, after a nice dinner at the Minnesota State Fair, a man in the restroom, apparently confusing the back of my leg for the urinal, did, well, what you'd usually expect to be done in a urinal, but on my leg. Had there been any consequences between my disgust (and my wife's disgust) and some aggressive doing of laundry, I do not think I assumed any of those risks. (I also do not think it was the State Fair's fault, though he was likely overserved.) Even with that less-than-ideal experience, I reiterate: the best State Fair anywhere. A colleague of mine, upon hearing the story, asked if I thought that was a battery. (I do.)
5. The *Dunbar* case treats inherent risks when they've been addressed in a statute. Of course, with tort law being mostly common law, many somewhat similar situations arise without a statutory overlay. You've already seen one—go back and read the *Murphy v. Steeplechase Amusement Co.* "Flopper" case in Chapter 1. But for a more modern gloss, we visit a haunted attraction in Saint Louis.

Munoz v. Six Flags St. Louis, LLC

670 S.W.3d 239 (Mo. Ct. App. 2023)

Sherri B. Sullivan, J.

Introduction

Carly Munoz (Munoz) appeals from the grant of summary judgment in favor of Six Flags St. Louis, LLC d/b/a Six Flags St. Louis and John/Jane Doe (collectively Six Flags) on Munoz's negligence claim. The trial court granted Six Flags' motion for summary judgment based on assumption of the risk due to the nature of the event, *i.e.*, actors scaring guests during the park's annual Fright Fest. Munoz appeals the trial court's ruling, alleging she was denied her right to trial by jury where there are factual disputes regarding the cause of the injuries she sustained during the event. We affirm.

Factual and Procedural Background

On October 19, 2019, Munoz attended Six Flags' Fright Fest with her cousin. Before attending Fright Fest, the Six Flags' annual Halloween-themed event, Munoz understood characters in the park would try to scare her. She knew and appreciated she would get surprised, startled, scared, and frightened and also understood people could have different and unpredictable reactions whenever they got surprised, frightened, startled, or scared.

On the day of her injury, Munoz arrived at the park with her cousin around 8:00 p.m. and her injury occurred around 11 p.m. In that three-hour period before her injury, Munoz had seen and encountered characters in the park who tried to scare and startle her. On at least 10 different occasions, she also saw characters interact with other guests and she saw guests scream and sometimes run after they encountered the characters. Everything Munoz witnessed in the hours before her injury was what she expected to occur at Fright Fest. She never expressed feeling uncomfortable, unsafe, or in danger, and in fact was having fun and did not want to leave.

Munoz recalled she was injured while she was walking toward the Mr. Freeze ride when a clown jumped out in front of her "out of nowhere" and started "chasing" after 10–15 other guests in that area, and then everyone in that area started to run. However, when asked to explain specifically what occurred, Munoz testified the clown was actually only six feet away from her when it popped out and moved toward her when she turned and ran away. Munoz confirmed she never actually looked back to see if the clown was "chasing" her. Munoz believed it was about 10 seconds after she started running that she tripped on a curb and injured herself. Similarly, Munoz's cousin testified she did not perceive the clown to be interacting with them. Munoz's cousin believed the clown to be "fast walking" or running toward another group of people near them. Munoz's cousin did not know if the clown actually made any movements or actions toward them before they started running. Munoz's cousin, like Munoz, never looked back to see if the clown was "chasing" them before Munoz's injury.

On August 27, 2020, Munoz filed her lawsuit against Six Flags in which she alleged defendant Doe (a still-unidentified individual), "dressed as a frightening clown[,] appeared and purposefully scared a crowd of approximately fifteen to twenty people." She further alleged Six Flags or its employee Doe "failed to conduct actor activities in a safe manner," including failing to "cease chasing guests once a group of guests began stampeding," failing to warn of or maintain a safe premises free of "dangerous stampedes of people," and failing to direct or train actors in a manner that kept guests safe.

On August 15, 2022, Six Flags filed its motion for summary judgment, arguing an implied primary assumption of the risk barred Munoz's alleged negligence claims against Six Flags. Specifically, Six Flags argued it could not be held liable because Munoz's injury arose out of the very acts and occurrences she knew about, expected, and personally witnessed while at Fright Fest before her injury. Therefore, the risk of being injured by running away after being frightened was inherent in Munoz's decision to attend and remain at the event.

On October 12, 2022, the trial court granted Six Flags' motion finding 1) there was no evidence the scare actor actually chased Munoz, and 2) the scare actor's actual movements were immaterial because Munoz was injured by actions she knew about and expected when she attended Fright Fest. The trial court found "characters at Fright Fest are expected to take action to frighten patrons, and [Munoz] testified that is what she expected." The trial court further found the summary judgment record was not sufficient to establish the scare actor was negligent; rather, the record showed Munoz voluntarily exposed herself to the inherent risks she knew before attending the event, which included risks related to her own actions or reactions, and those of other guests, associated with running. This appeal follows.

[The court discussed the standard of review.]

Discussion

In her sole point on appeal, Munoz argues the trial court erred in granting summary judgment in Six Flags' favor, claiming there was sufficient evidence to create a genuine dispute as to whether Munoz impliedly assumed the risk of participating in the themed event where guests are frightened because the court failed to consider the interactions of Munoz with the scare actor, which were not inherent to the activity. Alternatively, Munoz contends even if she assumed the risk of falling and injuring herself by attending the event, Six Flags increased or altered that risk when the scare actor chased after the group surrounding Munoz. We disagree on both grounds.

The implied primary assumption of the risk doctrine states "if a person voluntarily consents to accept the danger of a known and appreciated risk, that person may not sue another for failing to protect him from it." *Coomer v. Kansas City Royals Baseball Corp.*, 437 S.W.3d 184, 191 (Mo. banc 2014). The participant "is deemed to have assumed the risk of injury from the inherent risks of an activity that are known and understood." *Ferbet* [*v. Hidden Valley Golf and Ski, Inc.*], 618 S.W.3d at 606. "When the risk arises from the circumstances (e.g., from a condition on the defendant's property or the inherent nature of the defendant's activity), 'implied primary assumption of the risk' completely bars recovery by a plaintiff who knowingly and voluntarily encounters that risk." *Coomer*, 437 S.W.3d at 192 (citing *Krause v. U.S. Truck Co., Inc.*, 787 S.W.2d 708, 711–12 (Mo. banc 1990)). The defendant is not liable "for injuries stemming from such inherent risks because no duty is owed as to those risks." *Ferbet*, 618 S.W.3d at 606 (quoting *Coomer*, 437 S.W.3d at 197). However, the defendant "still owes a duty of reasonable care not to alter or increase such inherent risks." *Id.* (quoting *Coomer*, 437 S.W.3d at 197–98). Inherent risks are "structural or involved in the constitution or essential character" of the activity in question; they are something "belonging by nature or settled habit." *Coomer*, 437 S.W.3d at 202. A "particular risk cannot be 'structural' or 'involved in the constitution or essential character of something' one day but not the next." *Id.* at 201. "Once a risk is determined to be 'inherent' in something, it will remain so until there is a fundamental change in that thing's constitution or essential character." *Id.* The mechanism of injury can determine whether a particular risk was inherent to the activity. *Id.* at 202–03.

Courts generally apply this doctrine to bar claims for injuries resulting from recreational or sporting activities because the providers of these activities cannot eliminate their inherent risks. For example, in *Loughran v. The Phillies*, 888 A.2d 872, 876–77 (Pa. Super. 2005), a Philadelphia Phillies centerfielder intentionally threw a baseball into the stands after catching the final out of the top of the seventh inning. *Id.* at 874. That ball struck and injured a spectator. *Id.* The *Loughran* court suggested that, although it is not formally part of the game of baseball, players tossing balls to fans between half innings is a customary part of the game. *Id.* at 875–76.

In *Coomer*, the Missouri Supreme Court analyzed whether a baseball fan being struck by a hotdog thrown by a team's mascot was an inherent risk of attending a baseball game. The Missouri Supreme Court distinguished the activity in *Loughran*—a player throwing a ball into the stands—with an activity unconnected to the game of baseball—a mascot throwing hotdogs into the stands:

> Baseball is the reason centerfielder Marlon Byrd was there, just as it was the reason the fans were in the stands (including the many who were yelling for Byrd to toss the ball to them). Here, on the other hand, there is no link between the game and the risk of being hit by [the Royals' mascot's] hotdog toss. The Hotdog Launch is not an inherent part of the game; it is what the Royals do to entertain baseball fans when there is no game for them to watch.

Coomer, 437 S.W.3d at 202–03. Just as baseball was the reason the fans were in the stands in *Loughran*, here, "fright" was the reason Munoz was attending Fright Fest. Unlike the risk posed by the Royals' hotdog-throwing mascot, the risk that a Fright Fest scare actor might cause a guest like Munoz to run and fall was inherent to the event, and Munoz knew, appreciated, and voluntarily accepted that risk before and during her attendance. Similarly, in *Loughran*, the Pennsylvania Superior Court recognized there was an undeniable link between attending the game and the risk of being hit with a ball tossed into the stands. *Loughran*, 888 A.2d at 876. Therefore, the mechanism of injury—a ball being tossed into the stands—was inherent to the overall experience and not limited to when the ball was in play. *Id.* In contrast, the *Coomer* court recognized the tossing of a hotdog by a baseball team's mascot was not inherently linked to the game of baseball; instead, the "[plaintiff] and his 12,000 rain-soaked fellow spectators were not there to watch [the mascot] toss hotdogs; they were there to watch the Royals play baseball." *Coomer*, 437 S.W.3d at 203.

The implied primary assumption of the risk doctrine has been applied to other sports, such as skiing and snowtubing. For example, in *Bennett v. Hidden Valley Golf & Ski, Inc.*, 318 F.3d 868 (8th Cir. 2003), the court applied Missouri law and found that risks posed by a mogul or tree on a ski slope were inherent to the sport of skiing. *Id.* at 873–75. The court concluded a skier voluntarily assumed "the risks inherent in or incidental to skiing, regardless of her subjective knowledge of those risks." *Id.* at 877. "'Implied primary assumption of the risk' bars a plaintiff from recovery when the plaintiff has knowingly and voluntarily encountered risk that is inherent in the nature of the defendant's activity." *Ferbet*, 618 S.W.3d at 606 (citing *Coomer*, 437 S.W.3d at 192). "The plaintiff's consent relieves the defendant of any duty to protect the plaintiff from injury and as a result, the defendant cannot be negligent." *Id.* (citing *Coomer*, 437 S.W.3d at 193); see also *Lewis v. Snow Creek, Inc.*, 6 S.W.3d 388, 395–96 (Mo. App. W.D. 1999) ("If the risks of the activity are perfectly obvious or fully comprehended, plaintiff has consented to them and defendant has performed his or her duty.").

In *Ferbet*, plaintiff brought a negligence action against Hidden Valley Ski Resort after he broke his leg while riding a rubber inner tube down a snow and ice covered hill on the resort's property. *Id.* at 599. Plaintiff argued his injuries and damages were caused by Hidden Valley's negligent maintenance and operation of the tubing hill and the release was unenforceable as against public policy. *Id.* However, the trial court disagreed and granted summary judgment in favor of the resort, finding the release-of-liability contract signed by plaintiff at the time of purchasing his snowtubing ticket was enforceable. *Id.* On appeal, this Court considered whether the record supported plaintiff's claim that the ski resort's alleged negligence enhanced any inherent risks involved in snowtubing on an uneven sliding surface. *Id.* at 607. There, the record did not describe the size or configuration of the sliding surface, or of any alleged "riprap" or crevice where the injury occurred. *Id.* The record also was largely silent concerning the resort's care and maintenance of the surface, whether the resort was aware of any risks, or whether there had been any prior similar incidents. *Id.* In addition, this Court differentiated between a known and understandable risk of "an uneven area that simply adds to snow tubers' thrill by pitching them up, and occasionally out, of the tube," as opposed to "a divot that repeatedly and unexpectedly catches and fractures customers' limbs." *Id.* The Court recognized that while the latter likely exceeded the inherent risk that is part of snowtubing's structure and essence, the record did not contain sufficient evidence showing any alleged negligence which enhanced the inherent risks involved in the activity. *Id.* For the purposes of assumption of risk, however, the Court concluded an uneven sliding surface and the potential risks it creates for snow tubers are inherent risks of snowtubing because they are structural to the activity and involve the essential character of snowtubing. *Id.* at 608. Under such circumstances, the Court held the resort owed plaintiff no duty for the injury he sustained when his foot became lodged in a crevice on the tubing hill, and thus the release of liability provision was inapplicable and irrelevant because uneven sliding surfaces were an inherent risk to snowtubing. *Id.*

Here, the summary judgment record is similarly sparse, and the evidence presented is not sufficient to support a finding that Six Flags or its scare actor was negligent by "chasing" Munoz.

[In a footnote, the court noted that Six Flags' corporate representative who was responsible for training the scare actors testified that Six Flags' "characters are specifically instructed not to chase individuals in the park as part of their training but they are informed ... to interact with guests and move towards them to interact with them." She explained the specific "number of steps is not a hard and fast rule." "What we like to do is what we call the two-step. We can lunge towards them, you can move in their direction quickly, and then you stop." She further explained that the two-step demonstration "is more like a sort of a guideline for [actors] that they're supposed to move toward a guest and then stop." And even if permitted, "chasing" would be something "difficult to define especially in a classroom setting." Besides this testimony, the summary judgment record does not contain expert opinions discussing any standard of care for haunted attractions to follow; likewise, there are no expert opinions that the scare actor here violated Six Flags' training or any other standards.]

Munoz testified she knew about, comprehended, and expected scare tactics that could result in her or other guests screaming or running away. Indeed, for three hours before her injury, Munoz witnessed frightened patrons running from scare actors. These undisputed facts show Munoz knew and appreciated the risk that Fright Fest actors might also scare her into running. She personally witnessed it happening for several hours before her injury and yet chose to continue participating in the event. Just as the courts in *Coomer* and *Ferbet* applied the implied primary assumption of the risk doctrine, the trial court here correctly concluded Munoz's injury was caused by an inherent risk of attending Fright Fest. Six Flags cannot take the fright out of Fright Fest, just as baseball teams cannot remove their bats and balls without fundamentally changing the game. *Coomer*, 437 S.W.3d at 196. In the instant case, experiencing fright, which could in turn cause running and thereafter a fall leading to injury, was inherent to the Fright Fest event. *Ferbet*, 618 S.W.3d at 608. Before deciding to go to Fright Fest, and for three hours after arriving there, Munoz knowingly and voluntarily accepted these risks. In recognizing these facts and applying them to the law, the trial court correctly found Munoz knowingly and voluntarily encountered the specific risk that injured her. Therefore, Six Flags owed Munoz no duty to prevent the fright which caused her to run.

Additionally, Munoz's argument that there is a genuine issue of material fact as to whether the scare actor "chased" her in violation of park policy, thereby precluding summary judgment, is unavailing. Neither Munoz nor her cousin identified facts which would support an inference that the actor was "chasing" them or the group around them. Munoz testified she saw people in the other group turn around and start to run "a little bit before [she] turned around"; she could not describe the interaction, other than to say she turned and started running, and she was in the middle of or slightly outside the group. She testified the scare actor "popped out," after which Munoz "started running, and there [were] people surrounding [her] from almost every angle" until she fell after approximately 10 seconds. Importantly, she stated she never actually looked back to see if the scare actor was truly engaged in a "chase" after Munoz turned and ran. The testimony of Munoz's cousin is equally unhelpful. She testified she never saw the scare actor interacting with her or Munoz but instead she saw the scare actor focusing on a nearby group of people. Moreover, Munoz's cousin was unable to say whether the scare actor made any movement or took any action toward her or Munoz before they started running. And, like Munoz, she never looked back to see if the scare actor was actually "chasing" them before the injury occurred. Taken together, all the facts in the summary judgment record do not support an inference that Munoz was being chased and, therefore, the trial court did not err in granting Six Flags judgment as a matter of law. As discussed above, Munoz's injury was caused by the inherent risk she assumed, and not by any allegedly negligent act on the part of Six Flags or its scare actor. Merely alleging a defendant was negligent is not enough to overcome the implied primary assumption of the risk doctrine; instead, the alleged negligence must have changed the outcome. See *Bennett*, 318 F.3d at 873–75 (the risks of trees and moguls were inherent to the sport of skiing; therefore, the defendant owed no duty under the implied primary assumption of the risk doctrine without direct evidence that the defendant negligently maintained or exacerbated the condition that caused a skiing accident).

But even if there were a chase, it is not material. A defendant's duty in situations involving an implied assumed risk is only to "make conditions as safe as they appear to be." *Martin v. Buzan*, 857 S.W.2d 366, 369 (Mo. App. E.D. 1993). "If the risks of the activity are perfectly obvious or fully comprehended, plaintiff has consented to them and defendant has performed his or her duty. Plaintiff's consent is implied from the act of electing to participate in the activity." *Id.* (internal citations omitted). Here, Munoz knew of and accepted the risk of being around other guests who were likely to run from Fright Fest actors, something she witnessed and was "perfectly obvious" to her for three hours before she was injured. Therefore, the mechanism of the injury—guests running after becoming scared—was or became an inherent risk that Munoz was aware of. Just as the plaintiff in Bennett could not show the ski resort owed a duty to protect against inherent skiing risks like trees and moguls, or the plaintiff in *Ferbet* could not demonstrate that uneven sliding surfaces were anything other than an inherent risk to snowtubing, here, Munoz cannot show that Six Flags owed a duty to prevent her injury because the risk of injury was inherent to Munoz and other patrons becoming frightened by a Fright Fest scare actor and running away. *Bennett*, 318 F.3d at 873–75; *Ferbet*, 618 S.W.3d at 608.

Finally, while we found no Missouri cases involving assumption of the risk and "haunted" attractions, courts in other jurisdictions have found the attraction operators have no duty to protect a patron from her own reaction to scares that occurred within the confines of the attraction. In *Griffin v. The Haunted Hotel, Inc.*, 242 Cal. App. 4th 490, 194 Cal.Rptr.3d 830 (2015), the California court applied the same test Missouri courts apply for assumption of risk as a bar to recovery. *Id.* at 501, 194 Cal.Rptr.3d 830. There, the haunted attraction was an outdoor trail where actors jumped out of dark spaces holding scary props, such as knives, axes, chainsaws, or severed body parts. *Id.* at 493, 194 Cal. Rptr.3d 830. At the end of the attraction, and after passing what the plaintiff believed was the exit, an actor performed a "Carrie effect" scare and confronted the plaintiff unexpectedly to give "one more extreme fright." *Id.* at 493–94, 194 Cal.Rptr.3d 830. This was delivered by an actor wielding a gas-powered chainsaw (the chain had been removed), who approached the plaintiff, frightened him, and then chased the plaintiff as he ran away. *Id.* The plaintiff was terrified and felt physically unsafe because he thought he had already left the attraction. *Id.* at 496, 194 Cal.Rptr.3d 830. After a chase, the plaintiff tripped, fell, and broke his wrist. *Id.* He then sued the operator of the haunted attraction, alleging negligence and assault. *Id.* at 493, 194 Cal.Rptr.3d 830. The *Griffin* court affirmed summary judgment, noting that all scare activities occurred within the defendant's boundaries, even though the plaintiff was not aware of that fact. *Id.* at 497, 194 Cal.Rptr.3d 830. Though the plaintiff believed he had gone through an exit, he was still within the "scary experience he purchased" and purposefully attended. *Id.* at 498, 194 Cal.Rptr.3d 830. Importantly, the court found whether the plaintiff thought he was still in the attraction was not relevant to establish the defense, which was simply that he decided to attend the attraction knowing he could be frightened and then could run and fall at any time. *Id.* at 509, 194 Cal.Rptr.3d 830. Munoz argues *Griffin* is distinguishable because there, guests had been warned they might be chased, and employees understood chasing was part of the attraction. But whether chasing occurred was not the determining factor in Griffin, just as it is not here. In both cases, it was the fact that the plaintiffs had already agreed to accept any risk they might be frightened, run, and fall at the venue. As the *Griffin* court explained,

> [T]he very purpose of The Haunted Trail is to frighten patrons. Haunted Hotel informed patrons the event had "high impact scares." Patrons in a Halloween haunted house are expected to be surprised, startled, and scared by the exhibits. That is what Griffin paid money to experience. At bottom, his complaint here is Haunted Hotel delivered on its promise to scare the wits out of him.

Id. at 508, 194 Cal.Rptr.3d 830. The court concluded that because the plaintiff "voluntarily paid money to experience" getting scared, the attraction owed him no duty. *Id.* Likewise, here, Munoz knew beforehand—and accepted—the risk that she might be frightened and run, which in turn could lead to falling and becoming injured at Fright Fest. Six Flags owed Munoz no duty as a matter of law. Other "haunted house" cases have reached similar conclusions.

In *Mays v. Gretna Athletic Boosters, Inc.*, 668 So.2d 1207 (La. Ct. App. 1996), a Louisiana case, a patron inside a haunted house was injured when someone scared her, causing her to run into a cinder block wall. *Id.* at 1208. The court found the operator had no duty to protect the patron from running into a wall in a dark room: "Patrons in a Halloween haunted house are expected to be surprised, startled and scared by the exhibits but the operator does not have a duty to guard against patrons reacting in bizarre, frightened and unpredictable ways." *Id.* at 1209. In *Galan v. Covenant House New Orleans*, 695 So.2d 1007 (La. Ct. App. 1997), the plaintiff believed she had exited a haunted house when a character startled her with a chainsaw and caused her to fall in alarm. *Id.* at 1008. She argued the haunted house operator was negligent but the court disagreed, noting again that haunted house patrons expect "to be surprised, startled and scared by the exhibits," such that the operator had no duty to guard against patrons reacting in unpredictable ways. *Id.* Finally, in *Durmon v. Billings*, 873 So.2d 872 (La. Ct. App. 2004), a patron inside a "haunted" cornfield maze was approached by a costumed character with a running chainsaw (from which the chain was removed). *Id.* at 879. The patron attempted to run away, but she fell and injured herself. *Id.* The court found the owners of the maze owed no duty to the patron to warn or protect her from her reaction to being frightened by a costumed character, "an experience she expected to have and for which she paid an *additional* admission fee." *Id.*

Here, just as the cases cited from other jurisdictions, Munoz knew "characters at Fright Fest are expected to take action to frighten patrons," and knew the risk that frightened guests might run away and fall. In other words, she was aware of the risk she encountered, and expected to be surprised, startled, and scared. *Griffin*, 242 Cal. App. 4th at 508, 194 Cal.Rptr.3d 830; *Galan*, 695 So.2d at 1008; *Durmon*, 873 So.2d at 879; *Mays*, 668 So.2d. at 1209. Munoz knew frightened guests might run, which could lead to falling and which in turn could lead to injury. Whether or not the actor "chased" Munoz is not the determining factor. Munoz was exposed to the exact risk she knowingly and voluntarily exposed herself to by attending and remaining at Fright Fest for three hours. Munoz was an active participant in the festivities and understood the known and inherent risks in it, including the risk of injury. Case law from Missouri and other states concludes that when a person is injured during such activities, summary judgment is proper because they assumed such risks. Therefore, based on the record, the trial court did not err in awarding summary judgment to Six Flags as there was no duty to prevent Munoz's injury, which was caused by an inherent risk of attending and remaining at Fright Fest. Point denied.

Conclusion

The Judgment is affirmed.

NOTES AND QUESTIONS

1. The court, in discussing the *Ferbet* case, mentions releases. We will spend considerable time on waivers and releases—including one from a haunted attraction—later in the book.
2. One important discussion here is whether it would be relevant if the unidentified clown scare actor had chased Ms. Munoz in a way that was inconsistent with the training at Six Flags. The court concluded that it did not matter, because the *risk* she knew about (falling down due to fright) was the *risk* she encountered (falling down due to fright); the specific mechanism (a clown jumping at her for two steps versus a clown chasing her) that caused it was immaterial.
3. It is interesting that this was resolved on a motion for summary judgment after (probably expensive) discovery that appears to have extended for nearly two years. As noted previously, this form of assumption of risk is generally considered a purely legal issue (except when there are factual disputes about what the inherent risks are), and the court does not seem to think the factual development was important in figuring out what those inherent risks are—indeed, it rejects the notion that the particular scare actor's conduct was particularly relevant. Do you think Six Flags could have won the case on a motion to dismiss—put another way, do you think a court could have looked at the allegations and said, "You went to get scared and now you're mad that you got scared—that's an inherent risk, case dismissed"?

CHAPTER 5

Waivers and Other Contractual Measures

Parks, ski resorts, and other recreation providers often seek to reduce their liability contractually, with everything from signs hopefully declaring "Ride at your own risk" (like the one pictured in the Author's Note at the start of this book) to far more elaborate multi-page contracts listing in sometimes upsetting detail the things that the owners at least want you to think might happen to you. (More on that vague teaser in a bit.)

These contractual efforts vary not just in their form but in their efficacy. As you review them, think about not just whether they would be enforceable, but also about whether they provide other value to their drafters, even if they turn out not to be enforceable. Our first case helps emphasize how contractual efforts intersect with statutory provisions relating to recreation.

Rutherford v. Talisker Canyons Finance, Co., LLC

455 P.3d 474 (Utah 2019)

JUSTICE HIMONAS, opinion of the Court:

INTRODUCTION

Young Levi Rutherford crashed and was injured when he skied into a patch of thick, wet, machine-made snow. His parents brought claims for negligence and premises liability on his behalf against Talisker Canyons Finance Company and ASC Utah (collectively, Talisker). Talisker asks us to hold that the Rutherfords' claims are barred by (1) a release of liability signed by Levi's father or, alternatively, (2) Utah's Inherent Risks of Skiing Act, Utah Code sections 78B-4-401 to -404 (the Act). We decline Talisker's invitations.

Two of our decisions compel this result. First, in *Hawkins ex rel. Hawkins v. Peart*, 2001 UT 94, 37 P.3d 1062, *superseded by statute as stated in Penunuri v. Sundance Partners, Ltd., 2013 UT 22, 301 P.3d 984*,[] we unambiguously declared that it would violate public policy to allow a parent to "release a minor's prospective claim for negligence." *Id.* ¶ 10. Second, in *Clover v. Snowbird Ski Resort*, 808 P.2d 1037 (Utah 1991), we unanimously held that claims for injuries caused by "inherent risks of skiing" are barred only to the extent that the risk was integral to the sport of skiing. *Id.* at 1044–45. And three years later we loudly reaffirmed our commitment to *Clover* in *White v. Deseelhorst*, 879 P.2d 1371 (Utah 1994), *abrogated on other grounds by Penunuri v. Sundance Partners, Ltd.*, 2017 UT 54, 423 P.3d 1150. Today, Talisker asks us to abandon our holding in *Clover* and turn turtle three decades of precedent and the settled expectations of skiers and the ski industry in favor of an alternate approach to interpreting the Act. But because of our established practices in statutory construction and precedential decisions in *Clover* and *White*, we reject this substitute construction.

Instead, we hold that Talisker has not convinced us that *Clover* was wrong, much less met its heavy burden to persuade us to overturn such weighty precedent. We therefore uphold the court of appeals' decision that the district court was correct to apply *Clover*. We do, however, take this opportunity to streamline the implementation of *Clover*'s holding and remand this case to the district court with instructions to apply *Clover* in a manner consistent with this opinion. We also agree with the court of appeals' conclusion to affirm the district court's partial grant of summary judgment to the Rutherfords, finding the release unenforceable under Utah law—although we do so for reasons other than those stated by the court of appeals.

BACKGROUND

Ten-year-old Levi Rutherford was a member of the Summit Ski Team, an affiliate of the United States Ski and Snowboard Association (USSA), during the 2009–2010 winter season. Levi was an advanced skier who regularly skied "on the double blacks, which were the expert runs." Levi's father signed him up for the team online in the fall of 2009. In the process, Levi's father signed an "Assumption of Risk and Release of Liability" on Levi's behalf. The release purported to waive Levi's right to sue USSA, the ski team, and any ski area operator for any injury due to any reason, including the negligence of one of the above-named entities. [In a footnote, the court noted a dispute about the specific release signed by Levi's father, but concluded that such dispute didn't create a genuine issue of material fact.]

On January 15, 2010, Levi's parents dropped him off at The Canyons ski resort for ski team practice.[] Levi met up with his coaches, who told him to take a warmup run while they set up gates for training on the Retreat run. At this time, multiple snow-making machines were in operation on Retreat. The coaches did not ask The Canyons to turn off the snow-making machines because "in the past [The Canyons] kept running the snow guns until they saw that people were up there ... and then they would shut them off when they saw that [the ski team] was on that run." The coach in charge of training that day testified in her deposition that she would not have had the team ski through the gates if the snow-making machines were still running by the time the course was set up "[b]ecause of [the] bad visibility and inconsistent snow."

Levi took his warm up on Retreat while the snow-making machines were in operation, making visibility poor. Warning signs were posted at the top of the run, stating: "snowmaking in progress." Despite the warning, Levi headed down Retreat without making turns. He went into a tuck position with his knees bent, his poles tucked under his arms, and his head near his knees. Near the bottom of the run, Levi ran into a mound of sticky, wet, machine-made snow that was roughly a foot high, which caused him to crash. Levi sustained a brain injury from the crash.

The Rutherfords filed suit on Levi's behalf against the ski team and Talisker. After discovery, the parties filed multiple cross-motions for summary judgment. At issue here are the motions concerning whether the Rutherfords' claims for negligence and premises liability against Talisker are barred either by the release signed by Levi's father or by the Act.

Regarding the arguments for the release, the district court read this court's precedent in *Rothstein v. Snowbird Corp.*, 2007 UT 96, 175 P.3d 560, as meaning that all preinjury releases for recreational skiing are unenforceable, while, pursuant to *Berry v. Greater Park City Co.*, 2007 UT 87, 171 P.3d 442, *abrogated on other grounds by Penunuri v. Sundance Partners, Ltd.*, 2017 UT 54, 423 P.3d 1150, preinjury releases for competitive skiing are enforceable. Based on this understanding, the district court held that the preinjury release signed by Levi's father was unenforceable because the type of skiing Levi was engaged in at the time he crashed was more similar to recreational skiing than competitive skiing. The district court alternatively held that the release was unenforceable under *Hawkins ex rel. Hawkins v. Peart*, which held that a preinjury release signed by a parent on behalf of a minor was unenforceable for violating Utah public policy. 2001 UT 94, 37 P.3d 1062, *superseded by statute as stated in Penunuri v. Sundance Partners, Ltd.*, 2013 UT 22, 301 P.3d 984.[]

The district court also denied Talisker's motion in which it argued that the Act's machine-made snow exemption [which specified that "machine-made snow" is an example of "inherent risks of skiing"] barred the Rutherfords' claims. The court held that, pursuant to *Clover v. Snowbird Ski Resort*, 808 P.2d 1037 (Utah 1991), there was a disputed question of material fact as to whether a skier wished to confront sticky, wet, machine-made snow from a machine that was allegedly "not functioning properly" and whether that risk could be eliminated through the exercise of reasonable care.

Talisker appealed the district court's partial grant of the Rutherfords' motion for summary judgment and its denial of Talisker's motion for summary judgment. The court of appeals affirmed the district court's rulings.

With respect to the preinjury release, it affirmed on the ground that the 2006 amendment to the Act, coupled with our analysis in *Rothstein*, effectively overruled *Berry* and eliminated the distinction between preinjury releases for recreational and competitive skiing, making both types of releases unenforceable. *Rutherford ex rel. Rutherford v. Talisker Canyons Fin. Co.*, 2014 UT App 190, ¶¶ 34–35, 333 P.3d 1266. Additionally, the court of appeals "reject[ed] the trial court's determination that the ... release is unenforceable because it was signed by a parent on behalf of a minor; rather, the release is unenforceable based on the Act's policy statement." *Id.* ¶ 30. We granted certiorari to review the court of appeals' decision. Based on our review, we hold that the court of appeals reached the correct result, but that its declaration that preinjury releases signed by parents on behalf of children do not generally offend Utah's public policy was in error.

The court of appeals also affirmed the district court's ruling with respect to the Act's machine-made snow exemption, stating that there is a "question[] of fact regarding the applicability of the machine-made snow exemption" in the Act. *Id.* ¶ 18. We affirm the court of appeals' and the district court's reliance on *Clover* in making this determination. However, we take this opportunity to clarify the implementation of *Clover*'s core holding and therefore remand this case to the district court to make a determination under *Clover* consistent with this opinion.

We exercise jurisdiction under Utah Code section 78A-3-102(3)(a).

* * *

ANALYSIS

We first examine whether the release is enforceable. It is not. Absent a relevant, contrary expression of intent from the legislature, we adhere to our pronouncement in *Hawkins ex rel. Hawkins v. Peart* that a parent cannot release his or her minor child's prospective claims for negligence. 2001 UT 94, 37 P.3d 1062, *superseded by statute as stated in Penunuri v. Sundance Partners, Ltd.*, 2013 UT 22, 301 P.3d 984.

Second, we turn to interpreting the Act, relying on our time-honored tools of *stare decisis* and statutory interpretation. For purposes of our opinion today, we begin with our precedential tools. We do so because in *Clover v. Snowbird Ski Resort*, 808 P.2d 1037 (Utah 1991), this court has already done much of the important work of interpreting the Act. And we find its reasoning both reasonable and persuasive, especially in light of the ambiguity in the Act's construction and the historical context in which it was enacted. With this in mind, and in accord with our case law, we see no reason to abandon the *Clover* court's core interpretation of the Act.

We do, however, take this opportunity to clarify the test announced in *Clover* in a way that implements the core holding of *Clover* by simplifying *Clover*'s two-prong subjective-objective inquiry into a one-step objective inquiry. We believe this clarification respects both the core holding of *Clover* and the language of the Act. Accordingly, we remand this case to the district court for a ruling consistent with this opinion.

I. PREINJURY RELEASES SIGNED ON BEHALF OF MINOR CHILDREN VIOLATE PUBLIC POLICY

The release signed by Levi's father violates public policy and is not enforceable. "Preinjury releases from liability for one's negligence pit two bedrock legal concepts against one another: the right to order one's relationship with another by contract and the obligation to answer in damages when one injures another by breaching a duty of care." *Rothstein v. Snowbird Corp.*, 2007 UT 96, ¶ 6, 175 P.3d 560. With this tension in mind, we have stated that preinjury releases are enforceable unless the party challenging the release establishes an exception to that rule. *Pearce v. Utah Athletic Found.*, 2008 UT 13, ¶ 14, 179 P.3d 760 ("[P]eople may contract away their rights to recover in tort for damages caused by the ordinary negligence of others.") *abrogated on other grounds by Penunuri v. Sundance Partners, Ltd.*, 2017 UT 54, 423 P.3d 1150; *Berry v. Greater Park City Co.*, 2007 UT 87, ¶ 12, 171 P.3d 442 ("[A] person should retain the power to contract away the right to recover damages for the negligence of another" but that right is "subject to many conditions and limitations."), *abrogated on other grounds by Penunuri*, 2017 UT 54, 423 P.3d 1150.

Preinjury releases are generally governed by contract law. *Hawkins ex rel. Hawkins v. Peart*, 2001 UT 94, ¶ 5, 37 P.3d 1062 ("[P]arties may obtain contractual releases from liability for negligent action ... where one party agrees to release the other from liability for future injuries."); *Jacobsen Constr. Co. v. Structo Lite Eng'g, Inc.*, 619 P.2d 306, 310 (Utah 1980) (noting that "the field of contract law is more than adequate to deal with" preinjury releases). Nevertheless, preinjury releases remain subject to several exceptions. We have previously identified three such exceptions to preinjury release enforceability: "(1) releases that offend public policy ... (2) releases for activities that fit within the public interest exception ... and (3) releases that are unclear or ambiguous." *Pearce*, 2008 UT 13, ¶ 14, 179 P.3d 760 (citations omitted). And while some jurisdictions conflate the public interest and public policy exceptions, [citing examples], we have expressly distinguished the two in the context of preinjury releases. *See id.*; *see also Penunuri v. Sundance Partners, Ltd.*, 2013 UT 22, ¶ 25, 301 P.3d 984.

Our public interest exception applies the six-factor test found in *Tunkl v. Regents of University of California*, 60 Cal.2d 92, 32 Cal.Rptr. 33, 383 P.2d 441, 444–47 (1963), which was adopted in *Berry*, 2007 UT 87, ¶ 15, 171 P.3d 442, and further analyzed in *Pearce*, 2008 UT 13, ¶¶ 16–21, 179 P.3d 760. In contrast, the public policy exception remains "a doctrine of vague and variable quality" based on "constitutional or statutory provisions or the common law." *Penunuri*, 2013 UT 22, ¶ 26, 301 P.3d 984 (citations omitted) (internal quotations marks omitted). This delineation between the two standards is necessary to maintain the "fluid nature" of the public policy defense, available in other contract claims, and to avoid the conflation of that defense with the six *Tunkl* factors. *Cf. Wolf v. Ford*, 335 Md. 525, 644 A.2d 522, 527 (1994).[]

In the context of releases signed by parents on behalf of minors, we have unambiguously held that preinjury releases for negligence violate public policy. *See Hawkins*, 2001 UT 94, ¶ 13, 37 P.3d 1062. We based our conclusion on a number of observations, all of which remain equally forceful today. First, Talisker "has cited no source of law, and we are aware of none, granting parents in Utah a general[,] unilateral right to compromise or release a child's existing causes of action without court approval or appointment to that effect." *Id.* ¶ 11. Quite to "the contrary, Utah law provides various checks on parental authority to ensure a child's interests are protected." *Id.* Indeed, "[u]nder the Uniform Probate Code, for example, when a minor has a cause of action, the minor or another person interested in the minor's welfare may petition for the appointment of a conservator." *Id.*; *see also* Utah Code § 75-5-404. "Significantly, a parent may act as a minor's conservator, not as a matter of right, but only when appointed by the court." *Hawkins*, 2001 UT 94, ¶ 11, 37 P.3d 1062; *see* also Utah Code § 75-5-410(1). Furthermore, "we see little reason to base the validity of a parent's contractual release ... on the timing of [the] injury. Indeed, the law generally treats preinjury releases ... with greater suspicion than postinjury releases." *Hawkins*, 2001 UT 94, ¶ 13, 37 P.3d 1062.[]

Talisker raises but one argument in opposition. According to Talisker, by superseding *Hawkins* with respect to certain equine and livestock activities, the legislature has made clear that preinjury releases signed by parents on behalf of their children do not offend public policy. Talisker's logic does not follow, and this argument may hurt Talisker's case more than it helps. Indeed, it is difficult to logically conclude that the legislature's decision to allow for preinjury releases by parents for minors in one very narrow area translates to a general policy that all such preinjury releases are valid. The conclusion that the legislature meant to say that preinjury releases signed by parents for minors are valid only in the unique context of equine activities is equally likely. In short, the legislature's action sheds no light on its view of the public policy surrounding the larger question, and, absent any positive signal from the legislature, we are loath to forsake *Hawkins* and its reasoning.

Having concluded that the preinjury release Levi's father signed on Levi's behalf does not preclude the Rutherfords' claims, we turn to Talisker's argument that the Act stands as a bar to the Rutherfords' claims.

II. *CLOVER* IS ENTITLED TO *STARE DECISIS* RESPECT

[The court, at length, analyzed its *Clover* case, which focuses on the interpretation of the statute. The statute provided, among other things, an exemplary (but not exhaustive) list of the inherent risks of skiing. It concluded that *Clover* remained and should remain good law. It noted, interestingly, that the statute's application did not create *no duty* as to those inherent risks, but instead codified a rule that once a ski area has acted reasonably as to those risks—defined specifically in the case as warning of those risks via signs or otherwise—there is no duty beyond that warning obligation. That interpretation is *maybe* best seen as a limited duty rule, since a jury could presumably conclude that as to certain inherent risks, a reasonable operator would do more than warn about them—but it is also possible that the court is in fact saying that, as to those inherent risks, a reasonable warning is the only thing ever required. It then turned to the potential to tweak the test applicable under *Clover*; while that issue is more relevant to the prior chapter, it's interesting enough to leave a bit of that discussion here.]

III. *CLOVER'S* TEST CLARIFIED

Having acknowledged the ambiguity in the Act's definition of inherent risks of skiing, [] we now turn to the best way to resolve that ambiguity. As discussed earlier, *Clover* held that inclusion of a risk in the Act's exemplary list does not end the inquiry into whether that risk constitutes an inherent risk of skiing. 808 P.2d 1037, 1045 (Utah 1991). Rather, the Act requires a case-by-case analysis to determine whether the injury-causing risk is truly an inherent risk of skiing under the Act. *Id.* We agree with this holding.

To implement this holding, *Clover* announced a test that asks whether a skier "wishes (or does not wish) to confront" a certain risk. If a skier wishes to confront a risk, then it is an inherent risk. *Id.* at 1047. But if the risk is one a skier would not wish to confront, then it is an inherent risk only if a ski area operator could not eliminate the risk through the exercise of ordinary care. *Id.*

While *Clover*'s holding is faithful to the purpose of the Act, *see supra* [], we believe that the *Clover* test could be implemented in a way that more precisely tracks the legislative intent of the Act. In announcing this clarification, we do not aim to overturn the results of our prior decisions in this area. Instead, we aim to clarify the implementation of law and more clearly bring it in line with the intent of the legislature.

The two-prong analysis under *Clover* in which a court first makes a subjective determination of whether a skier wishes to confront a risk followed by an objective determination of the ability to eliminate the risk (in the event that the risk is one a skier does not subjectively wish to confront), can be effectively collapsed into a one-step objective inquiry. Specifically, this objective inquiry asks whether a skier reasonably expects to encounter the risk when skiing.[] If so, then the risk is an integral part of the sport of skiing and therefore an inherent risk of skiing. And by extension, the list of enumerated risks captures those risks that the legislature believed to be inherent risks of skiing when they are encountered in the way that skiers would reasonably expect to encounter them. We believe this test effectively captures the legislature's intent when it announced that skiers assume the inherent risks of skiing as a matter of law.[]

To determine the legislature's intent we can turn to the Act's definition of inherent risks of skiing in section 402. Along with the general definition of inherent risks of skiing, the Act also provides an exemplary list of inherent risks of skiing in section 402. Crucial to our understanding of the legislature's intent is the way in which the exemplary risks are presented: the risks listed in section 402 are presented in an entirely unremarkable manner. That is, all of the risks are presented in the manner in which a skier would reasonably expect to encounter them. [] This is useful for understanding exactly what types of risks for which the legislature intended to bar recovery.

For example, the Act bars recovery for injury caused by impact with lift towers. The relevant inquiry in a case involving an impact with a lift tower is whether the legislature meant for the Act to cover the kind of impact with a lift tower at issue in the case. In deciphering what kinds of impact with lift towers the legislature envisioned when drafting the statute, it is telling that the legislature chose to simply use "lift towers" with no other qualifying terms. This language conjures up images of standard lift towers as any skier would reasonably expect to encounter them. Similarly, the use of "impact" suggests that the types of impacts contemplated with lift towers are those impacts that a skier could reasonably expect to occur while skiing. Interpreting the exemplary risks in this manner dispatches with the possibility of the kind of absurd or unreasonable results that the legislature could not have intended when applying the Act. *See Anderson v. Utah Cty.*, 13 Utah 2d 99, 368 P.2d 912, 913 n.3 (1962) ("[I]t is a general rule that where a statute is ambiguous in terms and fairly susceptible of two constructions, the unreasonableness or absurdity which may follow one construction or the other may properly be considered. Unreasonable, absurd, or ridiculous consequences should be avoided." (citation omitted) (internal quotation marks omitted)).[] Instead of barring recovery for an impact with a lift tower lying on its side waiting to be erected or painted to blend in with its alpine setting, the Act bars recovery for impacts with lift towers as skiers reasonably expect to encounter them. By extension, instead of barring recovery for an injury in which the chairlift cable snaps and a skier is thrown from a lift chair into a lift tower, the Act bars recovery for impacts as skiers would reasonably expect them to occur, such as skiing out of control and crashing into an ordinary lift tower. []

In addition to tracking the commonplace descriptions of risks in section 402, requiring an analysis of whether a skier would reasonably expect to encounter a given risk aligns with the purpose of the Act. As section 401 states, the purpose of the Act was to "clarify the law" as it existed in 1979. As discussed earlier, the Act served to reassert the defense of primary assumption of risk with respect to ski injuries. *See supra* []. Under a primary assumption of risk analysis, the question is not necessarily whether a skier would "wish" to encounter a certain risk, but whether a risk is inherent or essential to the sport of skiing and therefore whether the risk is one that a skier reasonably expects to encounter when participating in the sport. *See, e.g.*, *Hansen v. Flying J Travel Plaza*, 57 Fed. App'x 214, 216 (6th Cir. 2003) ("A baseball spectator assumes the risk of injury because it is common knowledge that hard balls may be thrown or batted at great speeds into the stands."); *Fleury v. IntraWest Winter Park Operations Corp.*, 372 P.3d 349, 355 (Colo. 2016) (Marquez, J., dissenting) ("The many hazards listed in [Colorado's Inherent Risks of Skiing Act] as 'inherent dangers and risks of skiing' are common, everyday conditions that any skier ... reasonably can expect to encounter...."); *Morgan v. State*, 90 N.Y.2d 471, 662 N.Y.S.2d 421, 685 N.E.2d

202, 207 (1997) ("[B]y engaging in a sport ... a participant consents to those commonly appreciated risks which are inherent in and arise out of the nature of the sport generally...."); *Turcotte v. Fell*, 68 N.Y.2d 432, 510 N.Y.S.2d 49, 502 N.E.2d 964, 968 (1986) ("As a general rule, participants properly may be held to have consented, by their participation, to those injury-causing events which are known, apparent or reasonably foreseeable consequences of the participation."). Regardless of whether a skier wishes to confront the inherent risks of skiing, skiers nonetheless reasonably expect to encounter those risks that inhere in the sport....

Because the legislature described the listed risks in their ordinary forms and the Act served to reassert the availability of the defense of primary assumption of risk, we hold today that the inherent risks of skiing are those risks which a skier would reasonably expect to encounter while skiing. And with respect to the risks enumerated in section 402, those risks are inherent risks of skiing only to the extent that a skier could reasonably expect to encounter them. We believe that this clarification of *Clover* remains true to the core holding of that case while simultaneously interpreting the language of the Act in a way that comports with the intent of the legislature. And although we expect the outcomes under this clarified standard to be the same as the outcomes under the old standard, we nonetheless remand this case to the district court to determine whether a skier would reasonably expect to encounter the wet, sticky snow that Levi encountered at The Canyons.

The legislature, of course, retains the power to amend the Act and overrule our interpretation, which it has thus far declined to do. To the extent our current holding is not in line with the legislature's actual intent, "we [continue to] invite the Utah Legislature to revisit the [Act] to provide clarity in this area." *State v. McNearney*, 2011 UT App 4, ¶ 10 n.2, 246 P.3d 532.

CONCLUSION

We affirm the court of appeals with respect to the preinjury release. The preinjury release executed by Levi's father on his behalf is void as against public policy. We also affirm the court of appeals to the extent that it chose to apply *Clover* to these facts. We remand, however, for a determination in accordance with our clarified implementation of *Clover*'s holding as to whether there exists a disputed issue of material fact with respect to the machine-made snow exemption.

NOTES AND QUESTIONS

1. If the law is clear (and it mostly is) that a parent in Utah "cannot release his or her minor child's prospective claims for negligence," why do you think the ski resort attempted to make that happen in its form? Will the ski resort get other value out of the attempt?
2. As of this writing, the season pass application for the ski resort where this occurred (now under new ownership) includes a similar attempt to limit liability on a page captioned, "RELEASE OF LIABILITY, WAIVER OF CLAIMS, ASSUMPTION OF RISK WARNING AND INDEMNIFICATION AGREEMENT." It leads off: "I represent that I am either the pass holder or, if the pass holder is a minor/child, that I am the parent or legal guardian of the pass holder," and, without limitation as to the age of the skier, includes an agreement "to the greatest extent permitted by law" to waive, release, indemnify, and agree not to sue based on injuries or death including those resulting from negligence. https://www.parkcitymountain.com/-/media/park-city/products/brochure/waiver/042720epasfallpassapplication-rol20218.ashx.
3. The Lutsen Mountains ski resort, on Minnesota's beautiful north shore of Lake Superior, provides this paragraph in its Release of Liability Waiver: "**OPTIONAL FEE TO NOT SIGN THIS RELEASE.** I understand that, for a fee of $8.00 per day per lift ticket in addition to the normal lift ticket price, Lutsen Mountains offers an optional lift ticket that does not require me to sign a Release of Liability. In signing this Release of Liability, I acknowledge I am aware of this option offered by Lutsen Mountains and hereby waive my right to purchase the same." If you were counsel to Lutsen, why would you suggest including this provision? How would you suggest calculating the surcharge? (I understand from someone who skied there a few years ago that $8 is up from $5.) If you were skiing at Lutsen, would you pay the extra $8? The local lawyer (a defense lawyer) who told me about the surcharge reports that he pays the extra $8 when visiting Lutsen.

   Lutsen is, in fact, the site of our next case, and in this case, the waiver worked for the defendant.

Myers v. Lutsen Mountains Corp.

587 F.3d 891 (8th Cir. 2009)

PIERSOL, District Judge.

Douglas R. Myers ("Myers") appeals an adverse grant of summary judgment. Myers was injured while skiing at Lutsen Mountains, a ski resort operated by Lutsen Mountains Corporation ("Lutsen"). He sued Lutsen, and the district court [] granted Lutsen's motion for summary judgment, holding that a release signed by Myers precluded him from pursuing his claims. This appeal followed. For the reasons set forth below, we affirm the judgment of the district court.

I

We review *de novo* a district court's grant or denial of summary judgment. *Med. Liab. Mut. Ins. Co. v. Alan Curtis LLC,* 519 F.3d 466, 471 (8th Cir. 2008). Summary judgment is appropriate when the record, viewed in the light most favorable to the non-moving party, demonstrates that there is no genuine issue of material fact and the moving party is entitled to judgment as a matter of law. *Id.;* Fed.R.Civ.P. 56(c).

II

The facts of this case are essentially undisputed. On December 28, 2006, Myers and two of his friends left their homes in Thunder Bay, Ontario, Canada, and drove approximately two hours to Lutsen, Minnesota. The three friends arrived in time to buy ski tickets before 9:30 a.m., when the ski lifts open at Lutsen. Myers has no memory of that day, but he agrees that he purchased a lift ticket and signed a written release of liability waiver. The release includes the following language:

> PLEASE READ CAREFULLY BEFORE SIGNING. THIS IS A RELEASE OF LIABILITY AND WAIVER OF CERTAIN LEGAL RIGHTS.
>
> I understand that skiing in its various forms, including snowboarding, involves risks, dangers and hazards that may cause serious personal injury or death and that injuries are a common and ordinary occurrence. Risks include, but are not limited to, changes in terrain, weather and snow surfaces, ice, moguls, bare spots, debris, fences, posts, trees, lift equipment and towers, rope tows, light poles, signs, buildings, roads and

walkways, ramps, half-pipes, padded and non-padded barriers, jumps and other terrain features, grooming equipment, snowmobiles, collisions with other persons and other natural and man-made hazards. I acknowledge that the risks in the sport of Alpine skiing can be greatly reduced by taking lessons, abiding by the Skier Responsibility Code, (known as Your Responsibility Code), and using common sense.

In consideration of the purchase of a lift ticket for Lutsen Mountains and use of its facilities, I RELEASE AND FULLY DISCHARGE Lutsen Mountains Corporation, its owners, officers, shareholders, agents and employees from any liability resulting from any personal injury to myself, including death, or damage to my property which is caused by the BREACH OF ANY EXPRESS OR IMPLIED WARRANTY or the NEGLIGENT ACT OR OMISSION of Lutsen Mountains Corporation, its owners, officers, shareholders, agents or employees in the design, location, construction, inspection, maintenance and repair of the conditions on or about the premises or ski area or the operations of the ski area, including but not limited to:

- the design, location, construction, inspection, maintenance and repair of trails, ski runs, slopes, ramps, half-pipes and other terrain features;
- grooming, snow-making, snowmobile operation, ski-lifts, rope tows and ski-lift and rope tow loading and unloading operations;
- padding or non-padding of natural and man-made obstacles and hazards;
- posting or failure to post warnings, signs, fences or other barriers;
- classification and labeling of trails and ski runs; or
- maintaining or modifying variations in the surface, steepness and pitch of trails, ski runs, slopes, ramps and terrain features.

I accept full responsibility for any injuries or damages which may result from the participation in the sport, and it is my intent to HOLD HARMLESS Lutsen Mountains Corpora-

> tion, its owners, officers, shareholders, agents or employees for any injury sustained by me, including death, while participating in the sport. I agree not to bring any action or suit against Lutsen Mountains Corporation, its owners, officers, shareholders, agents or employees for any injury or damage.
>
> In accordance with Minnesota law, nothing in this Release of Liability should be construed as releasing, discharging or waiving any claims I may have for reckless or intentional acts on the part of Lutsen Mountains Corporation, or its owners, officers, shareholders, agents or employees.
>
> I HAVE CAREFULLY READ THIS RELEASE OF LIABILITY AND UNDERSTAND ITS CONTENTS. I AM AWARE THAT BY SIGNING THIS RELEASE OF LIABILITY, I AM WAIVING CERTAIN LEGAL RIGHTS, INCLUDING THE RIGHT TO SUE LUTSEN MOUNTAINS CORPORATION, ITS OWNERS, OFFICERS, SHAREHOLDERS, AGENTS OR EMPLOYEES FOR CERTAIN CLAIMS.
>
> CAUTION: READ BEFORE SIGNING! THIS DOCUMENT AFFECTS YOUR LEGAL RIGHTS AND WILL BAR YOUR RIGHT TO SUE!

At the bottom of the release, Myers printed his name, signed the document, and listed his age as 32.

At approximately 3:30 p.m. on December 28, 2006, Myers, a self-described expert skier at the time of the accident, was on Lutsen's Lower Meadows trail when he skied over an edge of the course. At oral argument, Myers' counsel indicated that this is an intermediate slope. Myers apparently lofted into an area containing rocks and small trees, and he was injured. He filed a personal injury lawsuit against Lutsen in Minnesota district court based on diversity jurisdiction. The parties filed cross-motions for summary judgment. Concluding that the release Myers signed is valid under Minnesota law, the district court granted Lutsen's motion for summary judgment and dismissed Myers' complaint with prejudice. On appeal, Myers argues that the district court erred by holding the release is enforceable under Minnesota law.

III

Minnesota law applies in this diversity case. *See Integrity Floorcovering, Inc. v. Broan-Nutone, LLC,* 521 F.3d 914, 917 (8th Cir. 2008). Exculpatory clauses are enforceable in Minnesota as long as the clause (1) is not ambiguous, (2) does not release intentional, willful, or wanton acts, and (3) does not violate public policy. *See Schlobohm v. Spa Petite, Inc.,* 326 N.W.2d 920, 923 (Minn. 1982).

Myers first argues the release is ambiguous because it could be interpreted as waiving Lutsen's liability for all types of claims and not just negligence. We disagree. The language of the release expressly and unambiguously excludes from its coverage claims arising from reckless or intentional acts, and the district court correctly found the release is not ambiguous.

Myers next asserts the release violates public policy because he had no bargaining power; he had to sign the release or not ski at Lutsen. The Minnesota Supreme Court considers two factors to determine whether exculpatory agreements violate public policy: (1) whether there was a disparity of bargaining power between the parties (a compulsion to sign the contract with an unacceptable provision and a lack of ability to negotiate the elimination of that provision), and (2) the type of service being offered or provided through the contract (one who provides a public or essential service is less likely to be exempted from liability for harm caused by negligently providing that service). *See Schlobohm,* 326 N.W.2d at 923. Regarding the first factor, the Minnesota Supreme Court has explained that a disparity of bargaining power does not exist if the offered service is not necessary or if it could have been obtained elsewhere. *See id.* at 925. In *Schlobohm,* the court concluded there was no disparity in bargaining power when Schlobohm voluntarily joined a fitness center and signed a contract containing an exculpatory clause because there was no showing that the center's services were necessary or that the services could not have been obtained elsewhere. *See id.*

Relying primarily on *Yang v. Voyagaire Houseboats, Inc.,* 701 N.W.2d 783 (Minn. 2005), Myers contends a disparity in bargaining power existed because it would have taken him over two hours to drive from Lutsen to the closest ski hill. In *Yang,* the Minnesota Supreme Court invalidated an exculpatory clause in the context of a houseboat rental agreement. *See id.* at 786. The court suggested there was a disparity in bargaining power because the plaintiff had paid a deposit of "a couple thousand" dollars, had not known about the release until he arrived at the place of business, several hours away from the plaintiff's home, and the next nearest business providing the same services was over 65 miles away, *see id.* at 789 n.3, but the essential nature of the service was the dispositive factor in the court's conclusion that houseboat rental involves a public interest sufficient to invalidate the exculpatory agreement. *See id.* at 789. *Yang* lends little support to Myers' argument that a disparity of bargaining power existed in this case. As did the Minnesota Supreme Court in *Schlobohm,* we find no disparity of bargaining power because the service provided by Lutsen is not necessary, and Myers could have gone elsewhere to ski.

This brings us to the second factor considered by Minnesota courts to determine whether a release violates public policy: the type of service provided. Myers does not argue that Lutsen provides a public or essential service, and we predict the Minnesota Supreme Court would hold skiing is not a public or essential service. When considering whether a service is public or essential in this context, "courts consider whether it is the type [of service] generally thought suitable for public regulation. Types of services thought to be subject to public regulation have included common carriers, hospitals and doctors, public utilities, innkeepers, public warehousemen, employers and services involving extra-hazardous activities." *Schlobohm,* 326 N.W.2d at 925. In *Schlobohm,* the Minnesota Supreme Court held the services furnished by the health club are not the type generally thought suitable for public regulation and do not involve an activity of great importance or of practical necessity. *See id.* at 925–26.

Yang is instructive on this issue. The Minnesota Supreme Court held the rental company was acting both as a resort and as an innkeeper providing a public service when it offered houseboats for daily and weekly rentals. *See Yang,* 701 N.W.2d at 790. As a matter of public policy, the company could not circumvent its duty to protect guests by requiring them to release the company from liability for its negligence. *See id.* at 791. The court distinguished these types of services from those involving recreational activities which courts generally have held "do not fall within any of the categories where the public interest is involved." *Id.* at 789 (quoting *Schlobohm,* 326 N.W.2d at 925–26). The court specifically rejected the argument that renting houseboats is a purely recreational activity and is not a necessary or public service. *See id.* at 790.

Whether recreational activities involve a public interest is a question the Minnesota Supreme Court has not yet squarely addressed. If the Minnesota Supreme Court has not spoken on an issue, the federal court must determine what decision the state court would make if faced with the same facts and issue. *See Kovarik v. American Family Ins. Group,* 108 F.3d 962, 964 (8th Cir. 1997). The federal court should consider relevant state court decisions, "analogous decisions, considered dicta, ... and any other reliable data." *Id.* at 964 (quoting *Ventura v. Titan Sports, Inc.,* 65 F.3d 725, 729 (8th Cir. 1995)). The Minnesota Court of Appeals has upheld liability releases in contracts for various types of recreational activities, finding the activities are not of great importance to the public or of practical necessity to anyone. *See, e.g., Beehner v. Cragun Corp.,* 636 N.W.2d 821, 828 (Minn. App. 2001) (horseback riding); *Malecha v. St. Croix Valley Skydiving Club, Inc.,* 392 N.W.2d 727, 731 (Minn. App. 1986) (sky diving). We recognize that skiing is an activity enjoyed by many, but we believe the Minnesota Supreme Court would conclude it is not a necessary or public service and would find the release signed by Myers does not violate public policy.

Finally, we disagree with Myers' arguments that the release is invalidated by two Minnesota statutes, the Plain Language Contract Act and the Consumer Credit Sales Act.

Myers does not contest that the release, if valid, encompasses his claims against Lutsen. The release is valid under Minnesota law and, thus, we affirm the district court's summary judgment for Lutsen.

NOTES AND QUESTIONS

1. Do you think an amusement park or haunted house or the like would be deemed a necessary or public service in Minnesota?
2. The following is the text of a waiver that is (at least sometimes) presented to patrons of legendary music venue Toad's Place in New Haven, Connecticut:

You acknowledge and indicate that you are aware that sometimes liquids may hit the floor or other hard surfaces at Toad's Place making them slippery and you will at all times during this part of the performance assume there is a chance of liquids on the floor and will at all times exercise appropriate reasonable caution. You acknowledge this may result in a risk of a slip and fall type injury and you expressly agree to hold Toad's Place, its owners, managers, employees, agents and principals harmless from any injuries or losses you thereby suffer as a result of your willing participation in this activity and acknowledge that you have hereby been put on proper notice of the possible existence of these conditions at the venue during the performance.

You further acknowledge that Toad's Place has a strict 'no moshing policy' and agree to abide by this policy. Moshing does from time to time break out at performances and will be stopped promptly by staff. Offenders of this policy are subject to removal from the premises without refund of their admission price. If spontaneous moshing does occur before the Toads security can stop it, you assume all risk and you expressly agree to hold Toad's Place, its owners, managers, employees, agents and principals harmless from any injuries or losses you thereby suffer as a result.

Please sign here that you are in agreement ____________

Please PRINT name here ____________ Date: ________

Witnessed ________________

A form like this provides the venue both a (potentially) helpful contractual waiver and some evidence that it made an effort to inform patrons about what kinds of inherent risks there are.

We turn now to a notorious haunted house and its attempts to do, well, various things in the form of something that looks like a contract.

Megan Seling, *Tennessee's McKamey Manor: Torture on Demand*

Nashville Scene, Feb. 22, 2018

Before he gets started, the first thing Russ McKamey[, proprietor of "extreme haunted house" McKamey Manor,] has to do is call the cops. From the front porch of a trailer in Summertown, Tenn., he dials a number—"Lawrence County Dispatch," the woman answers—and informs the operator he's about to start his show.

"Please, if you get any crazy phone calls from the neighbors, don't come out here guns a-blazin'," says McKamey. "We had that happen once before. We don't wanna do that again."

The operator laughs.

"Yes, we were working that day," she says.

* * *

Between his two-acre lot in Summertown and a mysterious second location in Huntsville, Ala.—McKamey won't say much about that one—McKamey says he owns all manner of courses and contraptions designed to push people to their breaking points.

Some visitors might have to swim through a 200-yard muddy trench that's home to a few caimans, including a 2-and-a-half-foot male named Ralphie. "He's a biter," McKamey warns. Others might take a dip in a giant tank full of moray eels that "won't bite you, but they will wrap around your face." []

But before a contestant makes it through McKamey Manor's door, he or she must go through the tedious process of reading aloud and signing a 20-plus-page legal waiver that lists more than 100 disgusting, dangerous and disturbing scenarios they may face. The contract itself is so daunting that some people quit right then. But [patron] VanOver is enthusiastic, almost giddy.

* * *

In the hours it takes to make it through the waiver, he agrees to exposure to extreme temperatures (No. 73), having plastic wrap tightly held over his face (No. 74), and having his hands and feet zip-tied (No. 75). The only thing VanOver won't stand for—everyone gets to pick two "freebies"—is tooth-pulling and needles. McKamey hesitates to let VanOver call no needles, dramatically hemming and hawing about how it'll mess up the show, but McKamey finally agrees, reassuring VanOver that he can just drug him orally if need be.

* * *

NOTES AND QUESTIONS

1. McKamey Manor moved from California to Tennessee and a supposed second location in Alabama, though it's not clear the second location actually exists or if, in fact, there is any real "Manor" anymore (assuming it existed in California). A YouTuber known as "Reckless Ben" has, as of this writing, provided some evidence that McKamey now abuses people in the pre-admission part so comprehensively that they all back out prior to going "in" to the manor. *See* YouTube, Reckless Ben, https://www.youtube.com/@RecklessBen. Reckless Ben also found some evidence that McKamey was prohibited from using his barn for the haunt due to the lack of sprinklers—based on a code provision that probably followed from a tragic fire at Six Flags Great Adventure decades earlier, an incident we will discuss in Chapter 13. His inquiries may have led to an investigation by the Attorney General of Tennessee that started just as this book went to press. *See* Eli Motycka, *McKamey Manor Faces Probe From State Attorney General*, NASHVILLE SCENE, Nov. 3, 2023, available at https://www.nashvillescene.com/news/pithinthewind/mckamey-manor-attorney-general-investigation/article_16b6ca76-7a69-11ee-bcdb-3fe8952cc8ba.html. We will touch on this investigation again later in the book.

2. The packet of material sent to patrons (available on RecreationAndRisk.com), in addition to a slightly more narrowly-tailored release than set forth below, discusses various pre-tour activities that may be designed as much to make it so patrons are already exhausted upon arrival, which would be consistent with the hypothesis presented by Reckless Ben.

3. The "Manor" (whatever its reality is) has a lengthy waiver that it seeks to keep from being distributed, but there are two versions I've obtained. This is the older version; the newer version (which is not terribly different) is available, along with other materials, at RecreationAndRisk.com. As far as I can tell, the newer version is in addition to the packet referenced in Note 2. As you review excerpts from it, consider what McKamey is trying to do with it.

McKamey Manor [California location]
Mandatory
Waiver, Release, and Indemnity Agreement

1. REGISTRATION OF PARTICIPANT AND PURPOSE OF AGREEMENT: By signing this contract, (hereafter "agreement [*sic*]) I __________ ______________ (participant name) (Hereafter "participant"), do herein voluntarily, agree to participate in the below listed activities that will take place at "McKamey Manor" [].

Participant's signatory below agrees that they have been provided full and fair consideration for entering into this agreement.

I have set forth any and all pre-existing physical, medical conditions and any mental conditions in their entirety below. If none of these aforesaid conditions are listed then I am expressly waiving any and all claims as more fully set forth in General Release below as against the listed due to this failure to disclose and misrepresentation on my part.

2. SCOPE OF AGREEMENT AND DEFINITIONS: This agreement shall be legally binding upon the participant, their heirs, assignees and agents and any and all family members, spouses and next of kin. The participant represents that they are in fact not a minor, and are otherwise competent to enter into this agreement with no legal impediment.

3. PARTICIPANT AGREES THAT IF THE POLICE ARE CALLED OR APPEAR ON SCENE, THAT PARTICIPANT ACKNOWLEDGES THAT THIS IS JUST A GAME.

4. EXPRESS ASSUMPTION OF RISK OF INHERENTLY DANGEROUS ACTIVITY: Participant agrees and understands that participation in this event is both physically dangerous and could have a negative impact on one's mental health. By signing this agreement, the participant expressly assumes all risk of physical, mental or bodily harm despite this acknowledgment of the known risks.

5. ACCIDENTAL DEATH AND DISABILITY AND OTHER MEDICAL INSURANCE: Should any medical, emergency or otherwise, treatment be required, I understand and agree and represent that I have my own medical and/or health insurance that includes both accidental death, and disability insurance. I agree to pay all incurred expenses that may result of my participation and expressly agree to pay all costs associated therewith including deductibles.

6. GENERAL RELEASE: Release by party participant to this agreement. In addition, [*sic*] to the express terms of this agreement but including the provisions, terms, and conditions of, and obligations under and/or in connection with this Agreement, in further consideration of the matters set forth above, the participant and their past or present agents, heirs, representatives, successors, assigns, employees, and attorneys/counsel of record hereby release, acquit, and forever discharge each other, individually and collectively, and each of their past or present agents, representatives, officers, directors, shareholders, predecessors, successors, assigns, owners, partners, subsidiaries, employees, attorneys/counsel of record, heirs, executors, administrators, and descendants, from any and all known, unknown, and unanticipated claims, damages, demands, obligations, actions, causes of action, rights, liabilities, costs, losses of services and/or income, liens, injuries and/or damages caused by, arising out of, associated with, relating or pertaining to or resulting from any and all acts or omissions in connection with this participation by participant and any matter set forth in this agreement.

The parties hereto expressly waive and assume the risk of any and all claims for damages which exist as of this date, but of which the Parties do not know or suspect to exist, whether through ignorance, oversight, error, negligence, or otherwise, and which, if known, would materially affect the Parties' decision to enter into this Waiver, Release and Indemnity Agreement. The Parties further agree that they assume the risk that the facts or law may be other than they believe.

7. SPECIFIC RELEASE FOR ACTIVITY: Including but not limited to the above general release participant additionally understands and comprehends that by signing this agreement that as the undersigned he or she does hereby voluntarily RELEASES, DISCHARGES, WAIVES, AND RELINQUISHES any and all actives or causes of action for personal injury or loss of my property, property damage or wrongful death occurring to him/herself arising as a result of engaging or receiving instructions in said activity or any activities incidental thereto.

IT IS THE INTENTION OF PARTICIPANT BY THIS INSTRUMENT TO EXPRESSLY ASSUME ALL RISK OF SUCH PERSONAL INJURY, DEATH, OR PROPERTY DAMAGE UPON HIM/HERSELF, TO THE EXCLUSION OF MCKAMEY MANOR AND TO EXEMPT AND RELIEVE MCKAMEY MANOR AND ALL OF IT'S ACTORS FROM LI-

ABILITY FOR PERSONAL INJURY, PROPERTY DAMAGE OR WRONGFUL DEATH CAUSED BY NEGLIGENCE.

* * *

The participant hereto expressly waive [*sic*] and assume [*sic*] the risk of any and all claims for damages which exist as of this date, but of which the Participant does not know or suspect to exist, whether through ignorance, oversight, error, negligence, or otherwise, and which, if known, would materially affect the Participant's decision to enter into this Agreement. The Participant further agrees that they assume the risk that the facts or law may be other than they believe.

8. REPRESENTATION OF PHYSICAL AND MENTAL CONDITION: The undersigned, [*sic*] participant represents unequivocally that they are physically and mentally fit to participate in this attraction, and that the undersigned has no current or past medical condition, (i.e., heart conditions, back or neck problems, pregnancy, subject to seizures (strobe lights), paralysis, restrictive use of arms or legs, etc.) and that participant will act at all times in a civilized and reasonable manner.

9. STATEMENT OF COMPREHENSION OF THIS AGREEMENT AS A BINDING LEGAL DOCUMENT: In entering into this Waiver, Release and Indemnity Agreement, each Party represents that Party has relied upon the advice of his/her/their attorney, who is the attorney of their own choosing, concerning the legal consequences of this Waiver, Release and Indemnity Agreement and Release; that the terms of this Waiver, Release and Indemnity Agreement have been completely read and explained to the Parties by their respective attorneys, or they have waived the advice of an attorney. The terms of this Waiver, Release and Indemnity Agreement are fully understood and voluntarily accepted by all Parties.

10. HOLD HARMLESS AND FULL INDEMNIFICATION: To the full extent permitted by California Law the participant agrees to defend, pay on behalf, fully indemnify MCKAMEY MANOR and its agents and assigns, as well as it's [*sic*] actors, as they are more fully described in General Release, against any claims, causes of action, demands suits or loss including costs associated in any way associated with any activity occurring at MCKAMEY MANOR and/or this agreement both known and unknown.

* * *

17. Participant fully understands that MM is an extremely physical [*sic*], and that participant may will [*sic*] leave MM with bumps, bruises, cuts or other possible injuries ... including possible broken bones. Participant understands that injuries are never on purpose at MM and participant is fully aware of the risks and takes full responsibility.

18. Participant fully understands that MM is not a fight club and will refrain at all times from fighting with the actors.

19. Participant was warned numerous times about the intensity of MM by the Owners and other members of the crew and that YOU REALLY DON'T WANT TO DO THIS.

20. Participant agrees and understands that your life in reality is not in danger and this is just a game.

* * *

23. Participant understands and agrees that they are not being beat up, kicked, slugged, or actually physically harmed. You will be roughed up but no one is there to hurt you. Knowing that, MM is very rough and not for the meek. Participant will have bumps, bruises, possible black eyes, swelling of the face, etc.

24. Participant understands and agrees that they are never being held against their will.

* * *

27. Participant understands and agrees that the characters they come in contact with during the Tour are just actors that are there to provide a performance for Participant and other guests and actually is not reality.

28. Participant fully understands that by signing this waiver that they are giving MM permission to keep nothing off of the table (except sexual or inappropriate situations). Everything else imaginable can and will happen inside of MM. You are aware of this and are giving full permission for any action that may happen inside of MM.

* * *

35. Participant acknowledges and agrees to be submerged in 60 feet of open water. Participant acknowledges and agrees that their breathing apparatus will be removed and that it is Participant's responsibility to make their way to the surface on their own. If done incorrectly there is a real chance of Participant drowning or receiving decompression sickness (The Bends) which could cause permanent injury or even death.

36. Participant acknowledges and agrees that it [*sic*] **100% the Participant's responsibility** to use the safe phrase if they feel they are suffering from any bodily injury, from any mental impairment, or if the Tour becomes too much for Participant in any way.

* * *

39. Participant understands for this specific show only, that Participant is being offered a safe phrase. It is up to the Participant to use this phrase due to their weakness if they feel they need such a weak precaution as a safe phrase.

Yes ___ No ___

* * *

41. Participant agrees that their entire Tour will be viewed by a live audience in Las Vegas, the Philippines, and/or Thailand and that they will act appropriately.

* * *

47. Participant fully understands that they may incur injuries resulting from scare tactics where Participant may react by pulling away, resulting in falling on the ground, into walls, onto props or actors, etc. and that they will not hold MM libel [*sic*].

* * *

51. Participant fully understands that injuries may occur during their Tour of MM, which may include, but not limited to, head, neck, and back injuries, death, stroke, traumatic brain injury, brain aneurysms, cerebral or retinal hemorrhage, subdural hematoma, loss of consciousness, whiplash, harmful heart reactions, nausea, headache, dizziness, lacerations, broken or sprained bones, torn ligaments, bleeding wounds, scrapes and/or cuts, heatstroke, or drowning and does not hold MM responsible.

* * *

64. Participant fully understands and agrees that MK ultra (mind control) may be used.

* * *

90. Participant fully agrees to continue the Tour, and challenges themselves during the MM experience even though at a specific moment in time, participant requests the Tour to stop and to leave MM. Participant agrees to have the Tour continue no matter what participant may say at any time of their panic state of mind [*sic*].

91. Participant fully understands and agrees that there is no quitting until the staff of MM stops the show due to completion or because participant is at a physical or psychological level that it is best that the Tour is stopped.

* * *

94. Participant has been told several times and on more than one occasion by Russ McKamey and others not to take the MM Tour. Participant has heard all of his warnings, and refuses to listen to his recommendations not to take the MM Tour.

95. Participant fully understands and agrees that it is participant's responsibility to read and sign the complete MM waiver before ever taking the Tour. Participant agrees that they will see the waiver on the day of their Tour, and participant agrees that they will not be provided a copy of such waiver for any reason including legal action.

96. Participant fully understands and agrees that everything participant does related to MM will be videotaped, and participant agrees that they will never be provided a copy of any video or pictures for any reason including legal action.

* * *

100. Participant, having spent time with Russ McKamey and other staff of MM, and through other people and what participant has read, know that Russ McKamey and the staff of MM truly has my best intentions at all times [*sic*?]. Participant gives their permission to MM to challenge them both physically and emotionally to the highest degree. Participant does not want to quit MM unless there is no other choice. Participant wants to stay with the Tour no matter what they may say while they are distressed inside MM.

* * *

112. Participant agrees that if selected to participate in Houdini's Chinese Water Torture apparatus which will include being submerged upside down by your ankles with a straight jacket in a cylinder with live moray eels. There is a real possibility of drowning if Participant is unable to control their breath.

* * *

129. Participant will be given a safe phrase. If Participant uses this safe phrase the Tour will stop [*sic*] slowly come to a stop but harassment, shoving, etc. will continue until Participant completes their walk of shame.

* * *

137. If Participant is asked by law enforcement or any concerned individual during their walk of shame, they will say nothing except to point to the paper attached to their clothes explaining what has taken place, that they have failed McKamey Manor's Extinction, and the walk of shame is their punishment.

* * *

Participant acknowledges that they have freely and voluntarily entered into this Agreement after an adequate opportunity to review and discuss the terms and conditions and all factual and legal matters relevant hereto and freely and independently has chosen to execute this Agreement without fraud, duress, undue influence or coercion of any kind or nature whatsoever having been exerted by or imposed upon any party....

[signature block]

To briefly recap this Agreement, Participant understands that MM is advising Participant not take this Tour and that after everything Participant has read regarding the severity of the Tour, that Participant is going to get hurt in one form or another, i.e. cuts, bruises, possible broken bones, black eyes, rope burns, exhaustion, dehydration, even possible death. Basically Participant is basically going to, for lack of better wording, going to be body hardened [sic, so many sics]. That Participant is likely going to have their hair removed. Once again, MM is telling Participant that after reading the entire contract that Participant should not do this. Participant is agreeing to not hold MM or any other party liable for anything involved, that Participant will not involve the police because Participant understands what they are getting into and Participant has decided to do it anyway. Participant will not complain afterwards about anything that happens because Participant completely understands that they have been told that they do not want to do this. That Participant understands all risks and that everything is on the table which could involve injury or even possible death.

* * *

PERSONAL RELEASE FORM

I hereby authorize and grant to Russ McKamey ("the Producer") and McKamey Manor the right to record me (picture and/or voice) on film and/or videotape, for audio only, audio and visual, visual only reproduction, and/or textual transcription ("the Recording"), and to edit the recording into a film/video program (which may include other recordings and material) for purposes such as Facebook, YouTube, or other publication on public websites and for personal use ("the Program").

* * *

[signature block]

NON-DISCLOSURE AGREEMENT

[] The Recipient hereto desires and agrees to be an Actor and/or Builder and/or Attendee in relation to secure McKamey Manor's secrets (the "Transaction").

Throughout the duration of this Agreement, the Disclosing Party may deem it necessary to disclose or share certain proprietary information with the Recipient. Therefore, in consideration of the mutual promises and covenants contained within this Agreement, and other good and valuable consideration, the receipt and sufficiency of which is hereby acknowledged, both parties hereto agree as follows:

Confidential Information

For all intents and purposes of this Agreement, "Confidential Information" shall mean and include any data or information that is deemed proprietary to the Disclosing Party and that which is not generally known to the public, whether in tangible or intangible form, whenever and however disclosed, including, but not limited to [lengthy list of categories of things that do not seem to have anything to do with a haunted house]. The Receiving Party acknowledges that the Confidential Information is proprietary to the Disclosing Party and, as such, the Disclosing Party regards all of its Confidential Information as trade secrets.

* * *

Confidential Information Usage

The Receiving Party herein agrees to make use of the Confidential Information solely for the purpose and in connection with the current or contemplated business relationship between both parties and not for any purpose other than that which has been stipulated and contained herein this Agreement, unless otherwise authorized by prior written consent by an authorized representative of the Disclosing Party. There shall be no other right or license, whether expressed or implied, in the Confidential Information granted to the Receiving Party hereunder.

[Omitted: many paragraphs about confidential information that make no sense in the context of a haunted house.]

* * *

Non-Disparagement Agreement

* * *

Participant agrees that during their Tour of McKamey Manor and for twenty (20) years after their departure from the Tour, that Participant shall not, through any form of communication with the press, public, clients, media, blogs, or social media, disparage McKamey Manor in any way.

Participant understands that forms of communication include but are limited to social media websites, public forums, suppliers, vendors, conventions, interviews, or record statements. Participant understands that disparagement includes but is not limited to critiques, derogatory statements, ridicule, slander, jokes or insults at the expense of McKamey Manor, management, personnel, products or services.

Participant understands that if they violate this Agreement that Participant agrees to pay McKamey Manor $50,000 as damages. Similarly, McKamey Manor has the right to sue Participant in the San Diego County Superior Court system if damages are not paid.

[signature block]

NOTES AND QUESTIONS

1. The newer version of this document (again, available at RecreationAndRisk.com) seems more likely to have been reviewed by an attorney, but still is far longer than a typical type of waiver and has retained most of the more unusual features of the excerpted one above.
2. Not to get too colloquial, but I hope this sentence made you LOL, and perhaps even ROFL, when it appeared (twice!): "The Parties further agree that they assume the risk that the facts or law may be

other than they believe." The updated version contains that same sentence. Similarly, the attempt to get someone to agree, in advance, that a video of a visit will never be made available, even through legal process, is just silly.

3. A quick search of news databases in Westlaw comes up with about a hundred articles that reference McKamey Manor. Roughly two-thirds of the articles mention the waiver, often as the main focus. A *Daily Mirror* piece from 2019, for example, has as its headline, "World's scariest haunted house is so terrifying you must produce doctor's note," with the subheadline, "Events held at McKamey Manor are so terrifying that participants must sign a 40-page waiver."
4. We'll discuss intentional torts and criminal law in more detail in subsequent chapters. When reviewing the waiver excerpts above, think about how much of it is dedicated to various potential topics—negligence claims, intentional tort claims, criminal conduct, releases with respect to video or other recordings, non-disclosure efforts, and non-disparagement efforts. Since one can't effectively waive intentional tort claims by contract (as we'll discuss), what purpose (or purposes), if any, does the laundry list of mean things the Manor might do to patrons have?
5. If Russ McKamey hired you to revise this document, what questions would you have for him? What would you recommend changing?
6. In the "Reckless Ben" video series referenced above, the titular Ben (who, indeed, seems somewhat reckless) receives the current version of the waiver in Word format. Concerned about the non-disparagement provision, he deleted the $50,000 in liquidated damages provision and replaced it with $1. After signing it, he returned it to Russ McKamey, who executed it without looking to see if it had been changed. Do you think Ben's changing of the contract would cause trouble for him if there ended up being a dispute?
7. The waiver, among other interesting features, is wildly self-contradictory, asserting on the one hand that participants may suffer "head, neck, and back injuries, death, stroke, traumatic brain injury, brain aneurysms, cerebral or retinal hemorrhage, subdural hematoma, loss of consciousness, whiplash, harmful heart reactions, nausea, headache, dizziness, lacerations, broken or sprained bones, torn

ligaments, bleeding wounds, scrapes and/or cuts, heatstroke, or drowning," but on the other hand, "Participant agrees and understands that your life in reality is not in danger and this is just a game."

Similarly, the participant is given a safe phrase (though it comes with an insult: "Participant understands for this specific show only, that Participant is being offered a safe phrase. It is up to the Participant to use this phrase due to their weakness if they feel they need such a weak precaution as a safe phrase.") but also seemingly agrees that the Manor can ignore it ("Participant wants to stay with the Tour no matter what they may say while they are distressed inside MM."). Do you think a court would enforce the latter? In the updated version of the waiver, the participant is given an option, with that sentence prefaced with, "If NO SAFE PHRASE is selected, participant does not want to quit MM unless there is no other choice." Is that enforceable? Should it be?

Do you think a court would consider the internal contradictions and general sloppiness of this waiver as relevant to evaluating its enforceability and scope?

8. As far as I can tell, McKamey Manor has not been a defendant in litigation, though of course not all courts are easily searchable.

9. Various other "extreme" haunts have waivers that are much shorter and straightforward. See, for example, the 13th Floor Haunted House's (currently available at https://13thfloor.formstack.com/forms/13th_floor_denver_2023_waiver). Of note, that form only expressly references negligence in the context of Covid-19 risks, but has a broad release of liability. ("In consideration and acceptance of entrance into the attraction I agree to release 13th Floor Haunted House, its parent corporations, affiliates, officers, directors, employees and landlord from any liability for any harm, injury or death, cost or expense whatsoever that may arise directly or indirectly from attending this event or any of the attractions at this location.") They also are consistently much clearer about the availability of safe words/safe phrases. The "Monster Inside" documentary referenced above explores the safe words/safe phrases issue.

10. What are your thoughts about the legal intersection of tort law with activities involving consented-to intentional torts? Many people suggest that, wholly apart from the civil liability questions, it should

be illegal for a business to offer something that in other contexts would be considered abusive or violent, even criminally so. Do you agree? Are there some slippery slope issues in play here? Who should decide which sorts of contacts should be permissible with appropriate consent?

11. We'll look at waivers again in Chapter 9, related to the Haunted Mine Ride tragedy in Colorado (which, despite its name, is not a haunt but a ride).

The next case looks at another contractual (or maybe quasi-contractual?) way to attempt to limit liability: the "Common Adventure" concept.

Ruth v. Hutchinson Gas Co.

296 N.W. 136 (Minn. 1941)

PETERSON, Justice.

This appeal involves five cases in which recovery was sought upon the grounds of defendants' alleged negligence. Plaintiff Joseph Julig sues for personal injuries. The other four plaintiffs sue for the wrongful death of their respective decedents.

Julig, Frank J. Ruth, Lyle H. Schoeneman, Walter M. Spannaus, and Lewis P. Jergens were friends. Some of them were businessmen, and the others held responsible business positions with firms at Hutchinson. In November, 1938, they arranged to go deer hunting near Big Falls in the northern part of the state. Each was to bring his own bedding, except the mattresses, and his arms and ammunition. Each contributed to a common fund or 'kitty' of which Ruth was the custodian and out of which the expense of travel, food, and incidentals was to be paid. The testimony was that 'each fellow had an equal voice in the running of the trip.'

The five men planned to travel in a motor truck with a brooder house attached from Hutchinson to the place where they intended to hunt and to use the brooder house as their living quarters while they were hunting. Julig obtained the use of the brooder house from a lumber company and of the truck to which it was attached from his employer. The brooder house, as its name indicates, was a small structure such as is used by chicken raisers and was approximately 14 feet long, 8 feet wide, and 7 feet 4 inches high with a cubical content of about 600 feet. It had one door and five windows. There was a hole in the roof eight inches square to which a 'smokestack' had been attached, but this had been knocked off by contact with the structure above the door of a garage into which the truck had been driven.

Julig arranged with the corporate defendants for heat and fuel. They loaned and installed without charge a Radiantfire heater, a cooking plate, and two drums of propane gas for fuel. They donated as much of the gas as was to be consumed on the trip. The only obligation on the part of the men was to return the equipment and the unused gas. All the equipment was of standard type, design, and construction, in good shape, and free from defects. No claim was made that there was anything wrong with the gas.

The equipment was installed at the plant of the corporate defendants, where the truck with the brooder house attached was taken for that purpose. The defendant Luedtke, manager of the Hutchinson Gas Company and in charge of the business of both corporations at Hutchinson, arranged for the gratuitous installation of the equipment and the gift of the gas to be used. The installation was made under his direction by the defendant Rolander, an employe[e] who had been a gas service man for 15 years. He tested the equipment after it was installed and found it in good working order. He had made thousands of similar tests and had installed over 100 heaters, including three or four of the type here involved.

At the time of the installation there was the 8-inch square hole in the roof of the brooder house where the smokestack had been. During the progress of the work a tinsmith representing Julig and the other men measured the hole in the roof for the purpose of installing some sort of ventilator or cover. After the installation of the heating and cooking equipment the truck was driven away with the hole in the top of the brooder house unclosed. Later the tinsmith attached a cover over the opening which operated on a hinge and could be raised and lowered by means of a wire and kept open as desired by fastening the wire to a nail.

The heater had a collar to which a pipe or vent could be attached to carry off combustion gases or, as they were called, 'flue products', but no such pipe was attached or installed. The evidence showed that Luedtke and Rolander knew that the burning of the gas gave off flue products, but that they did not know the exact nature thereof or that, as it appeared here, the flue products consisted in part of carbon monoxide gas.

The heater had been used previously without a vent pipe with no injurious results. It had been sold to a customer who used it in his kitchen with propane gas as fuel during 1933 and 1934. Sometimes the kitchen door was closed and sometimes open. The customer returned the heater because he was in default on his payments. Thereafter the heater was installed without a vent pipe in the office of the Hutchinson Gas Company. The service was satisfactory and without ill effects in both instances, although the heater was not vented.

In the presence of all the men who went on the hunting trip except Spannaus, Rolander explained the use of the equipment to Julig. Rolander and other witnesses testified that he then instructed Julig to keep the brooder house well ventilated and to keep the door or a window open. This Julig positively denied.

Early on the morning of November 13, 1938, the hunting party left Hutchinson for Big Falls, which was some 300 miles distant. Two of them rode in the driver's seat and three of them in the brooder house attached to the truck. The heater was on all the way en route without any distressing results. The evidence does not show whether the roof ventilator was kept open en route or to what extent the brooder house was ventilated, except inferentially that the only ventilation was through cracks around the windows and an opening under the door. Apparently the windows and door were kept closed. Nor does the evidence show what the temperature, wind, or other atmospheric conditions were.

After reaching their destination the truck was parked. It was then cold, the temperature being below zero, and still. There was about six inches of snow on the ground. The heater was turned off while the men prepared their supper. After supper the heater was lighted again. The ventilator was kept open. The parties retired for the night with the heater burning. Julig, who slept alongside of a window where there was some draft, woke up during the night from nausea. There was evidence that he attempted to communicate with his companions. Receiving no response, he assumed that they were sleeping soundly and went to sleep again himself.

On the morning of November 14 two game wardens opened the door of the brooder house and found Julig unconscious and the other four men dead. The ventilator had been shut and the windows and door of the brooder house had been closed tight.

It was ascertained later that Julig's condition and the deaths of his four companions were caused by inhaling carbon monoxide gas given off by the heater while burning propane gas during the night.

Plaintiffs claimed that defendants were guilty of negligence in failing to install a pipe, vent, or other means to carry the carbon monoxide gas from the heater to the outside and in failing to warn Julig and the decedents of the carbon monoxide gas that would be given off by burning the gas in the heater and of the dangers incident thereto if the gases were not eliminated from the brooder house. The corporate defendants were charged as suppliers of the equipment and the gas and the individual defendants as agents and employe[e]s of the corporate defendants in accomplishing those purposes.

The evidence showed that the burning of propane gas in the heater gave off, among other flue products, carbon monoxide gas, which, because it had not been carried to the outside, freely circulated with the air inside. Carbon monoxide gas is colorless and to most people practically tasteless and odorless. Its effect upon the human system depends upon its density. "A concentration of one-fifteenth of one percent. is dangerous to human life, two-tenths of one percent. is usually fatal, and one percent. is regarded as fatal within a very short time." The density of a particular concentration in a given place depends not only upon the amount of carbon monoxide gas produced there, but also upon the extent of the elimination of the carbon monoxide gas and the introduction of fresh air. There was no affirmative showing here as to the amount of carbon monoxide gas given off by the heater or the amount of fresh air introduced through the roof ventilator, the opening under the door, and the cracks around the windows. Such means of ventilation proved sufficient while the party was en route from Hutchinson to Big Falls. There was not sufficient ventilation with the roof ventilator closed when the truck was at rest. The evidence does not show that there would have been sufficient ventilation if the roof ventilator had been kept open during the night, but an inference of the affirmative is permissible in view of the fact that no member of the party experienced any ill effects or distress while the ventilator was kept open.

* * *

The court further charged that if the parties were engaged in a joint adventure each was chargeable with the acts and omissions of the others. There was a verdict for defendants. Plaintiffs appeal from the order denying their motion in the alternative for judgment notwithstanding the verdict or for a new trial.

* * *

The evidence made the question of joint enterprise one of fact. Each party had a common object and purpose with the others which they sought to accomplish by the co-operation of all. Each contributed his share of the expense. Each had some task in connection with the trip assigned to him. The testimony is explicit that each one of them had an equal voice in the running of the trip. There is a joint enterprise where all the parties have a community of interest in the purposes and objects of the undertaking and an equal right in its control and management. As to third persons, each member of a joint enterprise is the agent of the others, and the acts of one within the scope of the enterprise are the acts of all. *Murphy v. Keating*, 204 Minn. 269, 283 N.W. 389. If there was a joint enterprise, the warning to ventilate given to Julig was imputable to all. Likewise, the negligence of one was attributable to all. Hence, if one of them negligently closed the ventilator, all were charged with such negligence. Restatement, Torts, § 491.

* * *

The order should be affirmed.

Affirmed.

NOTES AND QUESTIONS

1. According to Ron Watters, the former director of the Idaho State University Outdoor Program, at least one origin of the contemporary common adventure concept was a 1972 memo prepared by Richard Wyman for the director of the University of Oregon Outdoor Program, Gary O. Grimm. That document, "A Memorandum Regarding the Tort Liability of Self-Directing University Outdoor Wilderness Programs," addresses a range of liability theories (*e.g.*, common carrier, misrepresentation, contractual duty) and potential defenses (*e.g.*, sovereign immunity, express assumption of risk, implied assumption of inherent risks, comparative fault), providing hypotheticals for each. The memorandum advised the Outdoor Program about

facts that would "support the contention that participants are common adventurers in court," providing for a defense to any claim by a participant against other persons in the outing:

1. Equal payment of all members for any rental of group equipment
2. Equal responsibility for the control and maintenance of the boat equipment
3. Equal position and status among the members; the absence of any reliance relationship such as teacher-student
4. Equal understanding of what risks are to be faced in the common adventure

Wyman, *A Memorandum Regarding the Tort Liability of Self-Directing University Outdoor Wilderness Programs*, 1972 (on file with author, courtesy of Ron Watters) (handwritten revisions on original incorporated above). Note that Wyman does not contend the establishment of those facts would necessarily provide a defense to the University for any claims but, as in the *Ruth* case, they would help make it more difficult for one participant to successfully sue other participants.

2. Watters, in a 1999 piece (available at http://www.ronwatters.com/CALitReview.htm), suggests that this memo had some interesting consequences. Some interpreted it as identifying a path for universities or other organizers to avoid liability—almost certainly overstating the level of protection that the "common adventurer" structure in fact provides. The approach outlined in the memo also became almost a dogma for the "right" way to do outdoor programs, apart from (indeed, seemingly without awareness of) any legal protections—it just became the way some people in that community thought trips *should* be organized:

> [I]t was not authoritarian and participants shared decision making. It attempted to simplify and dispense with bureaucracy. It was the opposite of commercialism. No one made money. People shared expenses. It is no wonder that it caught on, and the numbers of students participating in common adventure trips increased exponentially in the 1970s.

Id. Some people still rely on the common adventure concept today including references on, as my friend and former colleague Professor Erin Buzuvis points out, the websites for kayak adventures. *See, e.g.*, https://paddlinggals.com.

3. Do you think there might be a way for a court to adopt a no-duty or limited-duty rule related to a common adventure program to help cabin liability? Should one do so?

CHAPTER 6

Regulations and Investigations

When I talk about this class (and this casebook) with friends, after the usual bits ("Yes, I still ride roller coasters" and "No, I don't think you should be afraid of amusement parks or carnivals" and "No, I don't ride the Zipper or other flat rides much, but it's because I'm old and they make me feel gross; I think they're plenty safe" and "Yes, it's weird that I write about haunts a lot but never want to go to one"), I talk about how the subject matter is not just a rehash of tort doctrine—that it touches on a bunch of different areas of law, and that the regulatory aspect is particularly interesting.

What's always particularly fascinating to me is how many people—including lawyers in highly regulated industries—assume that all of the rides are regulated at the federal level in some way. Not so.

Kathy Fackler, *Carnival Fatality Investigations by Steve Jr.*

SaferParks.org, June 5, 2005*

Early last year, I wrote about the unexplained death of Monique Mendoza, a 22-year-old Arizona woman who lost consciousness and died while riding a Wisdom Sizzler owned and operated by Steve Broetsky's carnival Frazier Shows. According to the police report, the ride owner's son, Steve Jr., inspected the ride following the woman's death and cleared it to reopen 45 minutes later. The Prescott Valley police had

* Copyright 2005 Kathy Fackler, Saferparks. Reprinted by permission.

witness testimony and video tapes pointing to a possible over-speed problem, but lacked legal authority to order the ride closed pending an independent public safety inspection. The ride owner's son assured police that his 45-minute look-see showed the ride to be operating within approved tolerances.

By allowing his own son to clear the ride, Mr. Broetsky acted in compliance with all federal, state, and local laws. Arizona does not regulate the safety of amusement rides. Lt. Janik of the Prescott Valley Police Department spent four hours looking for a public safety agency he could turn the case over to. In that time, he found two agencies that would have taken jurisdiction immediately if the dead person had been a carnival employee. No government agency in Arizona is empowered to protect paying customers.

Steve Jr. is 23 years old and has a NAARSO Level I certification. That means he correctly answered at least 112 of 150 questions covering general interest (ability to read and understand instructions, basic math, measurement systems, etc.) and basic amusement ride safety concepts. NAARSO level I certification is analogous to Red Cross life saving training. Basic lifesaving is a great starting point when training lifeguards, but if somebody dies at a commercial water park, you wouldn't want the public safety investigation carried out by the owner's son who's taken a CPR course. And no matter how high the kid scored on his CPR test, you really don't want the owner's son to be the sole technical investigator in *two* unexplained fatalities on the same piece of equipment.

Yet that is exactly what happened last Saturday evening in Durango, Colorado after 14-year-old April Benally was removed unconscious from Mr. Broetsky's Sizzler at the Durango Fiesta Days carnival. She died a short time later at Mercy Hospital. Steve Jr. put his NAARSO Level I certification to use again, inspecting his dad's Sizzler so it could re-open before close of business that night. Local paramedics assisted in a speedy re-opening by clearing the body within 12 minutes of the first emergency call. Commenting on the quick response, Mr. Broetsky told the press, "I have nothing but accolades for the authorities out here."

* * *

Colorado's amusement ride regulations do not require immediate reporting of deaths or injuries, and the state does not have a ride inspection or accident investigation program. Ride owners must register with the state, insure the ride, and show that it's been inspected by a NAARSO-certified inspector—that's right, Steve Jr.

* * *

Epilogue

The Durango Police Department's report on the second fatality listed cause of death as Cardiac Arrhythmia. The manner of death was ruled natural.

The Consumer Product Safety Commission (CPSC) investigated the second death on Frazier Shows' Sizzler ride. Highlights:

- The ride, manufactured in 2001, has a central pole that spins in a clockwise direction. Three sweeps attach to the center pole, with spindles hanging down from each sweep and four cars attached to each sweep (total of 12 cars). The entire ride is driven by one 20 hp motor. In addition, each of the three spindles is powered by its own hydraulic motor.
- On May 29, 2005, maintenance records show that the ride owner replaced the motor on the blue spindle, which eliminated any chance of determining whether an overspeed condition may have contributed to the fatalities in Colorado or Arizona. The ride played out the remainder of its allotted contract through May 30, 2005.
- On June 3, 2005, the ride manufacturer, Wisdom, sent a representative to inspect the ride. The new motor was found to be spinning the ride at an acceptable speed. Wisdom's report noted scratch marks on a set screw which may indicate that the flow control had been adjusted. When questioned by the CPSC investigators, ride operators indicated that the set screw controls the flow of hydraulic fluid which in turn controls the speed of the amusement ride, but the operators told CPSC they had never adjusted the set screw and did not know it existed until the manufacturer's representative came out to examine the ride following the second fatality.
- On June 22, 2005, two investigators from the U.S. Consumer Product Safety Commission performed an inspection of the Sizzler, and found the new motor to be spinning the ride at an acceptable speed.

Kathy Fackler, *Regulatory Roulette*

SaferParks.org, June 23, 2007*

On June 21, a cable snapped on a drop tower at Six Flags Kentucky Kingdom. The broken cable hit a 13-year-old rider, severing both of her legs just above the ankles. The ride happened to be located in a state that has a government ride inspection program. According to news reports, the park staff is working with the Kentucky Department of Agriculture to determine the cause of this tragedy. Two theme park corporations, Six Flags and Cedar Fair, have voluntarily shut down similar drop towers pending resolution of the technical investigation.

The gruesomeness of the outcome gives this accident more public play than most. I've received requests for interviews from mainstream news programs, but also from tabloid shows and in-your-face talk shows looking to capitalize on this family's bad luck. I took a pass on most of the requests, but did agree to two minutes on a CNN morning show. The interviewer and I talked about regulatory exemptions for a bit and then he asked the stock questions provided to the press by the industry to mitigate PR fallout in the wake of accidental tragedies:

- *Accidents happen everywhere. Don't patrons accept certain risks when they choose to board a thrill ride?*
- *Thrill rides are statistically safe. Why stir people up over something so inconsequential?*

I have been asked some version of those two questions more times than I can count, but never in the early aftermath of something of this magnitude. I was truly taken aback at the timing. Can you imagine any parent considering the amputation of their child's feet to be an acceptable risk at a family amusement park?

What happened to that little girl highlights the high price of even a single failure. The only brag-worthy statistic for limb loss on an amusement park ride is zero. Cables don't just snap. If they do, something has gone badly wrong in the system. There's a history behind every serious accident that, if uncovered, can illuminate a path to prevention—not just on that ride or in that park, but on similar equipment across the globe. Public records ensure that safety-critical information is available to all who need it, expanding the knowledge base of the engineer and inspector communities, and allowing consumers the right of informed choice in the marketplace.

Uncovering that history means digging into all the available evidence without regard to what it might cost your company or your client, without preconceived notions about who or what to blame. This is the job of the government, not the companies who built, operated, and insured the ride. Yet government accident investigations and public accident reports are only allowed in certain geopolitical areas of this country. U.S. amusement park rides are exempt from all federal safety oversight. In the quarter century since Congress granted the exemption, only 27 states have created regulatory programs that require government officials to investigate amusement ride accidents.

Human lives and limbs are too precious to entrust to this kind of patchy regulatory roulette, especially when we're talking about children.

The Intamin drop ride in Kentucky is regulated by [state] government ride safety officials, but the Intamin drop ride at Elitch Gardens in Colorado is not. Elitch was part of the Six Flags chain until early this year when the park was sold, along with several others, to a real estate investment trust called CNL Income Properties. Colorado has a ride licensing law on the books, but no government ride inspection or accident investigation program. If one of the rides at Elitch Gardens accidentally maims a child, there isn't any government safety agency authorized to investigate.

What if this had happened at another Six Flags park? Some are subject to government oversight, some are not. Six Flags operates two amusement parks in Texas. Neither has an Intamin drop ride, but between them they boast a 325-foot-tall-85-mph roller coaster, a 325-foot-tall freefall combo tower, and almost a hundred other amusement rides. Texas, like Colorado, has no government ride inspection or accident investigation program. Parks manage their own accidents without pesky government interference.

What about the other corporate park chains? How accountable are they to the public?

Disney and Universal Studios operate thrill rides at parks in California and Florida. California investigates theme park thrill ride accidents, but Florida does not. All accidents at the Florida theme parks are handled privately by the company. All findings remain confidential.

Busch Entertainment operates theme parks in Virginia, Texas, Florida, and California. State accident investigation reports are only available for the park in California.

Cedar Fair operates parks in eight states. Some have laws authorizing state ride inspectors to investigate serious accidents; some do not.

Under what conditions is it unreasonable or undesirable to require a thorough public safety investigation of a machinery accident that maims a child? Why are many theme park thrill rides subject to less stringent government safety oversight than the plush toys and hot dogs sold in their shops?

Despite my reputation in some corners, I'm not a big fan of overregulation. I'm asking for an honest, thoughtful, respectful public policy discussion about the gaping holes in the current system. Congress, industry, the existing regulatory community, and consumer representatives should be willing to do that much to protect the millions of children who climb on board U.S. thrill rides every year.

NOTES AND QUESTIONS

1. Ms. Fackler, the author of the two editorials excerpted above, for many ears ran a website called SaferParks.org. As of this writing, her site is still operational but has not been updated in some time. She became an activist when her young son's foot was seriously injured when riding Disneyland's Big Thunder Mountain Railroad in the late 1990s. The ride came to a temporary stop and her son, thinking he was supposed to get ready to exit, put his foot out the open side. The ride move forward and his foot was jammed between the platform and the track. Later in the year, a patron at the park died after a cleat flew off another ride. The park, discussing that tragedy, said it was the first "serious injury" of a guest in four years. Fackler was understandably confused about how her son's injury wasn't counted as serious. And so her activist path was set, and she spent many years involved in the issue (including serving on industry committees), largely focused on policy efforts that would make reliable information available.

2. SaferParks was also (to my knowledge) the only source of exhaustive information about the regulatory scheme in effect in every state until she more or less retired a few years ago. As you will see shortly, for this book, I (with the invaluable assistance of a research assistant) put together what was, at the time it was written, an exhaustive summary of states' regulatory schemes.
3. As I mentioned above, the folks I talk to—assuredly not representative of the population as a whole—tend to be surprised, even shocked, that there isn't federal oversight of fixed-site amusement rides, and at the variability of regulation of rides at the state level. As you read the materials, if you are inclined to think that there should be more regulation, think about what you'd want that regulation to include. Should regulators be involved at the ride design stage? Should they be inspecting rides? If so, how often? What level of incidents should be investigated, and by whom? How should reports be issued, and how often? How should they be funded? And so on.
4. Regardless of your initial response to the idea of additional regulation, are there particular metrics that you would find relevant to evaluating the question, or to evaluating whether additional regulations were "successful"? If it were possible to reliably compare the per capita injuries or deaths that took place under one regulatory scheme compared to another, would that be useful or persuasive to you? (I will note that, in part because of the lack of a single warehouse of data about incidents and a lack of consistent definitions, it is not in fact possible to make such a comparison, at least not reliably—this is, of course, part of what Ms. Fackler advocated for.)
5. Note that not all of the data cited in Ms. Fackler's editorials is still accurate; states often adjust their regulatory schemes, sometimes making them stricter, sometimes less strict. Colorado, as we will see later, now does have investigations of accidents. Less immediately importantly, as of this writing, Six Flags and Cedar Fair have announced their intention to merge into a single regional theme park chain. That will, one assumes, make it so that changes to a ride in one park would get rolled out across all of the chain.

Ronald J. Cereola & Reginald Foucar-Szocki, *Fixed Site Amusement Rides; Who Regulates Safety?*

25 *Hospitality Review* 47 (2007)

There is currently no national regulation of fixed site (ex. roller coaster) amusement ride safety. The current regulatory system is highly fragmented and consists of many disparate efforts by State and local agencies, judicial intervention in the form of tort litigation and industry self regulatory compliance. The Federal government has no authority over fixed site ride safety.

* * *

According to a Consumer Products Safety Commission (CPSC) Report in September 2005, there were 67 documented fatalities for the years 2003 and 2004: 46 from fixed-site rides, 13 from mobile rides, and 8 from unknown-site rides. Data for 2005 was not available at the time of the report. The CPSC defines fixed-site rides as those permanently affixed to a site, such as are found in amusement parks as opposed to mobile rides, which are moved from site to site and typified by rides found at fairs and carnivals. It should be noted that the CPSC has jurisdiction over mobile rides but not over fixed site rides. The so called "Roller Coaster Loophole" of the Consumer Products Safety Commission Act of 1981 exempted fixed site rides from CPSC jurisdiction.

Among all the products exempted from CPSC regulation, fixed site amusement rides were the sole product exemption not regulated by any other Federal agency. Regulatory jurisdiction was then and still is specifically left to the individual states. According to the CPSC July 2006 Directory of Amusement Park Safety Officials, 39 States utilize state, local and private inspectors, 3 states rely solely on private inspections and 9 states have either no regulatory scheme or no required inspections.

There is currently no national reporting requirement or repository for collecting ride fatality or injury information. The CPSC statistics are derived indirectly since it has no direct access to amusement park fixed ride fatality and injury data. Reports to the CPSC of fixed ride incidents are not required nor is the CPSC permitted to investigate such incidents. It must compile that information through the National Electronic Injury Surveillance System (NEISS), which gathers information from a statistical sampling of hospital emergency rooms and then estimates national numbers. Additionally, according to Safer Parks, a consumer organization advocating Federal regulation of fixed site amusement rides, the CPSC has decided to no longer publish reports on amusement park deaths and fatalities in the United States.

H.R. 2861 To restore the jurisdiction of the Consumer Product Safety Commission over amusement rides which are at a fixed site, and for other purposes

September 7, 2011, introduced by
Rep. Edward Markey

Be it enacted by the Senate and House of Representatives of the United States of America in Congress assembled,

SECTION 1. SHORT TITLE.

This Act may be cited as the "National Amusement Park Ride Safety Act of 2011".

SEC. 2. JURISDICTION OVER FIXED SITE AMUSEMENT RIDES.

Section 3(a)(1) of the Consumer Product Safety Act (15 U.S.C. 2052(a)(1)) is amended by striking ", and which is not permanently fixed to a site. Such term does not include such a device which is permanently fixed to a site." and inserting a period.

SEC. 3. AUTHORIZATION OF APPROPRIATIONS.

There are authorized to be appropriated to the Consumer Product Safety Commission $500,000 for each fiscal year to enable the Commission to carry out the Consumer Product Safety Act as amended by this Act.

NOTES AND QUESTIONS

1. H.R. 2861 has not been made law. Edward Markey is now a U.S. Senator and has not pursued this legislation in the Senate. The most recent reference to amusement parks on his current website is from September 2012, when he was still in the House, calling for this legislation after passengers were stranded (safely) 300 feet up on a ride at California's Knott's Berry Farm. Press Release, *Markey Renews Call for Passage of Roller Coaster Safety Legislation*, https://www.

markey.senate.gov/news/press-releases/markey-renews-call-for-passage-of-roller-coaster-safety-legislation. The ride in question, perhaps notably, is not a roller coaster, but a swing ride; it now operates at the park chain's Worlds of Fun in Kansas City.

2. The conservative/libertarian *National Review* published an editorial about now-Senator Markey's work relating to amusement ride regulation, with the writer, Charles C.W. Cooke, characterizing the work as Markey being "hell-bent on ruining my fun." Cooke, *Ed Markey's Peculiar Crusade*, National Review, Feb. 9, 2013. "Markey found his eccentric calling during a horrifying but statistically aberrant week in 1999 during which four people were killed in amusement-park accidents. Drawing on his unholy blend of ignorant outrage and unwavering belief in the federal government's capacity to fix all ills, the congressman immediately began agitating for federal oversight of all 'fixed-site amusement rides,' blaming the tragedies on the increased speed, height, and intensity of the nation's roller coasters." Cooke summarized (with his own gloss) some of the research that the industry funded:

> In 2003, alarmed by the ignorance of Markey's campaign—and the willingness of many in the press to give it a platform—the Six Flags chain commissioned both the American Association of Neurological Surgeons (AANS) and the engineering group Exponent Failure Analysis Associates (EFAA) to conduct in-depth studies of the issue. For Markey, the results were devastating. The AANS concluded flatly that "there is no proof that roller coasters cause neurological injury and there is no significant public-health risk associated with amusement-park attendance." The association's spokesman, Dr. Robert Harbaugh, added that injury rates at amusement parks are "significantly lower" than those of "other activities such as owning bunk beds, skateboards, sleds, or bicycles." Presenting the EFAA's report, Dr. Lee Dickinson concurred, affirming that "roller coasters are safe" and explaining that "we did not find anything to suggest that a public-health issue exists." More specifically, he continued, "G-forces on

roller coasters are not a problem and the available government data do not support a problem."

Do those reports "devastate" Senator Markey's efforts, do you think?

3. The Consumer Product Safety Act was amended in 1981 to exclude fixed-site amusement parks from its purview after what was described at the time as a "successful lobbying campaign by the industry." Susan Bennett, *U.S. Safety Aide Raps 'Amusement-Ride Roulette,'* PHILADELPHIA DAILY NEWS, Aug. 7, 1984 at 5.

   The amendment came after a Fifth Circuit case found that the CPSC had expansive jurisdiction. In that case, *State Fair of Texas v. United States Consumer Product Safety Commission*, the Fifth Circuit found that an aerial tramway known as the Swiss Skyride at the State Fair of Texas was a "consumer product" within the meaning of the Consumer Product Safety Act, such that the CPSC could properly enter the fairgrounds to inspect it. 650 F.2d 1324 (5th Cir. 1981). Prior to the CPSC's attempt to investigate, an accident had occurred at the Fair in 1979, in which four gondolas collided and fell, leaving one patron dead. The Fifth Circuit concluded that the skyride qualified as a consumer product (noting that Congress defined the term "expansively" anchored on the question of whether a consumer is "expos[ed] to it," *id.* at 1328). The State Fair does not appear to have challenged jurisdiction based on Commerce Clause grounds.

   The Supreme Court, after the congressional amendment, granted *certiorari* with direction to vacate the opinion and dismiss the original case as moot. Due to that amendment, the Consumer Product Safety Commission has only some form of oversight of rides at traveling carnivals but not fixed-site parks. As noted in the article above, the CPSC has indeed ceased performing its annual estimate of deaths at amusement parks.

4. What was your reaction to the budget of $500,000 per year for the work as set forth in the legislation?

5. In 2022, I hired a research assistant, Alexander Yee, to do a 50-state survey on the status of amusement park regulation in the United States, since, as far as I could tell, that sort of research had not been updated in a number of years (after the at-one-time comprehensive SaferParks.org stopped being updated). What exists is what every

observer seems to be required to describe as a "patchwork." The full (extensive) package of information is available at RecreationAndRisk.com. But this count of how many states perform various types of regulation should give you a sense:

Program type:		**Inspections—Performed by:**	
Comprehensive gov. Oversight	33	Government inspector	36
Partial gov. oversight	11	3rd-party inspector	29
Private-sector oversight	3	Self-inspected	1
Electrical inspections only	1	**Operation:**	
No state agency w/ jurisdiction	7	Ride ops must be 18yo+	9
Ride safety advisory board	13	Patron responsibility rules	28
References ASTM (F24) Standards	41	**Accidents—Owner must report:**	
Regs Cover:		Severe injury or death	37
Theme park rides	47	Injury requiring ER or Dr's visit	29
Other fixed-site rides	46	Ride damage or malfunction	16
Portable rides	49	**Accidents—Investigation:**	
Inflatables	27	Gov. may investigate accidents	36
Waterslides	29	Owner must preserve acc. scene	30
Permits/Insurance:		Gov. may shutdown unsafe rides	38
Rides must be registered	40	**Accidents—Public records:**	
Insurance required	45	State provides public records	38
Inspections—Frequency:			
Annually (at least)	42		
At each setup (portables)	11		

According to the Roller Coaster Database (rcdb.com), the eleven states with the most total roller coasters are California (89 coasters), Texas (59), Pennsylvania (56), Florida (54), New Jersey (49), New York (49), Ohio (41), Missouri (32), Illinois (27), Georgia (25), and Virginia (25). Their programs can be compared:

This instruction does not affect the Freak Out (FRB16, all serials), Sicko (SCK24, all serials), XXL (all serials), Revolution (FRB32, all serials) and newer generation Afterburner rides (FRB24, serials 40 and up).

We trust to have you informed sufficiently.

Timothy Herrick, *Tyler Law Makes Ohio Amusement Ride Inspections Most Stringent in Country*

CarnivalWarehouse.com, June 24, 2021
https://carnivalwarehouse.com/newsserver/tyler-law-makes-ohio-amusement-ride-inspections-most-stringent-in-country-1624492800

In the long anticipated legislative response to one of the worst midway accidents in recent times, Ohio's "Tyler" law went into effect this fair season. Named after Tyler Jarrell, an 18-year-old from Columbus who died in a fatal accident at the 2017 Ohio State Fair, the new law sets what the Department of Agriculture describes as a new ASTM standard for ride inspections as well as increased inspections and mandating that either the manufacturer or a registered professional engineer review any areas of "fatigue or corrosion."

* * *

The key innovation to inspector protocols is: "Annually perform a complete visual inspection of a ride's structure including removing access panels where possible to do so. Special attention shall be given to structural members and their connections for signs of fatigue or corrosion. If fatigue or corrosion is found, the owner will discuss the findings with the ride's manufacturer and implement mitigation strategies."

* * *

The reality is that most manufacturers are either unable or unwilling to send an engineer onsite to inspect any issues, so documenting means photographing the corrosion and sending the pictures to the manufacturer for them to assess and prescribe the mitigation strategy. It's that step that is causing consternation and confusion among carnival industry members because it essentially is asking the manufacturer to make a determination based solely on photographical evidence, opening up the liability potential for the companies.... One manufacturer, who requested not to be named, told Carnival Warehouse, that they are not responding to any Tyler Law requests, under advice of legal counsel.

NOTES AND QUESTIONS

1. The KMG Fireball is a relatively modern ride, and the ride maker is still in existence, so KMG very likely knows where all of the rides it has sold are and by whom they are owned. This incident was also obviously a very high-profile case, such that anyone who was operating a similar model almost certainly learned about it right away. The Tyler law attempts to address some issues where the ride has been resold or reconditioned or when the manufacturer is no longer in business, deeming them "orphan rides" and setting forth a way to address corrosion issues in those situations.

2. Consider, though, the situation where there's an important safety update for a ride but the ride manufacturer is no longer in business and it's unknown where all of a particular ride is. Sometimes one might not even know who the manufacturer is; there are at least a half dozen different rides that closely resemble the Sizzler (which I've heard described as the most popular flat ride ever). The CPSC, while having "oversight" of portable rides, does not have a comprehensive database of them, and rides change hands regularly. What is the best way to get the word out about any updates? Who is responsible for doing so? Wisdom, the maker of one of the very popular versions of the Sizzler, has on its website 47 pages of Sizzler bulletins, many of them referring to makers other than the current Wisdom Rides of America (https://wisdomrides.com/pageserver/service-bulletins): there are bulletins on behalf of Wisdom Rides; Wisdom Industries, Ltd.; Wisdom FG, Inc.; and Wisdom Manufacturing, Inc. I do not know how the various entities are related, but the header on the Service Bulletin page suggests the current entity hopes to avoid being responsible for some of them:

   > As a convenience to our customers, Wisdom Rides of America makes available selected bulletins for rides designed and manufactured by other ride designers or manufacturers who are no longer operating.
   >
   > Wisdom Rides of America is not the manufacturer of these rides. The bulletins are being issued in the interest of avoiding a potential problem on rides whose manufacturer is no longer in business. These bulletins are in the interest

of safety and should in no way be construed as Wisdom Rides of America assuming the role of manufacturer of these rides.

3. The Sizzler, as noted, is wildly popular and economical to run. As you might reasonably infer from the extensive Service Bulletin compilation, it also had a fair number of issues, largely related to "patron ejection" that was associated with a reduction in minimum height requirements. The ride restraint system was designed for teenagers and adults and, the results suggest, did not work as well for smaller children, and some of the incidents resulted in criminal charges. The mitigation was the addition of seat belts (essentially made "mandatory" by Wisdom, though, again, query how to get that word out) and a filler plate added to the center of the lap bar. Since those additions, I have not heard about additional ejections from Wisdom Sizzlers.
4. This Ohio incident was, of course, on a portable ride that is under CPSC jurisdiction. Do you think the outcome would have been any different if the ride was in a fixed-site park?
5. Sometimes the inspectors become the target of civil and criminal cases. And sometimes the inspectors have discretion to set the boundaries of their jobs. The next reading describes what can happen in that situation.

William G. Childs, *When Criminal and Tort Law Incentives Run into Tight Budgets and Regulatory Discretion*

34. Cap. U. L. Rev 581 (2006)

Eight-year-old Greyson Yoe was electrocuted while waiting to get on the "Scooters" bumper car ride at the Lake County Fair in northeastern Ohio. The failure to ground the ride structure and damage to a light fixture on the ride caused his death. The day before the electrocution, two inspectors from the Ohio Department of Agriculture (ODA) inspected the ride and passed it as "safe to operate." That inspection was superficial and grossly inadequate, and the completed inspection form had serious misrepresentations. Indeed, the inspectors later admitted that they never reviewed the key electrical items that they checked off on the inspection form. The post-electrocution review not only showed that the electrical system had gross safety problems but also that the ride's management and operators knew of and ignored these problems.

This Article is not about the electrocution; it is not about the botched inspection; nor is it about the ignored problems. The lay press covered those well. Instead, this Article is about the response of the responsible authority, the ODA, to the civil and criminal actions brought or promised against it and its employees. The ODA appears to have chosen to protect itself and its employees by getting out of the business of protecting the public from similar electrical hazards. [In particular, after the prosecutions of its employees, the ODA removed the grounding section from its inspection form entirely, while adding a notice to ride owners reminding them that the ride owner is responsible for, among other things, ensuring that rides are properly grounded.]

Such actions, under a prominent theory regarding the foundations of tort and criminal law, are predictable and unsurprising. Further, the ODA's acts should call into question certain assumptions about the incentives created by criminal and tort law.

Traditional tort and criminal law jurisprudence assume that the potential for, and reality of, civil or criminal liability changes behavior.... In particular, many scholars contend that liability makes the injuries or harms caused by a violation of tort or criminal law standards less likely to occur in the future by way of what is sometimes called "specific deterrence" in the case of the individual defendant or "general deterrence" in the case of others....

This Article explores one instance of what may be a broader problem for such deterrence theory: a defendant who controls the standards by which it is judged, in an age of tight budgets and financial pressures, where government is expected to operate "like a business." In that scenario, incentives can combine to make the situation post-litigation more dangerous rather than less dangerous.

NOTES AND QUESTIONS

1. Since the Fireball incident, Ohio has overhauled its ride regulation dramatically, as noted above, including moving amusement ride regulation into its own department, no longer part of the Department of Agriculture.

2. Other than a requirement of various levels of insurance, among the most common regulatory requirements among those states that do regulate fixed-site parks is the option for the state to perform investigations after incidents. The experience of investigators varies widely, as you would expect—some states have few if any incidents that would trigger an investigation in any given year, so investigations may be one of a number of job responsibilities, many of which may have nothing to do with amusement rides. The lead investigator on the fatality we will discuss in Chapter 9 is, per his LinkedIn profile (https://www.linkedin.com/in/scott-narreau-26835995/), the program manager for both amusement ride safety and explosives regulations. That is not to say he isn't competent (indeed, the report issued in that incident is thorough).
3. The level of expertise and specialization in amusement ride incident investigations is in contrast to, for example, the "Go Team" approach taken by the National Transportation Safety Board. The NTSB investigates about 2,000 aviation incidents yearly and 500 accidents in other transportation forms, with 400 employees. They are able to loop in others to their teams as well. The teams have an investigator in charge (a senior investigator with both NTSB and industry experience), with specialty investigators for specified portions of the investigation. Specialty areas include operations, structures, powerplants, systems, air traffic control, weather, human performance, and survival factors. *See* https://www.ntsb.gov/investigations/process/Pages/goteam.aspx.

   Many of those topics are equally relevant (or at least analogous to) issues that arise in amusement ride accidents. Consider whether an agency modeled on the NTSB would be effective, or perhaps simply adding amusement ride accidents to those investigated by the NTSB if they involve a certain level of severity. In the next two chapters, you will see excerpts from reports generated by state-level investigators; consider how those compare to NTSB reports. You may wish to sample NTSB reports; they are available at https://www.ntsb.gov/investigations/AccidentReports/Pages/Reports.aspx.
4. We will spend considerably more time on the fact pattern in Chapter 13, but the tragedy that took place at Six Flags Great Adventure's Haunted Castle walk-through attraction provides an example of the

failure of regulations drafted in general terms to address a specific problem, and what appears to have been a successful regulatory response to that problem.

Precisely what caused the deadly fire is still not wholly clear, but this summary—based largely on a 2014 article (Samuel S. Dannaway, *Amusement park fire still haunts after 30 years*, August 7, 2014, available https://www.phcppros.com/articles/1954-amusement-park-fire-still-haunts-after-30-years)—seems to capture most of the consensus, and tracks the more formal investigation you will read later: The Haunted Castle was, briefly, a traditional walk-through haunted house—dark and confusing passageways with various displays and actors. It was initially installed as a temporary attraction (a designation that becomes important), made up of sixteen commercial truck trailers connected by plywood and wood framing. The interior, too, was constructed of plywood and wood stud walls, with plywood ceilings, all of it covered with various (mostly flammable) materials. It had emergency exits and illuminated exit signs, and emergency lighting that would kick in if the power failed. It had no smoke alarm or sprinkler systems. A success in its first year, the Haunted Castle was expanded and became effectively a permanent attraction—but it was still considered temporary for regulatory and inspection purposes, and so its lack of sprinklers was acceptable.

A fire broke out one evening in the spring of 1984, its cause never fully identified. It was well known, though, that kids would use lighters to find their way through (and that is Dannaway's conclusion). Eight of the roughly thirty people who were in the attraction died. Reports suggested that some patrons thought the flames were an effective illusion. The emergency lights did not turn on, because the power did not go out, and, as noted, there were no smoke alarms to alert patrons of what was going on.

Fire guidelines—largely in response to this tragedy—now generally have special provisions for attractions like haunted houses—they typically specifically require sprinkler systems and a smoke detection system that, if triggered, notifies an employee *and* turns on the lights and quiets any other confusing sounds.

Haunts are, of course, a good example of a theme seen throughout the materials in this book: attractions and rides designed to confuse and scare and distract patrons, and intended to make you think you are in danger when, the vast bulk of the time, you are not. Those specific features make it trickier to provide the right type of warnings and instructions when things are working correctly, and the right type of communications when they go wrong, than when you're talking about, say, a shopping mall. If the reports are correct that some patrons believed the flames were an impressive effect rather than an imminent danger, it is a precisely on-point example of the issue.

5. The Haunted Castle tragedy raises questions other than regulatory (and criminal law) questions as well. We will discuss design and warning defect/negligence allegations in Chapter 8, but it is worth planting the seed to think about how a ride or attraction designer, manufacturer, or operator should anticipate issues with how to deal with (a) attractions that are expressly designed to be dark and disorienting; (b) non-restrained patrons who may choose to interact with the environment in "incorrect" ways; and (c) communication to patrons of *actual* risk as opposed to intentionally-generated fictional risk—and all three in the context of what I referred to previously as the "bubble," where patrons may think of the context as essentially risk-free.

Tafaro v. Six Flags Great Adventure, LLC

2018 WL 1535289 (D.N.J. Mar. 29, 2018)

Freda L. Wolfson, U.S.D.J.

Before the Court, in this case involving Plaintiff Sharon Tafaro's ("Plaintiff") allegations of injuries sustained by her minor daughter, G.T., while riding a rollercoaster in the theme park of Defendant Six Flags Great Adventure, LLC ("Six Flags"), are (1) the motion of Six Flags for partial dismissal of Plaintiff's Amended Complaint; (2) the motion of Defendants Intamin; Intamin, Ltd.; and Interride, LLC (collectively "Intamin"), for dismissal of all claims in the Complaint as raised against Intamin; and (3) the Cross-Motion of Plaintiff for leave to file a Second Amended Complaint to replead her claim against Intamin under the New Jersey Product Liability Act, N.J.S.A. 2A:58C ("NJPLA"). For the reasons set forth below, Defendants Six Flags' and Intamin's Motions are granted, and Plaintiff's Cross-Motion is denied. Plaintiff may, however, within thirty days, file a renewed motion seeking leave to file a Second Amended Complaint, consistent with the rulings in this Opinion.

I. FACTUAL BACKGROUND & PROCEDURAL HISTORY

* * *

Plaintiff alleges that Intamin manufactured, designed, and installed the El Toro rollercoaster ride on the premises of Defendant Six Flags' Great Adventure theme park in Jackson, New Jersey. Amended Complaint ("Am. Compl."), ¶¶ 4–5. Plaintiff further alleges that Defendant Rocky Mountain Construction Company participated in the construction of El Toro. *Id.* at ¶ 10. On July 12, 2016, minor G.T. paid for admission to Six Flags' theme park, rode El Toro, allegedly suffered serious, debilitating injuries, and was permanently disabled as a result. Plaintiff brings five causes of action to recover for those injuries.

In Count I of the Amended Complaint, Plaintiff brings a claim against all Defendants under the NJPLA, alleging that El Toro was defective in its design and manufacture, as well as in the warnings provided to its riders, and that G.T. was injured as a result of those defects. *Id.* at ¶¶ 14–20. In Count II, Plaintiff brings a claim against all Defendants for common law negligence, alleging that El Toro was negligently and improperly maintained, leading to G.T.'s injuries. *Id.* at ¶¶ 21–22. In Count III, Plaintiff brings a claim against all Defendants for common law negligence, alleging that El Toro was negligently and improperly operated. *Id.* at ¶¶ 23–25. Count IV is confusingly pleaded, but it appears that, therein, Plaintiff seeks to bring a claim against all Defendants for failure to comply with the Carnival-Amusement Rides Safety Act ("the Safety Act"), N.J.S.A. 5:3-31 to 59, Am. Compl., ¶¶ 26–32, and against Six Flags for fraudulent concealment for failure to undertake an investigation into, and keep proper documentation of, Plaintiff's injuries sustained while riding El Toro. *Id.* at ¶¶ 33–36. In Count IV, Plaintiff also seeks to recover for the infliction of severe emotional distress, *id.* at ¶ 37, and seeks an award of punitive damages against all Defendants, *id.* at ¶ 38. In Count V, Plaintiff brings a claim against all Defendants for loss of consortium, alleging that she has been deprived of the services of her daughter, G.T., as a result of the injuries G.T. allegedly sustained while riding El Toro. *Id.* at ¶¶ 39–41.

On August 1, 2017, Defendant Six Flags moved to partially dismiss the Amended Complaint, arguing (i) that Plaintiff's Count I NJPLA claim must be dismissed as raised against Six Flags because Six Flags is not a product manufacturer, distributor, or seller subject to liability under the statute, and (ii) that Plaintiff's Count IV claim for failure to comply with the Safety Act, fraudulent concealment, intentional or negligent infliction of emotional distress, and punitive damages, should be dismissed for failure to state a claim. Plaintiff opposed the motion. On December 12, 2017, Defendant Intamin filed a separate motion to dismiss the Complaint. Intamin moves to dismiss (i) Plaintiff's Count I NJPLA claim as inadequately pleaded; and (ii) Counts II, III, IV, and V as not properly brought against Defendant Intamin, subsumed under the NJPLA, and/or inadequately pleaded.

On December 28, 2017, Plaintiff opposed Defendant Intamin's Motion and cross-moved for leave to file a Second Amended Complaint to attempt to remedy the pleading deficiencies of her Count I NJPLA claim against Defendant Intamin. Intamin opposed Plaintiff's Cross-Motion as futile, on January 22, 2018. All three motions are now fully briefed and before the Court for consideration.

[The court described the standard of review under the Federal Rules.]

III. Analysis

The Court first considers Defendant Six Flags' motion to dismiss Counts I and IV and then proceeds to consideration of Intamin's motion to dismiss all claims against it in the Amended Complaint.

A. Count I, NJPLA Claim Against Six Flags

Six Flags moves to dismiss Count I of the Amended Complaint, which alleges claims sounding in product liability, on the grounds that all such claims are subsumed under the NJPLA and that Six Flags, as an amusement park owner and operator, is not a manufacturer, distributor, or "seller of a product" subject to liability under that statute. In opposition, Plaintiff advocates for a broader definition of "seller of a product," encompassing Six Flags, but does not appear to dispute that Six Flags is not a manufacturer or distributor of El Toro.

Courts that have considered the boundaries of the definition of "product seller" under the NJPLA are unanimous in their conclusion that an amusement park owner and operator—and indeed Six Flags in particular—is not a manufacturer, distributor, or seller of the rides and attractions to which it sells access. [Citations]

In reaching their decisions, each of these courts was guided by the same statutory language. Under the NJPLA, only "[a] manufacturer or seller of a product shall be liable" for injuries caused by a product, which is defectively designed, defectively manufactured, or fails to contain adequate warnings. N.J.S.A. § 2A:58C-2. A "seller of a product" or "product seller," as defined under the Act, does not include "a provider of professional services in any case in which the sale or use of a product is incidental to the transaction and the essence of the transaction is the furnishing of judgment, skill or services." *Id.* § 2A:58C-8. In determining whether amusement park owners and operators are "product sellers" under the Act, courts are therefore called upon to rule whether the rides and attractions at issue are incidental to the defendant's provision of amusement services. Beginning with *Doerflein* [*v. Six Flags Great Adventure*, No. A-0522-04T2, at *3 (N.J. Super. Ct. App. Div. Feb. 22, 2006)], every court to have considered the question has found that the products at issue—various rides and attractions—are indeed incidental to the amusement parks' provision of services to their customers. This Court agrees with the reasoning of those decisions and adopts it in this case.

* * *

Count I, as raised against Defendant Six Flags, is, therefore, dismissed with prejudice.

B. Count IV Against Six Flags

It is unclear from the allegations in Plaintiff's Amended Complaint how many causes of action Plaintiff intended to raise in Count IV. Reading the Amended Complaint as broadly as possible in favor of the non-moving party, the Court can discern four distinct claims: (i) an action for noncompliance with the reporting requirements of the Safety Act; (ii) a common law action for fraudulent concealment; (iii) a common law action for intentional or negligent infliction of emotional distress; and (iv) a common law action for punitive damages—possibly in conjunction with any or all of the prior three actions. As the parties have briefed Six Flags' motion to dismiss Count IV on all available bases, the Court will address each in turn.

1. The Safety Act

In paragraphs 27 through 34 of the Amended Complaint, Plaintiff details Defendant Six Flags' alleged failure to comply with the Carnival-Amusement Rides Safety Act, N.J.S.A. 5:3-31 to 59. Defendant Six Flags moves to dismiss on the grounds that the Safety Act does not provide Plaintiff with a private cause of action.

Plaintiff alleges that she submitted an incident report and provided notice to Defendant Six Flags after G.T. was allegedly injured riding El Toro, as required under N.J.S.A. 5:3-57(a). Am. Compl., ¶ 27. Plaintiff alleges that, despite having alerted Six Flags to the incident, Six Flags failed to notify the State of New Jersey of Plaintiff's incident report, as required under N.J.S.A. 5:3-39, or to perform its own investigation and draft its own incident report to be filed with the State, as required by N.J.S.A. 5:3-47. *Id.* at ¶¶ 31–32. Plaintiff characterizes this behavior as in violation of state law and a "cover up," designed to harm Plaintiff's ability to prosecute her claims. *Id.* at ¶¶ 33–34. As a threshold matter, the Court must therefore address Plaintiff's implicit contention that Defendant's alleged failure to comply with the reporting requirements of the Safety Act provides Plaintiff with a private right of action to bring a claim against Defendant Six Flags. N.J.S.A. 5:3-47 provides that

> It shall be the duty of every owner and ride operator to report immediately, on a form to be provided by the department, any accidents and resulting injuries or fatalities incurred during the operation of any carnival-amusement ride, other than minor incidents, as defined by rule, or any mechanical malfunction of any ride while in use necessitating suspension of operation for diagnostic or corrective work, and to cease operation of any ride whose breakdown or malfunction causes a fatality or serious injury to any person, subject to rules and regulations promulgated by the department.

N.J.S.A. 5:3-47. A rider claiming injury is entitled to a copy of the accident report, to be furnished by the Department of Labor. N.J.S.A. 5:3-57(c).

Contrary to Plaintiff's apparent position, the New Jersey Supreme Court has held that these provisions of the Safety Act do not give rise to a private right of action for injured amusement park goers. *Steinberg v.*

Sahara Sam's Oasis, LLC, 226 N.J. 344, 360 (2016) ("We reject plaintiff's implied argument that a violation of the Carnival-Amusement Rides Safety Act (the Safety Act), N.J.S.A. 5:3-31 to -59, standing alone, gives rise to a private right of action."). Instead, that Court has explained that the amusement park operator's violation of a statutory duty of care imposed by the Safety Act, while not independently actionable, may be admissible as evidence of negligence. *Id.* at 363 ("In sum, in given circumstances, 'the violation of a statutory duty of care' may be admissible as evidence of negligence. In this case such evidence is permissible because the aggregation of alleged negligent acts or omissions may be considered in determining whether Sahara Sam's conduct reached the level of gross negligence." (quoting *Waterson v. Gen. Motors Corp.*, 111 N.J. 238, 263, 544 A.2d 357 (1988))). This Court therefore finds that Plaintiff cannot state a claim against Defendant Six Flags for Six Flags' alleged failure to comply with the Safety Act. This finding, however, does not preclude Plaintiff from relying upon those allegations in support of some other recognized cause of action.

2. Fraudulent Concealment

Six Flags also moves to dismiss Count IV to the extent raised as a claim for fraudulent concealment. Spoliation "is the term that is used to describe the hiding or destroying of litigation evidence, generally by an adverse party." *Rosenblit v. Zimmerman*, 166 N.J. 391, 400–01 (2001). In order to remedy spoliation, a litigant is allowed to file a separate tort action for fraudulent concealment against an adversary that hides or destroys evidence during or in anticipation of litigation. *See id.* at 403, 406–07; *Williams v. BASF Catalysts LLC*, 765 F.3d 306, 320 (3d Cir. 2014) ("New Jersey permits plaintiffs to recover in an independent action for harm caused in a prior proceeding by an adversary's spoliation."). In order to prove fraudulent concealment, the plaintiff must establish five elements:

(1) That defendant in the fraudulent concealment action had a legal obligation to disclose evidence in connection with an existing or pending litigation;
(2) That the evidence was material to the litigation;
(3) That plaintiff could not reasonably have obtained access to the evidence from another source;

(4) That defendant intentionally withheld, altered or destroyed the evidence with purpose to disrupt the litigation;
(5) That plaintiff was damaged in the underlying action by having to rely on an evidential record that did not contain the evidence defendant concealed.

Rosenblit, 166 N.J. at 406–07....

Here, any claim for fraudulent concealment is either inadequately pleaded or clearly premature. Plaintiff alleges that Six Flags "covered up the incident, covered up the severity of [G.T.'s] injury and intentionally did not perform an investigation and intentionally did not file the appropriate paperwork under New Jersey law." Am. Compl. ¶ 33. Plaintiff characterizes this conduct as a failure to maintain or investigate evidence of Plaintiff's injuries. *Id.* at ¶ 34. To the extent that Plaintiff seeks to allege that Defendant Six Flags destroyed or failed to maintain evidence prior to the initiation of litigation in this matter, her allegations are bare, legal conclusions, without factual support. The only factual allegation raised is that Six Flags did not file an accident report with the State concerning the injuries suffered by G.T. From this alone, Plaintiff seeks to infer Six Flags' malicious intent not to collect or preserve evidence of any incident involving G.T. Plaintiff presents no law giving rise to such a presumption.

To the extent that Plaintiff seeks to allege that Defendant Six Flags has failed to provide to Plaintiff any evidence of the investigation, or lack thereof into the incident involving G.T. on El Toro, such allegations are premature before the exchange of discovery. *See Huzinec v. Six Flags Great Adventure, LLC*, No. CV162754FLWDEA, 2017 WL 44850, at *6–7 (D.N.J. Jan. 3, 2017) (dismissing Plaintiff's fraudulent concealment claim, without prejudice, as premature, where "[t]o the extent that Plaintiff intended to allege that Defendants have destroyed evidence prior to the start of litigation, Plaintiff simply has not pled Defendants' concealment in that regard with particularity[;] [and] [t]o the extent Plaintiff alleges that Defendants have not turned over the evidence that Plaintiff sought prior to the filing of the Complaint, Plaintiff has failed to allege any legal obligation on the part of Defendants to fulfill Plaintiff's requests for evidence outside of the discovery process."). Accordingly, Plaintiff's claim for fraudulent concealment is dismissed without prejudice as inadequately pleaded and premature.

3. Intentional or Negligent Infliction of Emotional Distress

[This will be included in the next chapter.]

* * *

IV. CONCLUSION

For the foregoing reasons, Defendant Six Flags' Partial Motion to Dismiss the Amended Complaint of Plaintiff Tafaro and Defendant Intamin's Motion to Dismiss the Amended Complaint are granted. Accordingly, as raised against Defendant Six Flags, Count I of the Amended Complaint is dismissed with prejudice and Count IV is dismissed without prejudice. All claims in the Amended Complaint are dismissed as raised against Defendants Intamin, Intamin, Ltd., and Interide, LLC: Count I is dismissed without prejudice; Counts II, III, and V are dismissed with prejudice as subsumed by the NJPLA; and Count IV is dismissed with prejudice. Plaintiff's Cross-Motion for leave to file the proposed Second Amended Complaint is denied. Plaintiff may file a motion seeking leave to file a new Second Amended Complaint, consistent with the rulings in this Opinion, within thirty days. Because Defendant Six Flags has not moved to dismiss Counts II, III, or V, this case shall remain open even if Plaintiff elects not to seek leave to file a Second Amended Complaint. An appropriate Order to follow.

CHAPTER 7

Emotional Distress Claims; Liability for Employee Conduct

If you step back for a bit, many amusements are essentially designed to perform (or at least simulate) intentional torts and to cause something that is at least adjacent to emotional distress. We'll do more on intentional torts in Chapter 12, but consider: haunted houses are made to make you fear or anticipate harmful or offensive contact (and sometimes in fact actually experience that contact): that is an assault and often intentional infliction of emotional distress. (It would be outrageous to just confront random people with scenes of torture and horror, no?) Likewise, rides bounce you around in ways that, if done in other contexts, would arguably be battery. As we will see, consent is the key to making it so that, say, Austin, Texas's "House of Torment" is not put out of business as a "House of Torts." (I am sorry for that joke.)

This chapter focuses *not* on those consent-oriented cases—we will get to those later—but on attempts to create liability for emotional distress when ordinary negligence theories might not suffice. As we saw in Chapter 4's discussion of limited-duty rules, the courts have created constraints on claims that seek recovery for purely emotional distress (whether asserted to be negligently or intentionally caused).

We also look at vicarious liability, in part because the issues arise together and in part because neither of them is frankly quite enough to be a chapter on its own.

Connell v. Sea World Parks & Entertainment, Inc.

Case No. 2010-CA-19146-O
(9th Jud. Cir. Fla. Aug. 30, 2011)

ORDER DISMISSING CASE WITH PREJUDICE

* * *

This case raises the question of whether a theme park spectator can bring a claim for emotional distress against the theme park when the spectator witnesses an unfortunate incident while visiting the theme park. Plaintiffs, Suzanne and Todd Connell, bring this action on behalf of their minor son, RTC, as a result of emotional distress he suffered while watching the unfortunate drowning of Mrs. Dawn Brancheau, a SeaWorld Trainer, during the Dine with Shamu show on February 24, 2010....

Sea World argues that the complaint fails to state a cause of action for negligent and intentional infliction of emotional distress. The Court will separately address each cause of action below.

Negligent Infliction of Emotional Distress

Florida law recognizes the tort of negligent infliction of emotional distress as an exception to the impact rule. [Citation.] To state a cause of action for negligent infliction of emotional distress, a complaint must allege the following elements: (1) the plaintiff must suffer a physical injury; (2) the plaintiff's physical injury must be caused by the psychological trauma; (3) the plaintiff must be involved in some way in the event causing the negligent injury to another; and (4) the plaintiff must have a close personal relationship to the directly injured person. [Citation.]

The question presented in this case is whether RTC had a "close personal relationship" with Mrs. Brancheau that would allow the complaint to proceed forward. Florida courts have held that mother/daughter, father/daughter and stepfather/stepchild relationships qualify as close personal relationships. [Citations.] Other courts have held that a fiance, "live in" ladyfriend, and girlfriend do not have the type of close personal relationship with the injured party that would support a claim for negligent infliction of emotional distress. [Citations.] The court has not found, and the parties have not submitted, any case where a complete stranger to the injured party was allowed to proceed forward with a claim of negligent infliction of emotional distress.

The central allegations establishing the contact between RTC and Mrs. Brancheau are found in paragraphs 1 and 50 of the complaint. In paragraph 50, the Connells allege that the Dine with Shamu show is an "intimate experience." The complaint further alleges that the "intimacy of the situation is intended to create a feeling of a close bond or personal relationship between RTC and the trainer." In paragraph 11, the Connells allege "Dawn was delightful and personable and as intended, bonded with minor Plaintiff RTC, making a very deep, positive impression during the performance."

The Connells concede that neither they nor their son are related to Mrs. Brancheau or that they ever met Mrs. Brancheau. The question then becomes whether the allegations in paragraphs 1 and 50 are sufficient to establish the "close personal relationship" needed to allow the Connells claim to proceed forward with their claim.

As noted above, various courts have recognized that family members, including step-parents, have the type of close personal relationship that can support the cause of action. Here, the Connells are not in any way related to Mrs. Brancheau. Moreover, their complaint is devoid of any allegations that would even suggest that they met her and developed a close personal relationship with her prior to her unfortunate death. Indeed, other than the allegations in paragraphs 1 and 50, the complaint contains no allegations that would establish any personal relationship at all between RTC and Mrs. Brancheau, other than one of spectator/performer. As such, the Connells have failed to state a cause of action for negligent infliction of emotional distress against SeaWorld.

Intentional Infliction of Emotional Distress

Florida law recognizes the tort of intentional infliction of emotional distress. [Citation.] To state a cause of action for intentional infliction of emotional distress, a complaint must allege four elements: (1) deliberate or reckless infliction of mental suffering; (2) outrageous conduct; (3) the conduct caused emotional distress; and (4) the distress was severe. In order to satisfy the requirement for outrageous conduct, a plaintiff must allege that the defendant's conduct was so "outrageous in character, and so extreme in degree, as to go beyond all possible bounds of decency" and further that it would be regarded as "atrocious, and utterly intolerable in a civilized society." [Citation.] Whether the conduct alleged is sufficiently outrageous and extreme to withstand a motion to dismiss is purely a question of law for the court to decide. [Citation.] In analyzing whether SeaWorld's conduct was outrageous and extreme, the court has reviewed and considered all of the allegations of the complaint, including the allegations that SeaWorld knew of the aggressive and violent tendencies of the killer whale before it allowed the whale to be near Mrs. Brancheau. See, paragraphs 53–57 of the Complaint. Given their length, the court will not recite all the allegations here. At best, these allegations support a claim of negligence on SeaWorld's part. Negligence, however, does not satisfy the requirement that the conduct in question be outrageous and extreme in order to support a cause of action for intentional infliction of emotional distress. *See, Eastern Airlines v. King*, 557 So.2d 574, 576 (Fla. 1990) (passenger who was on flight when all three engines failed failed to state a claim against airline for reckless or intentional infliction of emotional distress; allegations that airline failed to properly inspect, maintain and operate its aircraft rose no higher than negligence, and fact that there may have been at least one dozen prior incidents of missing O-rings causing engine failures did not reflect extreme and outrageous conduct intentionally or recklessly causing emotional distress).

Even if the conduct alleged in the complaint was outrageous and extreme, the Connells' claim fails because the alleged acts or omissions were not directed at them. Florida courts require the plaintiff to be the recipient of the insult or abuse in order to recover for intentional infliction of emotional distress. In *Habelow v. Travelers Insurance Company*, 389 So.2d 218 (Fla. 5th DCA 1980), the wife's claim for intentional infliction of emotional distress was dismissed because the abuse was directed at her husband. The Court stated that "in all cases we have found in Florida recognizing the tort of intentional infliction of emotional distress, the plaintiff was the recipient of the insult or abuse." *Id.* at 220. [Citations.]

Here, the Connells do not allege outrageous conduct directed toward RTC. Rather, they allege a serious of acts and omissions committed by SeaWorld in breach of its duty to its employees, including Mrs. Brancheau. See, paragraph 63(a)–(t) of the Complaint. Absent any allegations that outrageous or extreme conduct was directed toward RTC, the Connells cannot state a cause of action for intentional infliction of emotional distress against SeaWorld.

Conclusion

As noted above, the Connells and their son were guests at SeaWorld when Mrs. Brancheau's life was unfortunately taken. The Court has no doubt that RTC was traumatized by witnessing this event. However, given the status of the parties to this litigation and the pleading deficiencies noted above, the Connells have failed to state a cause of action against SeaWorld for negligent or intentional infliction of emotional distress. The Court concludes that these deficiencies cannot be corrected and thus, any further amendment of the complaint would be futile. Accordingly, it is hereby ORDERED AND ADJUDGED that Defendants' Motion to Dismiss Plaintiffs' Complaint is granted. This action is dismissed with prejudice. The Court retains jurisdiction to award attorneys' fees and costs if applicable.

NOTES AND QUESTIONS

1. As a matter of policy and deterrence, do you think this outcome is sensible? It seems certain that the Connells' son was, as the court concedes, traumatized by seeing this tragic event, and it also seems at least plausible that his trauma was caused by the negligence (or even recklessness) of the park. Does it make sense for that trauma to be worth nothing in civil litigation? Why or why not?
2. As is presumably not news to you, this is a reminder that not all harms are compensable and not all wrongs can be righted in the tort system.

Tafaro v. Six Flags Great Adventure, LLC

2018 WL 1535289 (D.N.J. Mar. 29, 2018)

FREDA L. WOLFSON, U.S.D.J.

[The background from this case is in Chapter 6.]

3. Intentional or Negligent Infliction of Emotional Distress

Six Flags next moves to dismiss Count IV of the Amended Complaint to the extent it was intended to raise claims for intentional or negligent infliction of emotional distress. Plaintiff alleges that "plaintiff ... has sustained severe emotional distress which is compensable under New Jersey law." Am. Compl., ¶ 37. To plead a claim for intentional infliction of emotional distress under New Jersey law, a plaintiff must allege four elements. "Initially, the plaintiff must prove that the defendant acted intentionally or recklessly. For an intentional act to result in liability, the defendant must intend both to do the act and to produce emotional distress. Liability will also attach when the defendant acts recklessly in deliberate disregard of a high degree of probability that emotional distress will follow." *Buckley v. Trenton Saving Fund Soc.*, 111 N.J. 355, 366 (1988) (citations omitted). "Second, the defendant's conduct must be extreme and outrageous. The conduct must be so outrageous in character, and so extreme in degree, as to go beyond all possible bounds of decency, and to be regarded as atrocious, and utterly intolerable in a civilized community." *Id.* (citations omitted). "Third, the defendant's actions must have been the proximate cause of the plaintiff's emotional distress." *Id.* (citations omitted). "Fourth, the emotional distress suffered by the plaintiff must be so severe that no reasonable man could be expected to endure." *Id.* (citations omitted). A claim for negligent infliction of emotional distress similarly requires a plaintiff to plead four elements: "(1) the defendant's negligence caused the death of, or serious physical injury to, another; (2) the plaintiff shared a marital or intimate, familial relationship with the injured person; (3) the plaintiff had a sensory and contemporaneous observation of the death or injury at the scene of the accident; and (4) the plaintiff suffered severe emotional distress." *Jablonowska v. Suther*, 195 N.J. 91, 103–04, 948 A.2d 610, 617–18 (2008) (citations omitted). For both types of claims, "[s]evere emotional distress means any type of severe and disabling emotional or mental condition which may be generally recognized and diagnosed by professionals trained to do so, including ... posttraumatic stress disorder." *Taylor v. Metzger*, 152 N.J. 490, 515, 706 A.2d 685, 697 (1998) (internal quotation omitted). "It is not enough to establish that a party is acutely upset by reason of the incident. In order to be actionable, the claimed emotional distress must be sufficiently substantial to result in physical illness or serious psychological sequelae." *Aly v. Garcia*, 333 N.J. Super. 195, 204, 754 A.2d 1232, 1236–37 (App. Div. 2000). "The genuineness and severity of emotional distress can present threshold questions of law." *Decker v. Princeton Packet, Inc.*, 116 N.J. 418, 430, 561 A.2d 1122, 1128 (1989). "Thus, the court decides whether as a matter of law such emotional distress can be found, and the jury decides whether it has in fact been proved." *Buckley*, 111 N.J. at 367 (citation omitted).

Here, the allegations of emotional distress are clearly insufficient to state a cause of action under New Jersey law. The sole allegation of emotional distress in the Amended Complaint comprises one sentence: "[t]he plaintiff has been seriously permanently injured and has sustained severe emotional distress which is compensable under New Jersey law." Am. Compl., ¶ 37. There are no allegations establishing the requisite severity of distress necessary for a cause of action under either type of action under New Jersey law. Any such claim for intentional or negligent infliction of emotional distress is therefore dismissed, without prejudice. This ruling, however, does not restrict Plaintiff's ability to seek recovery for emotional distress as an element of damages on Plaintiff's surviving negligence claims.

Department of Public Safety Accident Report

Commonwealth of Massachusetts 2004

DATE AND TIME: May 1, 2004, 1500 Hours
LOCATION: Six Flags New England, [address]
INJURED/DEAD: [Redacted on report; Stanley Mordarsky]
OBJECT UNDER INVESTIGATION: Superman Ride of Steel roller coaster
MANUFACTURER: INTAMIN AG, [Switzerland address]
WITNESSES: See supplemental investigation summary
INSPECTORS: Mark F. Mooney (lead inspector)
Thomas G. Gatzuins
LOCAL INVESTIGATING POLICE: Lt. Draghetti, Agawaman Police Department

INCIDENT SUMMARY

On the above date and location, at approximately 1500 hours, as the Superman Ride of Steel roller coaster was approaching the final turn in the cycle, [Mordarsky] was ejected from the front row seat of the coaster. As a result of the ejection, he struck the #6 support column (as identified on sketch #1) and was fatally injured.

Ride maintenance logs and operator logs were found to be in order. The overall condition of the ride was good, with no apparent mechanical defects. The seat belt restraints appeared to be in good condition with no signs of wear or mechanical failure. The "T" Bar hydraulic lap restraint appeared to be functioning as designed and showed no signs of leakage or damage.

ACCIDENT INVESTIGATION

On May 1, 2004 at approximately 1500 hours, a roller coaster accident occurred at Six Flags New England []. Within one hour, park officials [] contacted the Massachusetts State Police [about] the incident pursuant to Massachusetts Regulation 520 CMR 5.00. A preliminary investigation was started by Mr. Mark F. Mooney, Assistant Chief of Inspections of the Massachusetts Department of Public Safety on May 1, 2004 at 1845 hours[, assisted by Gatzuins, Commissioner of Public Safety]. The victim of the accident ... was given medical treatment at the scene and was later pronounced dead.... The scene was secured by Agawam police department, who also interviewed the guests shortly after the incident.

Upon investigation it appears that the victim [redacted] arrived at the Superman Coaster ride on a scooter/mobile chair []. Several ride attendants were aware of [redacted] and his scooter/mobile chair and made reasonable accommodations to allow him to park his scooter where he then walked to the front seat of the coaster. Based on witness testimony, it appears that [he] was guided into his seat by a ride attendant, and entered the ride by himself. The ride attendant was "going to sit him in the 2nd or 3rd car" however due to his larger size, the attendant sat him in the front seat because "those cars have a larger seatbelt so he would not have any problems buckling." It was observed, after the accident, that [his] seat belt was still connected and latched. The position of the latching mechanism was pulled between the seat, and the side restraint. The ride photo [] taken by an automatic camera on the coaster 10 to 20 seconds prior to the accident demonstrated that the seat belt was secured around [Mordarsky]. It appeared that upon his ejection from the seat, his foot caught the seatbelt and pulled the belt into the final position []. [His] sock was also tangled with the seatbelt. One shoe was still in the car at the time of the investigation. This could have been knocked off by the lap restraint or the seat belt upon ejection. The second shoe was found on the ground near the point of ejection.

According to witness statements, during boarding, a second patron ... was asked to move from his original seat to the seat in the 1st row next to the victim. This was also "because he was larger and could not fit into his seat belt," "standard procedure." It should be noted that measurements taken by Department of Public Safety Inspectors indicated that the front row of each car seat belts had [eleven] extra inches to adjust compared to the seats in the second row because they are secured at different locations. Since [the second patron] had already attempted to pull the "T" bar lap restraint forward, to move, the operator had to release the restraints from all passengers. Once [the second patron] was in his new seat, the park procedure required ride attendants to check all the passengers['] seat belts and "T" bar restraints. The ride operator as well as several patrons provided statements as such, however[,] there were some statements that indicated that seatbelts were not pulled tight enough or the "T" bar lap restraints did not get pushed against the patrons firm[ly] enough. [Mordarsky] did not speak to anyone during boarding and remained quiet throughout the ride. Once the ride attendants did their checks, they signaled to the operator "all clear." The operator then started the ride and the coaster left the station.

As the ride was underway, the patron behind the victim ... saw that [Mordarsky] was "getting air" on some of the hills and grabbed his suspenders in an attempt to keep him in his seat. [The second patron] indicated that [Mordarsky] was leaning forward in his seat the entire duration of the ride. On approaching the final bunny hills, [the second patron] noticed that [Mordarsky] was coming out of his seat high enough to take notice. At the last bunny hill approaching the last turn, [Mordarsky] "came up too much" and he began to fall out of the left side. Both [of the other patrons] attempted to hold onto [Mordarsky] as the ride came into the last turn, however the forces applied on [Mordarsky's] body were too great for them to hold on and his body was quickly thrown from the ride. The maximum peak instantaneous negative value in that section of the ride was -0.4 G, and the maximum peak instantaneous positive value in that section of the ride was +2.9 G according to ride accelerometer data.

As [Mordarsky] came out of his seat, the ride track begins to turn, which caused his body to move out of the car. As the coaster comes down the last bunny hill, the design of the track causes the coaster to pitch into the turn []. At the point when [Mordarsky] was exiting the coaster, and the coaster began to bank into the turn, his left hand landed on the left track and the rear wheels of the 1st car struck his arm at his wrist, severing his hand. It should be noted that it is not physically possible for a hand to come in contact with the coaster wheels when a person is properly restrained in the seat restraints.... Once [Modarsky] was clear of the coaster, his head and upper torso struck the #6 support column and he then traveled 31 feet [] before striking the ground and traveling another 38 feet before striking a chain link fence bordering the property.... At the time of this report, we do not have any conclusive evidence that [he] did or did not suffer any loss of consciousness prior to being ejected. As the coaster came into the braking area, the ride operator and ride attendants were made aware of the incidence and performed [an] "emergency stop" of the coaster.

Some patrons jumped a chain link security fence in an attempt to assist the victim. Park emergency response officials arrived on the scene and began to provide medical assistan[ce] until an ambulance arrived.... Due to the possibility of a pre-existing health condition that could have a significant influence as a contributing factor, the Department officials have requested the assistance from the Office of the Chief Medical Examiner in order to seek an autopsy of the victim. Complete results of the autopsy were not available at the time of this report.

Following the accident, the family indicated to the press that [Mordarsky] suffered from cerebral palsy, which is a medical condition that affects the muscles of a part or side of the body, sometimes the entire body. Uncontrolled reflex movements and muscle tightness (spasticity) occur with varying severity. [Mordarsky] was approximately 5'3" in height and weighed 225 pounds.

The hydraulic system of the "T" lap bar restraint was checked for proper function. The system appeared clean and free of leakage.... The seatbelt system was also checked and mechanically functioned properly. Ride operational and maintenance logs were reviewed as well as the status of the Allen Bradley PLC [programmable logic controller], however, a printout of the PLC alarm log was not available at the time of the investigation (the system does not have a local printer set up), but has been requested.

Based on this preliminary investigation, the Department has identified the following **contributing factors**:

1. **Girth of the victim.** The girth of the victim's lower torso was incompatible with the "T" bar restraint. Based on photographic evidence, it appears that the victim's body configura-

tion prevented the "T" bar restraint from being in a position that would adequately protect the patron from being ejected.

2. **Pre-existing medical condition.** Massachusetts regulations 520 CMR 5.03(6)(e) requires patrons to notify the ride operator of any pre-existing health conditions that may negatively [affect] the health and safety of the patron if they were to ride an amusement device. Based on witness testimony of ride operators, first responders and statements volunteered by his family to the press, [Mordarsky] failed to notify the ride operator of his pre-existing medical conditions that should have prevented him from getting on the ride.
3. **Varied Seat Belt Sizes.** The different sizes of seat belts enable people of unique size to enter the ride. The creates an opportunity for patrons, who may have a body size and type that is incompatible with the "T" bar restraint to ride the coaster, unaware of the potential hazard.
4. **Failure of ride attendant.** In order for the "T" bar restraint to work properly, it is necessary that the bar be positioned firm against the patron's upper thighs. In the case where individuals with large torso girth [are patrons], the lower abdomen can interfere with the proper position of the "T" bar restraint. There was a failure of the ride attendant to properly identify that the restraints were inadequately applied. Had the ride attendant identified that the "T" bar lap restraint was not in a position necessary to protect the patron from ejection, the patron would have been removed from the ride.

* * *

Following the investigation, the Department officials held a post-investigatory meeting with park officials to review what were identified as contributing factors and outline the steps the park had to take before being allowed to re-open the ride to the public.

Pursuant to Massachusetts General Law chapter 140 section 205A, the ride shall remain closed until the operators and/or manufacturer implement a corrective plan which is approved by Commissioner Gatzunis.

NOTES AND QUESTIONS

1. This low-quality diagram of the Track Layout for Superman: Ride of Steel is replicated from the investigation report. The station and final turn are where I have added text boxes below. The full report (which includes non-graphic photographs) is available in the "Resources" section of RecreationAndRisk.com.

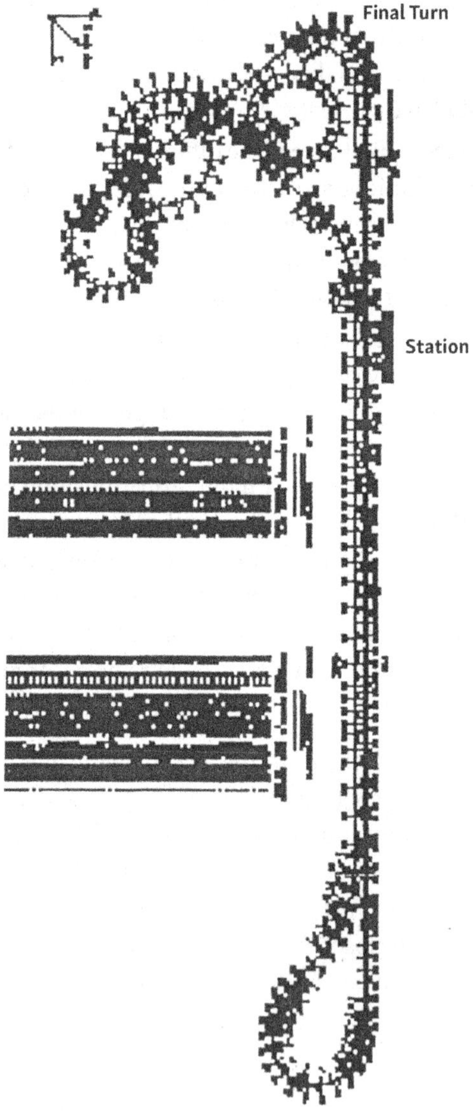

2. The report also includes a photo of the then-extant warning sign, which read, in relevant part):

> **[Superman "S" logo]**
>
> "An exciting roller coaster with high speed turns, steep drops and sudden stops"
>
> FOR YOUR PROTECTION, THIS ATTRACTION IS NOT RECOMMENDED FOR GUESTS WITH:
> [icons reflecting pregnancy, recent illness, heart trouble, etc.]
>
> ATTENTION ALL GUESTS:
> Read important safety information and follow instructions of attendants
> You must be 54" tall to ride, maximum height 78"
> DO NOT RIDE IF YOU:
> Have significant physical ailments or conditions
> Have had back or neck problems
> Have had high blood pressure, heart trouble, or nervous disorders
> Are an expectant mother
> Are under the influence of drugs or alcohol
> ALSO:
> Guests should be in good physical condition to ride
> Shirts, shorts, and shoes must be worn at all times
> Food and drinks are not permitted on this ride
> No smoking in line or on the ride
> Line jumping may cause ejection from the park
> If you are hearing impaired, ask the ride attendant for written ride instructions before boarding the ride
> Due to the restraining device on this ride, certain large guests may not be able to ride
> You must be able to properly utilize all restraint devices
> Cameras and video equipment are not permitted on ride
> Casts are not allowed on this attraction

3. The investigation report describes as a contributing factor to Mr. Mordarsky's death his failure to report his cerebral palsy to the ride operators. We will return to that (and more related to that), in the next chapter.

4. Did you come away from this investigation report satisfied? Do you think you know what caused this tragedy? Do you know the root causes of it? If you were in charge of operations at another park with a similar coaster with similar restraints, what, if anything, would you change?
5. Review the National Transportation Safety Board's reports on the 2018 "Stretch Duck 7" tragedy, where a World War II-era amphibious passenger vehicle that had been modified for tourist use sank, killing 17. That report is available at https://www.ntsb.gov/investigations/Pages/DCA18MM028.aspx. (Click on the "Related Reports" links and at least some of the "Recommendations.") How do you think the NTSB would have investigated the Superman: Ride of Steel death?
6. It is not entirely clear why the front row seatbelts were longer than others. It may have been to try to accommodate larger patrons or, as suggested by some, it may have been the consequence of the mounting having to be in a different location and the manufacturer failing to take into account that the location change would make the seatbelts accommodate larger patrons than would be safe. The complaint that followed alleges that the restraints were modified to accommodate larger riders. After Mr. Mordarsky's death, among other changes, they were made the same length as others such that he would not have been allowed to ride.
7. Sandor Kernacs, the U.S. president of Intamin (the ride maker) was quoted in the *Hartford Courant* in a story about the Mordarsky and other incidents on Intamin Rides in the same period of time. He said that 800 to 900 million people ride Intamin rides each year, and that:

> I believe the safety of the rides is very, very good. Up to this point we haven't found anything to indicate something is wrong with any of the rides....
>
> It's impossible to avoid an accident. Every accident is tragic and we should strive not to have any, but accidents do happen. The question is what is an acceptable number?

Dan Uhlinger, *Coaster Fall Was Not First for Company*, HARTFORD COURANT, May 4, 2004, A1. What is your reaction to that quotation? How would you feel about it if you represented someone suing Intamin? If you represented Intamin?

8. Unsurprisingly and wholly understandably, Mr. Mordarsky's survivors sued the park.

Complaint of Estate of Stanley Mordarsky v. Riverside Park Enterprises, Inc., Six Flags, Inc. and Intamin, A.G.

No. 3:04-cv-01453 (D. Conn. Sept. 1, 2004)
(paragraph numbers omitted)

The Parties

[Germaine Mordarsky, of Connecticut, was the mother of the decedent, Stanley Mordarsky, who resided in California. Riverside Park was the local entity that operated the park that by then was known as Six Flags New England, and was owned by Six Flags, Inc. Intamin A.G. was the U.S. business of a ride manufacturer based in Liechtenstein. Intamin made "Superman: Ride of Steel," installed at Six Flags New England. Does 1–3 "are believed to be the individual persons employed by the defendants at various locations who had various roles in the maintenance and modification of the 'Superman—Man [*sic*, Ride] of Steel Rollercoaster' located at Six Flags New England amusement park located in Agawam, Ma."]

* * *

COUNT ONE: Wrongful Death
[By Estate of Stanely Mordarsky]

On or about May 1, 2004, Stanley attended the SFNE amusement park located in Agawam, MA.

Stanley waited in line for the 'Superman' ride. Unknown to him, [defendants] had modified or permitted to be modified the ride to allow persons of larger stature to ride. In prior years Stanley would have been prohibited from riding this ride to his larger size.

Modifications to this ride either directly or as authorized by IAG changed the restraint system. This change resulted in spacing in the sides of restraint system that did not previously exist. The purpose of this modification was to allow larger people to ride. Plaintiff if informed, believes and thereon alleges that it was in the financial interest of all defendants to have as many people as possible to ride this popular and 'headliner ride' at SFNE so as to maximize revenue. If it became known that larger people could not ride this ride it would affect attendance at SFNE which would reduce the [defendants' profits].

Mordarsky was admitted to the ride and placed into a train which contained the modified restraint system. At the time he was placed in the train, the restraints were further not properly seated and he was not properly restrained in the seat. The [defendants] negligently failed to check the restraint system, and allowed the ride to leave the loading area with Mordarsky not properly restrained in the train.

During the course of the ride on May 1, 2004, at or about 1800 EDT, Mordarsky became dislodged from his seat since he was not properly restrained. He and others attempted to restrain him in his seat as the ride continued [its] course. Due to the sustained positive and negative 'G' forces, Stanley was thrown from the ride at approximately sixty miles per hour.

During the time he was dislodged from his seat and before his final plunge to the concrete below, his hand was severed by the train as he fell from his seat, and then he died as he struck the ground below.

An investigation by the Department of Public Safety of the State of Massachusetts determined that [the park] was negligent in allowing Mr. Mordarsky to leave the loading area without being properly restrained and for modifying the train without properly determining the risks to larger persons from the modified restraint system.

As such, Stanley has been damaged by the loss of his life in amount in excess of One million dollars by the defendants jointly and severally.

COUNT TWO: Negligence
[Against All Defendants]

* * *

In 1999 on an identical ride design at a SFI park at Darien Lake, a person was thrown from their seat and SFI was held to be 100% liable in that accident arising from improper verification of the seat restraints prior to the ride leaving. Despite having actual knowledge of the risk of modifying restraints and not ensuring proper restraint of riders, [defendants, including Does 1–3] permitted and/or approved the modification, and failed to have in place proper training and procedures to ensure that riders left the boarding areas properly restrained.

As a result of the negligence of the defendants Stanley has been damaged in an amount in excess of One million dollars for personal injury.

Pstanley [*sic*] further seeks punitive damages for the negligence of SFI having been on notice of the risk of larger patrons being ejected from this coaster and actively modifying the coaster to allow larger persons to ride without ensuring such modifications were safe. Such failure to take action after being faulted by both the State of New York and a jury was outrageous behavior given the speeds, g-forces and risks associated with high speed rides such as Superman.

* * *

COUNT FOUR: Intentional Infliction of Emotional Distress

* * *

Once Stanley began to come out of the seat, he was overtaken by feelings of fear and imminent personal injury. Said feelings turned to horror and fear of imminent death as he became more and more dislodged from the seat until he was flung to the ground, his hand severed and his body broken.

The actions heretofore mentioned leading up to Stanley's death were an intentional and wanton infliction of emotional distress by the defendants in the design, operation, maintenance and modification of the Superman ride. Any reasonable person would feel fear and terror at being first forced out of their seat and then ejected from a roller coaster at 60 mph.

As a further result of the events leading up to his death Stanley is and will be unable to care for his aged mother, provider her comfort in her declining years and otherwise be a good and loyal son and brother. Such would [cause] any reasonable person emotional distress and was the direct result of the events leading up to his death[.]

COUNT FIVE: Negligent Infliction of Emotional Distress
[Against All Defendants]

* * *

Any reasonable person would know that improperly modifying the ride, failing to properly inspect the ride, failing to ensure that Stanley was properly restrained and failing to monitor the video cameras positioned to ensure each ride is properly monitored could lead to personal injury or death. In fact, signs posted at the Superman ride state that failing to follow ride limitations and rider [*sic*, ride] operator instructions can lead to personal injury or death.

Such failures by the defendants caused the infliction of emotional distress of the kind described [above], and were the result of the negligence of the defendants as alleged herein.

Stanley seeks damages for the [negligent] infliction of emotional distress and punitive damages therefore, from all defendants.

[Counts Six through Nine alleged wrongful death on behalf of Stanley's mother and brother and negligent or intentional infliction of emotional distress on behalf of each of them. Count 10 alleged the breach of a settlement agreement.]

NOTES AND QUESTIONS

1. In 1999, a patron was, as noted in the complaint above, thrown from the similar Darien Lake version of Superman: Ride of Steel and suffered broken ribs. Investigators reportedly concluded that the lap bar had not been pushed far enough down due to his size. Ben Dobbin, *Army amputee thrown from NY roller coaster, dies*, Associated Press, July 8, 2011. The ride had just opened, and the restraints had not been modified, notwithstanding the Mordarsky complaint's allegations.
2. This complaint was filed on September 2, 2004. The docket reveals essentially no activity other than appearances and extensions of deadlines until January 20, 2005, when the parties filed a stipulation of dismissal, presumably reflecting a settlement.
3. Do you agree that the investigation report concluded that the park was negligent, as described by the complaint?
4. Assume that the law as to negligent and intentional infliction of emotional distress described in the Seaworld case is roughly the same as Massachusetts law (controlling in this case). If you were a judge and the defendants moved to dismiss the negligent infliction of emotional distress claim, asserting that the complaint failed to state a claim upon which relief can be granted, would you grant it? If defendants made a similar motion to dismiss the intentional infliction of emotional distress claim (and Massachusetts uses a traditional definition of that tort), would you grant it?
5. Still operating with you as the judge: Assume no motion to dismiss is brought, and further assume that discovery in this matter develops such that a jury could find the facts to be roughly as alleged. If the

defendants moved for summary judgment on the intentional infliction of emotional distress claim, would you grant it? How about on the negligent infliction of emotional distress claim?

6. If you were a juror and the evidence came in consistent with the complaint and investigation report and the jury instructions properly defined the claims, would you support a verdict for plaintiff on the intentional infliction of emotional distress claim? How about on the negligent infliction of emotional distress claim?
7. Assume that, had the ride operators followed their training, Mr. Mordarsky would *not* have been permitted to ride. Should the fact that they were acting contrary to their training mean that their employers should not be held vicariously liable for their alleged negligence?
8. Think about the ride operators you've seen at parks you've visited, or talk to friends or other students about ride operators they're familiar with if you haven't been to parks. How do you feel about them being entrusted with riders' safety? If the direction to them on a ride like Superman is "Ensure the 'T' Bar is pressing against the patrons' upper thighs, not their stomachs," is that a reasonable thing to ask them to enforce?
9. As noted, we will return to the design and warnings aspects of this case in subsequent chapters. The next item involves a patron being thrown from an effectively identical roller coaster in New York seven years later.

Report, District Office 08, Industry Inspection Bureau, Rochester, New York

July 9, 2011

On Friday, July 8, 2011, an accident occurred at the Darien Lake Theme Park.... At approximately 5:30 p.m., James Thomas Hackemer [] was ejected from the Ride of Steel, struck by the coaster train, and thrown to the ground, coming to rest between the track sections of the 2nd and 3rd hills. The coaster train continued to the end of the track, and Darien Lake staff sounded an alert to the incident. Mr. Hackemer's body was found face down and in a state of obvious death by Darien Lake security and EMS staff—no medical attention was rendered.

The Ride of Steel ... formerly known as the Superman Ride of Steel, is a roller coaster manufactured by Intamin [and marketed under the brand name Mega Coaster]. [The report describes the coaster, which is similar to, but not identical to, the coaster at Six Flags New England.]

Mr. Hackemer, a military veteran, did not have a left leg or left hip, and his right hip was amputated above the knee due to injuries suffered during his military service. Mr. Hackemer was not wearing prosthetic limbs while at Darien Lake, and was using a wheel chair during his visit to the park.

At approximately 4:05 pm on July 8, 2011, Mr. Hackemer entered the Guest Relations building near the entrance of the park and inquired about handicapped boarding policies. According to interview, the Guest Relations staff explained their "go up the exit" procedure, which permits those passengers with disabilities to enter ride platforms through the exit ramp. Guest Relations staff further offered Mr. Hackemer a copy of the brochure titled "A Guide to Fun at the Park for Guests with Disabilities" which outlines restrictions and polices [*sic*, policies] for patrons at Darien Lake. Mr. Hackemer refused the brochure and indicated that he already possessed a copy. Guest Relations staff explained to Mr. Hackemer the policy regarding the loading and unloading patrons onto their rides. Mr. Hackemer then exited Guest Relations.

At approximately 5:30 pm on July 8, 2011, Mr. Hackemer, along with his nephew, entered the Ride of steel through the exit ramp and stopped at the gate adjacent to the unload platform. The unload attendant notified the ride operator that a disabled guest needed to be loaded. Mr. Hackemer was loaded into the Red Train (car 11 seat 2) with the assistance of his nephew, who then seated himself next to Mr. Hackemer (car 11 seat 1). The rest of the Red Train was loaded in its usual manner with all restraints checked by the attendants and then launched. According to witnesses, shortly after cresting the 3rd hill, Mr. Hackemer was ejected from his seat. The Red Train continued along the track and completed its run. Upon stopping in the braking station, passengers began to inform the ride attendants of the accident and gave an approximate location of the incident as the train was brought into the station to unload. Ride staff began the notification of Darien Lake Emergency Response, to respond to the accident. [As noted above, Mr. Hackemer was obviously deceased. In order to unload the red train, the blue train, which was loaded with passengers, had to be dispatched and run through the cycle, and then the then-empty red train was also cycled in order to unload the blue train.]

I was notified by a text message from Sr. Inspector McEwan that an accident had occurred at Darien Lake. After talking with my Supervisor, I left several phone messages for Darien Lake staff that I was enroute to the accident. Upon my arrival, Imet with Darien Lake Ride Maintenance Staff and members of the Genesee County Sheriff's Office. I was brought up to speed as to what had happened and started my investigation of the accident with the assistance of Darien Lake Staff.

I proceeded to take photo documentation in the vicinity of the accident and surrounding area. I then went to the loading station and took photo documentation of the Red Train and both the loading and unloading stations, including both the regular entrance and ADA accessible entrance and all related signage. With the assistance of Ride Maintenance mechanics, the Blue Train was backed out of the station and the Red Train was brought into the station. I took additional photo documentation of the Red Train. Darien Lake Management provided copies of the "souvenir" pictures taken of the red train during its cycle in which the accident occurred. I requested that copies of numerous documents related to this device, including the owner's manual, operator training records and maintenance inspections be made available to me the next morning. Darien Lake personnel informed that they had already begun compiling the requested information. Under the direction of Supervising Inspector Frederick, I issued an order not to operate the device in order to facilitate the investigation, and made arrangement to perform a mechanical inspection of the device for the next morning.

On July 9, 2011, with the assistance of Sr. Inspectors Mc Ewan and Brown and after a brief meeting with Darien Lake and a representative from Herschend, the corporate management company of Darien Lake, I conducted a mechanical inspection of the Ride of Steel. With the assistance of Darien Lake Ride Maintenance mechanics, a complete review of the Red Train was conducted, with no deficiencies found. The Blue Train was not inspected at this time. Further review of the signage for the Ride of Steel was conducted, and I took additional photo documentation of the entrance and exit to the device, and also additional photos of the Red Train. Darien Lake supplied me with copies of the documents requested the previous night.

On July 11, 2011 after my complete inspection and photo documentation of the ride and area around ride, the ride was released to Darien Lake to allow operation for maintenance functions and cleaning, with the understanding that the ride was still not allowed to operate with patrons.

On July 12, 2011, Sr. Inspector Mc Ewan and I met at Darien Lake to interview the Ride of Steel attendants and operators who were working at the time of the accident. In addition to speaking individually with each employee, I requested that each employee provide[] a written statement, all of which occurred in the presence of a representative from Herschend. Sr. Inspector McEwan and I next completed a mechanical inspection of the Ride of Steel Blue Train, with no deficiencies found. Sr. Inspector McEwan and I then traveled to the Genesee County Sheriff's Office, where we met with Sgt. Steve Mullen and Sheriff Maha, along with the Undersheriff and the Chief of Operations. Mr. Clarke from the DOL was also present at the meeting. Set. Mullen provided copies of reports and statements that they had obtained in the course of their investigation. During the meeting, we discussed the mechanical inspection of the Ride of Steel and that we had found no deficiencies, we also indicated that we were still in the process of reviewing all documents provided by Darien Lake. Sheriff Maha informed us that his office had concluded their investigation, and that they were not planning on issuing any charges related to the accident, pending a review of their report by the Genesee County District Attorney's Office.

After considerable review of all documentation, as well as interviews with employees, it can be concluded that the accident was caused by operator error. While Mr. Hackemer used the appropriate entrance to board the Ride of Steel, he did not meet the minimum requirements to be a passenger on the Ride of Steel. Ride operators and attendants permitted Mr. Hackemer to board the Red Train with the assistance of his nephew, contrary to their training of the manufacturer's restrictions for passengers and Darien Lake's policies. Mr. Hackemer did not meet the minimum height requirements, nor did he possess the requisite two legs, as pointed out in the ride information signage provided at the regular and the "handicap access entrance", as well as the brochure distributed by customer services. The brochure states that passengers must possess two legs to ride this ride. It should be noted that part of the passenger restraint system on the ride is specifically designed to lock the passenger's shins in place to help ensure that a passenger cannot fall out or be ejected from the ride.

Over the days since the accident occurred, all documentation has been reviewed in various work sessions by me with assistance by Sr. Inspectors Mcwan and Brown, Supervising. Inspector Frederick, and Program Manager Guizzotti. After exhaustive review of all the documentation and interviews, it appears that the ride operator and ride attendant training materials met the requirements of the manufacturer; however, issues concerning the employee's comprehension of the training material and their ability to retain the associated requirements of their position, specifically in reference to rider restrictions, became apparent.

Numerous conversations were held with representatives from Herschend and Darien Lake to discuss suggestions to enhance the ride operator and ride attendant training programs for the Ride of Steel. Additionally, modifications to passenger warning signage and ways to provide visual reminders of rider restrictions for use by employees were discussed. Furthermore, Herschend brought additional corporate training and safety resources as well as outside consultants to the facility to review and enhance all facets of operation for not only the Ride of Steel, but all amusement devices at Darien Lake. Herschend has created a new "auditor" position at Darien Lake to review all training programs, and also to routinely audit employees related to the requirements for the amusement device and the employee's retention of the training information, pertaining to their respective assignment. Herschend has provided copies of all revised training materials and also copies of the new safety and audit procedures and forms, which Supervising inspector Frederick and I both found acceptable.

On July 19, 2011, Supervising Inspector Frederick and myself witnessed the revised training procedures to be implemented in a training session for operators and attendant positions for the Ride of Steel at Darien Lake. The enhanced changes to the program were acceptable to both of us; we observed the entire training session.

Mechanical deficiencies were not found with the amusement device during the course of the entire investigation.

A draft proposal of a Notice of Violation with two citations to be issued to Darien Lake has been forwarded to Supervising Inspector Frederick for review before they are issued.

NOTES AND QUESTIONS

1. Note the part of this report referencing "that part of the passenger restraint system on the ride is specifically designed to lock the passenger's shins in place to help ensure that a passenger cannot fall out or be ejected from the ride." That restraint system was added after the ejection of Stanley Mordarsky discussed above. Previously, the restraint was a "T" bar, designed to push down onto passengers' upper thighs, using the strength of the femur to keep patrons restrained. What appears to have happened with Mr. Mordarsky is that the "T" bar instead went onto his stomach, and his legs could straighten out and the G forces could eject him. With the shin restraint and an additional vertical bar keeping legs within the restraint, patrons are kept in a "Z" shape—*i.e.*, the knee joint would be kept at a roughly 90-degree angle, so that even if the "T" bar is not right up against the femur, the body is better constrained. (This restraint is shown about 20 seconds into this absurdly detailed video: https://www.youtube.com/watch?v=d5PVW7jPVdI.) That same video (at around minute 42) provides its view of the accident, including an animation that reflects how the "T" bar did not hold Mr. Mordarsky in. After those modifications (and some others), no additional similar incidents occurred. A few years later, the ride was outfitted with electronic verification to ensure that the restraints are adequately far down.
2. Do you agree with the investigator's conclusion that "the accident was caused by operator error"? Who else, if anyone, shares the blame?
3. As with the Mordarsky death, it appears that the ride operators' conduct was contrary to training—indeed, allowing Mr. Hackemer to ride was evidently contrary to the requirements posted at the ride entrance. Should the park be held civilly liable for its employees' apparent negligence in this situation?
4. Consider again the situation the likely teenager ride operators are faced with here: a double amputee, possibly identifiably a veteran, wanting to ride the coaster. Think about what that scenario was like for them.
5. Six Flags (and many other parks) now require patrons seeking accommodations to obtain an "accessibility card" (https://accessibilitycard.org), and then, based on their specific situation, receive an

"attraction access pass." You can see more about that at https://www.sixflags.com/darienlake/plan-your-visit/accessibility. The current park access guide is at https://static.sixflags.com/website/files/sfdl_ada-guidelines.pdf.

Amended Complaint of Nancy Hackemer v. CNL Income Darien Lake LLC et al.

No. 1:11-cv-0672 (W.D.N.Y. Aug. 24, 2011)
(paragraph numbers omitted)

* * *

At all times herein-relevant, defendants owned, operated, maintained and ran property and premises commonly known as the Darien Lake Theme Park located at 9993 Allegheny Road in Darien Center, Genesee County, New York.

At all times herein-relevant, defendants owned, maintained and operated a roller coaster ride commonly known as the "Ride of Steel".

On or about July 8, 2011, James Hackemer was a patron at the Darien Lake Theme Park and was permitted to be a passenger on the defendants' Ride of Steel roller coaster.

On or about July 8, 2011, James Hackemer was caused to be thrown from the Ride of Steel roller coaster while it was in operation and was caused to be thrown to the tracks and struck by the roller coaster and thrown to the ground below.

On or about July 8, 2011, James Hackemer died from injuries as a result of the incident described in the foregoing paragraph.

AS AND FOR A FIRST CAUSE OF ACTION AGAINST DEFENDANTS

* * *

James Hackemer died wrongfully as a direct result of the negligence and/or recklessness of the agents, servants and/or employees of the defendants.

The incident mentioned [] above occurred solely as a result of the negligence and/or recklessness of the defendants' agents, servants and/or employees, without any negligence attributable in any measure to the decedent James Hackemer.

* * *

Due to the wrongful death of decedent James Hackemer, as caused by the negligence and/or recklessness of the agents, servants and/or employees of the defendants, plaintiff is entitled to an award of damages in an amount which does not exceed the monetary jurisdictional limits of this Court and an amount which will be determined by the jury at the trial of this action.

AS FOR A SECOND CAUSE OF ACTION
AGAINST DEFENDANTS

* * *

James Hackemer suffered extreme mental shock and anguish, including fear of grave injury and/or impending death before his demise and also suffered conscious pain, suffering and resulting damages prior to his death; and said extreme mental shock, anguish, fear of grave injury and/or impending death, conscious pain and suffering and resulting damages were caused solely by the negligence and/or recklessness of defendants' agents, servants and/or employees.

As the result of James Hackemer's extreme mental shock, anguish, fear of grave injury and/or impending death, conscious pain and suffering and resulting damages, the plaintiff demands an award of damages which does not exceed the monetary jurisdictional limits of this Court and an amount which will be determined by the jury at the trial of this action.

NOTES AND QUESTIONS

As a reminder, bringing a claim for emotional distress that accompanies physical injury—in this case, emotional distress *as to Mr. Hackemer* before his death—does not implicate the same limited-duty rules. A claim for the negligent infliction of emotional distress on behalf of, say, his family members, on the other hand, would implicate those rules.

Answer to Amended Complaint in Nancy Hackemer v. CNL Income Darien Lake LLC et al.

No. 1:11-cv-0672 (W.D.N.Y. Aug. 25, 2011)
(paragraph numbers omitted)

[Defendants admitted the basic allegations about the parties, denied fault, and provided the following affirmative defenses.]

AS AND FOR A FIRST AFFIRMATIVE DEFENSE

Whatever injuries the plaintiff may have sustained as alleged in the Complaint herein were proximately caused, in whole or in part, by the culpable conduct, including contributory negligence and assumption of risk, of the plaintiff's decedent James Hackemer, and without any negligence or fault or want of care on the part of these answering defendants.

AS AND FOR A SECOND AFFIRMATIVE DEFENSE

Plaintiff's decedent actively and affirmatively assumed all the risks inherent in, and naturally associated with, engaging in a dangerous and hazardous activity, i.e., riding a roller coaster, when he knew, or with the exercise of reasonable caution should have known, that he was ineligible and not physically capable of doing so.

NOTES AND QUESTIONS

1. The lawsuit was settled in early 2013.
2. While we addressed comparative fault and assumption of risk in earlier chapters, this case obviously raises significant questions on both topics. Why do you think Mr. Hackemer—who told park staff he had previously received the guide to rides and, we can presume, at least could have seen the sign noting that patrons needed two legs to ride—still got on the ride?
3. If you were a juror hearing the facts alleged above, do you think you would find for Mr. Hackemer's survivors? Do you think he was contributorily negligent? Did he assume the risk (under either primary or secondary assumption of risk)? If you think the park would have a strong argument for barring recovery, why do you think the park still settled the case?

4. The next case provides a look at one portion of operations at Action Park, and a nice look at how one court addressed vicarious liability.

Gray v. Great American Recreation Association, Inc.

970 F.2d 1081 (2d Cir. 1992)

Van Graafeiland, Circuit Judge:

Great American Recreation Association, Inc. and its subsidiary, Vernon Valley Recreation Association, Inc. (hereafter "Great American"), appeal from a judgment of the United States District Court for the Southern District of New York, which followed a jury trial before Judge Griesa. David Gray and Victor Colicchio each were awarded $15,000 on their claims for assault, and Colicchio was awarded an additional $800 on his claim for conversion of his property. We vacate the judgment and remand the case to the district court for retrial.

Great American operates an amusement park in Vernon, New Jersey known as Action Park. On August 3, 1989, Colicchio and his wife, together with Gray and a female companion, visited Action Park. Because many of the Park attractions are water rides, it has what Mrs. Colicchio described as "rows and rows" of coin lockers in which patrons may check their non-swimwear and other articles not suitable for water exposure. The four visitors placed all of their property of this nature in locker number 2142, which they locked with the key provided. When they returned after about an hour, they found that the locker had been broken into and their property was missing.

Plaintiffs were informed by one or more of the guards that, because the lock on their locker had been broken, their belongings had been removed for safekeeping. They subsequently were informed that their property could be found at the Park's courtesy desk. However, when they asked the woman attendant at the courtesy desk whether their property was there, she said that nothing had been turned in. Because Gray believed that he saw plaintiffs' property behind the courtesy desk counter, he attempted to get at it by going through a latched gate or door into the restricted area behind the counter. He was prevented from so doing by a Park attendant, and apparently a brief scuffle took place involving the two plaintiffs and two attendants, which caused no injury of moment to anyone. With the exception of money and jewelry, which apparently had been stolen, plaintiffs' property was in fact behind the counter and was returned to plaintiffs.

The trial was a short one, lasting less than two days. However, it started off on the wrong foot and never recovered. Although Gray knew that the trial was to begin on a Wednesday morning, he left New York and flew to Florida on Tuesday night. No reason was given for his departure. In the words of the district judge, "he just decided to go." Over defendants' objection, the trial proceeded in the absence of Gray, who was represented by the same attorney as was Colicchio. Under the circumstances, the defendants were entitled to a charge that the jury might draw an adverse inference against Gray. "'The law creates a presumption, where the burden is on a party to prove a material fact peculiarly within his knowledge and he fails without excuse to testify, that his testimony, if introduced, would be adverse to his interests.'" *Meier v. CIR,* 199 F.2d 392, 396 (8th Cir.1952) (quoting 20 Am.Jur., *Evidence* § 190, page 193). [The court then discussed the error in not giving such an instruction.]

In any event, other egregious error, duly excepted to, mandates reversal.

With certain limited exceptions, an employer is liable for the acts of his employee only when the acts are within the scope of the latter's employment. New Jersey has adopted the *Restatement (Second) of Agency* definition of scope of employment, which states in part that the conduct of a servant is not within the scope of employment "if it is different in kind from that authorized ... or too little actuated by a purpose to serve the master." *Id.* § 228; *see Di Cosala v. Kay,* 91 N.J. 159, 169, 450 A.2d 508 (1982). These, say the New Jersey courts, are questions of fact to be decided by the jury. The court may decide whether a plaintiff has introduced sufficient evidence to make a question of fact; it may not, however, answer that question. As stated in *Cleaves v. Yeskel,* 102 N.J.L. 621, 624, 133 A. 393 (N.J.1926):

Whether the act was or was not such as might reasonably be held to be within the employment's scope is ordinarily one of fact for the jury's determination, excepting where the departure from the master's business is of a marked and decided character when the question may be within the province of the court to determine.

This statement of New Jersey law mirrors the approach taken by the *Restatement (Second) of Agency:*

> The question of whether or not the act done is so different from the act authorized that it is not within the scope of the employment is decided by the court if the answer is clearly indicated; otherwise, it is decided by the jury.

Id. § 228 cmt. d.

The district court refused to submit the issue of scope of employment to the jury and would not permit defense counsel to even discuss it in his summation. The court merely defined conversion and assault and asked the jury to decide, by answering specific interrogatories, whether these offenses had been committed by one or more Great American employees. When the jury answered the interrogatories in the affirmative, the district court held as a matter of law that Great American was liable. This was error.

On the conversion claim, the district court itself recognized that it had gone awry when, on the argument of the motion to set aside the verdict, it said: "No one contends that such a conversion would be within the scope of an employment." The district court's decision that it nonetheless could hold Great American liable as a matter of law on the ground that it owed plaintiffs a non-delegable duty to protect their property or, alternatively, that it aided in the theft of the property by supplying some of its security guards with master keys, merits little discussion. That was not the theory of liability on which the case was submitted to the jury. Moreover, Great American was neither an innkeeper nor a common carrier. *See Roth v. First Nat'l State Bank,* 169 N.J.Super. 280, 286–87, 404 A.2d 1182 (App.Div.), *certif. denied,* 81 N.J. 338, 407 A.2d 1212 (1979); *cf. De Wolf v. Ford,* 193 N.Y. 397, 406–09, 86 N.E. 527 (1908); *Gillespie v. Brooklyn Heights R.R. Co.,* 178 N.Y. 347, 352–59, 70 N.E. 857 (1904). Neither was it a bailee of the contents of the thousands of lockers it provided for its customers' use. The district court clearly erred in stating that the "undisputed facts are that the locker was opened by means of [a] master key" in the possession of defendants' security guards. The proof actually was that the lock's cylinder had been pulled and that a security guard said that the lock had been broken. We think it safe to say that an experienced thief would have little trouble in accomplishing entry into an ordinary metal locker in this fashion, and it is far from clear that this is not what occurred in the instant case. Finally, we take it as a given that master keys are an absolute necessity for any place of public assembly where lockers are furnished for public use.

The district court also erred in holding as a matter of law that the assault was within the scope of employment of Great American employees. In reaching this conclusion, the district court obviously felt that the alleged conversion and the alleged assault should be compartmentalized and the latter considered separate and distinct from the former. Perhaps the jury could have treated the two incidents in this manner. It was not for the court to do so as a matter of law. Plaintiffs alleged in their complaint that they were assaulted while they were attempting to retrieve their converted belongings. In his opening to the jury, plaintiffs' counsel described the loss of his clients' possessions from the open locker and stated that plaintiffs "in the course of their attempts to resolve the situation with park personnel" were assaulted. It cannot be said with certainty that there was no connection between the alleged conversion and the alleged assault. It would not have been illogical for the jury to have concluded that the latter followed directly from the former. Whether Great American was legally responsible for what occurred should not have been decided as a matter of law.

In *Holler v. Ross,* 68 N.J.L. 324, 53 A. 472, 474 (N.J.1902), a case similar in many respects to the instant one, the court said:

> For a willful act done by a servant, not within the line of his employment, and about which there is not a doubtful question of fact as to whether the act of the servant was or was not within the line of his duty, the court should control the case, and nonsuit or direct a verdict for the defendant. Whether there be evidence which raises a question to go to the jury, as to whether the act of the servant was within the line of his duty and employment, is for the court. If the court so determines, then it is a question for the jury whether, under the proof, the act was or was not within the line of the servant's duty or employment.

This clear-cut statement of traditional New Jersey law was a guidepost that the district court should have followed.

We cannot conclude our discussion of reasons for reversal without commenting briefly on the district court's charge relating to damages. Because there were no physical injuries or special damages, the district court addressed its comments to the "invasion" of plaintiffs' rights. In describing the value of this "invasion of rights", the district court said:

> It is not a matter of a nominal thing. It is not a matter of a dollar, nominal damages, or $10 nominal damages. It wouldn't be sensible to make it a million dollars. There are things that are so clearly out of bounds one way or the other, if you find that there was an assault, you don't want to trivialize it and have your verdict be so low that it would be a laughing stock. You want to take into account what is regarded as a serious amount of money in these times of our economy and what money means. By the same token, you wouldn't want to have it so high that it would be out of bounds and unfair to the defendant.

If there is any question why plaintiffs, particularly plaintiff Gray who did not even appear, were awarded $15,000 in damages, the answer lies in the above-quoted charge.

For all the above reasons, the judgment of the district court is vacated, and the matter is remanded to that court for retrial.

NOTES AND QUESTIONS

1. The law around vicarious liability (often also called *respondeat superior* by people who enjoy using Latin) varies enough that it is probably a fool's errand to try to summarize it. Overall, I think it is fair to say that the trend is towards allowing more employee conduct to be considered within the scope of employment for purposes of liability, as long as the conduct can be properly characterized as related to the work being done.
2. When there is employee conduct at issue, that doesn't mean the *only* way to establish liability on the part of the employer is by way of vicarious liability. Often, a plaintiff can show (or at least allege) negligence by the employer in hiring, training, supervision, and so on. In the *Hackemer* investigation, recall that the regulators required improved training of ride operators, concluding that the training had failed. While that training would itself probably not be admissible (because of Rule 702 of most Rules of Evidence), it's a decent hint that the training could have been better. So, when you're looking at a fact

pattern involving employees, don't *only* think about vicarious liability as a way that the employer's pockets might be available.

3. Ride operator training at major parks has largely been systemized. Some places use a model that has long been used for lifeguards, where the parks' trainers will themselves be trained by outside consultants, and the operations are themselves anonymously audited. One example (possibly the only major player) is International Ride Training, which has extensive information available at its website, ridetraining.com. Their clients become certified under the International Ride Operator Certification—their in-house trainers are certified as trainers by attending IRT classes ("Ride Camp"), and then IRT staff perform anonymous random audits, assessing operator performance. Having such a system can provide parks with useful evidence and documentation in the event of an incident occurring and litigation following. In a case discussed in Chapter 9, as in the Hackemer case, regulators required a park to implement new training for all employees prior to reopening—in a situation like that, a third-party training outfit is likely wise. Why would it also be useful in litigation?

CHAPTER 8

Design, Warnings, Experts

Especially when in the amusement park or carnival context, litigation often ends up being about the design of attractions or, maybe even more often, the warnings accompanying them. You've already seen discussions of both designs and warnings in the previous chapter, in the Mordarsky and Hackemer incidents (which we will revisit below).

Both design and warnings can be particularly challenging in the amusement context—here I'm talking not about the difficulty in litigation, but instead in the real world context of actually creating designs and crafting warnings in ways that will check all of the boxes—making it so patrons will have fun and have the information and equipment necessary to be kept safe (and, not incidentally, providing a good defense to injury claims). As we have discussed already, parks are largely designed to make patrons feel the rush of danger without (one hopes) actual danger, and that seems to result in patrons being inclined to feel emboldened and perhaps impervious to harm—increasing the need to anticipate misuse, and possibly expanding the realm of such misuse that could be deemed foreseeable.

Moreover, many patrons are children—many of them young enough to be incapable (legally) of negligence, or at least young enough to be presumed not to be negligent. And, more importantly, kids are unpredictable, more so when encountering new situations where they might get scared or excited. When you hear someone saying that most ride accidents result from "rider misconduct," remember that the term may well include a nine-year-old panicking on a ride and, in terror, getting out of a restraint that could well be designed more effectively, at least in terms of preventing a nine-year-old from escaping its hold. It fits in the "rider misconduct" bucket, sure, but it's a bit different than a 35-year-old standing up on a coaster on a dare from his buddy, right?

The challenges are even greater when formulating warnings. In the first place, warnings are routinely ignored, no matter how implemented, but defendants are still potentially held liable for their arguable failings. And it's all in the context of trying to communicate risks and instructions to distracted people filled with adrenaline (and sometimes alcohol), or kids of various levels of literacy and attention. Add in, as in our first case in this chapter, peer pressure, and it's a fraught world. Regardless, there are more and less sophisticated ways to craft warnings, and the difference between a decades old placard with dense text in one language thrown in front of a traveling Zipper ride and the multi-phase warnings system with images, animations, and multiple languages that you might see at, for example, Universal Studios, is stark.

Potential design and warnings defects are almost always presented by way of expert testimony, and so this chapter addresses all three topics.

Nilson v. Hershey Entertainment & Resorts Co.

649 F. Supp. 2d 378 (M.D. Pa. 2009)
(record citations omitted)

Sylvia H. Rambo, District Judge.

This is a personal injury action brought by Plaintiffs based on their allegation that Tyler Nilson, a minor, lost hearing in his left ear as a result of riding the Wildcat roller coaster at Hersheypark—an amusement park wholly owned by Defendant Hershey Entertainment and Resorts Company ("HE&R")—on or about August 1, 2003. For the reasons that follow, the court will grant Defendants' joint motion for summary judgment[].

[BACKGROUND AND FACTS]

The following facts are undisputed except where noted, and are viewed in the light most favorable to Plaintiff. Plaintiff Tyler Nilson ("Tyler") is a minor who, at the time of the events relevant to this case, was 11 years old. Defendant HE & R is the operator of the Wildcat roller coaster and the Hersheypark amusement park. Defendant Great Coasters International, Inc. ("Great Coasters") is the manufacturer of the Wildcat....

On August 1, 2003, Tyler visited Hersheypark with a friend, Bryan Romeike, Bryan's mother, brother, and a friend of Bryan's brother. While at Hersheypark, Tyler rode several rides, including the Lightning Racer, another roller coaster. Tyler rode the Lightning Racer two times. At first he did not want to ride the Lightning Racer due to his fear of heights, but facing peer pressure he "gave in" and rode it because his friends "kept asking and bugging [him] about it." As he boarded the Lightening Racer, Tyler read the posted signs located at the entrance.

Prior to leaving Hersheypark, Tyler rode on the Wildcat as his last ride for the day. Throughout the day, the other children went on various other roller coasters, but Tyler declined to go on any roller coaster other than the Lightning Racer and the Wildcat. Initially, Tyler did not want to ride the Wildcat because he was scared of heights, and because "it just looked like it was less safe," and he did not want to "fall out" of the ride. Ultimately, Tyler was convinced by his friends to ride the Wildcat because it was "the last one of the day," and because he did not "want to look like a little wimp not going on it." Before riding the Wildcat, Tyler understood that a roller coaster is "something that goes at high speed as they lift hill [*sic*] and drops you." While waiting in line for the Wildcat, Tyler read the signs stating that riders should not ride the Wildcat if they suffer from certain health issues and advising riders of "certain speed changes" that occur during the ride.

Tyler rode the Wildcat and sat with his feet flat on the floor of the car and his back against the seat of the car. He remained in this position throughout the duration of the ride. The Wildcat did not mechanically malfunction during the ride: the safety restraint stayed in place during the entire ride; no part of the ride came loose or struck Tyler; and the ride came to a slow, gradual stop at the end. Tyler's head did not make contact with any object during his ride on the Wildcat. While on the ride, and ascending the first hill, Tyler heard a loud clicking sound that he described as someone screaming in his ear. After reaching its peak, the ride descended quickly, shaking as it rounded several curves, causing the riders to shake as well. In his deposition, Tyler described the shaking as "violent ... like [he] was getting whipped back and forth by the ride." Tyler testified at his deposition that he would not have ridden the Wildcat if there had been a sign advising him that the ride had "violent shaking."

After Tyler exited the ride, he almost immediately realized that he suffered a head ache, although the head ache was not localized in one part of his head. About a minute or two after he got off the Wildcat, Tyler experienced a ringing in his left ear, but at that point he could still hear. The ringing in Tyler's left ear lasted "a couple of hours." Tyler mentioned his headache and the ringing in his left ear to his friend immediately, and to his friend's mother about 1 hour after going on the Wildcat. The group slept that night in a hotel room, and the ringing in Tyler's ear lasted until he went to sleep. When he awoke the next morning he did not have a headache or ringing in his left ear, but he could not hear from that ear. Tyler has not been able to hear from his left ear since before going to bed the night after he rode the Wildcat....

[MEDICAL EXPERTS]

On August 5, 2003, Tyler went to his family doctor because the hearing in his left ear had not returned, the office notes from that visit do not include any mention of Hersheypark, roller coasters, the Wildcat, or any other suspected cause of the hearing loss. The first mention of the roller coaster in any medical records appears in the office notes from Tyler's visit to Dr. Steven Handler on November 17, 2003—more than three months after Tyler's trip to Hersheypark. The tests performed at this visit indicated that Tyler suffered from normal hearing in his right ear, but had nearly complete hearing loss in his left ear. A CT scan was performed on December 2, 2003 and was normal. No follow-up occurred until November 2, 2004, when Tyler was taken to Philadelphia to see Dr. Thomas O. Wilcox, M.D. for a second opinion.

Dr. Wilcox, an otolaryngologist, confirmed that Tyler has almost complete hearing loss in his left ear, and recommended that Tyler have an MRI scan of his brain. The MRI scan came back normal. Dr. Wilcox did not see Tyler again until December 27, 2006, at that visit, Dr. Wilcox noted that Tyler's hearing had not improved. After this litigation commenced, on March 21, 2007, Dr. Wilcox wrote a letter to the attorneys for Plaintiff offering his medical opinion as to the cause of Tyler's hearing loss. Dr. Wilcox opined:

> It is my impression to a reasonable degree of medical certainty that Tyler Nilson sustained a left sensorineural hearing loss due to cochlear trauma from the roller coaster ride. I believe that the temporal onset of symptoms including tinnitus and

> hearing loss within one-half hour after exiting the ride supports this conclusion. Although there are no published cases of roller coaster induced hearing loss, there are several publications about roller coaster induced injuries.... It is my impression that intracranial pressure changes due to head trauma during the roller coaster ride were transmitted to the cochlea resulting in intracochlear membrane damage. The intracochlear membrane damage resulted in the severe-to-profound left sensorineural hearing loss and tinnitus.

The parties vigorously dispute whether Tyler suffered any membrane damage. Although Dr. Wilcox's March 21, 2007 letter mentions that there was membrane damage, Defendants point to Dr. Wilcox's office notes from Tyler's original visit with Dr. Wilcox in November 2004. The notes read, in relevant part: "I do suspect that Tyler sustained some inner ear membrane damage because of the head trauma from the roller coaster ride. This resulted in the hearing loss." According to Defendants, those notes indicate that it is "nothing more than a suspicion rather than a demonstrable fact" that Tyler suffered from inner ear membrane damage. Defendants also point out that none of the diagnostic tests (CT scan or MRI) revealed any inner ear damage. Finally Defendants point to the report of their medical expert, Dr. Robert Sataloff. After examining Tyler, Dr. Sataloff opined:

> In my opinion to a reasonable degree of medical certainty, Tyler Nilson's hearing loss was not causally related to his roller coaster ride. He sustained no head trauma or whiplash injury associated with the ride and he experienced no dizziness at the time of his alleged hearing loss.... [T]he absence of acute dizziness suggests that his hearing loss was not caused by an inner ear membrane break or fistula.

Dr. Sataloff opined that he could not determine the cause of Tyler's hearing loss without more testing, but the fact that Tyler's hearing loss "occurred after a roller coaster ride does not mean that it occurred because of the roller coaster ride."

[WARNINGS]

The parties do not dispute that the following signs were displayed at various points to the riders entering the Wildcat, and that Tyler saw these signs before riding:

THROUGHOUT THE RIDE RIDERS WILL
EXPERIENCE SPEED CHANGES
and UNEXPECTED FORCES.
STRICT ADHERENCE TO THE RULES and
INSTRUCTIONS IS REQUIRED TO
ENHANCE YOUR ENJOYMENT OF THE
RIDE and TO AVOID INJURY
PLEASE
REMAIN SEATED and
KEEP ARMS and LEGS
INSIDE THE RIDE VEHICLE
AT ALL TIMES.
SIT UPRIGHT AND HOLD ONTO THE GRAB BAR
FOR YOUR SAFETY
Please Keep ALL Parts of Your Body
Inside Vehicle at All Times
NO STANDING.

Defendant HE & R was in possession of First Aid incident reports indicating the park patrons had complained of headaches and neck pain after riding on the Wildcat, but this information was not communicated on any sign.

[ENGINEERING EXPERTS]

The parties retained engineers to opine about the adequacy of the warnings posted on the Wildcat. Plaintiff's expert, George P. Widas, P.E., concluded as follows in his June 25, 2008 report:

> The conditions that produced the subject injury were that Tyler Nilson was not provided with sufficient warning/information related to the character or severity of the forces associated with the Wildcat roller coaster....
>
> At the time of the conditions that produced the subject injury to Tyler Nilson there was no warning signage that com-

> municated to a rider how fast the ride traveled, nor what the rider could experience in terms of force or speed during the ride....
>
> The subject Wildcat roller coaster was provided to Tyler Nilson with improper, ineffective warnings, without regard for and/or contrary to accepted safe practices, and without regard for and/or contrary to cited, readily available, recognized, accepted, authoritative, applicable reference, standards and codes....
>
> Proper and adequate warnings would have specifically identified the hazard for injury by quantifying the character of the speed, motions and forces exerted on the rider by the ride, such as by assigning a severity number to the ride.

In a supplemental report dated August 8, 2008, Mr. Widas concluded that the signage at the Wildcat did not provide the necessary words of "caution," "warning," or "danger." Mr. Widas provided an exemplar sign that would have, in his opinion, appropriately warned Tyler Nilson:

WARNING!!!
THIS IS A HIGH SPEED RIDE WITH RAPID JOLTS IN SHARP TURNS AND HARD DIPS. DO NOT RIDE UNLESS YOU ARE PREPARED FOR THE MOST SEVERE LEVEL OF PHYSICAL IMPACT AND THRILL.

Defendants also retained an engineer to offer his expert opinion concerning the adequacy of the warnings on the Wildcat. Alan Dorris, P.E., Ph.D, offered a contradicting opinion from that of Mr. Widas. Dr. Dorris concluded, among other things, in his June 23, 2008 report:

> The warning signs posted at the entrance to the Wildcat provide appropriate precautionary information to prospective riders....
>
> In the materials reviewed to date I find no indication that Tyler Nilson's condition after riding The Wildcat was related to a known hazard associated with the roller coaster. Absent identification of a hazard, there is nothing to warn of. Without an identified hazard there can be no statement of how to avoid the hazard and no statement of consequences resulting from exposure to the hazard.

[Procedural history and the legal standard for summary judgment omitted.]

[ISSUES BEFORE THE COURT]

[T]he only counts remaining in this case are Counts I through III. In Count I, Plaintiffs allege that Defendants were negligent in the use, design, manufacture, assembly, testing, warnings, inspection, and/or distribution of the Wildcat roller coaster; and, that Defendants negligently failed to provide adequate warnings and/or instructions concerning the characteristics and/or dangers of the Wildcat roller coaster. In Count II, Plaintiffs allege generally a strict liability defective product claim stating that the Wildcat was "unfit, unsafe, and/or unsuitable for its intended or foreseeable uses and/or was otherwise defective in design, manufacture, distribution, sale, operation and/or warnings." Finally, in Count III, Plaintiffs state a strict liability failure to warn claim and state that Defendants "failed to exercise reasonable care to inform and/or warn expected or foreseeable users of the Wild Cat roller coaster of its dangerous condition or of the facts that made the Wild Cat roller coaster likely to be dangerous."

Aside from the generalized allegations in the Amended Complaint, Plaintiffs do not allege that the Wildcat malfunctioned in any way. Plaintiffs' engineering expert focuses not on any defect inherent in the Wildcat roller coaster itself, but rather that the ride suffered from inadequate warnings. Furthermore, in their statement of material facts, Defendants stated the following: "The Wildcat did not malfunction in any way during Tyler's ride." Plaintiffs' response was: "Denied. Plaintiffs submit that the Wildcat 'malfunctioned' in that the warnings/signage provided with it were inadequate. Plaintiffs contend that Tyler Nilson would never have even ridden the ride were it not for inadequate warning(s)." There is simply no evidence in the record suggesting that the Wildcat mechanically malfunctioned in any way during Tyler's ride. In light of this, and Plaintiffs' admission that the only "malfunction" at issue is the alleged failure to warn, the court will grant Defendants' motion for summary judgment as to Count II (product defect/product liability), and that part of Count I (negligence) premised upon anything other than the negligent failure to warn, without further discussion. Plaintiff has simply failed to adduce any evidence on these issues, and judgment will be granted in favor of Defendants.

[FAILURE TO WARN]

The crux of the dispute between the parties is whether the warnings provided by Defendants adequately advised riders of the Wildcat of the latent risks associated with riding the roller coaster. If the warnings were adequate, the Wildcat was not defective, and all of Plaintiffs claims fail. If the warnings were inadequate, the court must then analyze whether Tyler would have heeded other warnings, and whether there is sufficient evidence supporting causation. Plaintiffs' theory of the case is that Defendants failed to warn of latent dangers associated with riding the Wildcat roller coaster. Specifically, Plaintiffs assert that the warnings failed to advise Tyler "how violent and fast this ride might be." Had they done so, according to Plaintiffs, Tyler would have heeded the appropriate warnings, not ridden the Wildcat, and would still be able to hear from his left ear. Plaintiffs assert that Defendants are liable for their failure to warn under theories of negligence and strict product liability.

[The court described the elements of a negligence tort.]

The determination of whether a warning is adequate and whether a product is defective due to inadequate warnings are questions of law to be answered by the court. [] The adequacy of a warning is evaluated solely on the basis of whether the danger complained of was unobvious and reasonably foreseeable. *See Blake v. Greyhound Lines, Inc.* 448 F. Supp.2d 635, 641 (E.D.Pa.2006) ("Where a danger is open and obvious, there is no duty to warn.") [] Whether a danger is open and obvious is an objective inquiry that does not require examination of an individual user's actual knowledge or awareness of the danger. [] Rather, this inquiry examines whether an ordinary consumer with knowledge common to the community would have knowledge of the danger. [] "If the product is one customarily used by children, the danger must be one which children would be likely to recognize and appreciate in order to prevent them from recovering for a product related injury on the grounds that the danger was open and obvious." [Citations]

[ADEQUACY OF THE WARNINGS]

Here, the parties disagree about the nature of the warning that was needed, and Plaintiffs present an inconsistent picture of what it is that they believe to be the latent danger of the Wildcat. In his report, George P. Widas, Plaintiffs' expert, stated that Defendants inadequately warned Tyler about the character or severity of the forces of the ride[, as quoted above].

In response, Defendants argue that "the general danger on which Plaintiffs and their expert have focused—the speed and turbulence of the ride—is both obvious and sufficiently addressed in the existing warning." In their brief in opposition to Defendants' motion for summary judgment, Plaintiffs ratchet up the nature of the warning that they believe to be necessary, and argue that the warnings on the Wildcat roller coaster were inadequate because they did not caution that riders "would be shaken violently and would be subjected to trauma to their heads and necks," and that the "speed and violent nature of the ride was not so obvious that an inexperienced, first time young rider would know of the ride's violent nature." In their reply, Defendants argue that since Plaintiffs have "failed to adduce any evidence whatsoever that the ride was unsafe" they cannot argue that the necessary warning would have warned of "violent shaking" and "head trauma."

After reviewing the evidence in the light most favorable to Plaintiffs, the court finds that the warnings given by Defendants were adequate, and the warning suggested by Plaintiffs' expert would not have prevented the injury....

The court fails to appreciate any informative significant difference in Plaintiffs' expert's suggested alternative warning and the warning actually on the Wildcat. For his part, Mr. Widas—Plaintiffs' expert—stated that the Wildcat's "faded, nearly illegible, vague informational sign ... did not quantify the character of the speed, motions or forces exerted on the rider by the ride...." The irony is that Plaintiffs' expert's proposed alternative suffers the same flaws. Nowhere does Mr. Widas' sign quantify the character of the speed—except to state that it is "high," a characterization that needs a benchmark in order for it to have meaning, in other words, "high" as compared to what?—nor does it quantify the motions or forces exerted by the rider. Quite simply, it is not more—or less—specific than the sign already present, and since the adequacy of a warning is evaluated on the basis of whether a better warning would have prevented the injury[], the court finds that the proposed alternative would not have communicated materially different information such that Tyler would have chosen not to ride the Wildcat. Tyler's deposition testimony supports this conclusion.

Tyler testified at his deposition that he would not have ridden the Wildcat if there had been signs indicating that the ride would cause "violent shaking, or if it could cause something that could happen like happened to me...." Plaintiffs' expert had access to Tyler's deposition, and reviewed it in preparation of his report; nonetheless, Mr. Widas did not opine that an appropriate warning should include any mention of "violent shaking." Instead, he proposed a sign that communicates substantially similar information as the sign already on the Wildcat, a sign that did not deter Tyler from riding.

Moreover, Plaintiffs have failed to demonstrate that the defect complained of—the speed and force exerted by the ride—were unobvious. Here, Defendants are permitted to "assume that users ... will possess the common knowledge of the community," and they are only required to warn of latent risks. *Fletcher v. Raymond Corp.*, 424 Pa.Super. 605, 623 A.2d 845, 848 (1993). The court finds it incredible that anyone—even someone as young as 11—would not know that roller coasters go up and down hills at a fast speed, and that they exert forces on your body. This is obvious to any customer of Hersheypark or any other amusement park. In fact, it was obvious to Tyler. Tyler testified at his deposition that, before riding the Wildcat, he understood a roller coaster to be "something that goes at high speed as they lift hill [*sic*] and drops you." These observations are sufficient.

The danger complained of by Plaintiffs is not latent in the sense that one must be an expert to appreciate it; after all, this is not a case involving drug side effects, or the foreseeable misuse of a product such as the inhalation of aerosol or butane canisters. Instead, Plaintiffs allege that Defendants should have warned of the excessive speed and force imposed by the Wildcat. Plaintiff's flaw, however, is that they failed to adduce any evidence that the Wildcat imposed excessive speed or force. Plaintiffs do not dispute that at all times the Wildcat met ASTM standards[], or that the applicable ASTM standards were correct or adequate. Plaintiffs also introduced no evidence suggesting that the Wildcat is an inherently dangerous product. Absent some evidence of this sort, and some evidence that an ordinary patron of Hersheypark would not obviously appreciate that they would get jostled on the Wildcat while going very fast, Plaintiffs have failed to demonstrate that the Wildcat's warning was defective or that Defendants were negligent.

[REASONABLY FORESEEABLE DANGER]

In their brief in opposition to summary judgment, Plaintiffs try to redefine the Wildcat's danger to conform to the testimony of Tyler that he suffered violent shaking. While it may be true from Tyler's perspective that he suffered "violent shaking," none of the evidence in this case suggests that the Wildcat malfunctioned in any way, or that a warning that the Wildcat subjected riders to potential "violent shaking" or "head trauma" was reasonably foreseeable.

Plaintiffs' own expert opined that the inadequacy in Defendants' warning was that it failed to provide Tyler "with sufficient warning/information related to the character or severity of the forces associated with the Wildcat roller coaster." Later, in a supplemental report, Plaintiffs' expert suggested an alternative warning that does not suggest that patrons should be warned of violent shaking or head trauma. Plaintiffs' counsel's characterization that the inadequacy of the warning was its failure to advise of violent shaking and head trauma finds no support in the evidence, and is an argument that is unsupported even by Plaintiffs' own expert. Presumably, Plaintiff's counsel arrived at the conclusion that the warning should have contained language concerning violent shaking and head trauma because Tyler stated in his deposition that had there been a warning of this sort he would not have ridden the Wildcat. While this may have been true for Tyler, there is no evidence to support the conclusion that Defendants had a duty to warn of this danger because it was not reasonably foreseeable.

Plaintiffs introduced no evidence that the Wildcat subjected riders to dangerous forces. Defendants' expert report cited the Brain Injury Association of America's review of the Correlation between Brain Injury and Roller Coaster Rides, which concluded that the accelerations experienced by roller coaster riders are far below experimentally derived injury thresholds for healthy individuals. Furthermore, Defendants' expert opined that the Wildcat "meets industry and ASTM standards for acceleration as verified by two separate biodynamic reports." There is nothing in the record contradicting this evidence. While Plaintiffs generally aver that Defendants were in possession of First Aid Incident Reports indicating that riders of the Wildcat reported suffering from headaches and neck pain, they failed to make these reports available for the court to allow it to compare the severity of past injuries with the harm that they allege requires a warning. The only evidence of reported injuries from riding the Wildcat came from Jeffrey Budgeon, Defendant HE & R's corporate representative regarding the operation of the Wildcat. Mr. Budgeon testified at his deposition that he was aware, from First-Aid reports, that there were occasional injuries reported. When asked to specify, Mr. Budgeon testified that "[t]here's an occasional complaint of whatever type of injury, be it neck; be it headache; be it I bumped my elbow; be it I stubbed my toe; be it a bug flew in my eye." While not specific, the court has little trouble concluding that these injuries are not on par with the injuries suffered by Tyler. Plaintiffs have the burden of coming forward with evidence showing that it was reasonably foreseeable that an injury like the one complained of could occur by riding the Wildcat. [Citation] They have not done so.

To the extent that Plaintiffs contend that Defendants had a duty to warn Tyler that he could suffer hearing loss, the court concludes that this too was not a reasonably foreseeable danger. Plaintiffs have adduced no evidence that Defendants knew or could have reasonably foreseen that a person could suffer hearing loss as a result of riding the Wildcat. Plaintiff's own medical expert acknowledges that "there are no published cases of roller coaster induced hearing loss." Furthermore, Defendants' expert's report states that "[t]here have been no reported "loss of hearing" claims on the Hershey Park Wildcat Roller Coaster since its opening in 1996. Over 9,000,000 guests have ridden the ride since its opening." Plaintiffs refuted none of this evidence. There was simply no basis for Defendants to conclude that they needed to warn about potential hearing loss, violent shaking, or head trauma, and Defendants had no duty to warn of those dangers not reasonably foreseeable.

[SUMMARY]

The crux of Plaintiffs claims is Defendants alleged failure to properly warn of the latent dangers of the Wildcat. The court concludes as a matter of law that the Wildcat contained sufficient warnings given the information possessed by Defendants and the reasonably foreseeable risks of injury. As such, the Wildcat was not "defective" and Plaintiffs' claims fail as a matter of law. This conclusion applies equally to Plaintiffs' strict liability claims and its claims for negligence. With adequate warnings there was no defect in the Wildcat, thus defeating Plaintiff's product liability claim. Furthermore, because the risk of harm complained of was not reasonably foreseeable to Defendants at the time of the injury, Defendants did not have a duty to warn, and, therefore, cannot have been negligent.

The court does not want to appear dismissive of the injuries suffered by Tyler. A loss of hearing certainly is a significant detriment; however, neither the law of negligence nor the law of products liability imposes absolute liability on Defendants. Absent a duty to warn and inadequate warnings, Defendants cannot be held liable as a matter of law, and the court will grant Defendants' joint motion for summary judgment as to all of the remaining counts.

NOTES AND QUESTIONS

1. It is not universal that the adequacy of a warning is a matter of law for the court; indeed, in many states, a warning is considered an issue of fact for the jury. This case is helpful, even if an outlier, to show how a factfinder might evaluate that factual question.
2. ASTM (previously known as the American Society for Testing and Materials), referenced in the case, is a standards organization. It is non-governmental and produces consensus technical standards for a wide range of topics, including amusement rides. Its standards are written by committee, and membership is open to anyone who is interested. (As noted in Chapter 6, for example, Kathy Fackler, a concerned parent, was part of ASTM for years.) It is not a regulatory agency and does not enforce compliance with its standards, though regulators or other governmental entities may adopt its standards by reference (as is the case in Pennsylvania). For example, the Consumer Product Safety Improvement Act of 2008 made an ASTM standard mandatory for certain toys pending potential additional regulations from the CPSC.

   Several dozen ASTM standards directly affect amusement rides, and others likely do so implicitly. These range from F2374-22 ("Standard Practice for Design, Manufacture, Operation, and Maintenance of Inflatable Amusement Devices") to F3158-22 ("Standard Practice for Patron Transportation Conveyors Used with a Water Related Amusement Ride or Device") to F2137-19 ("Standard Practice for Measuring the Dynamic Characteristics of Amusement Rides and Devices") to F3214-23 ("Standard Practice for Characterization of

Fire Properties of Seating, Upholstery, and Padding Materials for Vehicles Associated with Amusement Rides and Devices").

All major ride manufacturers design their rides to be consistent with ASTM standards (and EN standards, roughly the European equivalent), because such compliance is required by virtually all purchasers of such rides. Insurers likely also require parks to only buy rides that are compliant with such standards. As noted, though, the ASTM does not itself test rides for compliance, and the compliance is often self-tested.

3. If you were in a state where the adequacy of a warning was a jury issue, and you were sitting on a jury hearing this case, what would you have concluded?
4. Do you think most eleven-year-old children review the warnings about roller coasters as thoroughly as the plaintiff in this case testified he did? Do you think he did? What risks do you think the plaintiff was in fact aware of, whether from warnings or from observing the ride?
5. From what you understand about this ride, how would you craft signs for patrons (even if you think the warning sign as it existed is adequate)? What about if the coaster was entirely out of sight of the park, where patrons cannot see any of it?
6. Do you think Hersheypark should add a warning about the potential of hearing loss to the signs for Wildcat? Why or why not?
7. Wildcat was transformed into "Wildcat's Revenge" in 2022, where the wooden structure was kept but the coaster was made into a steel-tracked coaster. If you want to see what the prior version was like, search for "Hersheypark Wildcat POV" on YouTube and be sure you find a pre-2022 video. It was not, by my recollection, an unusually rough wooden coaster.
8. Do you think the doctrine of *res ipsa loquitur* should have a place in a case like this?
9. As in many cases, the depositions in this matter were really the end of at least large parts of the case—and the importance of those events is often not obvious in law school. Being really good at taking the deposition of plaintiff and fact witnesses—or of company representatives and the like—is usually more important than being really

good at being the person who stands up and argues and asks questions at trial.

Pierre v. Hilton Rose Hall Resort & Spa

2016 WL 4742281 (E.D.N.Y. Sept. 12, 2016)
(record citations omitted)

VERA M. SCANLON, United States Magistrate Judge

In this diversity action, Plaintiff seeks damages for personal injuries that he allegedly sustained on August 9, 2013, while vacationing at a hotel in Jamaica that, at the time, was owned and operated by Defendants. For the reasons stated herein, Defendants' motion for summary judgment is **granted in part and denied in part**.

I. FACTUAL BACKGROUND

At all relevant times to the within action, Defendants owned and operated the Rose Hall Resort (the "Resort") in Montego Bay, Jamaica. On or about August 9, 2013, Plaintiff was a guest at the Resort while vacationing with his family when he decided to ride the waterslide at the Resort's pool. There was one Resort staff member stationed at the top of the slide, but there were no staff members positioned at the bottom of the slide or in the pool itself. Plaintiff did not receive any directions or instructions from the staff member stationed at the top of the slide, nor did he observe any warning signs. Plaintiff rode the waterslide and was injured when his foot hit the bottom of the pool after he entered the water from the waterslide. According to Plaintiff, had he seen any warning signs, he "probably" would not have gone down the waterslide.

II. RELEVANT PROCEDURAL HISTORY

Plaintiff's Amended Complaint mentions various theories of liability—*i.e.*, the waterslide was in a defective/dangerous condition; the water level was at an unreasonable level; Defendants failed to properly supervise the pool, provide warning signs and/or barrier, or remove a dangerous condition—which are all alleged in the alternative.

Plaintiff's Fed. R. Civ. P. 26(a) disclosures, which were served approximately one month after the filing of the Amended Complaint, contain a section entitled, "Theory of Liability." This section states as follows:

> Defendants were negligent in the design, construction, operation, and supervision of the slide the Plaintiff sustained injuries upon, waterslide [*sic*], in its main pool area in that the water levels from the slide terminus outward to 6 feet in front of the slide terminus was not at a sufficient depth to prevent the Plaintiff's injuries. Failure to design the slide by the terminus to have a maximum angle of the slide runway at the exit between zero degrees and eleven degrees measured downward from horizontal and the failure of the Defendants to comply with the standards that conform [to] the Consumer Product Safety Act. The Defendants were negligent in failing to maintain the water depth by the slide terminus at the maximum water level in that area, although said depth was still below standards established by the Consumer Product Safety Act[.] [T]he Defendants have failed to properly warn Plaintiff that the drop area for the slide was below standards established for the safety of the swimming pool designs and operation. Therefore, the force obtained from riding the slide was excessive and consequently dangerous for entering the water at depth of less than five (5) feet and as a result[,] injuries may occur to the lower extremities, such as what happened to the Plaintiff.

After the close of discovery, Defendants sought to preclude the testimony of Plaintiff's proposed liability expert, Matthew Diamond, under Federal Rule of Evidence 702 and *Daubert v. Merrell Dow Pharms., Inc.*, 509 U.S. 579 (1993). Mr. Diamond intended to "opine that the depth of the pool present[ed] a danger to its users."

Following the filing of the fully briefed motion, oral argument was held, during which the Court orally granted Defendants' motion to exclude the testimony of Mr. Diamond, with a written decision to follow. Questioning the procedural posture of the case moving forward, the Court [asked how the case would proceed without the expert].

III. STANDARD OF REVIEW

[A typical standard of review discussion is omitted.]

IV. DISCUSSION

Neither the Amended Complaint nor Plaintiff's opposition papers is entirely clear but, as explained below, it appears that Plaintiff now seeks to assert two additional theories of liability: a products liability claim based on the failure-to-warn and negligence.

1. Products Liability

[New York law provides four possible theories for products liability claims:] (1) express warranty; (2) implied warranty; (3) negligence; and (4) strict liability. [Citations.] Plaintiff proceeds on a negligence theory only [and so he must show defect and causation].

Here, Plaintiff asserts a products liability claim based on two possible theories: design defect and failure-to-warn. The Court will address each in turn.

[Defective Design]

Plaintiff does not specifically so state, but his opposition papers suggest, that Plaintiff believes both the waterslide and pool were defectively designed. "Under New York law, a plaintiff asserting a claim for defective design must show that: (1) the product, as designed, posed a substantial likelihood of harm; (2) it was feasible to design the product in a safer manner; and (3) the defective design was a substantial factor in causing the plaintiff's injury." *Valente v. Textron, Inc.*, 931 F. Supp. 2d 409, 437 (E.D.N.Y. 2013).... "The first two prongs are often referred to as the risk-utility balancing test and are used to determine whether a product is defective or 'unreasonably dangerous.'" *Sorto-Romero v. Delta Int'l Mach. Corp.*, 05 Civ. 5172 (SJF) (AKT), 2007 WL 2816191 (E.D.N.Y. Sept. 24, 2007).... "Critically ... this analytical framework requires a plaintiff to prove, via expert testimony, the existence or feasibility of an alternative design which would have prevented the accident." *Beruashvili v. Hobart Corp.*, 05 Civ. 1646 (ENV) (MDG), 2010 U.S. Dist. LEXIS 146015, at *37 (E.D.N.Y. July 15, 2010) (citing *Rypkema v. Time Mfg. Co.*, 263 F. Supp. 2d 687, 691–92 (S.D.N.Y. 2003)); *Hilaire* [*v. DeWalt Indus. Tool Co.*], 54 F. Supp. 3d at 252 ("New York law requires plaintiffs to use expert testimony as to the feasibility and efficacy of alternative designs in order to prove a design defect.")....

Having already had the testimony of Plaintiff's expert, Mr. Diamond, excluded, Plaintiff does not offer any evidence that the pool or waterslide was defectively designed—let alone that any such defect was a substantial factor in causing Plaintiff's injury—or any evidence of the feasibility of an alternative design that would have otherwise prevented the accident.... Plaintiff argues that, even without expert testimony, he can nonetheless establish a design-defect claim through lay testimony. More particularly, Plaintiff claims this matter to be a "clear example ... where [a] jury requires no expert assistance," equating such a constraint to requiring a home construction expert to "attest to whether a broken stair in a house [i]s dangerous."

In theory, Plaintiff is correct insofar as, in limited circumstances, expert testimony may not be required to prove a design defect. Indeed, "[i]n cases where lay testimony is sufficient to allow a reasonable jury to find that the elements of a product defect have been set forth, courts have allowed plaintiffs to proceed even without any expert testimony." *Castaldi v. Land Rover N. Am., Inc.*, 06 Civ. 1008 (JG) (KAM), 2007 WL 4165283 (E.D.N.Y. Nov. 21, 2007); *Valente*, 931 F. Supp. 2d at 437 ("A plaintiff is generally required to provide expert testimony in order to establish the feasibility and efficacy of an alternative design, unless 'a reasonable alternative design is both obvious to, and understandable by, a layperson.'" (quoting *Soliman v. Daimler AG*, 10 Civ. 408 (SJF) (AKT), 2011 WL 4594313 (E.D.N.Y. Sept. 30, 2011)). In such cases, however, the relevant defects are "within the common knowledge of a juror." *Buckley v. Gen'l Motors Corp.*, 98 Civ. 4366 (BSJ), 2004 WL 725933 (S.D.N.Y. Apr. 2, 2004) ("A plaintiff need not introduce expert testimony to establish that a vehicle should neither veer nor lean to one direction if the driver is not steering in that direction, that a vehicle should slow down when the brake is applied, and that a vehicle should not roll over under normal driving conditions; such a conclusion is within the common knowledge of the jury."); see, e.g., *Faryniarz v. Nike, Inc.*, 00 Civ. 2632 (NRB), 2002 WL 530997 (S.D.N.Y. Apr. 8, 2002) (allowing plaintiff to prove a prima facie case of product liability without expert testimony regarding causation when the claim was that sneakers were defectively designed such that their laces would catch on their pull-tabs); W. Page Keeton et al., Prosser & Keeton on the Law of Torts §41, at 270 (5th ed. 1984) ("[C]ommon knowledge may provide a basis from which the causal sequence may be inferred.")....

Here, on the other hand, a lay person would neither readily understand nor necessarily find obvious the nature of pool and/or waterslide design. Designing a pool and waterslide, particularly in conjunction with one another, requires specialized and technical knowledge taking into account, among other topics: the proper length and/or angle of a waterslide bearing in mind the speed a user may reach while descending; the effect of friction created by a user's body and/or bathing suit on the waterslide; whether such friction is affected by water flow on the waterslide itself and/or water tube; and the proper depth and/or angle of a pool floor, bearing in mind the varying weight of users and the speed at which such users will reach while riding the waterslide in order to allow for safe entry into the water.... To be clear, this is not a situation where Plaintiff has presented evidence that the angle of the waterslide or depth of the pool was so patently defective such that common knowledge could dictate a finding that Defendants are liable under this theory. [] In fact, neither party has provided the Court with competent evidence of the length/angle of the waterslide or the depth of the pool on the day of the accident.[]

As Plaintiff has provided no expert testimony as to a reasonable, alternative pool and/or waterslide design, and such evidence is required by New York law under the circumstances, his negligence claim, insofar as it is premised on the theory that Defendants' pool and/or waterslide was defectively designed, is dismissed.

[Failure to Warn]

In addition to a theory of products liability predicated upon a defective design, Plaintiff seeks to recover based upon a theory of failure-to-warn.

[The court concluded that Plaintiff had adequately, if inartfully, alleged a failure to warn claim such that the Defendants were on notice of the claim.]

As noted above, Plaintiff claims that Defendants failed to warn him of the "risk and dangers associated with the use" of the subject pool and/or waterslide and the "risk of striking the bottom of the pool."

"To establish a claim for failure to warn, a plaintiff must prove that: '(1) a manufacturer has a duty to warn; (2) against dangers resulting from foreseeable uses about which it knew or should have known; and (3) that failure to do so was the proximate cause of the harm."[] *Valente*, 931 F. Supp. 2d at 440....

"[W]hether warnings were adequate to deter potential misuse and whether the failure to warn was a substantial cause of the injury is ordinarily a question for the jury." *Clarke v. LR Sys.*, 219 F. Supp. 2d 323, 329 (E.D.N.Y. 2002) (citing *Howard v. Poseidon Pools, Inc.*, 530 N.E.2d 1280, 1281 (1988)); see *Mustafa v. Halkin Tool, Ltd.*, 00 Civ. 4851 (DGT), 2007

WL 959704 (E.D.N.Y. Mar. 29, 2007). "However, a court may dismiss a failure-to-warn claim as a matter of law if: (1) the defendant had no duty to warn because the hazard was patently dangerous or posed an open and obvious risk; or (2) the plaintiff cannot prove causation because 'the injured party was fully aware of the hazard through general knowledge, observation or common sense, or participated in the removal of a safety device whose purpose is obvious.'" *Clarke*, 219 F. Supp. 2d at 329 (quoting *Liriano v. Hobart Corp.*, 700 N.E.2d 303, 308 (1998)); see *Burke v. Spartanics Ltd.*, 252 F.3d 131, 137 (2d Cir. 2001) (no causation when plaintiff was actually aware of the danger of placing his hand in the cutting plane of a metal shearing machine); *Howard*, 530 N.E.2d at 1281 (no causation when the plaintiff, with general knowledge of pools and common sense, dove into shallow end and was injured). "In both of these scenarios, the duty to warn is effectively vitiated by the factual circumstances." *Rogers v. Westfalia Associated Techs.*, 485 F. Supp. 2d 121, 129 (N.D.N.Y. 2007).

Relatedly, "[u]nder the primary assumption of risk doctrine, 'by engaging in a sport or recreational activity, a participant consents to those commonly appreciated risks which are inherent in and arise out of the nature of the sport generally and flow from such participation.'" *Charles v. Young Life Lake Champion*, 11 Civ. 401 (VB), 2013 U.S. Dist. LEXIS 77067, at *9, 2013 WL 2362242 (S.D.N.Y. May 21, 2013) (quoting *Morgan v. State*, 685 N.E.2d 202, 207 (1997)); *Leslie v. Splish Splash at Adventureland*, 766 N.Y.S.2d 599, 599 (2nd Dept. 2003) ("A plaintiff is barred from recovery for injuries which occur during voluntary sporting or recreational activities if it is determined that he or she assumed the risk as a matter of law."); *Turcotte v. Fell*, 502 N.E.2d 964, 968 (1986) (noting participants consented "to those injury-causing events which are known, apparent or reasonably foreseeable consequences of the participation"). "The proprietor of a recreational venue therefore has only 'a duty to exercise care to make the conditions as safe as they appear to be. If the risks of the activity are fully comprehended or perfectly obvious, plaintiff has consented to them and defendant has performed its duty.'" *Charles*, 2013 U.S. Dist. LEXIS 77067, at *9, 2013 WL 2362242 (quoting *Morgan*, 685 N.E.2d at 207 & *Turcotte*, 502 N.E.2d 964 at 968). "This consent extends to 'readily appreciable' risks from open and obvious or 'less than optimal' conditions at the venue, but not to risks that are concealed, unreasonably enhanced by the proprietor, or 'unique and … dangerous condition[s] over and above the usual dangers that are inherent in the sport.'" *Id.* (quoting *Morgan*, 685 N.E.2d at 207); see *Martin v. State*, 878 N.Y.S.2d 823, 826 (3rd Dept. 2009) ("[I]t is irrelevant that a defendant could feasibly have provided safer conditions.").

Defendants argue that Plaintiff was fully aware of the risks associated with riding the waterslide, and assumed those risks, as he knew he would fall into the water after the riding the waterslide and knew he could be injured doing so. Plaintiff counters that risk of injuring his foot by hitting same at the bottom of the pool "could not have been 'comprehended' and ... was far from 'perfectly obvious[,]' as the law requires" in order to negate Defendants' duty to warn or to invoke the assumption of risk defense.

The Court agrees with Plaintiff that Defendants have not met their burden to establish that, based on the undisputed facts and construing those facts in the light most favorable to Plaintiff, the hazard of which Plaintiff complains was so patently obvious so as to negate Defendants' duty to warn, see *Clarke*, 219 F. Supp. 2d at 329, or that the relevant risks were readily appreciable such that Plaintiff assumed such risks, see *Charles*, 2013 U.S. Dist. LEXIS 77067, at *9, 2013 WL 2362242.

Defendants cite only one case, *Clarke v. LR Sys.*, 219 F. Supp. 2d 323 (E.D.N.Y. 2003), in support of their argument. In *Clarke*, the plaintiff was injured when he stuck his hand in a plastic grinding machine, which he had operated for several years, in order to clear a blockage without first turning off the power source. See *Clarke*, 219 F. Supp. 2d at 327–28. The District Court granted summary judgment on the plaintiff's failure-to-warn claim explaining that the plaintiff acknowledged several times in his deposition that "he knew it was dangerous to put his hand [in the machine] without first turning off the power," and thus, the plaintiff was "actually aware of the danger." *Clarke*, 219 F. Supp. 2d at 330. Analogizing the within matter to *Clarke*, Defendants argue that Plaintiff "was aware before using the waterslide of the chance of getting hurt riding it." Defendants cite to Plaintiff's deposition to establish this point:

> Q: Did you have an understanding there was a chance you c[ould] get hurt riding the waterslide before you went on it?
>
> A: I know I am going to—because I saw some people going down.

There are two problems with Defendants' argument. First, Defendants do not present a full statement of Plaintiff's testimony. For clarity sake, the entire colloquy is as follows:

> Q: Did you have an understanding there was a chance you c[ould] get hurt riding the waterslide before you went on it?
>
> A: I know I am going to—because I saw some people going down. It looks like they were having fun. I wasn't thinking[,] if I get on this tube[,] I'm going to end up breaking a leg or possibly seriously injured or even death. That didn't cross my mind at all.

Read in context, Plaintiff clearly did not acknowledge being aware of any danger prior to using the waterslide.[] At best, the portion of the transcript cited by Defendants is more appropriately described as a broken thought.

Second, even if Plaintiff was generally aware that he could be injured, this argument misses the mark. "[T]he issue here is not whether Plaintiff understood injury could result from using the [waterslide], as Defendants contend. Rather, the issue is whether, under the circumstances, Plaintiff knew or could foresee the risk he was undertaking." *Charles*, 2013 U.S. Dist. LEXIS 77067, at *11, 2013 WL 2362242. As succinctly stated in a factually similar, waterslide-based action:

> Here, [Plaintiff] was engaged in the recreational activity of riding down a waterslide. [Plaintiff], however, was not injured by coming into contact with the interior of the slide[,] ... he did not collide into another rider and was not injured by hitting a barrier clearly placed to keep riders from going too far in the splash pool. [] This is not a situation where the waterslide and splash pool functioned in the way they were intended to function, but an injury nonetheless occurred. Instead, [the waterslide and/or pool] did not function as it was intended. The dangerous condition posed by the ride was unique and over and above the usual dangers that are inherent in riding down a water slide. On this record, [the Court] cannot conclude that [Plaintiff] had an appreciation of the nature of the risks presented, and was aware of the risk that the ... pool

> would be inadequate to bring him to a safe halt upon his exit from the slide.

Mussara v. Mega Funworks, Inc., 952 N.Y.S.2d 568, 573 (2nd Dept. 2012) (internal quotations and citations omitted); see *Kriz v. Schum*, 549 N.E.2d 1155, 1160 (1989) (denying summary judgment on failure-to-warn claim where the plaintiff executed a headfirst belly slide through an inner tube into a pool rendering her a quadriplegic and no warning labels were affixed to the slide).

Accordingly, an issue of fact remains as to whether the legal cause of Plaintiff's injury was the allegedly negligent conduct of Defendants in failing to affix warnings to the waterslide and/or pool or to otherwise warn Plaintiff of the risk of striking the bottom of the pool when riding the waterslide. Therefore, Defendants' motion for summary judgment seeking to dismiss Plaintiff's negligence claim, insofar as it is premised on the theory that Defendants failed to warn Plaintiff, is denied.

NOTES AND QUESTIONS

1. Failure to warn claims and primary assumption of risk of inherent risks often overlap, as here, since obvious risks as to which no warnings are required often overlap with the "commonly-appreciated risks which are inherent in and arise out of such [sporting or recreational] activity generally, and which flow from the participation." *Leslie v. Splish Splash at Adventureland, Inc.*, 766 N.Y.S.2d 599 (Mem.) (2003).

2. The contexts in which expert testimony is or is not required to establish a defect (design or warning) vary and are the subject of much debate. The general concept—that it is required for anything that is beyond the "ken of the jury"—is relatively well-accepted, but what all fits into the "ken" box is unpredictable at best. (As an aside, this is also the only time I ever hear the word "ken" used in this sense, meaning, roughly, the understanding or knowledge of the jury.)

   In the context of design defect allegations, most courts agree that most cases involving the risk/benefit standard require experts, except for absurd situations. (The *Pierre* court, in a footnote, suggests the example that expert testimony might not be required "if Plaintiff presented evidence that the waterslide was built at a near 90 degree angle, or the pool depth at the waterslide terminus was 10 inches deep." *Pierce.* at n.7.)

But the requirement of expert testimony gets murkier when discussing the consumer expectations standard, applied in some states and in some contexts. That standard asks the jury to compare what a reasonable consumer would expect from a product and compare it to what happened, determining if the consumer expectations were satisfied. Such a standard best fits in cases with relatively simple products, such that a consumer would have reasonably discernible expectations. It is probably already obvious to you that determining when that is the case itself overlaps with cases where it would not be beyond the ken of the jury—again, for example, the 90-degree waterslide.

In *Huzinec v. Six Flags*, No. 21-1950, 2023 WL 1433633 (3d Cir. Feb. 1, 2023), the plaintiff alleged injuries while riding El Toro, a roller coaster at Six Flags Great Adventure in New Jersey, when another patron dropped her cell phone and it hit the plaintiff. His allegation centered on Six Flags's loose objects policy and its enforcement. The district court had concluded that the plaintiff's expert was not qualified to testify about the standard of care as to that policy and granted summary judgment, concluding that expert testimony was required on that topic. The Third Circuit reversed (in an unpublished opinion), applying New Jersey law, concluding that the issue is not so complicated as to require an expert: "We believe that the average person can understand the risk Six Flags created by permitting patrons to carry unsecured cell phones on a roller coaster. Thus, we conclude New Jersey law did not require Huzinec to produce an expert to identify the standard of care." *Id.* The other cases that the trial court cited were, the Third Circuit concluded, involved more complicated issues. For example, in *Velasquez v. Land of Make Believe*, 2012 WL 986982 (N.J. Super. A.D., 2012), the court had properly required expert testimony to address the state regulatory scheme, "as it bore on the plaintiff's allegations that overcrowding led to her being stepped on an[d] injured by another patron." *Huzinec* at *2. The expert was necessary to show what the staffing and operation was, compared to the regulatory requirements. In *Bomtempo v. Six Flags Great Adventure LLC*, likewise, an expert was necessary to establish the standard of care for a waterslide's maintenance and operations, all in the context of the more complex aquatic safety world. *Bomtempo v. Six Flags Great Adventure LLC*, 2016 WL 4729642 (N.J. Super. A.D., 2016).

3. Consider who the likely experts are in amusement ride or similar cases. For design defects, the obvious candidates are other ride designers, but of course, people in an industry tend not to want to testify against others in the industry, even if competitors. Ride inspectors (or retired ride inspectors) often appear in that role, though query whether that population is best equipped to testify about the design of rides as opposed to the maintenance or operation of rides. For warnings claims, specific expertise in the amusement field is probably less critical (though still helpful), making it so that experts with more general backgrounds are probably often adequate—but even there, experts who have done a lot in designing ride warnings are probably more appealing to a jury and more accessible to defendants.
4. In the *Pierre* case, Plaintiff's sole expert was named Matthew Diamond. Quoting from the Court's opinion excluding his testimony (omitting record citations):

> Plaintiff's expert disclosures did not contain Mr. Diamond's curriculum vitae or an explanation of his qualifications as required by Fed. R. Civ. P. 26(a)(2)(B)(iv), but Mr. Diamond testified to his background at his deposition.
>
> Mr. Diamond's highest level of education is high school, and he is currently self-employed as the owner of a pool service company called "The Pool Lady," which conducts service, maintenance and renovations on residential and commercial pools. Prior to owning The Pool Lady, Mr. Diamond was a "partner" at a general construction company in Florida from 2000–2009 called "Gold Coast Construction Services." Approximately 5% of the work completed by Mr. Diamond while at Gold Coast Construction Services pertained to pool construction repairs, none of which involved waterslides. From 1990–2000, Mr. Diamond worked for The Pool Lady, which, at the time, was owned by his mother.
>
> Simply stated, Mr. Diamond lacks any relevant qualifications to serve as an expert witness on the propriety of the subject pool and/or waterslide design. The entirety of Mr. Diamond's experience in this area amounts to providing

construction and maintenance pool services. During Mr. Diamond's 25-year career in the pool industry, he has never: (1) designed any structural specifications for pools; (2) designed any structural specifications for waterslides; or (3) approved any pool-design or pool-construction drawings. At best, Mr. Diamond's qualifications are limited to physically building a pool, a different task than designing a pool or a waterslide, which, as Mr. Diamond acknowledged at his deposition, he—unlike engineers or architects—is unqualified to do.

> In sum, while Mr. Diamond may be entirely qualified to offer testimony on whether a particular pool or waterslide was built according to predetermined specifications—a topic not at issue in this litigation—he is not qualified to opine on whether the design specifications of the subject pool and/or waterslide (design specifications which, as described below, he did not review) were designed in accordance with applicable safety standards (applicable safety standards with which, as described below, he was unacquainted) or whether the alleged failure to abide by the applicable safety standards caused Plaintiff's injuries (about which, as described below, he affirmatively stated he has no opinion). Accordingly, Mr. Diamond is not qualified to offer testimony regarding the standard of care or breach thereof related to the subject pool or waterslide design, or the designs' alleged causation of Plaintiff's injuries. This precludes his testimony in its entirety.

Pierre v. Hilton Rose Hall Resort & Spa, No. 14-Civ-3790 (VMS), Memorandum and Order, Mar. 28, 2016. While the rules of admissibility of expert testimony in full are beyond the scope of this casebook, the court's analysis of the factors is concise and instructive:

> [T]here is no decisive list of factors to be considered when evaluating a *Daubert* motion. *Daubert*, 509 U.S. at 593–94. "Nevertheless, whether the theory can and has been tested, whether it has been subject to peer review, the technique's potential rate of error, and whether the technique has been 'generally accepted' in the relevant profes-

sional or academic community have all been identified as relevant considerations." *Buchwald v. Renco Grp.*, 13 Civ. 7948 (AJN), 2015 U.S. Dist. LEXIS 110140, at *23 (S.D.N.Y. Aug. 19, 2015).... Here, Mr. Diamond's proposed testimony falls dramatically short of the required standards of reliability as he cannot satisfy any of these four factors.

Plaintiff seeks to have Mr. Diamond testify that the subject pool and/or waterslide were improperly designed so as to prevent Plaintiff from safely entering the water via the waterslide. In his report, Mr. Diamond provides opinions regarding the depth of the pool and the height of the water at the waterslide terminus, which, in essence, is his "theory." [] Yet, in support of his theory, he fails to provide any of the following: citations to applicable pool-design safety standards, citations to applicable waterslide-design safety standards, testing he conducted, science or engineering he consulted or utilized, methodology he used, or alternative pool and/or waterslide designs he created or reviewed. In other words, Mr. Diamond has not shown that his theory has been tested or subjected to peer review, whether the (non-existent) testing has been generally accepted by the relevant professional community or whether there is an identifiable rate of error. Along the same vein, Mr. Diamond's failure to provide an alternative pool and/or waterslide design, in and of itself, justifies the exclusion of Mr. Diamond's testimony....

Moreover, even if Mr. Diamond had provided any of this information, conducted appropriate testing, or created alternative designs, there is no information in the record as to how he would have correctly done so given the lack of facts and data given to him. See Fed. R. Evid. 702(b) ("A witness who is qualified as an expert ... may testify in the form of an opinion or otherwise if ... the testimony is based on sufficient facts or data."). According to Mr. Diamond, the only document he reviewed prior to offering his report was a single photograph of the "bottom section of the [water] slide." Mr. Diamond did not undertake his own investigation as he did not: (1) speak to or interview Plaintiff; (2) read Plaintiff's deposition transcript; (3) visit the resort or inspect the subject pool or waterslide; (4) read any other document produced in the litigation; (5) review, or even claim to be aware of, pool- or waterslide-safety standards, statutes or codes applicable in Jamaica; or (6) review any engineering specifications, drawings or blueprints of the pool or waterslide. Some or all of this information would be necessary to any expert's proposed opinion on the propriety and safety of the subject pool and/or waterslide designs and whether the designs played a part in causing Plaintiff's injuries. Mr. Diamond made no effort to collect the underlying facts or data necessary to undertake a scientific and disciplined approach to proffering a bona fide expert opinion.

In fact, Mr. Diamond candidly admitted that, without any of the necessary facts or data, he is unable [to] opine on the depth of the subject pool, the water level of the subject pool or the cause of Plaintiff's injury:

Q: You don't know the floor of this pool at Rose Hall because you never inspected or saw any spec[ification]s?

A: That's correct.

Q: This 3-foot 6-inch pool depth could be okay if the bottom of the pool was sloped accordingly?

A: If it is sloped accordingly, that is possible.

Q: Is it true that you couldn't render an opinion absolutely that this pool is not deep enough at 3 feet 6 inches because you don't know that other information?

A: I don't believe anybody could, correct.

****

Q: Is it fair to say that a synopsis of your opinion is that you didn't have enough information to determine whether the plaintiff was injured because this water-

> slide was unreasonably dangerous or defective in some way?
>
> A: That is correct.
>
> Simply stated, Mr. Diamond cannot assist the trier of fact where his opinions, whatever those opinions may be, amount to mere speculation as to whether an alternatively designed pool or waterslide would have led to a different result when Plaintiff used the subject pool and waterslide. Mr. Diamond's submissions lack any factual foundation that would demonstrate the reliability of his opinions; his opinions are conclusory and classic ipse dixit. [] Moreover, Plaintiff cannot use Mr. Diamond to complete the factual record.

Id. An amendment to Rule 702 went into effect on December 1, 2023, mostly addressing methodology issues and emphasizing the importance of trial courts acting as gatekeepers. Note that Mr. Diamond's lack of advanced education does not preclude him from qualifying as an expert, since experience can suffice. But he did not qualify on that path either. What additional experience do you think would have been enough?

5. Why do you think summary judgment was denied here but granted in the Hersheypark hearing loss case that preceded it?
6. Consider the Raven incident described in Chapter 3, where Tamar Fellner died after being ejected from the roller coaster at Holiday World. The trains in operation on that roller coaster had two forms of restraints, you will recall: an individual ratcheting lapbar and an individual seatbelt. The former, once pressed down onto the patron, could not be released except by the ride operators. The latter, in contrast, was, like car or airplane seatbelts, in the control of the rider. In the final investigatory report issued by local prosecutors, the car was described as follows: "Fellner's seatbelt was found unfastened and each end was tucked between the cushion and the sidewall on both sides of her seat. The lap bar where she had been sitting was down." The lawsuit that followed included these allegations about design:

> PTC owed a duty to Tamar, and to all riders of The Raven for that matter, to design and manufacture "restraints"

> within the cars of The Raven in such a manner that ejection therefrom during the operation thereof would be impossible.... PTC breached that duty by ... failing to safely develop, design, manufacture, test, and/or inspect the "restraints" within the cars for The Raven to prevent Tamar's ejection therefrom while riding the Raven.... As a direct and proximate result thereof, Tamar was killed.

Complaint, *Fellner v. Philadelphia Toboggan Coasters, Inc. and Koch Development Corporation,* No. 2:05-cv-02052-BMS (E.D. Pa. April 29, 2005).

Do you think it is a defective design to have a seatbelt that can be unfastened by a patron? Are there downsides to restraints that can only be removed by a ride operator, and, if so, are they downsides that are relevant to the determination of a design defect? If a ride has two restraints, is it reasonable to require that both of them be in place for effective protection from ejection? When designing restraints for a ride, how much rider "misconduct" should be anticipated? Does it matter to your answer to that question if the ride has a height requirement such that it will mostly have adults as riders?

Holiday World, where that incident occurred, now has this language on its coaster signs (among other things), citing Indiana's Rider Responsibility Statute: "Patrons have a duty to properly use all ride or device safety equipment provided. In addition, Holiday World & Splashin' Safari require Guests to exercise good judgment and act in a responsible manner while riding. Any Guest who tampers with a safety device (such as a lap bar or seatbelt) or fails to follow safety instructions will be escorted from the park without a refund."

7. Recall also the Superman: Ride of Steel case from Six Flags New England. Mr. Mordarsky had cerebral palsy, and the investigators included this as one of the contributing factors:

> **Pre-existing medical condition.** Massachusetts regulations 520 CMR 5.03(6)(e) requires patrons to notify the ride operator of any pre-existing health conditions that may negatively [affect] the health and safety of the patron if they were to ride an amusement device. Based on witness testimony of ride operators, first responders and

> statements volunteered by his family to the press, [Mordarsky] failed to notify the ride operator of his pre-existing medical conditions that should have prevented him from getting on the ride.

Do you think (setting aside only for now the overlay of accessibility requirements under U.S. law) that a ride design is reasonable if it requires patrons to have full control over their bodies? If a patron is able to get around the park, whether in a wheelchair or on foot or otherwise, does a reasonable ride design exclude them from being able to ride the ride?

To look at the question a different way, what if a patron unexpectedly passes out while a coaster is on the lift hill. Should the ride restraints ensure that the patron will get back to the station still in the car?

That final question was suggested to me by Dr. Kathryn Woodcock, a professor in Toronto Metropolitan University's School of Occupational and Public Health and director of the THRILL Lab (Tools for Holistic Ride Inspection Learning and Leadership). A human factors expert, she teaches and researches about accident theory, safety evaluation, and other topics. In 2018, Dr. Woodcock published one of her multiple articles about the intersection of disability and safety in amusement attractions. Its abstract reads:

> Eligibility to participate on an amusement attraction may be limited for patrons with certain characteristics, including size, age, disability, and health conditions. Human rights and equal access laws increasingly mandate the inclusion of people with disabilities in as many activities as possible, although safety is an accepted basis for exemption. This paper reports on practices and evidence pertaining to eligibility and safety of patrons with disabilities, including a content analysis of status quo criteria from 100 amusement ride manufacturers' manuals and prevalence of references to disability in reports of serious and fatal injury. The analysis found that restrictive criteria exclude people with disabilities broadly, while permitting other vulnerable populations to self-determine their participation. Publicly available injury data do not provide evidence to justify the

> extent of mandatory exclusion. Self-selection appears to be sufficient where it is used but expanding self-selection will require more communication to patrons about the functional requirements of each ride.

Woodcock, *Disability and participation in amusement attractions*, Journal of Themed Experience and Attractions Research 1, 38–53 (2018). She observes that ride manufacturers, seeking to avoid potential liability, have an incentive to set forth rider requirements that over-exclude in the interest of avoiding even unlikely risks, while ride owners have additional incentives due to their exposure to regulatory and other requirements relating to accessibility and patron interests (and the desire to have more, rather than fewer, people be able to ride). After a detailed analysis of admittedly limited data (including injury data and ride manuals, among other things), she concludes:

> Eligibility criteria that exclude "disability" or the equivalent are more prevalent than injury evidence appears to warrant, as there is no clear evidence that people with disabilities are at undue risk when permitted to self-select, given clear description of ride requirements. Although there are rides that are not suitable for some patrons, existing manufacturers' manuals lack the information needed to restrict only those patrons who cannot participate safely. Self-selection appears to be sufficient to exclude vulnerable riders with disabilities (although not all vulnerable riders, such as the adults overrepresented in the quarterly reports). However, patrons will need information about functional requirements of the ride to make appropriate, safe choices.

In an earlier paper, Dr. Woodcock advocated for a "human factors engineering approach" rather than a "medical approach" to evaluating eligibility to go on rides:

> The human factors engineering approach complements existing ride analysis methods used in existing standards and can be implemented by the designer/engineer. Unlike the medical approach, an exhaustive analysis of all disabilities and conditions is not required for the human factors engi-

> neering approach, and only those guests whose disability specifically limits a required function would be excluded from participation, which is easier to defend under equity legislation. The human factors approach is implemented through risk communication at the individual attraction, including operational practices, and may be supplemented with guest information materials such as printed matter and central guest-relations resources. Informed self-selection formalizes the responsibility of the guest or their agent, while focusing the manufacturer's and owner/operator's responsibility on clearly identifying and communicating the functional requirements needed for safely riding and the expected outcome of participation without the minimum required functional abilities. Transparent functional risk rationales may be more convincing to support guest self-selection and respects the dignity and autonomy of guests with disabilities, which may promote harmonious guest relations.

Woodcock, *Determining participation eligibility for amusement attractions*, PROCEDIA MANUFACTURING 3, 5389–96 (2015).

If you were advising a park or manufacturer on whether to consider a "medical approach" (where eligibility is based, basically, on what category of disability a patron has) or a "human factors approach" (where it is instead based on what the patron is able to do, largely based on their own views), which would you recommend and why?

8. The goals of having potential liability for a failure to warn is to facilitate fully informed choices by patrons and the promotion of safe use. One helpful articulation of the standard comes from *Pavlides v. Galveston Yacht Basin*, 737 F.2d 330 (5th Cir. 1984): "A warning must (1) be designed so it can reasonably be expected to catch the attention of the consumer; (2) be comprehensible and give a fair indication of the specific risks involved with the product; and (3) be of an intensity justified by the magnitude of the risk." *Id.* at 338.

   John Riggleman, a retired Universal manager, has helpfully broken down the categories of warning signs used at amusement parks as (a) primary, (b) secondary, (c) load, and (d) on-board. Of course, the extent to which parks or carnivals use a strategy like this is wildly variable; in my experience, most traveling rides have one sign that tries to do it all. But when there are these multiple stages of signs, the goals vary a bit as the patron goes through the queue.

The *primary* signs are at the entrance of each attraction and are largely focused on the informed choice aspect. Ideally, it has a description of the attraction, ridership requirements, and accessibility information. The description is particularly important when the attraction is not visible to patrons.

At Universal Studios, for example, the Harry Potter and the Forbidden Journey ride is entirely inside and what it entails is hard to describe—and the park, no doubt, wishes to avoid "spoilers" while still giving a clear description of what is to come. Here's what they ended up with for the primary sign:

Notice from the
Department of Magical Games and Sports
WARNING!
This ride simulates dramatic aerobatics.
The ride vehicle will suddenly accelerate, stop, turn,
climb, and drop.
Failure
to follow posted guidelines
may result in serious injury
Or expulsion from the park.

Some similar rides will have animated videos outside the ride showing the nature of the ride vehicle motion without actually showing what's going on in terms of the magical creatures and such.

The *secondary warning* signs are typically distributed throughout the queue, and focus again on ridership requirements. Access information and the ride description is typically not repeated, on the theory that the patron has made the choice to ride at the *primary* sign and the job now is to reiterate what they need to do in order to ride safely.

The *load* signs are often more abbreviated, and focus on how to safely ride. At this point, the notion is, the patrons have seen the signs and the instructions, and now it's about reminders of the key stuff. Most parks also have "spiels," which are either pre-recorded or live-read announcements describing how to load safely, with reminders about key safety issues.

Likewise, the *on-board* warning signs are about how to safely ride ("remain seated at all times," "keep your hands and feet inside the vehicle," etc.). Sometimes there will be specific reminders at specific places during rides—for example, on log flumes, I often see "Stay seated!" signs just before the final big drop, presumably trying to deter people from trying to get out to avoid the big splash.

How should parks address multi-lingual attendee populations? Attendees who cannot read at all?

What about rides that include content that will be upsetting to a small but not zero number of people? The Harry Potter ride referenced above, for example, includes images of hundreds or thousands of spiders. (Spoiler alert, I guess, for the very famous Harry Potter ride, introduced in 2010.) Dr. Woodcock has shared that she is scared of spiders and only knew about them because she had seen early design drawings for the ride. Should other arachnophobes be upset that the ride warnings do not talk about spiders? If they experience emotional distress, should that be actionable?

How many patrons do you think read the signs outside attractions? Should parks do more to try to increase that number? Do you think signs like this affect behavior?

A notable contrast with the phased and strategic warnings like those described above for the Harry Potter ride is, at least often, the single sign outside traveling rides. The Zipper is a very popular ride, first released in 1968, that fits on a single trailer. Its cars rotate on their own axis, travel on a track around the long boom, which is itself rotating around a central axis. (It's hard to describe, but easy to find videos of online.) At least at the Minnesota State Fair, it receives essentially the same sign as other attractions, including this portion:

GUEST SHOULD [*sic*] EXPECT
STRONG SIDE TO SIDE FORCES
RAPIDLY CHANGING TURBULENT FORCES
STRONG FRONT TO BACK FORCES
RAPIDLY CHANGING HEIGHTS

THIS ATTRACTION IS NOT RECOMMENDED FOR GUEST [*sic*] WITH:

HEART PROBLEMS	**HIGH BLOOD PRESSURE**
BACK & NECK PROBLEMS	**PREGACY [*sic*]**
NO SMOKING	**SICKNESS**
NO DRUGS	

I encourage you to find a video of the Zipper, but if there is one thing the ride does *not* have, it is "strong side to side forces." The forces are extreme but only in one plane. Apart from that, does this sign give useful guidance? If someone has a cold, should they be precluded from riding? What if they suffer from ADHD? If they have asymptomatic prostate cancer? Are people who are smokers precluded from riding as long as they are not smoking while on it?

Many (but not all) states follow a so-called heeding presumption: the notion that, in a warnings case, a jury can be told of a rebuttable presumption that, if a proper warning had been given, it would have been heeded (that is, followed by the plaintiff). This permits a plaintiff to establish causation even if the empirical evidence suggests that consumers do not follow warnings. It is adopted, in most cases, based on public policy (the desire to create incentives for good warnings) rather than on empirical evidence (any sort of belief that it reflects reality). *See Coffman v. Keene Corp.*, 133 N.J. 581, 597 (N.J., 1993) (agreeing with defendant that "the heeding presumption is not firmly based on empirical evidence" but that it "can be grounded in public policy").

> The heeding presumption thus serves to reinforce the basic duty to warn—to encourage manufacturers to produce safer products, and to alert users of the hazards arising from the use of those products through effective warnings. The duty to warn exists not only to protect and alert product users but to encourage manufacturers and industries, which benefit from placing products into the stream of commerce, to remain apprised of the hazards posed by a product. The use of the heeding presumption provides a powerful incentive for manufacturers to abide by their duty to provide adequate warnings.

Id. at 599.

CHAPTER 9

Strategy and Ethics

This chapter is different than most casebook chapters. After some introductory matters, it is made up of lengthy excerpts from primary source materials relating to a tragic case that occurred at Glenwood Caverns Adventure Park in Colorado in the fall of 2021, resulting in the death of a young girl on a drop ride. As I noted back in the introductory materials, a big part of litigation is navigating and interpreting things like the reports below, which can be dense and tricky to follow. Here's your chance to do so.

While we are not at the end of the course materials, you can think of it as a capstone to the course to date. As of this writing, the civil case is still pending. Your professor may use it in various ways, but regardless of assignments, I hope you will work through the materials thinking about how they would affect how you would approach the case if you represented the family, the park, the ride manufacturer, or someone else involved. Think also about how the lessons learned from the litigation should affect the park going forward, or others in the industry. Specifically, think about it also not just from the point of view of litigation, but also in the context of how such tragedies might be avoided in the future.

Minnesota Rules of Professional Conduct

Adopted by the Minnesota Supreme Court
October 1, 2005

RULE 3.1: MERITORIOUS CLAIMS AND CONTENTIONS

A lawyer shall not bring or defend a proceeding, or assert or controvert an issue therein, unless there is a basis in law and fact for doing so that is not frivolous, which includes a good faith argument for an extension, modification, or reversal of existing law....

Comment

[1] The advocate has a duty to use legal procedure for the fullest benefit of the client's cause, but also a duty not to abuse legal procedure. The law, both procedural and substantive, establishes the limits within which an advocate may proceed. However, the law is not always clear and never is static. Accordingly, in determining the proper scope of advocacy, account must be taken of the law's ambiguities and potential for change.

[2] The filing of an action or defense or similar action taken for a client is not frivolous merely because the facts have not first been fully substantiated or because the lawyer expects to develop vital evidence only by discovery. What is required of lawyers, however, is that they inform themselves about the facts of their clients' cases and the applicable law and determine that they can make good faith arguments in support of their clients' positions. Such action is not frivolous even though the lawyer believes that the client's position ultimately will not prevail. The action is frivolous, however, if the lawyer is unable either to make a good faith argument on the merits of the action taken or to support the action taken by a good faith argument for an extension, modification or reversal of existing law.

RULE 3.4: FAIRNESS TO OPPOSING PARTY AND COUNSEL

A lawyer shall not:

(a) unlawfully obstruct another party's access to evidence or unlawfully alter, destroy, or conceal a document or other material having potential evidentiary value. A lawyer shall not counsel or assist another person to do any such act;

(b) falsify evidence, counsel or assist a witness to testify falsely, or offer an inducement to a witness that is prohibited by law;

(c) knowingly disobey an obligation under the rules of a tribunal except for an open refusal based on an assertion that no valid obligation exists;

(d) in pretrial procedure, make a frivolous discovery request or fail to make a reasonably diligent effort to comply with a legally proper discovery request by an opposing party;

(e) in trial, allude to any matter that the lawyer does not reasonably believe is relevant or that will not be supported by admissible evidence, assert personal knowledge of facts in issue except when testifying as a witness, or state a personal opinion as to the justness of a cause, the credibility of a witness, the culpability of a civil litigant or the guilt or innocence of an accused; or

(f) request a person other than a client to refrain from voluntarily giving relevant information to another party unless:

(1) the person is a relative or an employee or other agent of a client; and

(2) the lawyer reasonably believes that the person's interests will not be adversely affected by refraining from giving such information.

NOTES AND QUESTIONS

1. As is emphasized in the comments to the Rules of Professional Conduct, the law changes and the lines that regulate lawyer conduct can be fuzzy.
2. In Chapter 3, you read excerpts from the book about Action Park. As noted there, the park was popular (or notorious, depending on your point of view) for giving patrons a lot of control over their experience and not giving them a lot of guidance about how to avoid danger. In this excerpt, we learn more about the park's legal strategy.

Andy Mulvihill with Jake Rossen, *Action Park: Fast Times, Wild Rides, and the Untold Story of America's Most Dangerous Amusement Park*

pages 161–67 (Penguin Books 2020)*

What [a look back] reveals is a man determined to remain sovereign, never to allow Action Park to become a homogenized area that only simulated risk. The thrill was not in being bolted down to the Alpine [slide]. The thrill was in deciding how fast you wanted to go without being constrained by rules or seat belts. What broke the reverie was when someone sped into trouble.

As my father added rides and expended the property, our once favorable newpaper coverage ... began to change. Now, when New Jersey newspapers mentioned Action Park, it was in relation to an injury. But here, as the result of man-made attractions, they became regular bulletins. The lawsuits piled up.

[Mulvihill lists nine lawsuits that occurred over about three years.] These were just a few of many....

Legal consequences, once rare, became something for which my father kept a file folder on his desk. We logged 110 reported injuries in 1985 and 330 in 1986, the latter making us responsible for half of all theme park accidents in New Jersey that year.

[Many incidents were minor or not ride-related.] More serious cases, such as someone being knocked out or breaking a bone, were herded onto golf carts equipped with stretchers and driven to the first-aid station.

This is where my father's preemptive actions began to take place. The park was required to report serious accidents to the state Department of Labor within forty-eight hours of the incident.... What qualified as "serious" was open to interpretation. Was a broken bone serious on its own, or only if it resulted in an overnight hospital stay? [Other parks, per the author, were also aggressive in defining incidents as non-serious.]

My father saw no reason to behave differently. We filed nothing that was not clearly mandated by law and, at times, stretched the definition of "non-serious" to include fractures.... My father did not want the state to decide what was too adventurous for people. He believed they could decide for themselves, and that the serious injuries were often self-inducted.

While the EMTs were treating an injury, a staff member would ask the guest what had happened. Inevitably, they would begin their story with, "I was horsing around," or, "I thought it would be funny if...." They might also admit to not knowing how to swim or steer, or having ignored safety instructions. The staff member would nod, taking copious notes.

[Many injuries were treated on site, reducing the potential for medical bills if awarded.]

My father stifled some [potential lawsuits] by enlisting a man named Eric Karg, who was the claims adjuster for the insurance company covering the park, London and World Assurance, Limited. A day or two after an accident, Karg would phone the individual and offer a nominal sum to cover medical costs and smooth over any lingering resentment. Someone who wiped out on the Alpine might agree to a $750 payout to let the matter drop....

Karg couldn't dissuade everyone, however. In those cases, my father dispatched a lawyer named David Chaffin.... His services were needed often enough that he kept an office across the street from the property. He'd open a dialogue with the plaintiff's attorney by informing him that he was going to challenge the claim every step of the way.

The opposing lawyer would scoff, incredulous that a major business would want a legal skirmish. That's when David would introduce the statement the plaintiff gave at the time of the accident.... He argued most all cases on the premise that the guest was assuming risk. If their assumption of risk involved goofing off, then the park was not at fault. At least, that's how a jury was likely to see it.

David made it clear that the suit would go before a jury. He didn't settle cases, which mean [attorneys] would be tied up for months or years in what they initially thought would be a quick phone call to get the park to admit wrongdoing. This insistence on not settling quickly made the rounds in the legal field. Action Park didn't do what big, liability-prone places are supposed to do, which is roll over. It became difficult for people to find attorneys to take on their case....

If a plaintiff and their counsel somehow cleared all those barriers and decided to pursue litigation, David flourished. He made sure park employees gave depositions like dullards, poorly dressed and slack-jawed. When they got to court, they were sharply dressed and well spoken, completely throwing off the attorney who had been counting on making the employees look stupid. When David deposed the opposing side, he exhausted them with questions. Depositions that should have taken an hour took a day or more....

David often jumped on an Alpine cart in the middle of the courtroom, demonstrating the brakes that allowed anyone to slow down to a crawl. "That's all you have to do," he'd say, "to avoid a problem." [] "It's called Action Park," he bellowed. "Of *course* you can get hurt if you're not careful!"

NOTES AND QUESTIONS

1. Were any of Chaffin's strategies or tactics potentially ethically problematic?
2. Do you think the strategies he used would still be effective today? Note that, unlike during the heyday of Action Park, far more depositions are recorded on video now.
3. Recall the Six Flags Great Adventure case in which the plaintiff alleged the park failed to report her injury. Query whether that was also due to different interpretations of the standards, as described above.

Dara Bitler & Vicenti Arenas, *6-year-old girl dies while riding Haunted Mine Drop at Glenwood Caverns Adventure Park*

KDVR, Sept. 8, 2021

The Garfield County Coroner's Office says a 6-year-old girl died on the Haunted Mine Drop Ride at the Glenwood Caverns Adventure Park Sunday.

* * *

How the child died is not clear. An investigation is underway into the circumstances that led to her death.

* * *

... The mine drop was the last ride of the day for Victoria Gallegos of Byers.

"When we were on it, it didn't feel secure. It didn't feel safe. It just has seatbelt buckles that strap you into the ride. It seemed extremely terrifying to me.... It feels like you are going to come out of the seat. It felt very unsecure," Gallegos said.

ACCIDENT INVESTIGATION REPORT

Colorado Division of Oil and Public Safety—
Amusement Rides and Devices Program
September 11, 2021

Accident Information

Accident Date:	September 5, 2021
Accident Report Date:	Verbal report on September 5, 2021 Written report on September 11, 2021
Permit Holder or Operator:	Glenwood Tramway LLC, dba Glenwood Caverns Adventure Park
Facility Address:	51000 Two Rivers Plaza Rd, Glenwood Springs, Colorado 81601
Accident Description:	Patron fatality on the Haunted Mine Drop amusement ride
Device Name and number:	Haunted Mine Drop, serial number #J0100
Investigators:	Scott Narreau, Amusement Rides and Devices Program Supervisor David Knight, Amusement Rides and Devices Audit Inspector Leslie Sohl, Amusement Rides and Devices Technical Specialist

Background

On September 5, 2021, at 8:41 pm, Mr. Scott Narreau with the Colorado Department of Labor and Employment, Division of Oil and Public Safety—Amusement Rides and Devices Program (OPS) received a phone call from Ms. Nancy Heard, manager of the Glenwood Caverns Adventure Park (GCAP) in Glenwood Springs, Colorado, stating that there had been an accident on the Haunted Mine Drop (HMD) ride on September 5, 2021, at approximately 7:15 pm. Ms. Heard reported that a patron (Ms. Wongel Estifanos) suffered injuries that led to a fatality and that no additional details were known at that time.

The HMD was immediately shut down and, following recovery of Ms. Estifanos from the HMD shaft by first responders, the scene was preserved. First responders, the Garfield County Sheriff's office (GCSO), Case # 21-14438, and the Garfield County Coroner's Office (GCCO), Case # 21-09-05, also responded to the accident. GCAP additionally closed its entire facility from September 6–10, 2021, in light of the fatality.

The HMD is a drop tower style ride that uses gravity to create freefall. The HMD carries 6 passengers and drops 110 feet into a shaft in the ground. Operators are responsible for fastening and checking two separate seatbelts for each passenger prior to dispatching the ride. When Ms. Estifanos, a six-year old girl, sat down on the ride, operators did not notice she was sitting on top of both seatbelts. The control system of the ride prevented the operators from dispatching the ride and alerted them to a seatbelt safety issue on Ms. Estifanos' seat. Operators took several incorrect actions and reset the ride seatbelt monitors which allowed them to dispatch the ride. Because Ms. Estifanos was not restrained in the seat she became separated from her seat and fell to the bottom of the HMD shaft, resulting in her death. This fatal accident was the result of multiple operator errors, exacerbated by several factors detailed in this report.

Investigation Authority and Scope

The Colorado Revised Statutes (CRS) 8-20-1002 require OPS to promulgate the Amusement Rides and Devices Regulations found at 7 Colorado Code of Regulations (CCR) 1101–12. Statutes and regulations can be viewed at *www.colorado.gov/ops/RegulationsStatutes*. Operations and devices at GCAP must comply with the standards adopted by these regulations, the manufacturer's recommendations (if applicable) and all applicable federal, state and local safety, fire, health, building codes, and standards. These rules and regulations apply to the construction, inspection, operation, repair and maintenance of the ride involved in this accident. Regulations require that every owner/operator of regulated amusement rides or devices first register the rides with OPS and receive a permit from OPS in order to operate in Colorado. The permit application approval process includes verifying that the owner/operator has current and appropriate liability insurance and that every ride has received an annual ride inspection that was conducted by an OPS-certified third-party inspector.

The intent of this investigation is to determine:

- The cause of the accident;
- If violations of the Amusement Rides and Devices Regulations occurred; and
- If additional safeguards are warranted to prevent the possibility of future accidents.

Investigation Timeline

The timeline for the OPS investigation of the accident is described below. Further details of the investigation may be listed within other sections of this report.

- On September 7, 2021, Mr. David Knight and Mr. Narreau met with Ms. Heard, Mr. Jordan Lipp (GCAP counsel), Mr. Matt Jenness (GCSO), and Mr. Rob Glassmire (GCCO) at GCAP to initiate the investigation by first viewing HMD surveillance video. The parties then evaluated the condition and operation of the HMD ride. Mr. Narreau, Mr. Jenness and Ms. Heard interviewed the ride operator (Operator 1) responsible for initially loading the patrons (passengers) on the ride when the accident occurred. The operator who dispatched the ride (Operator 2) was not interviewed at this time but had previously been interviewed by GCSO, according to Mr. Jenness. Mr. Narreau had further discussions with Ms. Heard regarding training of the operators.
- On September 8 and 9, 2021, Mr. Narreau visited GCAP to further review the HMD surveillance video and conduct interviews with additional staff, including the Attractions Trainer and the Director of Maintenance.
- On September 10, 2021, Mr. Narreau visited GCAP to again review the HMD surveillance video and to visit the HMD to understand the operation of the restraint system (seatbelts). OPS emailed GCAP a shutdown notice for the HMD and requirements to reopen the other rides not involved in the accident at GCAP. GCAP submitted documents to OPS as requested.

- On September 11, 2021, GCAP submitted the official GCAP incident report to OPS. OPS authorized GCAP to reopen all rides except the HMD.
- On September 13, 2021, Mr. Narreau visited GCAP to review the HMD surveillance video of operations prior to the accident.
- [On] September 14, 2021, OPS requested that GCAP submit all documentation received from the manufacturer regarding the commissioning of the HMD and all correspondence from the manufacturer since January 1, 2020. OPS also requested and received the HMD—Operator training checklists for Operator 1 and Operator 2 from GCAP.
- On September 15, 2021, OPS staff met virtually with ownership and management from Altitude Rides and Attractions, LLC (Altitude Attractions) to understand their involvement post-accident. Altitude Attractions' legal counsel was present for this meeting, as were staff from the State of Colorado's Attorney General's office. At the time of this meeting, Altitude Attractions had not investigated the accident, and OPS was not able to get a clear answer about the letter[] sent to Soaring Eagle clients regarding Altitude Attractions' status as the manufacturer or not. OPS was given access to interview recordings from GCSO, as well as the additional documents that OPS requested from GCAP on September 14, 2021. OPS reviewed recorded interviews completed by GCSO of Operators 1 and 2 and other GCAP staff that responded to the accident.

During the investigation GCCO received and forwarded an email to OPS from a person that was a passenger on the HMD in 2019. Mr. Narreau spoke by phone with the person on September 13, 2021. In visits to GCAP, Mr. Narreau communicated with GCAP staff to determine whether they were aware of the email. On September 20, 2021, Ms. Heard sent an email response to Mr. Narreau regarding the 2019 patron email.

Device Description and Operation

The HMD is a drop tower style ride where guests experience a freefall while seated in amphitheater style chairs. Once passengers are loaded into the passenger cart the operator dispatches the ride, the floor below the cart retracts, and passengers experience a freefall drop down a shaft into the ground for 110 feet, after which they are hoisted back up to the top to unload. Duration of the ride is approximately 120 seconds. The HMD consists of: a tower; a hoist system; a passenger cart; a lift cart; a sliding floor; a brake system; and controls. The control panel includes a Human Machine Interface (HMI) screen, dispatch button, and manual controls. The HMI is a specialized touch-screen that tells the operator what is happening on the ride, including any issues (errors) with the monitored seatbelt. The passenger cart includes six seats, each of which have two separate seatbelts. The HMI Screen monitors one seatbelt; this seatbelt has a rod (also known as a pin in the manual) which pushes into and is held by a buckle (known as a restraint block in the manual) next to the passenger's seat. The other seatbelt mimics an automotive lap seatbelt and is not monitored by the HMI screen.

When the passenger cart arrives back at the top to unload, the restraint block automatically unlocks so that rods can be removed. The control system is set up so that after a brief amount of time (less than a minute), the restraint block is automatically relocked. If the seatbelt rods are not removed from the restraint block within that unlock window, the rods are locked back into place and the HMI screen will denote that with a *restraint cycled* error (red indicator light). Rods that are removed from the restraint block in that unlock window, once a new passenger is seated, must be placed into the restraint block to be locked. Any rods not inserted will cause the HMI screen to denote that with a *restraints* error (a different red indicator light). Each seat has its own set of indicator lights for each of these scenarios on the HMI screen.

According to *Section 2: Cave Drop Overview* of the Soaring Eagle Operation & Maintenance Manual2, Rev D July 2017 (hereafter referred to as the manufacturer's operating manual), "The Cave Drop Ride contains unprotected heights, high voltage electronics, automated machinery, and other hazards.... It is critical that the Owner/Operator have a complete understanding of this manual before operating any of the rides that are part of the Cave Drop."

Equipment Evaluation

GCAP has been operating for more than 15 years. The HMD was added to the annual GCAP permit effective July 21, 2017. The application for the permit to operate the HMD included a certificate of inspection dated July 21, 2017, which was conducted by the manufacturer of the ride, Soaring Eagle Zipline Inc. In commissioning the ride, Soaring Eagle issued a document, dated August 7, 2017[], to GCAP, stating that the HMD was designed and manufactured to meet ASTM F2291 Standard Practice for Design of Amusement Rides and Devices, which is one of several ASTM standards adopted in the Colorado Amusement Rides and Devices Regulations.

Each year thereafter, OPS issued an annual permit to the GCAP which allowed it to continue operating the HMD. Annual inspections for the HMD occurred on June 15, 2018, June 8, 2019, June 16, 2020, and June 8, 2021. The Certificates of Inspection indicate that the ride was inspected in accordance with the Colorado Amusement Rides and Devices Regulations (7 CCR 1101–12) and that any deficiencies identified or noted at the time of the inspections were corrected.

Additional documents received and reviewed by OPS during this investigation include:

- All third-party inspection reports for the history of the ride.
- Commissioning inspection report for the ride.
- Maintenance records and daily inspections for a period of 30 days prior to the accident and including the day of the accident.
- Accident reports for the last three years prior to the accident.
- Manufacturer drawings.
- Familiarization training documentation issued by the manufacturer to GCAP in 2017.

Mr. Knight and Mr. Narreau observed an unloaded ride cycle on site, post-accident, on September 7, 2021. The HMD functioned according to specifications.

Operation Evaluation

Operation Procedures & Training

Upon request by OPS, GCAP provided OPS a copy of the manufacturer's operating manual, as well as a site-specific Haunted Mine Drop—Operations Manual, revised April 12, 2021 (hereafter referred to as the operations manual).

GCAP uses a training checklist for each ride which must be initialed and signed by the trainer, signed by the operator, and signed by the manager.

According to correspondence with GCAP, Operator 1 was hired on July 9, 2021 and received training on August 5, 2021. Operator 2 was hired on August 21, 2021 and received training on August 22, 2021.

During the investigation and review of both manuals and training checklists, the following was noted:

- "Operations manual (refer to written procedure)" is the first item on the HMD—Operator checklist. This item was initialed for Operator 2 and not for Operator 1.
- Operating procedures in both manuals instruct the operator to:
    - Pull the seatbelt over the passenger and insert rod into the restraint block.
    - Gently tighten the seatbelt against the passenger.
    - Repeat this step for each of the passengers.
- Operating procedures in both manuals instruct the operator to visually check to confirm that each passenger has a seatbelt over their lap.
- Neither manual details a procedure that operators must follow between ride cycles in regards preparing the seatbelts for the next group of passengers.
- The manufacturer's operating manual notes that the restraint block automatically unlocks when the ride is being unloaded; it does not include the fact that after a brief period the restraint block is automatically relocked.
- Operating procedures in both documents instruct the operator to verify that the HMI screen shows no errors.
    - The manufacturer's operating manual details what the various lights (indicators) on the HMI screen represent, and it does not detail what the procedure is when errors occur (when indicators are red).
    - The operations manual does not include an explanation of the various lights (indicators) on the HMI screen, and it

does not detail what the procedure is when errors occur (when indicators are red).

- Except for telling operators to check the HMI screen for errors, there is no procedure in the operations manual to follow if an error is found. The operations manual has a *fault procedure* and an *unplanned downtime procedure.* Neither procedure denotes when to specifically apply each. Step 1 of the unplanned downtime procedure is to unload passengers.
- Restraint Release Selector Switch's purpose is described in the manufacturer's operating manual; however, neither manual describes under what circumstances and by whom this action can be done.

GCAP Incident Reports, Interviews and Other Correspondence

GCAP submitted internal incident reports to OPS. Reports were completed by Operator 1, Operator 2, Ms. Heard, and the staff acting as the queue line attendant. After reading the reports and conducting interviews, Mr. Narreau noted the following:

- GCAP's September 11, 2021, incident report stated that during loading of passengers, Operator 1 did not notice Ms. Estifanos was sitting on both seatbelts. The incident report also stated that when Operator 2 arrived they removed and reinserted the rods for each monitored seatbelt and still did not notice that Ms. Estifanos was sitting on the seatbelts. The ride was dispatched, and following the retraction of the cart, Ms. Estifanos was not in the seat.
- GCAP staff are provided copies of the GCAP operations manual during training, and portions of the document are posted in the control room. Ride operators are not provided with copies of the manufacturer's operating manual.
- The Attractions Trainer does not reference the manufacturer's operating manual during training.
- An explanation of the HMI Screen and its various indicator lights is not a part of the GCAP operations manual.
- Terminology for key components of the HMD operating procedures, including the rod (on the end of the seatbelt), the

HMI screen indicator lights, and errors, were either not known by Altitude Attractions and GCAP management, or they were referred to by other terms that were inconsistent with the terms used in the operating procedures in both manuals. Not using consistent terminology or referencing ride parts by their names hinders operators' ability to learn and consistently execute a procedure. It also prevents staff from clearly distinguishing between different types of scenarios for which they may be responsible.

- When asked what the procedure for the seatbelts is between ride cycles, the Attractions Trainer said there were no specific requirements. Mr. Narreau watched surveillance video with the Attractions Trainer that showed an operator who was not involved in the accident unbuckling and moving seatbelts from seats that were unoccupied. All seatbelts for the ride were pulled away from the seats and laid alongside to leave the seats cleared before new passengers were allowed in the space. In video surveillance reviewed by OPS staff, this process was performed consistently by other operators who operated the HMD, including Operator 2 when they operated the ride earlier on September 5, 2021.
- The email complaint from a former patron that was sent to GCCO on September 8, 2021, was originally sent to GCAP on August 15, 2019. In the email, the patron described an incident on August 14, 2019, when they were a passenger on the HMD. The patron stated that when they were loaded onto the ride, they sat on the seatbelts and told the operator that they were not buckled in. The operator pulled on the tightening strap of the seatbelt and disputed that the patron was not buckled in. After persistence from the patron, the operator did verify that the patron was not buckled in and mitigated the issue prior to dispatching the ride.
- Inadequate training was a factor in the accident occurring. For that reason, OPS required GCAP to provide refresher training to the staff operating the other rides in the park prior to GCAP reopening the rides that were not involved in the accident (see State email from September 10, 2021).

Operator Surveillance Video Review

- Mr. Narreau watched the following videos of HMD operations:
  - September 3, 2021, from 10 am through the closing of ride for the day
  - September 4, 2021, from the opening of the ride through 5:45 pm
  - September 5, 2021, from 6 pm through the time of the accident.
- In video surveillance leading up to and including the accident, the following was observed:
  - In ride cycles immediately prior to the accident, Operator 1 inconsistently used the process of unbuckling and moving all seatbelts to clear the seats.
  - On the HMD, passengers often attempted to help fasten their own seatbelts. Operators did not appear to try and stop this from occurring.
  - In the ride cycle immediately prior to the accident, seat #3 was unoccupied and the operator fastened both seatbelts, inserting the rod into the restraint block to allow the ride to dispatch.
  - After passengers exited the ride cycle immediately prior to the accident, Operator 1 moved directly from the control room to the entry door to load more passengers; the process of managing the seatbelts was not completed at all—leaving seat #3's seatbelts locked on the seat.
  - Ms. Estifanos sat in seat #3 on top of the seatbelts and put the tail of a seatbelt across her lap.
  - Operator 1 assisted passengers in locking rods into restraint blocks and clipping unlocked secondary seatbelts and then proceeded to check that all rods were in the restraint block.
  - When Operator 1 got to seat #3, Operator 1 looked at the restraint block and pulled the tails of the seatbelts and did not notice that Ms. Estifanos was only holding the tail of one seatbelt across her lap. As Operator 1 tightened the

seatbelts, the tail was pulled out of Ms. Estifanos' hands, and Operator 1 did not notice that the seatbelts were not positioned across her lap.

- When Operator 1 went to the control room, the HMI screen showed an error on seat #3 due to not being cycled. Per the manufacturer's manual, this meant the rod was not removed from the restraint block after the previous cycle.
- Operator 1 returned multiple times to check the rods on all seats and pushed the rods into the restraint blocks. Per the interview with Operator 1, they did not believe the error because they were convinced the restraint had been cycled and that the issue was improperly inserted rods.
- When Operator 2 arrived, Operator 1 noted that there was an error preventing the ride from dispatching.
- Operator 2 chose to unlock the restraint block using the manual Restraint Release Selector Switch, and then went and removed all rods from the restraint block next to the seats and immediately reinserted them, without understanding and resolving the actual issue—that Ms. Estifanos did not have the seatbelts across her lap.
- In checking seatbelts, Operator 2 checked Ms. Estifanos' seatbelts by repeating the same actions as Operator 1 did in the first check. Ms. Estifanos had placed the tail of a seatbelt back across her lap; Operator 2 also did not notice that neither of the seatbelts were positioned across her lap.
- Operators 1 and 2 returned to the control room, and the HMI screen showed no errors; Operator 2 then dispatched the ride.

Findings

There were several factors that contributed to this fatality. A summary of these factors are in the findings listed below:

1. **Operator 1 did not prepare the seatbelts before allowing Ms. Estifanos and the other passengers to be seated. Because of this inaction Ms. Estifanos sat on a previously unoccupied seat, on top of the still locked seatbelts.**

- While not formally a part of the documented procedures or training, other GCAP operators appear to have adopted a process of unbuckling and moving all seatbelts to clear the seats, including removing rods from the restraint block on unoccupied seats prior to allowing passengers to enter the ride. Operator 1 had done this inconsistently on earlier ride cycles and did not do this on the accident ride cycle.
- OPS sees this process as critical for several reasons including:
  - Seatbelts are ready and able to be positioned for the next passengers properly.
  - Ensuring rods have been cycled
  - Prevents the automatic relocking of rods on previously unoccupied seats
  - Allows the ride to operate in automatic mode without operators using the Restraint Release Selector Switch.

2. **Both Operator 1 and 2 did not follow the operating procedures noted in the manufacturer's operating manual, which is a violation of Amusement Ride and Devices Regulations. Because of this the HMD seatbelts were not positioned over Ms. Estifanos.**
   - Section 2-5-1(B) of the regulations states, "Amusement Ride and Device Operators are required to operate each ride or device in accordance with these regulations, adopted codes and any applicable manufacturers' recommendations."
   - Specific procedures not followed were:
     - Pull the seatbelt over the passenger and insert the rod into the restraint block.
     - Visually check to confirm that each passenger has a seatbelt over their lap.
   - These procedures indicate that the operators of the HMD are required to perform this task as they are the trained professionals. Passengers cannot be expected to know or correctly execute the safety procedures for this ride.
3. **Training for both Operators 1 and 2 did not appear to emphasize the inherent risks of the ride, nor did it include reviewing the manufacturer's operating manual, which is a violation**

of Amusement Ride and Devices Regulations. Because of this Operators 1 and 2 did not fully understand their responsibility regarding passenger safety. Not having a complete understanding of the HMI screen and reasons for the various errors, the operators were not equipped to operate and dispatch the ride.

- Section 2-5-1(A) of the regulations states, "Ride Operators shall be trained in accordance with these regulations, adopted codes and standards, and any applicable recommendations provided by the Amusement Ride or Device manufacturer."
- Specific manufacturer recommendations not adequately trained on were:
  - The procedures described in Finding #2.
  - Information about the HMI screen and indicator lights.
- The *restraint cycled* error on the HMI screen for seat #3 indicated that the seatbelt's rod had not been removed from the restraint block before Ms. Estifanos sat down. The fact that the seatbelt had not been removed from the restraint block means it cannot have been positioned properly on the next passenger. The HMI screen error appears to be designed to warn operators of this fact.
- In the accident ride cycle video, OPS observed Operator 1 incorrectly attempting to resolve the *restraints cycled* error. The HMI screen tells operators exactly what seat had the error (seat #3). Operator 1 did not need to focus on any other seat, and yet they attempted to push rods further into the restraint blocks for random seats, including seat #3. The action of pushing rods is used to resolve an unrelated error (a *restraints* error) and does not address the fact that the seatbelts on seat #3 were not cycled.

4. **Having multiple operators making decisions and participating at different steps within the ride cycle was unusual and took the focus away from passenger safety.**
   - The decision to focus on the rods and the restraint block, rather than on whether the seatbelts were positioned properly, indicates that Operator 2 did not have a complete understanding of the various HMI screen indicator lights.

- When Operator 2 joined Operator 1 during the accident ride cycle, they chose to restart mid-procedure and appear to have switched the Restraint Release Selector Switch from locked to unlocked, without unloading passengers to determine what the issue was.
- Due to the fact that Operator 1 did not know how to deal with the *restraint cycled* error indicated on the HMI screen, it might have been considered "unplanned downtime". If Operator 1 had followed the unplanned downtime procedure, they would have unloaded passengers before proceeding.

5. **The restraint system (seatbelts) and the accompanying documentation (manufacturer's operating manual) contributed to the accident in the following ways:**
    - The manufacturer's operating manual does not instruct operators on how to properly address errors. The failure of the manual to instruct operators on how to address errors hinders operators' ability to effectively utilize the safety in place within the system.
    - Based on the location of pieces of the seatbelts, it is possible to lock both the seatbelts when they are incorrectly positioned.
    - Neither the manufacturer's manual nor the operating manual instructed that it was the operator's responsibility to buckle the unmonitored seatbelt across the passenger.

Conclusions

These conclusions were formulated based on the assessment of the evidence available at the time of the investigation.

This investigation was able to conclusively identify the factors that caused the accident and resulted in a fatality. The fatal accident was the result of multiple operator errors, specifically failure to ensure proper utilization of the passenger restraint system (seatbelts), and a lack of understanding and resolution of the Human Machine Interface (HMI) screen error conditions on the control panel.

Factors that led to the operator error were:

- Lack of procedures
- Inadequate training

- More than one operator taking responsibility of a ride during a ride cycle
- The restraint system involved

The Haunted Mine Drop (HMD) will remain closed until OPS repermits the ride, which will require the factors that caused the operator error to be addressed and a Certificate of Inspection to be submitted.

This investigation did identify violations of the Colorado Amusement Rides and Devices Regulations. Enforcement will be pursued via the statutory process.

OPS will share learnings from this accident with industry stakeholders in the interest of public safety. According to OPS records, there are no other HMDs (or similarly designed drop rides) manufactured by Soaring Eagle in Colorado. For the purpose of disseminating the findings to other owners/operators with this type of ride, Altitude Attractions will also be provided a copy of this report; they are the only company that has access to Soaring Eagle records which may include a client list and ride locations.

NOTES AND QUESTIONS

1. The designer of the ride, the late Stan Checketts, was quoted when the ride opened as saying, "We don't put shoulder restraints on the side of your head, which makes it a little bit more scary, a little bit more exciting." Rob Low, *Colorado park where 6-year-old died was designed without shoulder restraints*, KDVR, CBS17.com, Sept. 27, 2021.
2. You might want to spend some time online figuring out more about the agency doing the investigation, what their jurisdiction includes, and who the specific people involved in the investigation are. The report tells you a lot, but, regardless of who you represent or what your interests are, it is the start, not the end, of your process.
3. Most of the documents related to this incident, including those cited but not included, are available in the "Resources" section of RecreationAndRisk.com. There are no graphic photographs.

INCIDENT STATEMENT

Ride Operator 1

Sept. 7, 2021

The ride operator wrote that they were "leaving mine drop heading to MOD shack" at the time of the incident, and wrote:

DESCRIPTION OF INCIDENT

Describe what you observed: When I relieved [redacted] for break I finished the group [redacted] started and proceeded to let in the Next group. They were excited and moved past me before I could stop them there was about a dozen people in the room I was able to get extra people out and when I turned around they were all seated So I walked threw strapping them in. When I went to start the cycle it told me 1 of the restraints hadn't been cycled I checked the restraint and those around it and they were all locked, When I went back to the terminal it still showed the restraint hadn't been cycled and that is when [redacted] returned from break. I asked [redacted] why it was going off [redacted] said to just restart and try again. [redacted] unlocked restraints and pulled them all loose.

I re-locked restraints and walked in to help [redacted] lock restraints. I double checked the right to passengers and went to double check third but said [redacted] was right there also and so I didn't crowd [redacted] I walked to the end of the room to check terminal. Everything was good. [redacted] told me I could go so I left. I walked to the MOD shack and clocked out and as I was leaving heard one of the leads yell to some other employees that they would meet them down there as a few people took off towards The Giant Canyon Swi As I got to bottom of gondola I hard alot of Sirens so I asked the employee at the bottom wat happened and [redacted] said [redacted] thought [redacted] heard them say someone Fell down Mine Drop.

INCIDENT STATEMENT

Ride Operator 2
Sept. 5, 2021

The ride operator wrote that they were at the Haunted Mine Drop at the time of the incident, and that "screaming" was what drew their attention to the incident, and wrote:

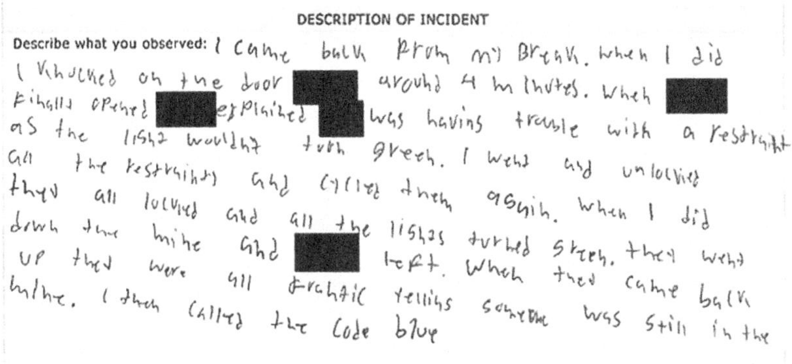

DESCRIPTION OF INCIDENT

Describe what you observed: I came back from my break. When I did I knocked on the door [redacted] around 4 minutes. When [redacted] finally opened [redacted] explained [redacted] was having trouble with a restraint as the light wouldn't turn green. I went and unlocked all the restraints and cycled them again. When I did they all locked and all the lights turned green. They went down the mine and [redacted] left. When they came back up they were all frantic yelling someone was still in the mine. I then called the code blue

Email from Patron

August 15, 2019

[The Investigation Report above notes an email from a former patron. This is that email, which was forwarded to the investigators after Ms. Estafaianos's death.]

Hello,

I am writing you today because of a serious security issue I experienced at the adventure park. Yesterday while my family and I were getting seated to ride the Mine Drop, everyone was getting strapped in their seats. [Redacted] came around and was buckling-in people, when it came to my turn [Redacted] buck[l]ed-in my seat belt... but my belt was not around my waist. I called [Redacted] attention to this (I was sitting on the belt and [Redacted] didn't even give me a chance to get up and put the belt around me) and said I'm not buckled in, [Redacted] disputed this and said no I've buckled it in. I said no again its not, [Redacted] pulled on it not bothering to check if it is indeed around my waist, and then said see its secure. I told that the strap was underneath me, [Redacted] response was "oh that's awkward" and then went back to unlock the buckles and re buckled me in. During the whole ride all I could think of was what if I didn't insist on [Redacted] checking again? I had no idea what the ride was, I didn't know that the floor was going to drop. This could have ended in tragedy for everyone. We were the last ones on the ride before the park closed.

Another incident worth mentioning is that while my [Redacted] was waiting to go on the same ride earlier that day [Redacted] was sitting on floor waiting to go in, had his head back on the wall and [Redacted] eyes closed. A [Redacted] tapped him on the shoulder and said to [Redacted] "please check your own seat belts because the [Redacted] inside is not doing a good job checking the seat belts and you could fall". [Redacted] also mentioned that [Redacted] almost had a similar experience but my [Redacted] could not remember exactly what it was. Needless to say, the fact it was a recurring theme was disturbing.

I urge you to look into this, otherwise you could have customers who will get seriously injured or even worse, dead. Safety is and should always be the prime objective of any work place and I have serious reservations about your park. Staff who take these issues lightly reflects on management and the owner.

I think a person like [Redacted] should not be working machines like this, [Redacted] displayed complete indifference to the safety of customers as well as incompetence when it comes to [Redacted] job. In addition, all your rides have safety measures in place to prevent such mistakes (e.g. the canyon swing and cliff hanger). I suggest you alter your equipment as a mitigation to human error.

I would like to hear back from you about the steps you have/are taking to ensuring this does not happen again, and hope to see the results next time I am there. I am not looking for any monetary gain or refunds, I simply want to make sure no one ever gets hurt during these rides.

If you need to contact me my email is a good way to do so.

Thank you for your attention to this matter.

NOTES AND QUESTIONS

1. When forwarding the email above, the patron reported that he never heard back from the park after sending the email.
2. Often, you'll find yourself having to try to read things like the handwritten notes above in litigation; that's largely why I've included them (rather than transcribing them).
3. Consider how, if at all, the facts in the following article would play out in litigation.

Changes Planned to Haunted Mine Ride at Glenwood Caverns Adventure Park After 6-Year-Old's Death

CBS 4, April 22, 2022

... On Friday, the amusement park announced it would completely overhaul the Haunted Mine Shaft drop tower ride.

* * *

In a news release the park announced that drop tower ride modifications include:

- [Changes to the entry area to improve visibility].
- The addition of a retractable shoulder seat belt....
- Retractable lap seat belt, part of the new shoulder belt....
- Ride carriage enclosure, moving up and down with the ride carriage, creating an elevator-type enclosure.

NOTES AND QUESTIONS

1. As of this writing, the Haunted Mine Drop has not reopened, despite the announcement that it would do so. The belt additions described were to be computer monitored "to confirm belt engagement."
2. Do you think the report's references to the ride's "inherent risks" is relevant to any evaluation of assumption of risk?
3. Every patron of Glenwood Caverns Adventure Park in 2021 was required to execute the following waiver. (It has not materially changed since then, as of this writing, except that it no longer lists the Haunted Mine Drop.)

ACTIVITIES WAIVER

2021, Glenwood Caverns Adventure Park

WARNING, ASSUMPTION of RISK, LIABILITY RELEASE, INDEMNITY And HOLD HARMLESS AGREEMENT

PLEASE READ CAREFULLY BEFORE SIGNING. THIS IS A RELEASE OF LIABILITY AND WAIVER OF CERTAIN LEGAL RIGHTS.

The person who is participating in the ATTRACTIONS: CLIFF-HANGER ROLLER COASTER, WILD WEST EXPRESS FAMILY COASTER, MINE WHEEL, ALPINE COASTER, GIANT CANYON SWING, CLIMBING WALL, SOARING EAGLE ZIP LINE/RIDE, LASER TAG, SLUICE BOX, GIDDY UP/FROG HOPPER, SPELEOBOX CAVE SIMULATOR, 4D MOTION THEATER, GLENWOOD CANYON FLYER SWING, HAUNTED MINE DROP or a CAVE TOUR at Glenwood Caverns Adventure Park shall be referred to hereinafter as "PARTICIPANT". "THE UNDERSIGNED" means only the PARTICIPANT when the PARTICIPANT is age 18 or older OR it means both the PARTICIPANT and the PARTICIPANT's parent or legal guardian when the PARTICIPANT is under the age of 18. THE UNDERSIGNED agree and understand that the CLIFFHANGER ROLLER COASTER, WILD WEST EXPRESS FAMILY COASTER, MINE WHEEL, ALPINE COASTER, GIANT CANYON SWING, CLIMBING WALL, SOARING EAGLE ZIP LINE/RIDE, LASER TAG, SLUICE BOX, GIDDY UP/FROG HOPPER, SPELEOBOX CAVE SIMULATOR, 4D MOTION THEATER, GLENWOOD CANYON FLYER SWING, HAUNTED MINE DROP or a CAVE TOUR or any of them, (hereinafter the "ACTIVITY") can be HAZARDOUS AND INVOLVE THE RISK OF PHYSICAL INJURY OR DEATH.

THE UNDERSIGNED agree and understand that there are risks associated with strenuous physical exertion and with participating in the ACTIVITY and that falls, INJURIES AND/OR DEATH may result from engaging in the ACTIVITY or any of them. THE UNDERSIGNED agree and understand that risks include, but are not limited to: use of equipment and ropes, equipment failure, improper use of equipment, slipping, falling, varied surfaces on the climbing wall, natural and man-made hazards, surface and environmental conditions, changing weather conditions, uneven and/or slippery ground or track conditions; varying slopes and surface conditions; variations in terrain; bumps, collisions with natural and manmade objects, the condition of the PARTICIPANT, dehydration, and high elevation.

In consideration for allowing the PARTICIPANT to participate in the ACTIVITY, THE UNDERSIGNED hereby ASSUME ALL RISKS associated with the PARTICIPANT's participation in the ACTIVITY. Additionally, THE UNDERSIGNED AGREE TO HOLD HARMLESS, RELEASE, DEFEND AND INDEMNIFY GLENWOOD CAVERNS ADVENTURE PARK, GLENWOOD CAVERNS HOLDINGS, LLC, GLENWOOD TRAMWAY, LLC, POW, INC. AND GLENWOOD CAVERNS, INC., affiliated organizations and companies, and each of their respective insurance carriers, agents, employees, representatives, assignees, members, managers, officers, directors, and shareholders (each hereinafter a "RELEASED PARTY") FOR ANY AND ALL LIABILITY and/or claims for injury or death to persons or damage to property arising from the PARTICIPANT's participation in the ACTIVITY, including those claims based on any RELEASED PARTY's alleged or actual NEGLIGENCE or BREACH OF any express or implied WARRANTY.

THE UNDERSIGNED take full responsibility for any injury or loss to PARTICIPANT, including death, which PARTICIPANT may suffer, arising in whole or in part out of the ACTIVITY. By signing this release, THE UNDERSIGNED AGREE NOT TO SUE any RELEASED PARTY and agree they are releasing any right to make a claim or file a lawsuit against any RELEASED PARTY. THE UNDERSIGNED further AGREE TO DEFEND AND INDEMNIFY each RELEASED PARTY for any and all claims of THE UNDERSIGNED and/or a THIRD PARTY arising in whole or in part from the PARTICIPANT's participation in the ACTIVITY. THE UNDERSIGNED agree to pay all costs and attorney's fees incurred by any RELEASED PARTY in defending a claim or suit brought by or on behalf of THE UNDERSIGNED.

THE UNDERSIGNED recognize that seat belts are required on the ZIP LINE/RIDER, HAUNTED MINE DROP, GLENWOOD CANYON FLYER SWING, ALPINE COASTER, and/or GIANT SWING and PARTICIPANT agrees to wear a seat belt at all times while participating in the ACTIVITY. THE UNDERSIGNED understand and agree that a seat belt IS IN NO WAY A GUARANTEE OF SAFETY and that no seat belt can protect the wearer against all foreseeable impacts to the head or body, and that the ACTIVITIES and other related activities can expose the user to forces that exceed the limits of protection provided by a seat belt. THE UNDERSIGNED also understand that a seat belt does not guard against injury to the neck, spine or any other part of the body, and that these limitations are INHERENT RISKS of the ACTIVITY.

THE UNDERSIGNED represent that the PARTICIPANT is in good health and there are no special problems associated with his/her care. THE UNDERSIGNED authorize any RELEASED PARTY and/or their authorized personnel to call for medical care for the PARTICIPANT or to transport the PARTICIPANT to a medical facility or hospital if, in the opinion of such personnel, medical attention is needed. THE UNDERSIGNED agree that upon the PARTICIPANT's transport to any such medical facility or hospital that the RELEASED PARTY shall not have any further responsibility for the PARTICIPANT. Further, THE UNDERSIGNED agree to pay all costs associated with such medical care and related transportation provided for the PARTICIPANT and shall indemnify and hold harmless the RELEASED PARTY from any costs incurred therein, or any claims arising therefrom.

In consideration for allowing the PARTICIPANT to participate in the ACTIVITY and for using the Glenwood Caverns Adventure Park facilities, THE UNDERSIGNED agree that ANY AND ALL CLAIMS for injury and/or death arising from the PARTICIPANT's participation in the ACTIVITY shall be GOVERNED BY COLORADO LAW and EXCLUSIVE JURISDICTION of any claim shall be in the DISTRICT COURT residing where the alleged incident occurred or in the FEDERAL COURT FOR THE STATE OF COLORADO.

In the case of a minor PARTICIPANT, the undersigned parent or legal guardian acknowledges that he/she is also signing this release on behalf of the minor PARTICIPANT and that the minor PARTICIPANT shall be bound by all the terms of this release. Additionally, by signing this release as the parent or legal guardian of a minor STUDENT, the parent or legal guardian understands that he/she is waiving certain rights on behalf of the minor that the minor otherwise may have. The undersigned parent or legal guardian agrees that but for the foregoing, the minor PARTICIPANT would not be permitted to participate in the ACTIVITY.

By signing this release without a parent or guardian's signature, the PARTICIPANT represents that he/she is at least 18 years of age, or, **if signing as the parent or guardian of the PARTICIPANT, you represent that you are the legal parent or guardian of the minor PARTICIPANT AND ACCEPT FULL RESPONSIBILITY.**

* * *

This release shall be binding to the fullest extent permitted by law. If any part of this release is deemed to be unenforceable, the remaining terms shall be an enforceable contract between the parties. This release shall be binding upon the assignees, subrogors, distributors, heirs, next of kin, executors and personal representatives of THE UNDERSIGNED.

* * *

I HAVE CAREFULLY READ THE FOREGOING LIABILITY RELEASE, UNDERSTAND ITS CONTENTS, AND AM AWARE THAT I AM RELEASING CERTAIN LEGAL RIGHTS THAT I OTHERWISE MAY HAVE.

Waiver signature required for **EACH AND EVERY PARTICIPANT.**

Participants over 18 must sign their own name. Under 18, a parent or legal guardian must sign for the child.

[Signature blocks]

ONCE ALL PARTICIPANTS HAVE SIGNED THE LIABILITY WAIVER, PLEASE GIVE THIS FORM TO THE GLENWOOD CAVERN'S ATTENDANT AND THEY WILL APPLY A WRISTBAND TO THE ARM OF THE PARTICIPANTS.

Colorado Statutes

§ 13-22-107 Legislative declaration—definitions—children—waiver by parent of prospective negligence claims

(1)

(a) The general assembly hereby finds, determines, and declares it is the public policy of this state that:

(I) Children of this state should have the maximum opportunity to participate in sporting, recreational, educational, and other activities where certain risks may exist;

(II) Public, private, and non-profit entities providing these essential activities to children in Colorado need a measure of protection against lawsuits, and without the measure of protection these entities may be unwilling or unable to provide the activities;

(III) Parents have a fundamental right and responsibility to make decisions concerning the care, custody, and control of their children. The law has long presumed that parents act in the best interest of their children.

(IV) Parents make conscious choices every day on behalf of their children concerning the risks and benefits of participation in activities that may involve risk;

(V) These are proper parental choices on behalf of children that should not be ignored. So long as the decision is voluntary and informed, the decision should be given the same dignity as decisions regarding schooling, medical treatment, and religious education; and

(VI) It is the intent of the general assembly to encourage the affordability and availability of youth activities in this state by permitting a parent of a child to release a prospective negligence claim of the child against certain persons and entities involved in providing the opportunity to participate in the activities.

(b) The general assembly further declares that the Colorado supreme court's holding in case number 00SC885, 48 P.3d 1229 (Colo. 2002), has not been adopted by the general assembly and does not reflect the intent of the general assembly or the public policy of this state.

(2) As used in this section, unless the context otherwise requires:

(a) "Child" means a person under eighteen years of age.

(b) For purposes of this section only, "parent" means a parent, as defined in section 19-1-103; a person who has guardianship of the person, as defined in section 19-1-103; a person who has legal custody, as defined in section 19-1-103; a legal representative, as defined in section 19-1-103; a physical custodian, as defined in section 19-2.5-102; or a responsible person, as defined in section 19-1-103.

(3) A parent of a child may, on behalf of the child, release or waive the child's prospective claim for negligence.

(4) Nothing in this section shall be construed to permit a parent acting on behalf of his or her child to waive the child's prospective claim against a person or entity for a willful and wanton act or omission, a reckless act or omission, or a grossly negligent act or omission.

Hamill v. Cheley Colorado Camps, Inc.

262 P.3d 945 (Colo. Ct. App. 2011)

[Plaintiff Chelsea] Hamill attended summer camp at Cheley in 2002, 2003, and 2004. Before attending camp each summer, Hamill and her parents signed a Liability/Risk Form (the agreement).

In July 2004, when Hamill was fifteen years old, she fell off a Cheley horse and broke her arm. Hamill sued Cheley for negligence and gross negligence, arguing that a Cheley wrangler had inappropriately saddled the horse she rode. The district court granted Cheley's motion for summary judgment on the two negligence claims, ruling that although Hamill was a minor, the agreement barred her claims and that there was no gross negligence as a matter of law.

Hamill appeals the district court's judgment, claiming that because she was a minor and her mother did not make an informed decision, the agreement did not extinguish her negligence claims and that disputed material facts preclude the grant of summary judgment on her gross negligence claim. We disagree and therefore affirm the judgment.

* * *

We analyze the validity of an exculpatory agreement, including those involving a minor child, by examining four factors: (1) the existence of a duty to the public; (2) the nature of the service performed; (3) whether the contract was fairly entered into; and (4) whether the intention of the parties is expressed in clear and unambiguous language. []

The first *Jones* factor requires that we determine whether a duty to the public existed in the instant case. *Jones* [*v. Dressel*], 623 P.2d at 376. Our supreme court has held that businesses engaged in recreational activities that are not practically necessary, such as equine activities, do not perform services implicating a public duty. *Chadwick v. Colt Ross Outfitters, Inc.*, 100 P.3d 465, 469 (Colo.2004).

The second *Jones* factor examines the nature of the service performed. *Jones*, 623 P.2d at 376. Here, Cheley provided recreational camping services, including horseback riding. The services were "not a matter of practical necessity for even some members of the public," because horseback riding is not "an essential service." *Jones,* 623 P.2d at 377–78 [].

[The third factor is fairness.] A contract is fairly entered into if one party is not so obviously disadvantaged with respect to bargaining power that the resulting contract essentially places him at the mercy of the other party's negligence. *Heil Valley Ranch, Inc.* [*v. Simkin*], 784 P.2d at 784[]. Because horseback riding is not an essential activity, Hamill's mother was not "at the mercy" of Cheley's negligence when signing the agreement....

By her own admission, Hamill's mother voluntarily chose to sign the agreement expressly giving permission for Hamill to participate in horseback riding activities....

In assessing fairness, courts may also examine whether the services provided could have been obtained elsewhere. *See Jones,* 623 P.2d at 375 (that a contract is offered on a "take-it-or-leave-it" basis does not, by itself, cause it to be an adhesion contract). The availability of other camps and other providers of horseback riding excursions is highlighted by Hamill's mother's deposition testimony that Hamill previously attended other camps. The record supports the district court's conclusion that the agreement was entered into fairly.

[The fourth *Jones* factor is the intention of the parties.] Hamill contends that the parties' intention was not clearly stated in the agreement. Her claim that she only intended to release claims for "things that Cheley would have no control over" does not create a fact issue and is contradicted by the record.

In reviewing a contract, we must enforce the plain meaning of the contract terms. *USI Properties East, Inc. v. Simpson,* 938 P.2d 168, 172 (Colo.1997); *B & B Livery, Inc.* [*v. Riehl*], 960 P.2d at 136. We must also determine whether its terms are ambiguous, that is, susceptible of more than one reasonable interpretation. *B & B Livery, Inc.,* 960 P.2d at 136. The parties' disagreement over the meaning does not in and of itself create an ambiguity in the contract. *Kuta v. Joint Dist. No. 50(J),* 799 P.2d 379, 382 (Colo.1990).

The language of the agreement here is unambiguous, and we give effect to its plain meaning. *USI Properties East, Inc.,* 938 P.2d at 172; *Kuta,* 799 P.2d at 382 (courts establish the meaning of a contract by examining the entire instrument as a whole, and not by viewing clauses or phrases in isolation)....

[T]he agreement here is not inordinately long—three and a half pages. The legal jargon is minimal. Along with the statutory release language of section 13-21-119(5)(b), the agreement identifies many risks associated with camping activities, including horseback riding. The agreement, like that in *Chadwick*, broadly states an intent to release claims of liability for "any injury," and like that in *B & B Livery, Inc.*, it includes all degrees of potential injury, including the "death" of the participant. Hamill and both of her parents signed the agreement on April 27, 2004. Indeed, they also signed agreements containing the same language each of the two previous years.

The agreement covers "inherent and *other risks*," noting that "[m]any, *but not all, of these risks are inherent*," and stating that it is impossible to delineate a full list of risks, inherent or otherwise. Finally, the agreement repeatedly states that, by signing, Hamill's mother agreed to release prospective claims against Cheley for "*any legal liability*," "*any injury*," and "*any claim*." (Emphasis added by italics.) The agreement sufficiently placed Hamill's mother on notice that the "[e]quipment used ... may break, fail or malfunction" and that "counselors ... may misjudge ... circumstances." The breadth of the release persuades us that the parties intended to disclaim legal liability for negligence claims. Indeed, misjudging a situation can amount to negligence....

In 2002, the Colorado Supreme Court held that it was against public policy for parents to prospectively waive liability on behalf of minor children. *Cooper v. Aspen Skiing Co.*, 48 P.3d 1229 (Colo.2002). The following year, the General Assembly superseded *Cooper* by enacting section 13-22-107(3), C.R.S.2010, which allows parents to "release or waive the child's prospective claim for negligence." The statute declares "that parents have a fundamental right to make decisions on behalf of their children, including deciding whether the children should participate in risky activities." *Wycoff* [*v. Grace Community Church*], 251 P.3d at 1264; *see* § 13-22-107(1)(a)(I)–(V). The statute states that "[s]o long as the [parent's] decision is voluntary and *informed*, the decision should be given the same dignity as decisions regarding schooling, medical treatment, and religious education." § 13-22-107(1)(a)(V) (emphasis added). However, the statute does not allow a parent to waive a child's prospective claim for "willful and wanton, ... reckless, ... [or] grossly negligent" acts or omissions. § 13-22-107(4), C.R.S.2010; *Wycoff*, 251 P.3d at 1264.

Relying on the "informed" language of the statute, Hamill asserts that Cheley's failure to identify the possibility that she might fall from a horse in the manner she did invalidates her mother's consent.

We assume that the General Assembly was aware of the *Jones* test when it enacted section 13-22-107(1)(a)(V), *Vaughan v. McMinn*, 945 P.2d 404, 408 (Colo.1997), but required something *more* for the waiver of a minor's prospective negligence claims.... A parent's decision is informed when the parent has sufficient information to assess the potential degree of risks involved, and the extent of possible injury. *Wycoff*, 251 P.3d at ___; *see also Black's Law Dictionary* 346 (9th ed. 2009) (defining "informed consent" as "agreement to allow something to happen, made with full knowledge of the risks involved and the alternatives").

In *Wycoff*, a minor was injured while being pulled behind an ATV on an inner tube over a frozen lake. The mother did not know her child would engage in the activity. The exculpatory agreement the mother signed in advance made no reference to the activity. *Wycoff*, 251 P.3d at ___. Thus, the mother was unable to assess the risks, or the degree of possible injury, before signing the release. *Id.* Accordingly, a majority of the division in *Wycoff* found that release legally insufficient to bar the daughter's personal injury claims. *Id.* The instant case is unlike *Wycoff*. [The court summarized the differences, focusing on the fact that Hamill (and her mother) were aware of the specific risks at issue in the release.]

That Hamill's mother may not have contemplated the precise mechanics of her daughter's fall does not invalidate the release and does not create a genuine issue of material fact. She knew her daughter would be riding horses and she was advised that there were risks, known and unknown, associated with the activity. Indeed, Hamill's mother acknowledged in her deposition testimony that when horseback riding, there is "a risk of a child being thrown or falling off a horse." Hamill's argument that her mother did not give informed consent, despite her signature on the agreement and the language in the agreement indicating the contrary, is not persuasive and does not create a genuine issue of material fact. As a matter of law, the agreement sufficiently informed Hamill's mother about the risks involved in horseback riding.

[The court also concluded that the release adequately described the extent of possible injuries.]

First Amended Complaint and Jury Demand, Estifanios v. Glenwood Caverns Holdings LLC et al.

No. 2022-CV-4, District Court, Garfield County, Colorado,
April 22, 2022
(Paragraph numbers omitted)

PARTIES, JURISDICTION, AND VENUE

At all times relevant hereto, Wongel Estifanos was a healthy, happy, and active 6-year-old girl who resided with her loving natural parents Estifanos Dagne and Rahel Estifanos in El Paso County, Colorado.

At all times relevant hereto, Defendant Glenwood Caverns Holdings, LLC d/b/a Glenwood Caverns Adventure Park (hereinafter "Glenwood Caverns") was and is a foreign limited liability company formed in Delaware.

Defendant Glenwood Caverns identifies a principal street address at 51000 Two Rivers Plaza Rd., Glenwood Springs, Colorado.

Defendant Glenwood Caverns owned/used/possessed the real property where Glenwood Caverns Adventure Park is located in Glenwood Springs, Colorado.

Defendant Toby Williams was an employee of Defendant Glenwood Caverns and was operating the Haunted Mine Drop on September 5, 2021.

Upon information and belief, Defendant Toby Williams is a resident of the state of Colorado.

Defendant Steve Ochoa was an employee of Defendant Glenwood Caverns and was operating the Haunted Mine Drop on September 5, 2021.

Upon information and belief, Defendant Steve Ochoa is a resident of the state of Colorado.

Defendant Soaring Eagle, Inc. (hereinafter "Soaring Eagle") was a foreign corporation with a principal street address of 326 West 2500 North, Logan, Utah. It was the manufacturer, designer, and seller of the "Haunted Mine Drop" ride sold and installed at Defendant Glenwood Caverns.

Defendant Altitude Rides and Attractions, LLC (hereinafter "Altitude Rides") is a foreign limited liability company with a principal street address of 326 West 2500 North, Logan, Utah. It is the successor entity of Defendant Soaring Eagle.

The Court has ruled that jurisdiction and venue are proper in Garfield County, Colorado.

FACTUAL ALLEGATIONS

Glenwood Caverns Adventure Park is an amusement park in Glenwood Springs, Colorado which is owned, operated, managed, and controlled by Defendant Glenwood Caverns.

Glenwood Caverns further represents that it has a "crowd-pleasing assortment of rides" and its "high elevation thrill rides are among the most heart-pounding anywhere."

One such ride is the "Haunted Mine Drop"—a drop tower style ride that uses gravity to create freefall.

The "Haunted Mine Drop" carries six passengers and drops 110 feet into a shaft in the ground.

Soaring Eagle, by and through its founder Stan Checketts, designed the Haunted Mine Drop ride.

Upon information and belief, Stan Checketts died on January 2, 2022.

Soaring Eagle sold the Haunted Mine Drop to Glenwood Caverns in 2017.

Altitude Rides purchased the Soaring Eagle product line and rights to the Soaring Eagle name in January 2020.

Glenwood Caverns invites and encourages young children to ride the Haunted Mine Drop.

It is very common for 6-year-old children to ride the Haunted Mine Drop.

Glenwood Caverns even allows young children to ride the Haunted Mine Drop alone.

The Glenwood Caverns height requirement for the haunted mine drop is forty-six inches.

The passenger cart for the Haunted Mine Drop includes six seats, each of which have two separate seatbelts.

When the passengers board the ride there is a floor underneath the seats.

When the ride is launched by the operator the floor is pulled away, causing the passengers to freefall 110 feet straight down a shaft in the ground.

Soaring Eagle designed the Haunted Mine Drop, including its seatbelt restraint system.

The restraint system includes two lap belt-style seatbelts.

The vast majority of drop rides in use at amusement parks utilize an over-the-shoulder restraint system.

Over-the-shoulder restraint systems are safer for use in drop rides than the lap belt restraint system utilized in the Haunted Mine Drop.

Soaring Eagle's lap belt design was defective and dangerous in that it allows passengers to sit on top of the restraints.

Soaring Eagle's lap belt design was defective and dangerous in that one of the seatbelts has a long tail, thereby creating confusion among riders and operators as to whether it was properly secured.

Soaring Eagle's lap belt design was defective and dangerous in that it is possible to lock both seatbelts when they are incorrectly positioned.

Soaring Eagle's restraint design was defective and dangerous in that it allows operators to manually override error indicator lights.

The Haunted Mine Drop should have been designed and manufactured to meet applicable ASTM (American Society for Testing and Materials) standards.

ASTM standards required Soaring Eagle to conduct a hazard analysis of the lap belt restraint system.

Soaring Eagle either failed to complete this analysis or its analysis was insufficient to address the defective and dangerous designs stated above.

ASTM standards required Soaring Eagle to conduct a mitigation analysis of the lap belt restraint system.

Soaring Eagle either failed to complete this analysis or its analysis was insufficient to mitigate the defective and dangerous designs stated above.

Soaring Eagle's operating manual does not instruct operators on how to properly address error indicator lights.

Soaring Eagle failed to provide operations maintenance manual and instructions required under ASTM.

Soaring Eagle's operating manual fails to sufficiently instruct operators as to their responsibility to buckle the unmonitored seatbelt across the passenger.

The Haunted Mine Drop ride was defective both in design and warnings.

If a passenger is not wearing a seatbelt when the ride deploys, the passenger will be ejected from the ride from 110 feet to their death.

The State of Colorado investigated the death of Wongel on the Haunted Mine Drop and issued an Accident Investigation Report.

Operators are responsible for fastening the two separate seatbelts prior to dispatching the ride. (Colorado Division of Oil and Public Safety Accident Investigation Report p. 1) (hereinafter "Accident Investigation Report").

Operators are responsible for checking two separate seatbelts for each passenger prior to dispatching the ride. (Accident Investigation Report p. 1).

Operators are required to pull the seatbelt over the passenger and insert the rod into the restraint block. (Accident Investigation Report p. 7).

Operators are required to visually check to confirm that each passenger has a seatbelt over their lap. (Accident Investigation Report p. 7).

The operators of the Haunted Mine Drop are required to perform this task as they are the trained professionals. (Accident Investigation Report p. 8).

Passengers cannot be expected to know or correctly execute the safety procedures for this ride. (Accident Investigation Report p. 8).

One of the two seatbelts for each passenger (the seatbelt with the rod) is electronically monitored. (Accident Investigation Report p. 3).

The control panel for the Haunted Mine Drop includes a specialized touch screen ("HMI Screen") that tells the operator about any errors with the monitored seatbelt for each passenger. (Accident Investigation Report p. 3).

Each seat has its own set of seatbelt indicator lights on the HMI screen. (Accident Investigation Report p. 3).

Before launching the ride, the operator is required to view the HMI screen to confirm that there are no errors with any of the seatbelts. (Accident Investigation Report p. 5).

Glenwood Caverns knew prior to September 5, 2021, that if the ride was dispatched before a rider had been restrained with a seatbelt that rider would fall at least 110 feet to their death.

The operators of the haunted mine drop knew prior to September 5, 2021, that if the ride was dispatched before a rider had been restrained with a seatbelt that rider would fall at least 110 feet to their death.

On Sunday September 5, 2021, the Estifanos family took their first trip since the start of COVID. Wongel's Father and Mother, Estifanos and Rahel, took Wongel and her two-year-old brother to the Glenwood Caverns Adventure Park. They were joined on the family trip by Wongel's uncle, aunt and their young children. All paid the full admission price.

On September 5, 2021, Mr. Williams and Mr. Ochoa were employed by Glenwood Caverns as Haunted Mine Drop operators.

Wongel's uncle eventually took Wongel, two of his own children, his wife and another relative onto the Haunted Mine Drop. They properly followed the directions given to them by Mr. Williams and Mr. Ochoa.

When Wongel and her family boarded the Haunted Mine Drop, Mr. Williams and Mr. Ochoa were acting within the course and scope of their employment with Glenwood Caverns.

When Wongel and her family boarded the Haunted Mine Drop, Mr. Williams and Mr. Ochoa were acting pursuant to the authorization of their employer Glenwood Caverns as to the manner of their actions while operating the ride.

When Wongel boarded the Haunted Mine Drop, she sat on top of the two lap belts.

Wongel's aunt specifically observed what she believed to be Mr. Williams or Mr. Ochoa buckling Wongel into the ride.

Mr. Williams and Mr. Ochoa went to Wongel's seat at least four times prior to launching the ride.

Prior to launching the ride, Mr. Williams and Mr. Ochoa knew Wongel's restraint system had a system error indicator.

Despite knowing Wongel's seat had a restraint system error indicator, Mr. Williams and Mr. Ochoa spent less than a combined 10 seconds over four separate trips to her seat to investigate or remedy the issue.

Without solving the issue, Mr. Williams and Mr. Ochoa performed a manual override of Wongel's restraint warning light.

Mr. Williams and Mr. Ochoa then dispatched the ride, causing the restrained passengers to fall in their seats 110 feet down the mine shaft.

When the ride came to a stop at the bottom of the mine shaft, Wongel's uncle checked to see whether Wongel had enjoyed the ride. He was stricken with terror to see that Wongel was not in her seat.

Wongel's uncle then saw Wongel's battered body at the bottom of the mine shaft. Wongel had fallen to her death, suffering numerous fractures, brain injuries and internal and external lacerations.

As Wongel's uncle and other relatives on the ride screamed in horror and tried to get out of the ride to run to Wongel, the ride would not release them and pulled them 110 feet back up to the top of the mine shaft[.]

Wongel's Death Was Caused By Reckless Acts

The State of Colorado Division of Oil and Public Safety ("Colorado Investigators") investigated the death of Wongel on the Haunted Mine Drop.

The Colorado Investigators determined that Wongel was killed because of multiple failures by the Glenwood Caverns. (Accident Investigation Report p. 9).

Each of those acts was reckless, as it was plainly foreseeable that the failure to properly restrain a rider would cause that rider to fall 110 feet to her death.

The Colorado investigators concluded that:

a) The operators (Mr. Williams and Mr. Ochoa) were responsible for fastening and checking the two separate seatbelts that should have been around Wongel when the ride launched. (Accident Investigation Report p. 1,7,9).

b) Passengers cannot be expected to know or correctly execute the safety procedures for this ride. (Accident Investigation Report p. 8).

c) The operators did not put either seatbelt over Wongel prior to deploying the ride (Accident Investigation Report p. 2).

d) Because the operators did not fasten either seatbelt over Wongel before deploying the ride Wongel fell to the bottom of the mine shaft where she died of the injuries from the 110-foot fall. (Accident Investigation Report p. 1,2).

e) Before the operators deployed the ride without restraining Wongel, a warning light had alerted them that there was a problem with Wongel's seatbelt in particular (Accident Investigation Report p. 1,3,7).

f) After the warning light notified the operators of an error with Wongel's seatbelt in particular, the operators still failed to put either of the two seatbelts on Wongel.

g) Instead of placing the seatbelts on Wongel, the operators took several incorrect actions and reset the ride seatbelt monitors, which allowed them to deploy the ride with Wongel completely unrestrained. (Accident Investigation Report p. 1,5,6,9).

h) The operators deployed the ride with Wongel completely unrestrained, and both seatbelts underneath her. (Accident Investigation Report p. 1,5,6,9).

According to the Accident Investigation Report, the Glenwood Caverns' Operations Manual for the Haunted Mine Drop:

a) failed to instruct the operators as to what each of the warning (error) lights mean;
b) failed to instruct the operators what to do when a warning (error) light came on;
c) failed to instruct the operators on the use of the HMI screen;
d) failed to instruct the operators as to what to do with the seatbelts between ride cycles, to ensure that the next rider did not sit on top of the belts.

(Accident Investigation Report p. 5,6,7,8).

The Colorado Investigators concluded that Glenwood Caverns did not train the operators in the inherent risks of the ride, and on their responsibility for passenger safety. (Accident Investigation Report p. 8)

The Colorado Investigators concluded that due Glenwood Caverns' failure to properly train the operators of the Haunted Mine Drop, "the operators were not equipped to operate and dispatch the ride." (Accident Investigation Report p. 8).

Soaring Eagle and Altitude Rides Knew Before Wongel Was Killed That the Lap Belt Restraint System Used on the Haunted Mine Drop was Defective

Upon information and belief, Soaring Eagle and Altitude Rides experienced a similar incident with their lap belt restraint system as occurred on the Haunted Mine Drop.

Upon information and belief, in 2016 a boy sat on top of the same lap belt restraint system on a ride designed, manufactured, and sold by Soaring Eagle and Altitude Rides.

Upon information and belief, when the boy sat on top of the lap belt restraint system, he was ejected and seriously injured.

Upon information and belief, neither Soaring Eagle nor Altitude Rides issued a bulletin to its customers as required by ASTM standards.

Upon information and belief, neither Soaring Eagle nor Altitude Rides notified Glenwood Caverns of the incident.

Upon information and belief, neither Soaring Eagle nor Altitude Rides changed the double seatbelt restraint system utilized on the Haunted Mine Drop.

Upon information and belief, neither Soaring Eagle nor Altitude Rides changed its warnings and instruction in order to avoid such incidents from happening in the future.

Glenwood Caverns Knew Before Wongel Was Killed That the Operators Were Failing to Put Seatbelts on Some Riders

Prior to dropping Wongel to her death, Glenwood Caverns had been put on notice by multiple angry and terrified customers that the operators of the ride had been prepared to launch the ride before putting the seatbelts on the riders.

For example, in July of 2018 Glenwood Caverns was put on notice by a terrified mother of a failure of the Haunted Mine Drop operators to put seatbelts on a rider.

That mother sent an email to Glenwood Caverns on July 25, 2018 reporting that when she took her 6-year-old on the Haunted Mine Drop, the operators put everyone on the ride and then left the room to deploy the ride without securing the seatbelts of a teenage boy on the ride.

That mother informed Glenwood Caverns in 2018 that all of the riders started screaming "wait!" "wait!" at the operators but that the operators left the room anyway.

That mother informed Glenwood Caverns that when the operators walked out, ignoring their cries for help, "... I sat there knowing that the floor was about to roll away with him not buckled in. I understood the ride went faster than freefall so was immediately thinking about how to try to protect my small child from what was about to be a large flailing body that was about to come crashing down onto our heads."

The operators of the ride did then come back into the room and apologized and put the seatbelts on the unrestrained rider, stating that they would not start the ride without everyone buckled.

The General Manager of Glenwood Caverns emailed the mother back on July 25, 2018, acknowledging that they had received notice that the operators had left one of the passengers completely unbuckled.

The Glenwood Caverns General Manager then falsely assured the mother that the ride had a safety feature which ensured that the ride could not begin until all of the riders were restrained by seatbelts. The General Manager went on to say in July of 2018:

> "I know this doesn't excuse us from ensuring all belts have been secured and all guests are safe on this and all of our rides."

The Glenwood Caverns General Manager also wrote at that time:

> "I can assure you that this email will allow us to retrain and continue to assure the utmost safe operation of this ride and other aspects of the park."
>
> "Again I appreciate you bringing this to our attention and we will take any necessary steps to improve the safety of our operation."

In August of 2019, another concerned passenger sent an email to Glenwood Caverns, putting Glenwood Caverns on notice that its operators failed to seatbelt a rider.

During the investigation into the death of Wongel on the Haunted Mine Drop, Colorado Investigators discovered that in August of 2019 a Haunted Mine Drop passenger had sent an email to Glenwood Caverns reporting that when they were loaded onto the ride they sat on the seatbelts, and told the operator that they were not buckled in.

The operator, who was prepared to launch the ride with the passenger not buckled in, argued with the passenger and insisted that the passenger was buckled in. The passenger continued to insist that he was not buckled in, and finally the operator checked further and confirmed that the passenger was not buckled in. (Accident Investigation Report p. 3,6).

This 2019 incident was the exact same scenario that killed Wongel in 2021: a rider sitting on the seatbelts and the operator recklessly failing to secure the seatbelts on the rider.

On September 10, 2021, the Colorado Investigators ordered Glenwood Caverns to produce all complaints received regarding the Haunted Mine Drop, since it began operation.

Glenwood Caverns did not disclose that 2019 similar failure to the Colorado Investigators. They learned of it only because after Wongel was killed, the 2019 patron sent the Garfield County Coroner a copy of the email that the patron had sent to Glenwood Caverns in 2019. (Accident Investigation Report p. 3,6).

When Colorado Investigators asked Glenwood Caverns whether it had received the 2019 email, Glenwood Caverns said that it had, and had not provided it to Colorado Investigators due to an issue with their email system. (Accident Investigation Report p. 3).

It appears that Glenwood Caverns also did not disclose to Colorado Investigators the 2018 failure to put seatbelts on a rider, despite the September 10, 2021 order from the State of Colorado to produce all prior complaints.

Despite knowledge in August of 2018 that the operators had failed to put the seatbelts on a rider, and the public assurance that the operators would be retrained, Glenwood Caverns elected not to properly train the operators, and to allow the Haunted Mine Drop to continue to operate in an unsafe manner.

The decision by Glenwood Caverns managers and employees not to make the necessary changes after the 2018 incident caused the 2019 failure to seatbelt a passenger, and eventually caused the death of Wongel.

<u>Felonious Killing</u>

Plaintiffs incorporate by reference all other paragraphs as though fully set forth herein.

The Defendants' actions constitute a felonious killing because the Defendants recklessly caused Wongel to fall 110 feet to her death.

The fatal 110-foot fall was caused by multiple acts of the Defendants which constituted a reckless disregard of a substantial and unjustifiable risk that their actions would cause death.

The reckless acts of the Defendants which caused Wongel to be dropped 110 feet to her death include but are not limited to:

a) The decision to manufacture and sell a defective product in both design and warnings.
b) The decision not to notify and warn customers of the prior incident wherein someone was seriously injured due to the restraint system's defective design.
c) The decision not to place seatbelts on Wongel prior to dispatching the ride, as required by the operations manual.

d) The decision to dispatch the ride despite the error light warning that there was a seatbelt error in Wongel's seat.
e) The decision to dispatch the ride without looking at Wongel to confirm whether she was wearing the seatbelts.
f) The decision not to properly train operators to place seatbelts on each passenger before deploying the ride, even after Defendants were put on written notice by customers in both 2018 and 2019 that operators had been prepared to launch the ride with completely unrestrained passengers.
g) The decision by Defendants to operate the ride with operators who the State of Colorado determined "were not equipped to operate and dispatch the ride."
h) The decision of Defendants not to train operators of the ride on the meaning of the warning lights on the control screen.
i) The decision of Defendants not to train operators as to how to properly respond to warning lights on the control screen

WHEREFORE, Plaintiffs pray for further relief as set forth below.

FIRST CLAIM FOR RELIEF

Plaintiffs against Defendants Glenwood Caverns, Williams and Ochoa
Premises Liability—Wrongful Death

Plaintiffs incorporate the previous paragraphs as fully set forth herein.

At all times material hereto, Defendant Glenwood Caverns was a landowner, as defined by C.R.S. § 13-21-115, of the premises where Wongel died.

At all times material hereto, Defendant Toby Williams was an employee of Defendant Glenwood Caverns, and specifically was an operator of the Haunted Mine Drop at the time Wongel was killed.

As an operator, Defendant Williams was an authorized agent of Defendant Glenwood Caverns.

As an operator, Defendant Williams was responsible for the activities conducted or the circumstances existing on the real property and specifically the Haunted Mine Drop.

At all times material hereto, Defendant Steve Ochoa was an employee of Defendant Glenwood Caverns, and specifically was an operator of the Haunted Mine Drop at the time Wongel was killed.

As an operator, Defendant Ochoa was an authorized agent of Defendant Glenwood Caverns.

As an operator, Defendant Ochoa was responsible for the activities conducted or the circumstances existing on the real property and specifically the Haunted Mine Drop.

On September 5, 2021, Plaintiffs and Wongel lawfully entered Glenwood Caverns Adventure Park as a paid business guest of the park.

At the time Wongel died, she and Plaintiffs had the status of an invitee as defined by C.R.S. § 13-21-115(5)(a).

Defendants owed Wongel and Plaintiffs a duty to properly restrain Wongel to the Haunted Mine Drop prior to deploying the ride.

Defendants Glenwood Caverns owed Wongel and Plaintiffs a duty to supervise and train operators to ensure they had a complete understanding of proper operating procedures of the Haunted Mine Drop.

All Defendants knew or reasonably should have known that failing to properly restrain passengers to the Haunted Mine Drop prior to deploying the ride constitutes a dangerous condition.

Defendants Glenwood Caverns knew or reasonably should have known that on at least two prior instances its operators failed to properly restrain passengers on the Haunted Mine Drop, resulting in a dangerous condition.

Defendants Glenwood Caverns knew or reasonably should have known that their failure to properly supervise and train Haunted Mine Drop operators on proper safety procedures constitutes a dangerous condition.

At all times material hereto, the Haunted Mine Drop constituted a dangerous condition, which created an unreasonable risk to the health or safety of Wongel which was known to exist, or should have been known to exist, in the exercise of reasonable care by Defendants. The dangerous conditions include: failing to properly restrain Wongel prior to deploying the ride; failing to follow all operating procedures prior to deploying the ride; deploying the ride when Wongel was not properly restrained; and failing to properly supervise and train its operators on safety procedures of the ride.

Defendants Williams and Ochoa breached their duty by recklessly failing to properly restrain Wongel to the ride before deploying it on September 5, 2021.

Defendants Glenwood Caverns, by and through the Haunted Mine Drop operators, breached their duty by recklessly failing to properly restrain Wongel to the ride before deploying it on September 5, 2021.

Defendants Williams and Ochoa breached their duty by recklessly failing to follow all operating procedures of the ride before deploying it on September 5, 2021.

Defendants Glenwood Caverns, by and through the Haunted Mine Drop operators, breached their duty by recklessly failing to follow all operating procedures of the ride before deploying it on September 5, 2021.

Defendants Williams and Ochoa breached their duty by deploying the ride when they knew or should have known Wongel was not properly restrained on September 5, 2021.

Defendants Glenwood Caverns, by and through the Haunted Mine Drop operators, breached their duty by deploying the ride when it knew or should have known Wongel was not properly restrained on September 5, 2021.

Defendants Glenwood Caverns, by and through the Haunted Mine Drop operators, breached their duty by recklessly failing to properly supervise and train its operators on safety procedures of the ride.

All Defendants failed to use reasonable care to protect against the dangerous conditions on the property on September 5, 2021.

Defendants' reckless failure to properly secure Wongel to the Haunted Mine Drop on September 5, 2021 was the direct and proximate cause of her death.

Defendants' reckless failure to follow all operating procedures prior to deploying the Haunted Mine Drop on September 5, 2021 was the direct and proximate cause of Wongel's death.

Defendant Glenwood Caverns' reckless failure to properly supervise and train its operators on safety procedures of the Haunted Mine Drop on September 5, 2021 was the direct and proximate cause of Wongel's death.

Defendants' reckless acts and reckless failures to act constitute gross negligence.

Defendants' reckless acts and reckless failures to act constitute a felonious killing.

Wongel is not comparatively negligent for her death.

Plaintiffs are not comparatively negligent for Wongel's death.

As a result of Defendants' reckless acts and failures to act, Plaintiffs suffered injuries, damages, and losses, including the death of their 6-year-old daughter.

<u>SECOND CLAIM FOR RELIEF</u>
Plaintiffs Against Defendants Soaring Eagle and Altitude Rides
Negligence—Wrongful Death

Plaintiffs incorporate the previous paragraphs as fully set forth herein.

Defendants Soaring Eagle and Altitude Rides were negligent by failing to exercise reasonable care to prevent the Haunted Mine Drop from creating an unreasonable risk of harm to the person one might reasonably be expected to ride it as it was being used in the manner Soaring Eagle and Altitude Rides reasonably expected.

The injuries and damages to Plaintiffs and Wongel were caused by the reckless and negligent acts and omissions of Soaring Eagle and Altitude Rides.

The reckless and negligent acts and omissions include and are not limited to:

a) Recklessly and negligently designing, manufacturing, assembling, distributing, delivering and selling the Haunted Mine Drop ride in a defective and unreasonably dangerous condition;
b) Recklessly and negligently failing to adequately, properly, and/or safely inspect or test the restraint system, or to make necessary corrections and adjustments, which would have revealed or remedied the dangerous condition;
c) Recklessly and negligently failing to discover defects in the restraint system;
d) Failing to provide and attach warning of the dangers associated with the restraint system;
e) Recklessly and negligently failing to exercise the requisite degree of care and caution in the designing, manufacturing, assembling, distributing, delivering and selling the Haunted Mine Drop;
f) Recklessly and negligently failing to adequately design, manufacture, assemble, distribute and sell the Haunted

Mine Drop in order to provide a safe product when used in a foreseeable manner;

g) Failing to establish warning and training programs for the use of the Haunted Mine Drop ride and its restraint system by consumers;

h) Recklessly and negligently failing to warn consumers of the dangerous condition of the Haunted Mine Drop ride when Soaring Eagle and Altitude Rides knew or should have known of the dangerous condition;

i) Recklessly and negligently failing to remove the Haunted Mine Drop ride from the market or stream of commerce when Soaring Eagle and Altitude Rides knew or should have known of the dangerous condition;

j) Designing, manufacturing, delivering and/or selling a drop ride with a defective restraint system; and

k) Failing to adequately inform or warn purchasers and end users of the Haunted Mine Drop as to the proper procedures for operating the ride.

Defendants' reckless acts and reckless failures to act constitute a felonious killing.

Wongel is not comparatively negligent for her death.

Plaintiffs are not comparatively negligent for Wongel's death.

As a result of Defendants' reckless acts and failures to act, Plaintiffs suffered injuries, damages, and losses, including the death of their 6-year-old daughter.

WHEREFORE, Plaintiffs seek economic and non-economic wrongful death damages, past and future, including but not limited to: grief, loss of companionship, impairment of quality of life, inconvenience, pain and suffering, emotional stress, fear and anxiety, funeral and burial expenses, and financial loss. Plaintiffs further seeks a finding that the acts causing the death of Wongel Estifanos constitute a felonious killing. Plaintiffs further seek prejudgment interest, post-judgment interest, costs and attorney fees as permitted by law, and any further relief as the Court may deem just and proper.

PLAINTIFFS REQUEST A JURY OF SIX TO HEAR ALL ISSUES IN THIS CASE

[Signature Block]

NOTES AND QUESTIONS

1. Colorado law provides limitations on the amount of noneconomic damages (and limits punitive/exemplary damages to the same amount) "unless the wrongful act, neglect, or default causing death constitutes a felonious killing, as defined in section 15-11-803(1)(b), C.R.S., and as determined in the manner described in section 15-11-803(7), C.R.S., in which case there shall be no limitation on the damages for noneconomic loss or injury recoverable in such action." Colo. Rev. Stat. § 13-21-203. Felonious killing can be found either via a criminal proceeding or by a civil jury finding the elements by a preponderance of the evidence. Do you think the facts as alleged constitute a felonious killing?
2. The Complaint does not reference the waiver form at all. Do you think anything in the Complaint is intended to address it?

Defendant Glenwood Caverns Holdings, LLC's Answer and Jury Demand to Plaintiffs' First Amended Complaint and Jury Demand, Estifanios v. Glenwood Caverns Holdings LLC et al.

No. 2022-CV-4, District Court, Garfield County, Colorado, June 10, 2022
(Paragraph numbers omitted)

[Defendant admits routine matters and denies most substantive allegations. Some specifically interesting paragraphs are included here. I'm not noting all paragraphs omitted below; the full documents are available at RecreationAndRisk.com.]

FACTUAL ALLEGATIONS

Glenwood Caverns admits that it purchased the Haunted Mine Drop Ride from Soaring Eagle in 2017 but notes that Soaring Eagle and/or Altitude Rides continued to service, maintain, and provided updated information and manuals for the Haunted Mine Drop Ride after Glenwood Caverns purchased the ride from Soaring Eagle.

Glenwood Caverns admits that the Haunted Mine Drop has a minimum height requirement of forty-six (46) inches, as set forth by the manufacturer, and as such children who meet the height requirement may ride the Haunted Mine Drop. Except as so admitted, Glenwood Caverns denies the allegations contained in Paragraphs 20–23.

Paragraph 62 of the First Amended Complaint states a legal conclusion to which no response is required. To the extent a response is required, Glenwood Caverns admits that Mr. Williams and Mr. Ochoa were acting within the course and scope of their employment with Glenwood Caverns while operating the ride and denies the imposition of any further duties or implications not consistent with Colorado law.

[Footnote in response to one paragraph that referred to Ms. Estifanos being "killed":] The First Amended Complaint is replete with the words "kill", "killed," and "killing." And it primarily uses this pejorative and inflammatory language completely disconnected with the allegations involving C.R.S. § 13-21-203(1)(a). Such inflammatory language is not proper or appropriate in a civil action. *E.g., BNSF Ry. Co. v. LaFarge Sw., Inc., No.* CIV. 06-1076 MCA/LFG, 2009 WL 9144604, at *13 (D.N.M. Feb. 16, 2009) (the defendant "asks the Court to instruct counsel that they may not use the word 'kill' (or similar inflammatory terminology suggesting a crime) to describe the manner of the decedents' deaths. The Court agrees that such terminology is improper, and counsel is instructed not to use it.").

Glenwood Caverns admits that an email was sent to it on July 25, 2018, and another email was sent to it in August of 2019. Those emails speak for themselves. Except as so admitted, Glenwood Caverns denies the allegations contained in Paragraphs 87–92 of the First Amended Complaint.

[Defendant denies liability for the claims for relief.]

GENERAL DENIAL

Glenwood Caverns denies all allegations of the Complaint not specifically admitted herein, including any allegations made in the prayer for relief.

AFFIRMATIVE DEFENSES

Plaintiffs' claims should be dismissed for failure to state a claim upon which relief can be granted.

Plaintiffs' claims are barred in whole or in part because the alleged damages and losses were proximately caused by intervening events attributable to persons, firms, and/or corporations other than Defendant.

Plaintiffs' claims are barred, in whole or in part, or recovery of damages and losses must be reduced by the relative fault of other persons, including responsible parties and non-parties, as provided at C.R.S. §§ 13-21-111, 13-21-111.5, and otherwise, and also by C.R.S. § 13-21-111.7, and otherwise.

Plaintiffs' claims are barred in whole or in part by release, contract, and waiver.

Plaintiffs' recovery of damages and losses, if any, must be reduced by the amounts received from collateral sources.

Plaintiffs' recovery of damages and losses, if any, are subject to applicable statutory caps and constitutional limitations.

Glenwood Caverns reserves the right to assert additional affirmative defenses to Plaintiffs' claim as further investigation and discovery warrant.

JURY DEMAND

Pursuant to Rule 38 of the Colorado Rules of Civil Procedure, Defendants' demand a trial by jury on all issues raised by the pleadings in this action.

WHEREFORE, Defendant Glenwood Caverns Holdings, LLC respectfully requests that the Court enter judgment in its favor and grant such other and further relief as the Court deems just and proper.

[Signature block]

NOTES AND QUESTIONS

1. As of this writing (late 2023), this case is still pending. I will continue to post about it on RecreationAndRisk.com as I learn more.
2. If you were representing Glenwood Caverns, what would you say about their chances of success on asserting that the waiver bars lia-

bility? If you represented the plaintiffs, what arguments would you make against its applicability under Colorado law?

3. If you were representing Glenwood Caverns, would you recommend any changes to its waiver?
4. Glenwood Caverns concedes in its Answer that the employees' conduct was in the scope of employment. What considerations do you think went into that?
5. What experts do you think you would want to retain (whether testifying or consulting) if you were involved in this case for either side?
6. What do you think are the strengths and weaknesses of this case for plaintiffs? For defendants?
7. If you were representing the plaintiffs and were preparing an opening statement, how would you briefly describe what led to Wongel's death in terms that a lay jury would understand?

CHAPTER 10

Insurance

As we have seen, one of the most common requirements of state regulations of amusement parks is the simple possession of insurance coverage (usually with minimum limits), sometimes requiring inspections to be done by the insurers (or people hired by the insurers).

While lawyers representing or advising (or suing) providers of recreation generally do not need to be insurance experts, the policies can affect operation and litigation in ways that are sometimes unexpected. And, one presumes, insurers of amusements can sometimes be surprised by what leads to claims.

And sometimes judges, as now-Supreme Court Justice Gorsuch below, have some fun writing the opinions.

Western World Insurance Co. v. Markel American Insurance Co.

677 F.3d 1266 (10th Cir. 2012) (record citations omitted)

Gorsuch, Circuit Judge.

Haunted houses may be full of ghosts, goblins, and guillotines, but it's their more prosaic features that pose the real danger. Tyler Hodges found that out when an evening shift working the ticket booth ended with him plummeting down an elevator shaft. But as these things go, this case no longer involves Mr. Hodges. Years ago he recovered from his injuries, received a settlement, and moved on. This lingering specter of a lawsuit concerns only two insurance companies and who must foot the bill. And at the end of it all, we find, there is no escape for either of them.

The problems began at the front door of the Bricktown Haunted House in Oklahoma City. There Mr. Hodges was working the twilight hours checking tickets as guests entered. When the flashlight he used began flickering and then died, he ventured inside in search of a replacement. To navigate his way through the inky gloom, Mr. Hodges used the light of his cell phone. But when an actor complained that the light dampened the otherworldly atmosphere, Mr. Hodges turned it off and stumbled along as best he could. He was aiming for the freight elevator, where (imprudently, it turns out) spare flashlights were stored. When he reached the elevator, Mr. Hodges lifted the wooden gate across the entrance and stepped in. But because of the brooding darkness, Mr. Hodges couldn't see that the elevator was on a floor above him and he crashed 20 feet down the empty elevator shaft.

It is here the insurance companies enter the picture. Mr. Hodges sued Brewer Entertainment, the haunted house's operator, for various torts. But no doubt wary of liability arising from its occult operation, Brewer had attended well to its insurance needs. It held two separate insurance policies, one with Western World Insurance Company and another with Markel American Insurance Company. Brewer quickly looked to them to defend the lawsuit and ultimately pay any award. For its part, Western World had thought far enough in advance to exclude from its haunted house coverage "any claim arising from chutes, ladders, ... naked hangman nooses, ... trap doors ... [or] electric shocks." But it hadn't thought to exclude blind falls down elevator shafts, so it admitted coverage and proceeded to defend Mr. Hodges's suit. Markel, however, balked, refusing to defend or pay any claim.

And that's the nub of the matter. Western World wants Markel to fork over half the cost it incurred in defending—and eventually settling—Mr. Hodges's claim. At summary judgment before the district court, Western World pointed out that Markel's policy covers Brewer for its haunted house operation and the very sort of accident that occurred here. In reply, Markel directed the court to an "escape clause" that, it said, allowed it to elude the liability that would otherwise arise from the terms of its policy. Ultimately, the district court agreed with Markel, found the escape clause a viable escape hatch, and entered summary judgment in Markel's favor—a decision, naturally enough, Western World now appeals.

First, though, we can identify some common ground. The parties agree that if the escape clause does not apply, Markel's policy affords coverage for the Hodges accident and requires it to reimburse Western World for its fair share of the attorney fees and the cost of the settlement (all in an amount the district court would have to determine on remand). That is because of the Oklahoma doctrine of equitable contribution, which "apportion[s] a loss between two or more insurers who cover the same risk so that each pays his fair share of a common obligation, and one co-insurer does not profit at the expense of the others." *United States Fid. & Guar. Co. v. Federated Rural Elec. Ins. Corp.*, 37 P.3d 828, 832 (Okla.2001). The only issue in this appeal, the parties agree, is whether the escape clause lets Markel escape liability.

Viewed in isolation, the clause seems to suggest as much. It provides that "[t]his insurance shall not apply to any entity that is already an insured under any other insurance provided by any company...." This seems a clear statement (or as clear a statement as one is likely to find in a densely drafted commercial insurance contract) disclaiming liability in the very circumstances we face.

But like so much else about this case, things are not always as they first appear. However appealing in isolation, Markel's argument faces serious problems when viewed in context. The escape clause does not appear in Markel's general commercial liability policy. Instead, the clause was added by a later endorsement with the following language:

> SECTION II, WHO IS AN INSURED, is amended by the following:
>
> A. Paragraph 2. Is amended to include the following as insureds:
>
>> e. Any legally incorporated entity of which you own at least 51% of the voting stock on the inception dates of this Coverage Form and on the date of any covered "occurrence," claim or "suit."
>
> This insurance shall not apply to any entity that is already an insured under any other insurance provided by any company or that would be an insured but for the exhaustion of its limits of insurance.

So following the endorsement's direction, we must place the new language in the context it belongs, in Paragraph 2 of Section II of the original policy, with its addition in italics for easy identification:

SECTION II: WHO IS AN INSURED

1. If you are designated in the Declarations as:

a. An individual ... owner.

b. A partnership or joint venture....

c. A limited liability company....

d. An organization other than a partnership, joint venture or limited liability company....

e. A trust....

[then you are insured.]

2. Each of the following is also an insured:

a. Your "volunteer workers" ...

b. Any person ... or organization while acting as your real estate manager.

c. Any person or organization having proper temporary custody of your property if you die....

d. Your legal representative if you die....

e. Any legally incorporated entity of which you own at least 51% of the voting stock on the inception dates of this Coverage Form, and on the date of any covered "occurrence," claim or "suit."

This insurance shall not apply to any entity that is already an insured under any other insurance provided by any company or that would be an insured but for the exhaustion of its limits of insurance.

Now Markel's contextual problem materializes before us. The escape clause appears only in Paragraph 2 and can be read as applying only to entities listed in that paragraph. To be sure, as Markel stresses, the escape clause uses broad language, stating "this insurance" shall not apply to "any entity" already insured under another policy. But it isn't clear what "this insurance" and "any entity" refer to.

[A lengthy and complex analysis of the policy language is omitted.]

And this leads us to the dispositive point. Even viewed in its best light, the applicability of the escape clause to an entity, like Brewer, insured under Paragraph 1 is far from clear. And in these circumstances, Oklahoma contract law tells us the tie must go to the insured. "[I]f an insurer desires to limit its liability under a policy, it must employ language that clearly and distinctly reveals its stated purpose." *Spears v. Shelter Mut. Ins. Co.*, 73 P.3d 865, 868 (Okla.2003). If (as here) the relevant limiting policy provisions are "unclear or obscure," then the objectively reasonable expectations of a person "in the position of the insured" control. *Id.* Put differently, when a policy's escape hatch is less a clearly marked exit than it is a hidden trap door, the reasonable expectations of an insured who has read and become familiar with the policy language supplies the rule of decision. *See Max True Plastering Co. v. U.S. Fid. & Guar. Co.*, 912 P.2d 861, 864–65 (Okla.1996). This doctrine does not, of course, negate the controlling effect of plain language. The plain terms of the contract are always the best evidence of the parties' intentions and always control. *Spears*, 73 P.3d at 868. But when the terms of the contract are unclear, or when the contract is susceptible to two reasonable interpretations, it is the expectations of the insured that control.

Applying the reasonable expectations doctrine to this case, we have no doubt a reasonable insured in Brewer Entertainment's shoes would have expected coverage from Markel. Expected coverage in light of Markel's general policy language promising Brewer coverage for accidents just like this one. Expected coverage in light of Section IV's promise that Markel will shoulder the burden of co-insurance. Expected coverage given the fact that the endorsement nowhere mentions Section IV and the escape clause is readily susceptible to a narrow reading. Neither are we directed to any counter-indication that Brewer understood (or should have understood) the escape clause as barring coverage here. In fact, to the extent that the extrinsic evidence points in any direction, it points decidedly against Markel. Markel's five page letter to Brewer explaining its decision to deny coverage rehearsed many other arguments—arguments it gave up the ghost on long ago—but the letter never once mentioned the escape clause. In fact, based upon the record the parties have presented to us it appears the first time Markel itself unearthed the escape clause from the depths of the contract and invoked it as a potential basis for evading liability was only after this litigation began.

We must and do readily concede Markel's complaint that the reasonable expectation doctrine tends to disfavor insurers, that it places a thumb on the scale of the insured seeking coverage. But some ambiguity-resolving rule of decision is necessary. And the Oklahoma Supreme

Court has adopted the rule it has because, often enough in its view, "[i]nsurance contracts are contracts of adhesion" forced by insurers on insureds with inferior bargaining power. *Spears*, 73 P.3d at 868. Neither may we, obliged to apply state law in this diversity action, rightly do anything other than faithfully follow that state policy direction.

Of course, few rules lack exceptions. And it's at least conceivable Oklahoma might someday choose to create an exception to the reasonable expectations doctrine for cases where (arguably as here) both parties to the insurance contract are sophisticated and able to vindicate their interests without any extra help. But no such exception yet exists, Markel has not argued for the adoption of one, and neither is it obvious whether Oklahoma would take up the invitation. After all, when it adopted the reasonable expectations rule the Oklahoma Supreme Court was surely well aware that not every insurance contract is an adhesion contract. And we can just as easily imagine Oklahoma would frown on an exception to its bright line and easily applicable (if overbroad) rule that invites parties to waste time and fortunes litigating a side-show about their relative bargaining power. Especially when sophisticated insurers (like Markel) can much more easily and inexpensively avoid the sting of the reasonable expectations doctrine by the expedient of drafting clear and plain escape clauses courts can enforce.

The district court's decision granting summary judgment to Markel is reversed and this case is remanded for further proceedings.

NOTES AND QUESTIONS

1. The exclusion of "any claim arising from chutes, ladders, ... naked hangman nooses, ... trap doors ... [or] electric shocks" from coverage suggests that the insurer here was paying pretty close attention to the business it was insuring. It also suggests that the insurance company was uninterested in insuring most risks that are particular to a haunt (as opposed to risks that inhere with almost any business enterprise).

2. Unsurprisingly, there are a number of insurance companies that specialize in insuring amusement parks and the like. When applying for coverage, they do request detailed information. The following includes just a few excerpts from an eleven-page application specific to amusement parks that requires considerable attachments as well.

Amusement Park Application

Philadelphia Insurance Companies, 2017

Submission Requirements

1. Complete ACORD Property, Auto and Umbrella Liability if coverages requested
2. Currently valued insurance company loss runs for the current policy period plus 4 years
3. Web site information, brochures and photos
4. Facility diagram
5. Schedule of all rides and attractions
6. Ride Inspection forms
7. Copy of most current independent ride inspection report
8. Copy of employee training manual
9. Latest financial statement
10. Emergency evacuation plan
11. Certificates of insurance from any sub-contractors/independent contractors

* * *

General Liability

[The form asks for annual attendance, season dates, payroll, number of employees, how much is made from various categories of sales, and so on.]

1. Any medical facilities provided or any employed physicians/nurses?
2. Any storage [] of hazardous materials?
3. Any operations sold, acquired or discontinued in the last [5] years?
4. Machinery, equipment or attractions rented to others?
5. Any watercraft docks (not bumper boats), floats on premises?
6. Is there a swimming pool on premises?
7. Are all swimming pools and spas compliant with Virginia Graeme Baker Pool and Spa Safety Act? If no, provide time table and action plan.

8. Any special events scheduled throughout the year?

* * *

Rides/Attractions

1. Do all ride signs comply with manufacturer recommendations with regard to age, height and exit requirements?
2. Does the Applicant or has the Applicant ever manufactured or retro-fitted any amusements/attractions...?
3. Are rides inspected daily?
4. Is an inspection log maintained?
5. Are there periodic inspections required by state inspectors?
6. Are maintenance manuals for all rides kept on premises?
7. Is there a qualified maintenance staff on site?

* * *

10. Are there rides where the operator controls the speed? If so, provide a list and operator training required.

[The application has a section about things like fireworks, zoos, driving ranges, and museums. It has a lengthy list of questions about cooking facilities. It has half a page about abuse and molestation histories and procedures. It has a page and a half about security, and another couple of pages about pyrotechnics. And so on.]

NOTES AND QUESTIONS

1. What do you think about those states where amusement park regulations are primarily oriented around ensuring that the parks have insurance of a certain sort and amount, without adding, for example, state inspections or investigations? What goals do such policies advance? Are there other goals that seem to be less important to policymakers who create these policies?
2. Sometimes there can be tension between the insured and the insurer, especially when the insured does not want to change how they do things or pay folks who encounter what they believe to be inherent risks. The comments in the next article from the founder of St. Louis's City Museum may echo, for you, the comments of Gene Mulvihill at Action Park.

Conor Dougherty, *This Museum Exposes Kids to Thrills, Chills and Trial Lawyers*

Wall Street Journal, May 1, 2010

ST. LOUIS—The City Museum here has a five-story jungle gym with two real-life jets kids can climb on. There's an enclosed "Monster Slide" that drops riders the length of three staircases....

The museum also has a reputation for occasionally being hazardous. One woman lost two fingers. A boy fractured his skull after a fall from the outdoor jungle gym, the "MonstroCity." The facility has been named in at least two dozen personal-injury lawsuits since 2005.

* * *

The injuries and lawsuits put the City Museum at the center of an enduring argument over the line between liability and personal responsibility. Some of the injured and their lawyers say the museum is deceptively dangerous and doesn't do enough to publicize its risks through signs or other warnings.

Mr. Cassilly [the museum's co-founder] counters that it is as safe as it can be without being a bore. "They [lawyers] are taking the fun out of life."

* * *

There's a price for this, of course. Annual insurance costs for the place have risen from about $36,000 since its founding in 1997, the museum says, to about $600,000 a year, representing about $1 of the $12 admission.

* * *

Recently, the museum installed video cameras to document accidents and discourage bogus claims. A sign near the admission gate gives the names and phone numbers of law firms that have represented people who sued the museum, blaming them for a 9% surcharge recently added to the cost of a ticket.

This defiance has drawn cheers from supporters....

NOTES AND QUESTIONS

1. I have been to City Museum (with my kids) a number of times and love it, as do they. It is also unquestionably a place where you almost certainly will get bruised or worse. I believe 2010 was my first visit; at that time, the signs at the entrance read:

> **Warning!**
>
> **City Museum is full of Creativity, Adventure and Learning ...**
> **And is fraught with**
>
> **DANGER.**
>
> Come explore, but keep these simple rules in mind:
>
> - Enter at your own **risk**.
> - Use Care, Caution, and Common Sense.
> - Children must stay under the supervision of their adult.
> - Have fun, but don't run!
> - City Museum does not take responsibility for accidents or injuries that may occur.
> - If you abuse the facility or other people, you will be directed to leave.

During my July 2010 visit, I got to see the signs posted by the museum featuring plaintiffs' lawyers, along with narratives describing the cases brought that the Museum considered frivolous.

My recollection, though I cannot read the smaller print on my photo (which you can see at RecreationAndRisk.com), is that the museum stated that its insurers insisted on resolving some of the matters over the Museum's objection.

In the same time frame, the City Museum posted several times on its Facebook page as well as its blog about lawsuits (though neither of the original postings are still up or accessible via the Wayback Machine). It posted a general comment and a series of three case descriptions, claiming them to be representative of its litigation portfolio:

> We understand that by creating a place where kids and adults can run, jump, and play, that there is a risk for injury.

> We are constantly doing everything we can to mitigate that risk all the while trying to protect the integrity of the museum. What exhausts us are the people that see the museum as an opportunity to perpetuate insurance fraud.
>
> * * *
>
> 1. Christina Ramage vs City Museum—It's your wedding night. You take the slide. Your husband, a body builder, doesn't wait until you clear the bottom and slams into you. The slide says "One at a time" and "Wait until bottom is clear."
> 2. Joli Sutter vs City Museum—You run and jump into the baby ball pit. Sign says "6 and under" and "Do not jump"
> 3. Timothy Walker vs City Museum—Your physical limitations should have told you that going down a slide, especially with knee problems in the past, is a bad idea

Aimee Levitt, *City Museum Fights Back Against 'Frivolous Lawsuits'—Via Facebook*, Riverfront Times, April 8, 2010.

I asked my kids about their memories of City Museum (as of this writing, we are planning another visit in about a month). My son, then about 8 (and now 21) said, "I remember feeling very proud that I went in the way small tunnels under the walkways outside and that y'all were freaked by it" and "being scared in the catacomb/cave area when I got separated. I remember the intricacies of the tunnels and how I felt like I didn't know where they would end up, and it was kinda scary but also exciting." My daughter said, "It felt like I was somewhere magical; it was like going on an adventure. A little bit scary, but that made it even more exciting."

I was back again in 2011, with a former student who was then in practice in Kansas City. I believe the sign was gone then but the place was as absurd as ever. That student notes that her kids (who are around the same ages as my kids) loved it and that she's "amazed they haven't been sued out of existence."

Consider those reactions to City Museum. Is it good for there to be places that are a little bit scary and maybe at least a little bit dangerous for kids? (I clearly think so but there are lots of reasonable responses to the question!) How should liability concerns affect such a place?

2. After the accidental death of City Museum's founder and co-owner, it was acquired by Premier Parks, a company that (in a prior form) had owned and operated the Six Flags chain and now operates a number of water parks and four smaller regional theme parks. My family returned in December 2023 and, to my surprise, the museum remains largely the same. There are perhaps a few more warning signs, and employees are possibly a bit more emphatic about preventing, for example, multiple people on a slide at once, but it remains, as I said in a social media post after our visit, fraught with mild danger. It also remains one of my favorite places. (And the kids had a blast still.)
3. In the last chapter, you'll recall how Action Park used the adjuster from its insurance company, London and World, to resolve some matters rapidly. Well, it turns out there's a story there as well.

Andy Mulvihill with Jake Rossen, *Action Park: Fast Times, Wild Rides, and the Untold Story of America's Most Dangerous Amusement Park*

Pages 203–08 (Penguin Books 2020)*

I learned of the insurance fraud through my Stanford classmate.... "Hey, Andy," he said. "Your dad's in some shit."

"You'll have to be more specific," I said. Adam handed me the newspaper. On page three was a headline:

RESORT HAD NO INSURER, STATE SAYS

* * *

For the past year, the New Jersey State Commission of Investigation (SCI) had been looking into allegations that London and World was not actually an independent insurer but one of Gene's own companies....

Asked to submit records of his various businesses, my father passive-aggressively sent over an entire moving truck full of documents. It took them three months to comb through it all. The SCI was looking for evidence of London and World's existence, but could find no trace of it. There was only a post office in the Cayman Islands.

* Copyright © 2020. Reprinted with permission of Penguin Books and the authors.

My father was cryptic on the topic of London and World. "Just because they can't find it doesn't mean it doesn't exist," he said, as though it were common for insurance companies not to have telephone numbers.

For those who knew him, there was little mystery as to why my father had done something so brazen. He hated insurance. Period. Premiums had skyrocked in the late 1970s, jumping 400 percent after a number of people injured at ski resorts won the resulting lawsuits.... The state's mandated amount of two million dollars in coverage for the park would have been incredibly expensive, even more so because of our spotty safety record. He theorized that it would be much cheaper to field claims himself and pay settlements out of his own pocket when needed, which wasn't often with the tenacious lawyer David Chaffin in his corner.

So, after the first couple of years of the park's existence, he opted out of conventional insurance. In this way, he avoided premiums, but it also meant that every time someone slid down the Alpine [slide] and stumbled off with weeping skin, the park was vulnerable to litigation.

NOTES AND QUESTIONS

1. Self-insurance is common today (and was not unheard of during Action Park's existence), but it does not, to be clear, mean a company can mislead regulators about the nature of its usage. Action Park also had obtained additional insurance of anything above London and World's coverage, which, since that company was notional at best, meant that Action Park had seemingly defrauded that (actual) insurance company.
2. Mulvihill, later in the same chapter, notes that a "battalion of lawyers who had active lawsuits against the park modified their complaints to note that the rides on which their clients were injured were only approved because of an insurance certificate from a company that was owned by the person seeking the ride permit [and] though it made the park even more at fault." *Id.* at 207. Does that theory make sense to you? Why or why not?
3. Several years later, a different park named Action Park—this one in New York—ran into an interesting, if small, insurance question.

State by Abrams v. Action Park, Inc.

540 N.Y.S.2d 396 (N.Y. App. Div. 4th Dept. 1989)

Each respondent operates a "fun center" consisting of a go-kart track, game room and snack bar.... At each establishment, a customer is charged a fee for use of the go-kart track.

In separate petitions, the State seeks to enjoin operation of the go-kart tracks. It is alleged that each respondent failed to procure a permit issued by the Commissioner of Labor as required by Labor Law § 870-d and failed to purchase sufficient liability insurance as required by Labor Law § 870-f. Supreme Court found that because respondents do not operate "amusement parks" within the meaning of Labor Law § 870-c(2) they are exempt from the permit and insurance requirements. We disagree, and we reverse and grant the petition in each case.

Labor Law article 27, in relevant part, applies to amusement devices at amusement parks "where an admission or fee is customarily or usually charged" (Labor Law § 870-b[1]). The parties agree, and Supreme Court found, that a go-kart track is an amusement device as defined by Labor Law § 870-c(1). An "amusement park" is defined as "a tract or area used principally as a permanent location for amusement devices or structures" (Labor Law § 870-c[2]). The agency charged with the enforcement of article 27 is the Department of Labor. The Commissioner of Labor has determined that the tract or area used by each respondent for operation of the go-kart tracks is an amusement park within the meaning of the Labor Law. Since that interpretation is not irrational or unreasonable, it must be upheld [citations].

Labor Law § 870-d provides that no amusement device "may be operated in the state without a permit" issued by the Commissioner of Labor. Before such a permit may be issued, the operator of the device must furnish proof of liability insurance in an amount not less than one million dollars (Labor Law § 870-f). Here, because each respondent has purchased liability insurance in the sum of only $300,000, the Commissioner is prohibited by law from issuing a permit for operation of either go-kart track. Since both respondents are acting in violation of law, the operation of both go-kart tracks must be enjoined.

CHAPTER 11

Punitive Damages and Damages Caps

Punitive damages (sometimes called exemplary damages) are awarded in a relatively small number of cases. Predicting both the cases in which they will be awarded and the amount of the awards is so difficult that a 2022 article was entitled *Bringing Predictability to the Chaos of Punitive Damages*. McMichael & Viscusi, 54 ARIZ. ST. L.J. 471 (2022).

While there's some disagreement about *how* unpredictable they are, in practice, there is broad agreement that they can be "a significant factor in litigation despite the fact that only a small fraction of cases in their sample involve punitive damage judgments." Polinksy, *Are Punitive Damages Really Insignificant, Predictable, and Rational?*, 26 J. LEGAL STUD. 663, 664 (1997). Put another way, the *possibility* of punitive damages can affect the conduct and settlement of lawsuits out of proportion to their *probability*, because litigants at least *think* that they are hard to predict. Consider: If you would ordinarily think a case had a predicted "value" of $10 million for compensatory damages but a 10% chance of a $100 million punitive damages award, that "unlikely" event doubles the expected verdict value to $20 million.

Similarly, non-economic damages (*e.g.*, pain and suffering) are less predictable than damages awarded for, for example, medical bills, and so they may affect decisions about pursuing and settling litigation out of proportion to their actual amount. These concerns (as well as general concerns about so-called "runaway juries"), helped prompt legislatures and courts in many jurisdictions to implement various controls.

Precisely how punitive damages are defined varies, and sometimes they are defined by statute and sometimes by common law. We won't cover the full waterfront on this issue here, of course.

What we will see is, first, some definitions of and standards for the awarding of punitive damages (as well as limitations for awarding both punitive and non-economic damages in the context of wrongful death). The amount of damages is one area where legislatures have dived in enthusiastically. We will then look at the facts of what is probably the most egregious case of recklessness I've ever seen in the context of amusement or water parks, the tragic death of Caleb Schwab.

Kansas Statutes §60-3701: Punitive and exemplary damages; separate proceeding for determination of amount; considerations; limitations; maximum amount of award; application limited

(a) In any civil action in which exemplary or punitive damages are recoverable, the trier of fact shall determine, concurrent with all other issues presented, whether such damages shall be allowed. If such damages are allowed, a separate proceeding shall be conducted by the court to determine the amount of such damages to be awarded.

(b) At a proceeding to determine the amount of exemplary or punitive damages to be awarded under this section, the court may consider:

(1) The likelihood at the time of the alleged misconduct that serious harm would arise from the defendant's misconduct;

(2) the degree of the defendant's awareness of that likelihood;

(3) the profitability of the defendant's misconduct;

(4) the duration of the misconduct and any intentional concealment of it;

(5) the attitude and conduct of the defendant upon discovery of the misconduct;

(6) the financial condition of the defendant; and

(7) the total deterrent effect of other damages and punishment imposed upon the defendant as a result of the misconduct, including, but not limited to, compensatory, exemplary and punitive damage awards to persons in situations similar to those of the claimant and

the severity of the criminal penalties to which the defendant has been or may be subjected.

At the conclusion of the proceeding, the court shall determine the amount of exemplary or punitive damages to be awarded and shall enter judgment for that amount.

(c) In any civil action where claims for exemplary or punitive damages are included, the plaintiff shall have the burden of proving, by clear and convincing evidence in the initial phase of the trial, that the defendant acted toward the plaintiff with willful conduct, wanton conduct, fraud or malice.

(d) In no case shall exemplary or punitive damages be assessed pursuant to this section against:

(1) A principal or employer for the acts of an agent or employee unless the questioned conduct was authorized or ratified by a person expressly empowered to do so on behalf of the principal or employer; or

(2) an association, partnership or corporation for the acts of a member, partner or shareholder unless such association, partnership or corporation authorized or ratified the questioned conduct.

(e) Except as provided by subsection (f), no award of exemplary or punitive damages pursuant to this section shall exceed the lesser of:

(1) The annual gross income earned by the defendant, as determined by the court based upon the defendant's highest gross annual income earned for any one of the five years immediately before the act for which such damages are awarded; or

(2) $5 million.

(f) In lieu of the limitation provided by subsection (e), if the court finds that the profitability of the defendant's misconduct exceeds or is expected to exceed the limitation of subsection (e), the limitation on the amount of exemplary or punitive damages which the court may award shall be an amount equal to 1½ times the amount of profit which the defendant gained or is expected to gain as a result of the defendant's misconduct.

(g) The provisions of this section shall not apply to any action governed by another statute establishing or limiting the amount of exemplary or punitive damages, or prescribing procedures for the award of such damages, in such action.

(h) As used in this section the terms defined in K.S.A. 60-3401 and amendments thereto shall have the meaning provided by that statute.

(i) The provisions of this section shall apply only to an action based upon a cause of action accruing on or after July 1, 1987 and before July 1, 1988.

Texas Civil Practice & Remedies Code §41.003: Standards for Recovery of Exemplary Damages

(a) Except as provided by Subsection (c), exemplary damages may be awarded only if the claimant proves by clear and convincing evidence that the harm with respect to which the claimant seeks recovery of exemplary damages results from:

(1) fraud;

(2) malice; or

(3) gross negligence.

(b) The claimant must prove by clear and convincing evidence the elements of exemplary damages as provided by this section. This burden of proof may not be shifted to the defendant or satisfied by evidence of ordinary negligence, bad faith, or a deceptive trade practice.

(c) If the claimant relies on a statute establishing a cause of action and authorizing exemplary damages in specified circumstances or in conjunction with a specified culpable mental state, exemplary damages may be awarded only if the claimant proves by clear and convincing evidence that the damages result from the specified circumstances or culpable mental state.

(d) Exemplary damages may be awarded only if the jury was unanimous in regard to finding liability for and the amount of exemplary damages.

(e) In all cases where the issue of exemplary damages is submitted to the jury, the following instruction shall be included in the charge of the court:

> "You are instructed that, in order for you to find exemplary damages, your answer to the question regarding the amount of such damages must be unanimous."

Tuttle v. Raymond

494 A.2d 1353 (Me. 1985)

VIOLETTE, Justice.

This action arises out of the serious injuries sustained by the plaintiff in an automobile collision involving the defendant. After a jury trial, the Superior Court, Androscoggin County, entered a final judgment ordering the defendant to pay the plaintiff $50,000 in compensatory damages and $22,000 in punitive damages. On appeal, the defendant challenges only the award of punitive damages. First, the defendant urges this Court to abolish common law punitive damages in Maine. Alternatively, the defendant contends that punitive damages are inappropriate as a matter of law on the facts underlying this case. Finally, should both of those arguments fail to persuade the Court, the defendant argues that several errors in the trial below nevertheless require reversal of the punitive damages award.

In several recent decisions, this Court has indicated its willingness, should the proper occasion arise, to re-examine "the judicially created rule of punitive damages ... in light of modern considerations and authorities." *Braley v. Berkshire Mutual Insurance Co.*, 440 A.2d 359, 361 n. 4 (Me.1982); *see, e.g., Hanover Insurance Co. v. Hayward*, 464 A.2d 156, 158 n. 2 (Me.1983); *Oliver v. Martin*, 460 A.2d 594, 595 n. 2 (Me.1983). This case presents such an occasion.... We refuse to abolish common law punitive damages in Maine. We do take this opportunity, however, to redefine and clarify the type of tortious conduct necessary to justify an award of exemplary damages. Furthermore, we heighten the standard of proof incumbent upon a plaintiff seeking such an award. We hold that, in order to recover punitive damages, a plaintiff must prove by clear and convincing evidence that the defendant acted with malice. We conclude that the conduct of the defendant in this case does not justify the imposition of an exemplary award.... Accordingly, we sustain the appeal.

* * *

Vigorous criticism of the doctrine of punitive damages is hardly a recent development in the field of jurisprudence. Arguments against the availability of such awards have been circulating for one hundred years and longer.... During those hundred years, commentators have exhaustively analyzed the doctrine.... Nonetheless, a substantial majority of jurisdictions today allow common law punitive damages in appropriate cases as a recovery beyond the amount necessary to compensate the plaintiff, for the purpose of deterrence or punishment or both....

One objection raised by the defendant is that the civil law is ill-suited to accomplish the goals that purportedly justify the doctrine of punitive damages. The defendant contends that the proper function of the civil tort law is to make plaintiffs whole, and that grave problems arise when it is used to extract from defendants something beyond full compensation for the victim. The defendant asserts that the primary purpose allegedly served by the doctrine of punitive damages, deterrence through punishment, is more properly left to the criminal law with its attendant procedural safeguards.

The bright line that the defendant attempts to interpose between the civil and the criminal law is in fact artificial. The courts of this country historically have not restricted the civil law to a compensatory function.... Furthermore, the lack of certain procedural safeguards, which are required in criminal prosecutions, does not render the civil law unfit to serve this deterrent function....

In a related argument, the defendant criticizes the doctrine of punitive damages because it permits a person to be punished twice for the same offense. The defendant observes that in the case at bar he was *both* convicted and fined in a criminal proceeding *and* assessed with punitive damages in a subsequent civil proceeding based upon the same conduct.... In the absence of constitutional compulsion, we can see no reason to bar actions for punitive damages based upon the fact that the underlying conduct is also subject to criminal prosecution....

Another objection to punitive damages raised by the defendant is that they bestow a windfall upon the plaintiff. As the defendant observes, such damages are awarded in Maine in excess of any amount necessary to compensate the plaintiff.... We find, however, that the extra recovery afforded to plaintiffs by punitive damages, rather than constituting a "windfall," serves a useful purpose. The potential for recovering an exemplary award provides an incentive for private civil enforcement of society's rules against serious misconduct....

The defendant next argues that the doctrine of punitive damages invites abuse because there is no objective standard by which to determine the amount of a proper award.... We, of course, do not advocate the availability of punitive damages on a completely open-ended basis.

The trial court must reject a claim for punitive damages as a matter of law unless the plaintiff presents adequate proof that the defendant acted in a sufficiently culpable manner. *See McKinnon v. Tibbetts*, 440 A.2d 1028, 1031 (Me.1982). Further, even after the plaintiff has satisfied his prima facie burden on the issue of exemplary damages, the fact finder must weigh "all relevant aggravating and mitigating factors" presented by the parties, including the egregiousness of the defendant's conduct, the ability of the defendant to pay such an award, and any criminal punishment imposed for the conduct in question....

In conclusion, we are not persuaded that we should abolish common law punitive damages in Maine....

Although we reject the defendant's contention that we should abolish common law punitive damages in Maine, we perceive cogent reasons for avoiding an overbroad application of the doctrine. Notions of fairness and efficiency weigh against allowing exemplary awards where the stated goal of deterring reprehensible conduct would be furthered only marginally or not at all.... Rather, punitive damages should be available based only upon a limited class of misconduct where deterrence is both paramount and likely to be achieved. With this in mind, we turn to a re-examination of the type of tortious conduct that can justify an exemplary award in Maine.

* * *

[In conclusion,] we retain the doctrine of punitive damages at common law in Maine, but not without substantial modification. Tortious conduct will justify an exemplary award only when the plaintiff can prove by clear and convincing evidence that the defendant acted with either express or implied malice.

NOTES AND QUESTIONS

1. Consider some the incidents about which you have already read in this course. If you were a juror in a state where punitive damages were permitted, would you have supported a finding of punitive damages if you heard a case where someone was injured on Six Flags Fiesta Texas's Rattler in its first season? Why or why not?

   What about in the case at Holiday World, where the coaster enthusiast Tamar Fellner died when thrown from the Raven coaster?

Or, say the McKamey Manor waiver was found inapplicable and someone was injured in the attraction after having said they were no longer consenting—would you support awarding punitive damages?

How about in the Ohio State Fair incident, where inspections failed to find corrosion and a former marine was killed?

In either of the Superman: Ride of Steel incidents (Darien Lake and Six Flags New England), where patrons were thrown to their deaths?

How about in the Glenwood Caverns tragedy covered in a previous chapter—would you award punitive damages against the park? The ride operators?

In any of the above where you think punitive damages might be appropriate, how much would you support? If there's someone nearby, describe the facts of some of the cases above and find out if they would agree with you about punitive damages.

2. As to those matters described in Note 1, what if you were a judge applying the standards described in either of the statutes identified above, or in the Maine case—would you send the question of punitive damages to the jury, or would you rule that they were not available as a matter of law? Why or why not?

3. States often impose caps on various categories of damages, whether punitive or otherwise. The United States Supreme Court has also held that the Due Process Clause of the U.S. Constitution imposes limits, albeit frustratingly vague limits, on punitive damage awards. Generally speaking, single-digit multipliers—that is, awards where the punitive damage award is no more than nine times the compensatory damages—are acceptable—but "because there are no rigid benchmarks that a punitive damages award may not surpass, ratios greater than those we have previously upheld may comport with due process where a particularly egregious act has resulted in only a small amount of economic damages.... The converse is also true, however. When compensatory damages are substantial, then a lesser ratio, perhaps only equal to compensatory damages, can reach the outermost limit of the due process guarantee. The precise award in any case, of course, must be based upon the fact[s] and circumstances of the defendant's conduct and the harm to the plaintiff." *State Farm v. Campbell*, 538 U.S. 408 (2003). Good luck providing concrete guidance on the issues based on the caselaw.

4. Kansas's limitation on punitive damages is included in the statute provided above. Kansas also imposes a limitation on wrongful death claims (those awarded to heirs), as seen here.

Kansas Statutes §60-1903: Amount of damages; jury instructions; itemized verdict

(a) In any wrongful death action, the court or jury may award such damages as are found to be fair and just under all the facts and circumstances, but the damages, other than pecuniary loss sustained by an heir at law, cannot exceed in the aggregate the sum of $250,000 and costs.

(b) If a wrongful death action is to a jury, the court shall not instruct the jury on the monetary limitation imposed by subsection (a) upon recovery of damages for nonpecuniary loss. If the jury verdict results in an award of damages for nonpecuniary loss which, after deduction of any amounts pursuant to K.S.A. 60-258a and amendments thereto, exceeds the limitation of subsection (a), the court shall enter judgment for damages of $250,000 for nonpecuniary loss.

(c) In any wrongful death action, the verdict shall be itemized by the trier of fact to reflect the amounts, if any, awarded for:

(1) Nonpecuniary damages;

(2) expenses for the care of the deceased caused by the injury; and

(3) pecuniary damages other than those itemized under subsection (c)(2).

(d) Where applicable, the amounts required to be itemized pursuant to subsections (c)(1) and (c)(3) shall be further itemized by the trier of fact to reflect those amounts awarded for injuries and losses sustained to date and those awarded for injuries and losses reasonably expected to be sustained in the future.

(e) In any wrongful death action, the trial court shall instruct the jury only on those items of damage upon which there is some evidence to base an award.

NOTES AND QUESTIONS

1. Obviously, cases that implicate punitive damages also often include criminal components. We will address criminal matters in the final chapter, but the central case in the rest of this chapter includes both.
2. There exist many videos online of Verrückt, the waterslide in Kansas that was the subject of the following. It is probably worth watching one of those videos to get a sense of just how fast and tall it was.

Emily Buder, *The World's Tallest Waterslide Was a Terrible, Tragic Idea*

THE ATLANTIC ONLINE, Aug. 13, 2019
https://www.theatlantic.com/video/index/595981/water-slide/

At 169 feet tall, Verrückt was the tallest waterslide in the world. Riders plummeted down the nearly vertical 17-story chute—taller than Niagara Falls—at speeds up to 70 miles per hour. German for "insane," Verrückt was designed to challenge the laws of physics. Visitors flocked to Schlitterbahn Water Park in Kansas City, Kansas, to experience its thrill.

That is, until August 7, 2016, when the raft that 10-year-old Caleb Schwab was riding went airborne and hit a metal pole supporting a safety net, resulting in his decapitation and instant death.

* * *

In 2012, the Schlitterbahn co-owner Jeff Henry, together with the senior designer John Schooley, fast-tracked Verrückt's construction to coincide with an appearance on a reality TV show about amusement parks. (They were also gunning for a Guinness World Record.) Although they had built rides before, neither Henry nor Schooley had a background in mechanical engineering. And according to state law, they didn't need those credentials to deem their own ride safe—unlike in the neighboring state of Missouri, water parks in Kansas do not require inspections by a state agency.

Indictment

State of Kansas v. Jeffrey Wayne Henry, John Timothy Schooley, and Henry & Sons Construction Co. Inc.
No. 18-cr-289, 18-cr-290, 18-cr-281, Mar. 21, 2018
(paragraph numbers omitted)

The Grand Jury for the 29th Judicial District, Wyandotte County, Kansas, charges:

[The indictment describes ASTM and notes that Henry & Sons was Schlitterbahn's private construction company.]

Henry, Jeffrey "Jeff" Wayne, Visionary and designer of the Verrückt project, and co-owner of the Schlitterbahn companies with siblings Gary Henry and Jana Henry Faber. HENRY dropped out of high school to work at his father's waterpark. HENRY possesses no technical or engineering credentials, yet he controls many key decisions regarding Schlitterbahn design and construction projects. Schlitterbahn consists of more than a dozen privately-held corporations owned and operated by the three Henry siblings. Although each corporation is technically a separate entity, the lines between those corporations are blurred....

Raft "B"—Verrückt rafts (also called boats) consist of two parts: an insert and a raft. The insert is manufactured by HSC and consists of the seats and restraints. One insert is installed inside each raft, and are labeled alphabetically A, B, etc. Since the insert label is prominently displayed on the back of the rear seat, staff refer to each raft by its alphabetical insert label. The rafts are soft inflatable rubber river rafts manufactured by Zebec of North America Inc., which are labeled numerically 1, 2, etc. Schlitterbahn kept approximately six rafts in operation at any given time, with about four others in reserve.

[The indictment describes the business entities and notes that John Timothy Schooley was the lead designer on the water slide despite having no engineering credentials. Tyler Austin Miles was the Director of Operations for Schlitterbahn Kansas City.]

Verrückt [vair-ROOKT]—Certified in 2014 by Guinness Book of World Records as the tallest waterslide on earth at 168 feet tall (17 stories; 264 stair steps). Verrückt is a hybrid of a roller-coaster and waterslide designed by HENRY, SCHOOLEY, and HSC.... Verrückt's slide path is enclosed with netting suspended over the top of metal hoops. Riders who were at least 54-inches tall began at the tower base where they were weighed into groups of two or three and totaling 400 to 550 pounds. Rider groups climb the tower steps and enter a raft. Rafts launch down the main descent into the invert. After the raft traverses the invert and ascends the "second hill" a series of high-pressure water blasters propel the raft over the top of the second hill and into the runout pool. Empty rafts are returned to the tower using conveyor belts. The crest of the second hill, which stands more than 50 feet above the concrete foundation, is where rafts would typically go airborne.

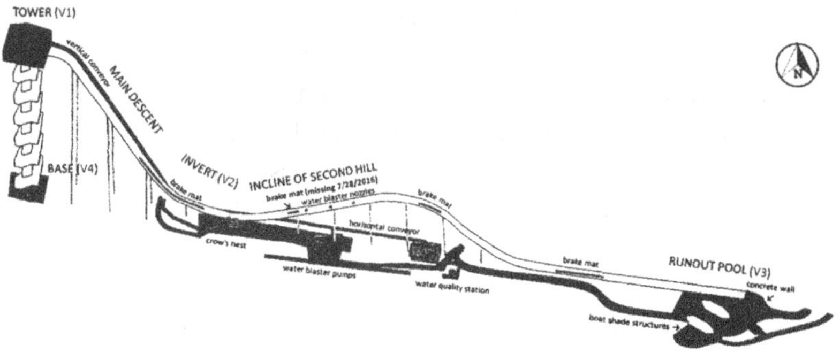

[The indictment provided a brief organizational structure summary.]

<u>Statement of Facts</u>

Introduction

On August 7, 2016, a 10-year-old boy, C.S. (xx/xx/2006), was decapitated and two adult women, Matraca Baetz and Hannah Barnes, were severely injured when raft B went airborne and collided with the overhead hoops and netting affixed to the Verrückt waterslide located at the Schlitterbahn Waterpark of Kansas City, Kansas.

A video recording of C.S.'s death confirms that, at the time of his death, C.S. was obeying all rider instructions.

The death of C.S. appeared at first to be an isolated and unforeseeable incident until whistleblowers from within Schlitterbahn's own ranks came forward and revealed that Schlitterbahn officials had covered up similar incidents in the past.

Experts in the field of amusement ride design and safety examined Verrückt and found physical evidence which indicated that other rafts had gone airborne and collided with the overhead hoops and netting before the fatality. These experts noted that Verrückt's design violated nearly all aspects of the longstanding industry safety standards published by ASTM. In fact, the design and operation of the Verrückt complied with few, if any, of the industry safety standards.

Armed with this knowledge, detectives from the Kansas City Kansas Police Department (KCKPD), special agents from the Kansas Bureau of Investigation (KBI), and special agents from the Kansas Attorney General's Office began reconstructing the design and operational history of Verrückt since its conception in November of 2012.

Evidence in the form of corporate emails, memoranda, blueprints, video recordings, photographs, and eyewitness statements revealed that this child's death and the rapidly growing list of injuries were foreseeable and expected outcomes; Verrückt's designers and operators knew that Verrückt posed a substantial and unjustifiable risk of death or severe bodily harm.

Those responsible for Verrückt's operation knew they were guilty of criminal misconduct, as evinced by their attempts to conceal evidence from law enforcement officers. These obstructions substantially delayed the investigation.

Design

On November 13, 2012, in a spur-of-the-moment bid to impress producers of the Travel Channel's Xtreme Waterparks series, HENRY concocted a plan to build the world's tallest and fastest water slide.

New and experimental amusement rides should be subjected to a thorough on-paper design process of dynamic (sometimes called "geometric") and structural engineering. Dynamic engineering involves calculating the physics a passenger will experience along the ride path, such as: speed, weight, distance, velocity, momentum, gravitational force, centripetal force, friction, and so on. Although time consuming, properly performed dynamic engineering yields a safer ride. Once the physics of the design is calculated, the designers adjust the blueprints before structural engineering begins. Structural engineering is then used to design the foundations and pillars to support the ride.

Records show that HSC was responsible for dynamic engineering under the direction of HENRY and SCHOOLEY. A third-party was hired for structural engineering. Investigators found ample evidence that structural engineering had been calculated. In stark contrast, investigators found nothing in Verrückt's project records indicating that dynamic engineering had been calculated, despite multiple court orders demanding that HSC disclose any such information.

HENRY and SCHOOLEY lacked the technical expertise to properly design a complex amusement ride such as Verrückt. Neither of the two men possessed any kind of technical or engineering credential relevant to amusement ride design or safety. As SCHOOLEY admitted, "If we actually knew how to do this, and it could be done that easily, it wouldn't be that spectacular."

HENRY was the principal designer and visionary, and was ultimately responsible for all decisions regarding Verrückt. HENRY was often described as a micromanager of the design and construction process. SCHOOLEY was lead designer and was responsible for designing Verrückt's slide path geometry....

Due to HENRY's and SCHOOLEY's lack of expertise and a desire to rush the timeline, they skipped fundamental steps in the design process. In place of mathematical and physics calculations, they rushed forward relying almost entirely on crude trial-and-error methods.

HENRY was responsible for the rushed timeline, as evinced by his emails. For example, on December 14, 2012, HENRY wrote two emails to SCHOOLEY and others: "We all need to circle on this[.] I must communicate reality to all. Time, is of the essence. No time to die." and "I have to micro manage this. NOW. This is a designed product for TV, absolutely cannot be anything else. Speed is 100% required. A floor a day. Tough schedule. Jeff." HENRY set a completion deadline for the entire project for June 15, 2013, a period of only 7 months. This timeline encompassed all design, construction, and testing.

Experts in the amusement park design industry who inspected Verrückt following the death of C.S. have stated that for a ride like the Verrückt, a team of approximately three to four members (including at least two fully-qualified and experienced engineers) would need three to six months of design calculations before the first ground is broken to construct a prototype of a proposed ride. After the prototype of a proposed ride is built, testing of the prototype can begin.

In comparison, not a single engineer was directly involved in Verrückt's dynamic engineering or slide path design. HENRY's statements and HSC's own project management records indicate that the design and construction of the Verrückt prototype began and was completed within 36 days of when HENRY first conceived of the idea for Verrückt.

* * *

Verrückt suffered from a long list of dangerous design flaws; however, the most obvious and potentially lethal flaw was that Verrückt's design guaranteed that rafts would occasionally go airborne in a manner that could severely injure or kill the occupants. HENRY, SCHOOLEY, and MILES all knew about this problem before the ride opened to the public. Investigators obtained video recordings of HENRY and SCHOOLEY in a raft going airborne during their personal test run on the Verrückt prototype. Test rafts went airborne on the prototype, the original slide profile, and the redesigned profile.

In 2014, Verrückt underwent a massive redesign because of the persistent airborne problem. Video footage shows SCHOOLEY sketching the raft's airborne flight path on a large whiteboard, explaining to MILES and others: "What we found in testing, was that the momentum of the higher weight testing carried [the raft] up over the top of the slide and into a path shown there. That is unacceptable. This is not an air-flying-ride; it's a raft-on-flume-ride."

In a separate interview, HENRY admitted the redesign was necessary because, "Too fast. Too many G's. *** And then when we get to the top, the boats just went sailing." When asked why HENRY and SCHOOLEY didn't have the design science down, HENRY answered, "I'm not quite sure yet. Many things, I think. There's a whole bunch of factors that creeped in on this one that we just didn't know about. Obviously things do fall faster than Newton said."

When rumors and news reports emerged about airborne rafts, a Schlitterbahn spokesperson publicly discredited these reports. Meanwhile, HENRY and SCHOOLEY began secretly testing at night to avoid scrutiny....

HENRY openly admitted that one of his principal motivations in building Verrückt was to flaunt his achievements in the faces of the other waterpark owners: "Hey guys, come on! Are you gonna let me have the bragging rights? Because I'm gonna brag a lot! We are the tallest ride in the world." To the owner of waterpark rival Beach Park, HENRY said, "You are now being bested by a guy in Kansas—not even Texas—okay, Kansas is number one. Wyandotte County Kansas is beating Beach Park."

HENRY admitted that he was ignoring established industry safety standards because he felt he could redefine those standards with his own achievements. While describing his vision of how Verrückt would change the industry, HENRY explained, "[We're going to set the standards up, and set the education up, and we're gonna redefine many of the definables that have been defined in the industry that we couldn't find good reasons for. Like a 48-inch height rule. Why 48 inches? I could never figure out why not 47 inches. It made no sense to me. And so we're gonna change all that now in this park, and hopefully change it worldwide in all parks and get back to rational reasonable scientific decisions as to why and how we run our facilities...."

HENRY remarked, "[Verrückt] could hurt me, it could kill me, it is a seriously dangerous piece of equipment today because there are things that we don't know about it. Every day we learn more. *** I've seen what this one has done to the crash dummies and to the boats we sent down it. Ever since the prototype. And we had boats flying in the prototype too. *** It's complex, it's fast, it's mean. If we messup, it could be the end. I could die going down this ride."

HSC hired an outside engineering firm to perform accelerometer testing of the rafts as they went down Verrückt. On July 3, 2014—one week before Verrückt's grand opening—the accelerometer test result data indicated that rafts in the weight range of 400 pounds to 550 pounds would likely go airborne at the crest of the second hill.

* * *

Business records obtained from the Verrückt project prove that MILES began assisting SCHOOLEY with logging test data before grand opening. SCHOOLEY and MILES logged the following airborne test rafts after the 2014 redesign:

Date	Type	Speed (mph)	Front (lbs)	Middle (lbs)	Rear (lbs)	Witness
06/25/2014	Sandbag	40	100	200	150	J. Schooley
07/06/2014	Human	43	160	0	230	J. Schooley
07/07/2014	Human	Not logged	160	200	200	T. Miles

* * *

[The indictment alleges that Schooley signed the commissioning document certifying its safety, and the operation manual, stating that it complied with ASTM standards. The indictment further alleges in detail the ways in which the waterslide did not comply with ASTM standards, specifically focusing on the placement of netting and hoops above the ride path, describing that design as "obviously defective and ultimately lethal."]

The presence of the overhead netting and support hoops speaks volumes about the designers' extreme disregard for the value of human life. ASTM directs that any structure located within the patron clearance envelope—meaning the area within which a rider could theoretically touch at any time during the ride—must be carefully scrutinized and any potential for physical contact with an obstruction during the ride must be eliminated. HENRY and SCHOOLEY did the opposite; they installed metal bars directly across the known flight path.

* * *

[The indictment alleges various flaws with the Operation and Maintenance Manual.]

Public Operation

On July 10, 2014, HENRY and SCHOOLEY opened the ride to the public. Video footage shows HENRY and SCHOOLEY standing together on an elevated platform between Verrückt's main descent and second hill. HENRY and SCHOOLEY both watch as a raft carrying guests traveled up and over the crest of the second hill. As they watched, HENRY remarked to SCHOOLEY, "Man, are they hitting that net up there? That boat flew. That boat looked like it flew."

On August 16, 2014, [a consultant hired by Schlitterbahn] wrote a report to HENRY warning him that Verrückt was unfinished and was still in an unsafe condition. HENRY obviously ignored the report because Verrückt remained in operation.

Injuries caused by Verrückt

[The indictment listed eleven incidents prior to the date of the decapitation.]

These injuries were caused by airborne rafts or other aspects of Verrückt's flawed design, such as problems with the raft design and violent collisions with the concrete wall at the end of the runout pool. Collisions occurred because the runout pool was incorrectly designed and violated ASTM standards. The raft's passenger compartment provided little protection or ability to brace, resulting in foot, leg, and head injuries.

[The indictment describes the injuries, some of which did involve riders going airborne; most of the injuries related to slamming down forcefully after going airborne. Patrons also reported seeing repairs being performed with duct tape and rubber bands. One patron specifically reported hitting a hoop, resulting in injuries. After that injury, the indictment alleges that park staff destroyed the initial reports and insisted that lifeguards and medical staff change their reports to exclude how the injury had occurred.]

Raft B

HENRY and SCHOOLEY selected the rafts for Verrückt. Not all rafts performed equally. Staff identified raft B as having a propensity for going abnormally fast and going airborne more frequently than other rafts. In 2016, MILES received written reports about raft B, advising [that it was abnormally heavy and ran faster than other rafts, including going airborne, and was linked to at least two of the prior injuries. Raft B was removed from service briefly after some injuries but returned and continued to have issues].

Maintenance Issues

[The indictment alleges extensive failures to maintain the ride, delaying any repairs that would take it out of service. The restraints were allowed to age so badly that they often failed. The brake system often was failing. A few weeks before the death, a manager flagged the brake system as an "urgent priority level 1 maintenance issue," but the park continued to operate the slide.]

Investigation of C.S.'s death

[Miles, the director of operations, was interviewed by both counsel for Schlitterbahn and by the police.]

On August 12, 2016, Kansas City Kansas Police Department Detective Jason Sutton interviewed MILES and asked, "Have you been aware of any complaints regarding Verrückt the ride in the last season? This season, this summer?" MILES answered, "I have not, sir." Det. Sutton asked MILES if complaints would typically be reported to MILES "in a written form or a verbal form?" MILES answered, "It would definitely come in a verbal form, sir."

At the time MILES made this statement, Det. Sutton was unaware that MILES had withheld thousands of written "ops daily reports" containing incriminating information against MILES and others....

On or about September 1, 2016, one of the lifeguards MILES had coerced into writing a coached statement, N.W. (age 17), came forward to Det. Sutton and revealed MILES's efforts to cover up the Groves incident in June of 2016. Investigators then interviewed J Groves, the lifeguards, and the medical staff who were involved in the Groves incident. Each person independently corroborated MILES's efforts to cover up....

In November of 2016, MILES loaded the ops daily reports into a vehicle and drove them from SWKC to a different corporation located in Texas which serves as HENRY's corporate headquarters.

* * *

Among the ops daily reports were dozens alerting MILES to airborne raft incidents witnessed by staff, problems with raft B, injuries, complaints, brake system failures, and pervasive maintenance problems on Verrückt....

[The indictment charged the defendants with 18 charges, including charges of second degree murder, aggravated endangering a child, and aggravated battery.]

NOTES AND QUESTIONS

1. In a separate indictment, Tyler Austin Miles and the waterpark itself were charged with involuntary manslaughter and other charges in a very similar indictment. Both indictments are available in full on RecreationAndRisk.com.

2. The indictments were dismissed by a judge, who concluded that it was improper for the grand jury to have been shown certain evidence, in particular the excerpts from television shows made to document the construction of the ride. "Defense attorneys said showing grand jurors the Travel Channel show was improper because it was scripted and dramatized to play up the riskiness of the ride" and the judge agreed. Steve Vockrodt, *Schlitterbahn charges tossed*, KANSAS CITY STAR, Feb. 22, 2019. "'Upon viewing the video, the court concludes this exhibit was not a likeness of what it pur-

ported to represent,' Burns said, 'and depicted a staged demonstration for entertainment purposes, not a factual depiction of the design and construction of the water slide.'" *Id.* The grand jury was also presented expert testimony that, apparently, suggested that ASTM standards were required under the law in Kansas, which was not true at the time.

3. The dismissal of the indictments did not preclude re-filing by the state (because jeopardy had not attached). The state has not brought new criminal charges for reasons that have not been made public.
4. Consider what you would do if you were a juror hearing a civil matter brought by Caleb's family. Setting aside for now any caps on damages, would you award damages to his survivors for non-economic damages like anguish, loss of emotional support, and the like? If so, how much? Why? How do you feel about the cap of $250,000 on such damages in Kansas?
5. Again setting aside any caps, would you want (as a juror) to award punitive damages based on what you know? How much? How do you feel about the cap of the lesser of the defendant's gross income or $5 million?
6. As you can see from the Kansas statutes above, the maximum Caleb's family was likely to be able to receive under Kansas law was limited, with noneconomic damages capped at $250,000 and likely a relatively small number for economic damages, given his young age and the consequential inability to prove economic damages.

   This is, I observe, an emotionally and ethically complicated consequence of how the law puts values on lives—money is the tool the civil justice system has, and to have that tool used in a way that is at all predictable or reviewable, it has to be based on something. That "something" is, in many aspects, reflecting the economic "value" of a life, which makes the young, the old, the disabled, the less educated, and others have less value under tort law.

   Consider for a bit how this might affect the liability exposure for attractions that primarily attract kids. Do you think Kansas law adequately reflects the damage done with the death of a child? Why do you think legislatures adopt caps like that? How much do you think the life of a child should be worth under the law? How did you come to that number?

Given that maximum of $250,000 for the non-economic damages and the single-digit multiplier as a limit on punitive damages, the maximum punitive award constitutionally was likely to be even lower than Kansas's statutory cap (which was likely $5 million in this case).

And yet the family settled with the various defendants for a total of just shy of $20 million, at least four times as much as the statutory caps would have suggested. *See* Steve Vockrodt, *Family of Caleb Schwab receives nearly $20 million in Verrückt settlements*, KANSAS CITY STAR, May 5, 2017. $14 million came from companies directly associated with Schlitterbahn, $5 million from Henry & Sons Construction, the general contractor, $500,000 from the ride manufacturer, and $232,125 from a consulting entity.

No lawsuit was filed—presumably the park and others recognized the overwhelming evidence of liability and agreed to negotiate without suit being filed—so we don't know what arguments might have been in the mix.

Why do you think the defendants agreed to a settlement so much larger than liability likely could have been under Kansas law? (Think back to the Holiday World discussion if you need a pointer.)

7. The legendary *Texas Monthly* journalist Skip Hollandsworth did a long article about the Schlitterbahn tragedy and, more, about Jeff Henry. It gives the history of Schlitterbahn—a central Texas waterpark I still love, founded by a Houston accountant who wanted to leave the city and bought land on the beautiful Comal River. Jeff Henry, the founder's son, grew up in the park and was involved in designing many rides there—rides that did not have anywhere near the forces of Verrückt and thus far fewer risks if something went badly. The article, while well beyond the scope of this casebook, provides a fascinating and sometimes upsetting look at the story and may help you see how things can go so badly—and you may, again, see parallels between Henry and Action Park's owner, Gene Mulvihill. I recommend it. *See* Skip Hollandsworth, *Schlitterbahn's Tragic Slide*, TEXAS MONTHLY, Aug. 2018.

8. Schlitterbahn Kansas City stayed open for two years after Caleb Schwab's death, though Verrückt never reopened. Verrückt was torn down in November 2018, and the park did not reopen in 2019.

Cedar Fair, a major amusement and water park operator, acquired Schlitterbahn's parks in New Braunfels, Texas (the original location) and Galveston, Texas, for a total of $261 million. *See* Press Release, Cedar Fair Completes Acquisition of Two Iconic Schlitterbahn Water Parks in Texas, July 1, 2019, cedarfair.com. Cedar Fair also had the right to acquire the Kansas City location for just $6 million more; it did not exercise that option, and the park has been demolished.

9. Prior to this incident, Kansas had some of the least extensive regulations of amusement rides in the country, leaving it almost entirely to the private sector—it required insurance and annual self-inspections. Caleb Schwab's father was a Kansas legislator—in fact, the Schwabs were at the park for a special day where state officials were invited to the park. The new regulations require independent inspections, change insurance requirements, require registration, and provide for an investigation if a death on a ride was due to a major malfunction. *See* K.S.A. §§ 44-1601 *et seq.*; *see also* Hunter Woodall, *In aftermath of Verrückt death, Brownback signs amusement ride bill*, Kansas City Star, Apr. 24, 2017.

   Kansas has no major amusement or water parks; it has various fairgrounds and family entertainment centers with kiddie coaster. Schlitterbahn was its only major park.

10. The full report is available on RecreationAndRisk.com.

CHAPTER 12

Intentional Torts

This is at least the third time we have addressed intentional torts, at least in passing. Chapter 5, addressing waivers, discussed aspects of the defense of consent, especially in the context of McKamey Manor's lengthy waiver. And Chapter 7 went into emotional distress claims, including intentional inflection of emotional distress.

Here, we will address other intentional torts (mostly battery and assault) and do a deeper dive on consent, which is, in some sense, the intentional tort equivalent of assumption of the risk—with important differences.

We start with a return to a case that first appeared back in Chapter 2.

Molenda v. Universal City Studios LLC

Case No. 2:20-cv-02554 (C.D. Cal. 2020)

The Honorable R. Gary Klausner, United States District Judge

Plaintiffs Melinda Molenda, Lisa Molenda, and Josiah Steele (collectively, "Plaintiffs") filed a Complaint in state court against Defendants Universal City Studios LLC and Universal Studios Hollywood (collectively, "Defendants" or "Universal"). [The Complaint includes allegations of assault and battery, among other things. This motion to dismiss followed removal to federal court.]

II. FACTUAL BACKGROUND

Plaintiffs' Complaint alleges the following:

Plaintiffs were actors at the Universal Studios Hollywood theme park who played zombies in a haunted house-like maze attraction based on the hit show The Walking Dead. While they were in character in the maze, Plaintiffs were physically assaulted and sexually harassed by park guests. For example, Plaintiff Melinda Molenda ("Plaintiff Melinda") was groped several times during her employment. On one occasion, a guest spat in her eye. Plaintiff Lisa Molenda was also groped by park guests. On one occasion, a guest threw soda in her eye, causing a severe eye infection. Plaintiff Josiah Steele was punched so hard by a park guest that he went to the hospital.

Plaintiffs reported many incidents of physical assault and sexual harassment to their supervisors. However, little action was taken in response. In fact, Universal contributes to the volatile situation in the maze. Indeed, [per the complaint,] Universal's website promotes the Walking Dead attraction by telling guests to "[p]repare to *fight* for survival in a fully immersive journey ... as you *battle* your way through nightmarish iconic landscapes."

III. JUDICIAL STANDARD

To survive a motion under Rule 12(b)(6), a complaint must contain "sufficient factual matter, accepted as true, to 'state a claim to relief that is plausible on its face.'" *Ashcroft v. Iqbal*, 556 U.S. 662, 678 (2009) (quoting *Bell Atl. Corp. v. Twombly*, 550 U.S. 544, 570 (2007)). A claim is facially plausible if the plaintiff alleges enough facts to permit a reasonable inference that the defendant is liable for the alleged misconduct. *Id.* A plaintiff need not provide "detailed factual allegations" but must provide more than mere legal conclusions. *Twombly*, 550 U.S. at 555. "Threadbare recitals of the elements of a cause of action, supported by mere conclusory statements, do not suffice." *Iqbal*, 556 U.S. at 678.

* * *

IV. DISCUSSION

Defendants move to dismiss Plaintiffs' Complaint in its entirety. The Court first considers Plaintiffs' assault and battery claim....

A. Assault and Battery (Claim 1)

Plaintiffs' first claim is for assault and battery. Defendants argue that this claim must be dismissed because ... Plaintiffs cannot state a claim for assault and battery against Defendants for actions taken by third parties (i.e., park guests).

1. Failure to State a Claim

Plaintiffs purport to state one claim for assault and battery. However, assault and battery are two distinct claims, each of which has its own elements. To state a claim for assault, a plaintiff must allege that: "(1) defendant acted with intent to cause harmful or offensive contact, or threatened to touch plaintiff in a harmful or offensive manner; (2) plaintiff reasonably believed she was about to be touched in a harmful or offensive manner or it reasonably appeared to plaintiff that defendant was about to carry out the threat; (3) plaintiff did not consent to defendant's conduct; (4) plaintiff was harmed; and (5) defendant's conduct was a substantial factor in causing plaintiff's harm." *So v. Shin*, 212 Cal. App. 4th 652, 668–69 (2013), *as modified on denial of reh'g* (Jan. 28, 2013). To state a claim for battery, the plaintiff must allege that: "(1) defendant touched plaintiff, or caused plaintiff to be touched, with the intent to harm or offend plaintiff; (2) plaintiff did not consent to the touching; (3) plaintiff was harmed or offended by defendant's conduct; and (4) a reasonable person in plaintiff's position would have been offended by the touching." *Id.* at 669. Assault and battery are both intentional torts. *Bartosh v. Banning*, 251 Cal. App. 2d 378, 385 (1967).

There are several theories of liability that a plaintiff can pursue when suing for assault and battery. Relevant here, the plaintiff can sue on (1) a direct theory of liability, (2) a *respondeat superior* theory of liability, and (3) an aiding and abetting theory of liability. In this case, Plaintiffs specifically disclaim that they bring their assault and battery claim on a *respondeat superior* theory.... Instead, Plaintiffs aver that they bring this claim on a direct theory and an aiding and abetting theory....

a. Direct Theory

Contrary to Plaintiffs' assertion, it does not appear that Plaintiffs bring their assault and battery claim on a direct theory of liability. Indeed, although the Complaint repeatedly alleges that Universal "aided and abetted" and "instigated" the assaults and batteries on Plaintiffs, it never alleges that Universal itself assaulted or battered Plaintiffs. (*See* Compl. ¶ 12 ("... Universal incites violence and instigates the commission of ... assault, and battery"); ¶ 14 ("Universal aided, abetted, counseled, and encouraged the assaults and batteries described below"); ¶ 48 ("In inciting the violence and instigating the commission of ... assault, and battery ... and in aiding, abetting, counseling, and encouraging the assaults and batteries....).) Accordingly, because Plaintiffs' Complaint does not allege assault or battery on a direct theory, the Court does not address the merits of any such claim.

b. Aiding and Abetting

Plaintiffs do bring their assault and battery claim on an aiding and abetting theory. "California has adopted the common law rule for subjecting a defendant to liability for aiding and abetting a tort." *Casey v. U.S. Bank National Ass'n*, 127 Cal. App. 4th 1138, 1144 (2005). Under this rule, liability for aiding and abetting an intentional tort may attach in two ways: "if the person (1) knows the other's conduct constitutes a breach of duty and gives substantial assistance or encouragement to the other to so act or (2) gives substantial assistance to the other in accomplishing a tortious result and the person's own conduct, separately considered, constitutes a breach of duty to the third person." *Id.* [quoting another source]. The key concepts are "knowledge" and "substantial assistance." To satisfy the knowledge requirement, the defendant must have "actual knowledge of the specific primary wrong the defendant substantially assisted." *Id.* This requires "more than a vague suspicion of wrongdoing." *In re First All. Mortg. Co.*, 471 F.3d 977, 993 n.4 (9th Cir. 2006). The definition of "substantial assistance" is somewhat unclear. *Id.* at 994. However, in *Casey*, the California Court of Appeal held that "even 'ordinary business transactions' ... can satisfy the substantial assistance element of an aiding and abetting claim if the [defendant] actually knew [that their actions] were assisting the [wrongdoer] in committing a specific tort. Knowledge is the crucial element." *Casey*, 127 Cal. App. 4th at 1145.

Here, Defendants argue, among other things, that Plaintiffs have not stated a claim for aiding and abetting assault and battery because they have not satisfied the "knowledge" requirement. The Court agrees. Plaintiffs allege that Universal had "knowledge of many violent assaults[.]" (Compl. ¶ 13.) However, at most, the Complaint plausibly alleges that Defendants knew about the assaults and batteries upon Plaintiffs *after the fact*—i.e., after Plaintiffs reported these incidents to their supervisors. The Complaint does not allege enough facts to permit a reasonable inference that Universal knew about these incidents before they took place, let alone that they knew the "specific primary wrong" that they were assisting. The Court therefore dismisses Plaintiffs' assault and battery claim.

NOTES AND QUESTIONS

1. What was your reaction to the complaint's use of language from the park's website—where guests were told they would "fight for survival" and "battle ... through nightmarish iconic landscapes"? If you were the judge, would you have concluded that language was sufficient to get past the Rule 12(b)(6) stage? Do you agree with how the court interprets the "knowledge" requirement?
2. This case identifies the lack of consent as an affirmative element of the tort of battery. As an element of the claim, the burden of proving the lack of consent is on the plaintiff. Some courts consider consent to be an affirmative defense as to which the defendant has the burden of proof. *See, e.g., Escue v. Northern OK College*, 450 F.3d 1146, 1158 (10th Cir. 2006). In practical terms, this probably doesn't make a huge difference.
3. Consent can be inferred and need not always be established through words. Do you think there is some contact to which an actor in a haunted house like Universal's consents? How about a patron going through a haunted house—is there some contact that would otherwise be a battery to which a factfinder might appropriately conclude a patron has consented? What evidence would be relevant to such a determination? If this case had proceeded into discovery, do you think the park would have or should have argued that the actors consented to at least some of the contact alleged to be tortious?
4. If this lawsuit was against the individual patrons who groped, punched, or otherwise came into offensive contact with the employees, do you have any question that a battery claim could be successful? Think about the range of potential contacts and consider what you think would and would not be a battery for which recovery

would be likely. Why isn't the employees' lawsuit against patrons? Again, do you think the patrons would have had a plausible argument for consent as to at least some of the conduct?

5. A reminder: these are "dignity" torts—the invasion of personal dignity is what is being protected, and so, unlike negligence claims, a plaintiff need not show actual damages.

6. In Chapter 4, we discussed assumption of risk in the context of haunted houses in the *Munoz v. Six Flags St. Louis, LLC* case. There, the plaintiff alleged that she was injured when an actor dressed as a clown scared her and then chased her (though how much of a chase took place was disputed). She did not include any intentional tort claims. Do you think she should have? Why or why not?

   The *Munoz* case referenced this next case in the context of assuming risk in a negligence context, but it also has an intentional tort aspect. As we will see, though, I think the court gets it a bit tangled up.

Griffin v. Haunted Hotel

242 Cal. App. 4th 490 (2015)

NARES, J.

In October 2011 appellant Scott Griffin purchased a ticket to experience "The Haunted Trail," an outdoor haunted house type of attraction where actors jump out of dark spaces, often inches away from patrons, holding prop knives, axes, chainsaws, or severed body parts. After passing what he believed was the exit and "giggling and laughing" with his friends about how much fun they had, Griffin unexpectedly was confronted by a final scare known as the "Carrie" effect—so named because, like the horror film Carrie (MGM 1976), patrons are led to believe the attraction is over, only to be met by one more extreme fright. This was delivered by an actor wielding a gas powered chainsaw (the chain had been removed), who approached Griffin, frightened him, and gave chase when Griffin ran away. Griffin was injured when he fell while fleeing. Griffin sued The Haunted Hotel, Inc. (Haunted Hotel), which operates The Haunted Trail, alleging negligence and assault....

[O]n this record there is no evidence creating a triable issue Haunted House [acted tortiously].

A. *The Haunted Trail*

Haunted Hotel operates four Halloween attractions in San Diego County, including The Haunted Trail located in Balboa Park. The Haunted Trail operates from September through October, ending on Halloween.

The Haunted Trail features actors in ghoulish costumes who frighten, startle and sometimes chase patrons amid loud noises and flashing strobe lights in a one-mile loop in Balboa Park. Patrons follow a narrow trail in the natural park setting, passing from one horror set to the next, each telling a different gruesome story. Along the way, actors jump out of dark spaces or spring from around corners, often inches away from patrons, holding bloody prop knives, axes or other weapons, or a severed body part.

If a patron becomes frightened and runs away, one of the actors will often chase after the person. The Haunted Trail played an orientation audiotape for every group of visitors who attended the attraction in 2011, which states:

> "Our creatures will not grab you, however, they may accidentally bump into you. Oh, you will be scared sh—less and try to run away, but in the end our creatures will chase you down like the chickens that you are!"

[Griffin testified that he did not remember this audio being played but conceded that evidence indicated it was played for every group.]

In 2011 the "Frequently Asked Questions" part of The Haunted Trail's Web site stated, "[Y]ou will not be grabbed or pushed," and warned, "Running is the main cause of minor injuries. Make sure to follow the rules and DON'T run and you should be fine!" Signs at the entrance stated, "Due to natural surroundings of the park the ground may be uneven with some obstacles such as tree roots, rocks, etc. Be careful."

The parties do not dispute that the ticket Griffin purchased states, "This attraction contains high impact scares" and "is not suitable for people with heart conditions or people prone to seizures; is not recommended for children under age 10; and pregnant women, infants and children being carried will not be allowed entry." The Haunted Trail instructs its employees to "stay away" if a child is crying, not to chase children at all, and to "stay clear of people who are crying." * * *

Photographs on The Haunted Trail Web site featured costumed actors holding chainsaws. Griffin purchased his ticket on the Web site. The chainsaw-wielding actors are the most popular feature of The Haunted Trail. The chainsaw scenes have been mentioned in radio advertising or shown on television.

At the final scene along the trail, three people with prop chainsaws—gas powered chainsaws with the chains removed—menace patrons as they walk to an opening in the temporary chain link fence, covered with a dark screen, that runs along the edge of the trail. That opening appears to be the exit, the end of the attraction.

What follows is something Haunted Hotel calls the "Carrie" effect, a final scare patterned after the closing scene of the horror movie Carrie when the audience is led to believe that the terror is over, only to be given one last jolting scare. When patrons have walked through the opening in the fence, they regroup on the park access road, thinking the attraction is over. But this is a fake exit. The access road is controlled by Haunted Hotel. A chainsaw-wielding actor with a gas powered chainsaw suddenly appears, starts the chainsaw, and charges at the patrons—providing a final scare. Although the chain has been removed from the chainsaw, it "still has the whole sound, the whole smell of a chain saw, and that's what gives the effect of—people think it's a real chain saw." During this last encounter, patrons are most prone to run away, with the actor giving chase.

The access road is visible to surrounding public space. Families "actually come and camp out and watch" because "it's fun to see when someone gets freaked out when a chain saw comes and chases an individual."

In the 14 years The Haunted Trial [*sic*, Trail] has been operating, over 250,000 patrons have attended the event. In the three years preceding Griffin's incident, between 10 and 15 people fell while running from the chainsaw-wielding actor in this final scare. Three people fell the night Griffin attended. None of the 15 who fell reported being injured.

B. *Griffin's Incident*

Near Halloween in October 2011 Griffin learned some friends were planning to attend The Haunted Trail. Griffin had previously attended Knott's "Scary" Farm and possibly "Fright Night" at Universal Studios. He had been to Balboa Park before, but he had never heard of The Haunted Trail and knew nothing about the attraction.

Griffin and his group entered the attraction, but Griffin recalled little about the preliminaries, acknowledging that he was "not paying attention" to his surroundings, but rather "laughing, visiting" with friends. As he walked through The Haunted Trail, Griffin was, to use his own words, "scared pretty darn good." He was not chased along the trail and said "it was fun."

At the final scene along the trail, Griffin heard chainsaws. At first, he was "shocked," but he just "walk[ed] through ... I knew we were almost ending ... we had already had so much fun already through the thingy, so it was okay."

After this final scene, Griffin headed for the "gate," which he believed was an exit, "ending the experience."

"[T]here was clearly, to me, an exit that the event is over because inside everything is roped off, you are on a path. It's very clear where you're going. And the gates and the exit, to me, were clear that we were done with the experience." [] This area, a "well-lit even surface," is actually controlled by The Haunted Trail and is part of the show.

Griffin testified in deposition that suddenly, a "gentleman" started a chainsaw and "came at me with it." Griffin tried to "back away from him" but "he just kept following me." Griffin asked the man to "stop" and when he did not stop, Griffin "started running away because it felt unsafe with his chainsaw because he was pointing it at me...."

Griffin testified,

> I started to try to get away from him, and, boy, he seemed to really enjoy that [and] I really got scared because he was really at me, with me at it, he was unlike the other people. And we had already exited the venue. He was right into my space.... He was literally coming at me. He selected me.... He was pointing [the chainsaw] right at me and it was live and active; you could literally smell the gas ... hear the sound and everything. Yes, I felt like he was handling that very dangerous [*sic*].... It was a real chainsaw.... This gentleman did not keep a safe distance ... and the more I backed away, the more he followed me. I asked him to stop; he wouldn't. I started running. He was literally running after me. And I really felt unsafe. And then I started getting really fearful that something was going to happen, because here's some stranger—I don't

> even know who he is—with a live, active chainsaw running after me with it. I was fearful for my safety big time.... I really felt that he could have tripped, that chainsaw could have fell down, and I could dangerously [*sic*] get hurt by it. That's what I felt.

While being chased and running an unspecified distance, Griffin fell, injuring his wrist. In deposition, Griffin acknowledged "it is the point of The Haunted Trail to scare the people who attend" and "not many people would attend the event if it were not scary."

A representative of The Haunted Trail testified in deposition, "you scare the hell out of them as much as you possibly can, and that's what they're paying us for, that's why they come." He stated Griffin "was never in harm.... He ran. He chose to run. You can't chase a human that doesn't run. If he had just stood there and said 'stop,' then it's not fun. You move on. You scare somebody else."

C. *The Trial Court Grants Summary Judgment*

[Griffin's complaint sought damages and punitive damages for general negligence, negligent hiring, training, supervision, and retention, and for assault. The trial court denied a motion to strike the inclusion of a claim for punitive damages, noting that the complaint alleged that "defendant trained employees to chase patrons beyond the exit" and that was sufficient to potentially support a claim for punitive damages. The Haunted Hotel later (after discovery) moved for summary judgment. Griffin opposed, arguing that he was not injured on the Haunted Trail, but instead was outside of it.]

After oral argument, the court granted the motion for summary judgment, stating, "the argument that defendant went beyond its boundaries is not supported by the evidence. It appears all the activities took place on and within defendant's boundaries, although plaintiff was unaware of that fact. That awareness, that subjective awareness is not what is required. And given further what the inherent nature of this event was, it does not appear inappropriate or actionable." In its order, the trial court added:

> "Patrons of The Haunted Trail pay for the opportunity to be scared and The Haunted Trail, by design, is scary. Plaintiff argues the assumption of risk doctrine does not apply because

> he was chased after he believed the event was over and 'even football fields have sidelines.' … [W]hile the plaintiff believed he had gone through an exit he was still within the scary experience he purchased. The risk that plaintiff might be scared enough to run away is inherent in the fundamental nature of a haunted house attraction. [¶] … [W]ho would want to go to a haunted house that is not scary?"

The court entered judgment in favor of Haunted Hotel. Griffin timely appealed.

DISCUSSION

[The court concluded that primary assumption of risk applied because the inherent risk of injury could not be eliminated without altering the "fundamental nature" of the activity, citing *Nalwa v. Cedar Fair, L.P.*, 55 Cal.4th 1148 (2012). In that case, the California Supreme Court concluded that the primary assumption of risk doctrine applied to bumper car rides and that—as a matter of law—the failure to prevent head-on collisions did not violate the limited duty not to unreasonably increase the risk of injury. The court rejected arguments by Griffin that duty was a factual issue; that because his fear was caused not by the "fun" fear that such events were designed for, but instead by his fear that this employee was creating real danger; and that there should be a bright line rule that haunted attractions should only engage in scary conduct within its clear boundaries. The court then turned to the intentional tort aspect of the case.]

4. *Revoked consent*

Finally, Griffin argues there is a triable issue he revoked his consent to assuming the risk of being frightened because he repeatedly told the actor chasing him to "stop." However, Griffin's argument fails because "[p]rimary assumption of risk focuses on the legal question of duty." (*Lilley v. Elk Grove Unified School Dist.* (1998) 68 Cal.App.4th 939, 943, 80 Cal.Rptr.2d 638.) Primary assumption of risk "does not depend upon a plaintiff's implied consent to injury, nor is the plaintiff's subjective awareness or expectation relevant." (*Ibid.*) For example, in *Cann v. Stefanec*, the plaintiff was injured by a weight dropped by a fellow swim team member during a workout session. The plaintiff argued primary assumption of risk did not apply because "she did not impliedly consent to having a weight dropped on her head." (*Cann v. Stefanec, supra,* 217 Cal.App.4th at p. 471, 158 Cal.Rptr.3d 474.) The appellate court rejected that argument, stating primary assumption of risk "'"does not depend upon a plaintiff's implied consent to injury...."' (*Ibid.*)

[In a footnote, the court notes:] For the first time in his reply brief, Griffin argues that fear of physical harm "is not something that is an inherent part of the *cultural experience of Halloween*." (Italics added, original emphasis omitted.) Arguments made for the first time in a reply brief are not considered. Moreover, this case does not involve the cultural experience of Halloween, i.e., pumpkin carving, trick or treating with young children, or even bobbing for apples. It involves an adult who pays money to experience extreme fright, and receives exactly what he paid for.

C. *There Is No Evidence Creating a Triable Issue That Haunted Hotel Unreasonably Increased the Risks Beyond Those Inherent in the Activity*

[The court rejects Griffin's argument that the Haunted Hotel made the risks go beyond those inherent in the activity.]

A basic part of the scares at The Haunted Trial [sic, Trail] is the startling, frightening, menacing and chasing of patrons by actors in ghoulish costumes, some carrying chainsaws with the chain removed. There is an inherent risk that a patron may decide to run and fall. Because there is no evidence that anyone associated with The Haunted Trail intentionally injured Griffin, and because being chased in the Carrie effect scene is neither reckless nor outside the range of ordinary activity involved in a scare attraction, the trial court properly determined that as a matter of law, Haunted Hotel breached no duty to Griffin.

Being chased within the physical confines of The Haunted Trail by a chainsaw carrying maniac is a fundamental part and inherent risk of this amusement. Griffin voluntarily paid money to experience it. "It is not the function of tort law to police such conduct." [Citation omitted.]

NOTES AND QUESTIONS

1. If, after class today, someone leapt out at you from around a corner revving a chainsaw (even one without a chain), is there any question in your mind that such conduct would be an assault? Did the court

here adequately address the assault claim that it noted Griffin included in his complaint? (Please do not do this to your colleagues.)

2. The defendants in this case contended that primary assumption of risk can apply to intentional conduct, citing *Avila v. Citrus Community College Dist.*, 131 P.3d 383 (Cal. 2006), which does observe that being intentionally hit by a pitch is an inherent risk of baseball, and *Gregory v. Cott*, 331 P.3d 179 (Cal. 2014), which found that the no-duty doctrine could be found to exclude liability to caregivers for intentional torts committed by Alzheimer's patients. In *Gregory*, the court was careful to note that even in that setting, calling the conduct intentional was iffy: "The assaultive conduct ... involving institutionalized Alzheimer's patients could be characterized as 'intentional.'" *Id.* at 190.

   It seems self-evident that conduct that would otherwise be an intentional tort is an inherent aspect of haunted attractions and many other amusements. Should that mean that a patron *cannot* revoke their consent to such conduct? Were you satisfied with how the court addressed Griffin's argument he revoked his consent?

   Consider other conduct that might take place in a haunted attraction beyond what was seen here—consider, for example, the McKamey Manor conduct, or that in other "extreme" haunts. Do we want tort law to endorse the notion that consent—or, more accurately, the revocation of consent—is irrelevant to possible liability if the conduct involved is deemed inherent to the attraction? Is that conduct fairly comparable to "brush-back" pitches in baseball or the kind of intentional torts committed by people suffering from dementia? Flip back to Chapter 2 to see how the *Overall v. Kadella* court addressed consent in hockey in what I think was a cleaner way than here.

3. The briefs on this case are available on Westlaw, and if you review them, you may agree with me that the parties did not give the court a particularly clear path forward on the question of intentional torts. As you may have inferred, I think there is value in keeping the line clean between primary assumption of inherent risks and consent. The former should (again just in my view) be applied to negligence claims and be evaluated as an objective factual question. The latter can certainly be inferred—as in consent to certain contact in hockey games or, in many cases, in things like haunted houses—but the

notion that the consent to inherent risks cannot be revoked seems to me to be problematic the further you get from things like sporting events. I do not think this court would probably conclude that, in the context of an attraction like McKamey Manor, it would be appropriate to ignore attempts to revoke consent, but that is what this case arguably points towards.

4. Why do you think the plaintiff in this case didn't also include an intentional infliction of emotional distress claim?
5. As an aside, this opinion twice refers to "The Haunted Trial" rather than "The Haunted Trail," which provides (a) a reminder that spell check is sometimes inadequate to the task and (b) an idea for a probably very dull haunted attraction.
6. Spoilers for a nearly fifty-year-old movie: For some reason, the *Carrie* reference is common in cases about surprise final scares like the one described above. In the film (which is better than most Stephen King adaptations, I'll say), the only survivor of the subject prom has a nightmare where the seemingly deceased title character's arm reaches from below the ground at a point when viewers think the scares are done. That scene was ranked as the eighth scariest movie moment of all time by Bravo.
7. Nightclubs have become much more vocal about informing patrons about issues related to consent, presumably both in an effort to do the right thing and to mitigate their own risk. A club I like a lot in Saint Paul, Amsterdam Bar & Hall, has this posted in multiple places:

**Consent is clear, coherent,
willing and ongoing.**

Wherever you are during tonight's event, your body autonomy is respected and valued in this space. We're all gathered here to enjoy ourselves, our community and live music; each and every person's boundaries and safety are a very important part of that.

If you feel uncomfortable about a situation that you or someone you know may be in, Amsterdam Bar & Hall staff are available to help.

The scenarios that the Amsterdam is presumably trying to address might be exacerbated if the assumption of risk/consent line is blurred as arguably occurred in the prior case.

Andy Mulvihill with Jake Rossen, *Action Park: Fast Times, Wild Rides, and the Untold Story of America's Most Dangerous Amusement Park*

269 (Penguin Books 2020)*

One day, on one of my regular patrols at the park, I noticed a number of people lying on the ground in Roaring Springs near the Colorado River Ride. Having heard of the plan [of people protesting potentially toxic waste nearby] to create a human speed bump, I thought perhaps some protestors were practicing. Upon closer inspection, I realized they were not moving. Quickly, medics and ambulances arrived and roused more than two dozen glassy-eyed people from the ground. We discovered that an ozone generator used to keep the water clear had been turned off so attendants could remove a woman who had injured her shoulder. Turning the machine back on—normally done before the park opened—release a toxic cloud of built-up ozone gas, felling twenty-eight people who were idling nearby.

"The thing about that," [an employee nicknamed] Smoke said, watching the last of the medics leave, "is that we're now putting people down nice and easy. No pain. They just go to sleep."

"Stop it," I said.

No one was seriously hurt—a few passed out, and some were nauseated—but the [Department of Environmental Protection] was not happy. It fined the park $10,000 for the accident and criticized us for failing to report it. The Occupational Safety and Health Administration fined my father another $960. He grumbled over this amount.

We did gas twenty-eight people. To me, $960 seemed like a steal.

NOTES AND QUESTIONS

1. Did Action Park (or its employees, as to whom the park would presumably be vicariously liable) commit a battery against those twenty-eight patrons?

2. When riding a roller coaster, it is very common (and wise!) for an employee to check the restraints—as the recording that plays before every coaster ride at my home park, Valleyfair, puts it in their prerecorded spiel, "An employee is coming around to physically check your lap bar and visually check your seatbelt." The employee often does come into contact with the patron (and, by definition, the lap bar restraint does). Assume a patron is genuinely offended by this contact. What, if anything, keeps it from being an actionable battery?

CHAPTER 13

Criminal Law Implications

When things go poorly in the context of amusement rides, they can go very poorly, just given the forces and heights involved—and, especially (but not only) when that happens to kids, law enforcement can get interested.

Indeed, one of the first ever criminal prosecutions of a company for a death was a case we saw briefly back in Chapter 6. We start with a look back at that case, this time with the National Fire Protection Association's investigation of the Haunted Castle tragedy. (The full report is available at RecreationAndRisk.com or at NFPA.org.) As you read it, consider both potential civil liability but also whether you think anyone involved should have faced criminal liability.

John Bouchard, *Fire in Haunted Castle Kills Eight*

FIRE JOURNAL, September 1985*

In the early evening hours on May 11, 1984, a rapidly spreading fire destroyed the Haunted Castle amusement facility at the 200-acre Six Flags Great Adventure Park in Jackson Township, New Jersey. At the

* John Bouchard is Assistant Division Director in the NFPA's Engineering Services Division.

This investigation was conducted by the NFPA under an agreement with the Federal Emergency Management Agency/United States Fire Administration (FEMA/USFA) and the National Bureau of Standards/Center for Fire Research (NBS/CFR). The investigation was jointly funded by these agencies and the NEPA.

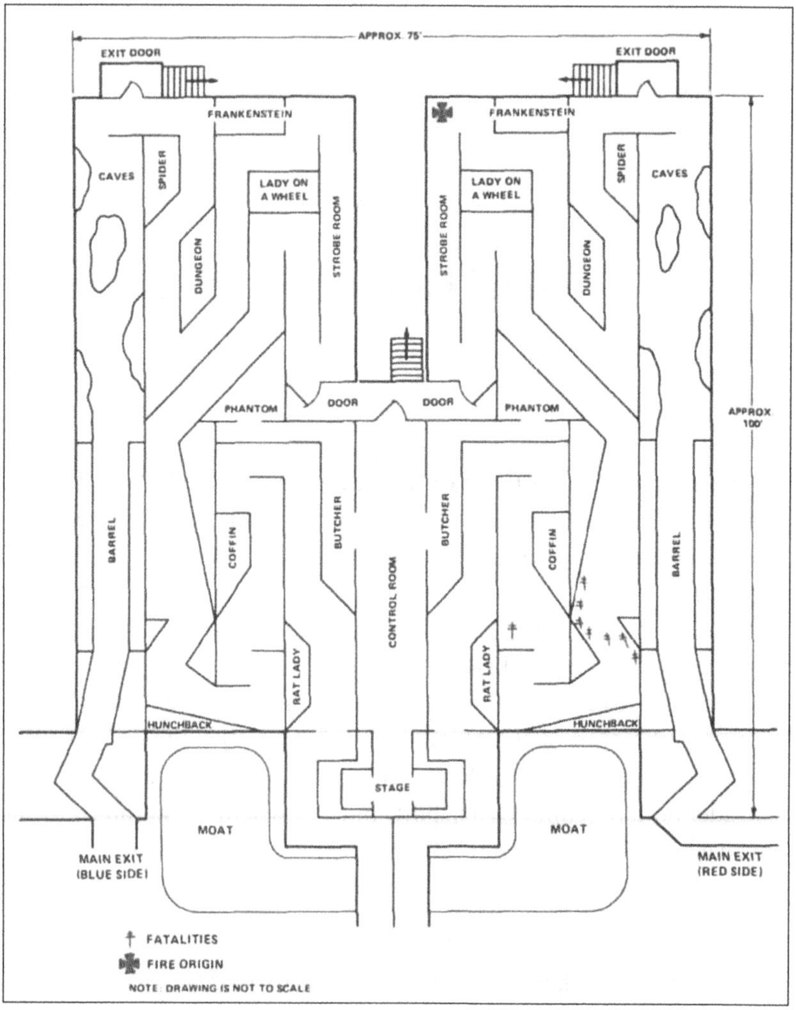

time of the fire, there were three employees and an estimated 28–34 visitors in the Haunted Castle. Eight of the visitors, unable to immediately exit from the structure, died in the fire.

The one-story structure was comprised of 17 commercial trailers that measured approximately 8 feet wide by 40 feet long by 8 feet high, connected together by means of plywood and wood framing. . . .

The interior of the Haunted Castle was constructed of plywood partitions that created a convoluted path of travel approximately 450 feet long. Materials used for the interior of the Haunted Castle included synthetic foam, various fabrics and plastics, plywood, and tarpaper.

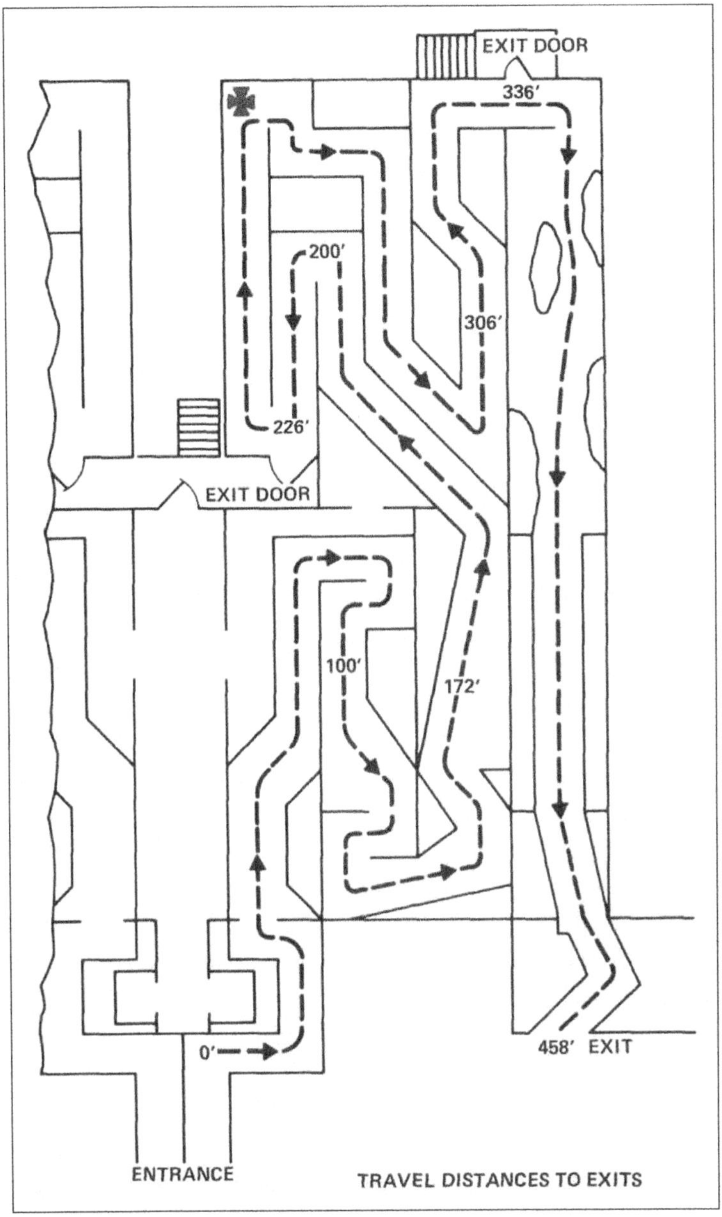

The structure had a total of seven exits, including the main entrance. Fire protection features included emergency lighting and portable fire extinguishers. No automatic detection or automatic sprinkler protection was provided in the facility.

County fire investigators determined that the fire was caused by accidental ignition of a wall-mounted polyurethane foam pad by a cigarette lighter. [The figure of the layout of the Haunted Castle included here shows where the fire was apparently started and where the fatalities took place. Note that later reports have been less certain about the origin of the fire. The second figure shows the traffic flow, along with showing the distance to the exit. Both are available on RecreationAndRisk.com to see with more detail.]

The Facility

[Six Flags Great Adventure is about 50 miles from New York City, and more than 3.3 million people visited in 1983.]

In the fall of 1978, a Haunted Castle facility consisting of four trailers was located at the park for several weeks. The attraction proved to be popular and a larger 17-trailer Haunted Castle facility was erected at the park in early 1979.... [It] was a single-story structure comprised of 17 used commercial trailers of various manufacture plus a wood-frame façade. Fifteen were box trailers, and two were open flatbed trailers. The trailers had been fabricated using either steel or aluminum bodies, with wood floors and ¼-inch plywood riveted to the interior of the trailer frame....

The trailer portion of the building was divided into two identical eight-trailer (mirror-image) sections, each of which constituted a complete and separate Haunted Castle. One or both of the sections (known as the Red Side and the Blue Side) could be in operation, depending on the crowd size. The seventeenth trailer served as the control room where employees donned their costumes and make-up prior to participating as haunted-house characters. The control room contained electrical panels [for both sections] as well as tables and chairs, lockers, a telephone, and two pressurized water fire extinguishers.

The trailers were connected by means of plywood and wood framing. The interiors were designed to simulate the atmosphere of a Haunted Castle through the use of a darkened, convoluted series of passageways that were intended to disorient and frighten visitors for amusement purposes as they progressed through the facility.

[The report provides more details about the construction as well as the various displays patrons would go through—"a rat lady, a butcher, [] a coffin display ... a Phantom of the Opera display[,] a corridor with strobe lights[,] the spider room[,] a [rotating] tunnel." Emergency exits were provided at the end of the strobe light corridor, about 226 feet from the entrance, and at the spider room, about 336 feet from the entrance. The full walk-through was about 450 feet long.]

In addition to the exit facilities described earlier, fire protection provisions included emergency lighting arranged to illuminate interior passageways in the event of power failure; due to the extent of fire damage, further details were not determined by the NFPA. No detection and alarm systems or automatic sprinklers were installed in the facility.

[The report then describes the park's internal fire-fighting brigade and the park's water supply.]

The Fire

On Friday, May 11, 1984, an average crowd of approximately 15,000 visitors thronged the Great Adventure Amusement Park. [The Red Side of the Haunted Castle] was open to the public, and three employees were on duty there.

A line of visitors was waiting to travel through the Haunted Castle, and employees were allowing approximately 10 visitors to enter per minute. At the time of the fire, it was estimated that there were about 30 visitors in the facility, based on an estimated travel time of approximately 3 minutes through this attraction. At approximately 6:30 pm, an employee positioned at the butcher display smelled smoke. He went to investigate and entered the passageway connecting the butcher display to the Phantom of the Opera display. As the employee traveled through the passageway, he saw heavy smoke coming from the Phantom area and went back through the butcher display to alert the other employees and instruct them to discontinue further entry of visitors. He then re-entered the Haunted Castle, went to the control room, and notified the Great Adventure Fire Brigade by telephone, then left the Haunted Castle by way of the control room door. Looking to his right, he saw smoke and flames around the emergency exit located at the strobe room. Meanwhile, an adult traveling through the darkened passageways discovered the fire, ran through the remainder of the castle, and alerted an employee at the front entrance.

Specific details on visitor evacuation were not determined; however, individuals and groups apparently left by way of the main entrance. One visitor was rescued from the coffin area by an employee....

Fire Brigade Operations and Mutual-Aid Fire Departments

[The report described the fire brigade response to the fire, which initially entered the Haunted Castle at the front entrance and was turned back by heavy fire. That brigade, along with the later-arriving fire departments from nearby towns, then attacked the fire from the rear of the trailers.]

Damage and Casualties

The 17 trailers and the façade that comprised the Haunted Castle facility were destroyed by the fire. [Photos, which are not graphic, are available in the full report you can find at the casebook website.]

According to the Ocean County Coroner's office, eight young adults, who ranged in age from 15 to 19, died as a result of smoke inhalation and carbon monoxide poisoning. Seven of the victims were found in the corridor near the hunchback display; the eighth victim was found in the vicinity of the coffin display....

Analysis

[The local investigators concluded that the fire was caused by accidental ignition of foam padding in the strobe room.]

According to investigators, on the night of the fire a 14-year-old youth was using a lighter to illuminate his path of travel. Apparently, it was common practice for visitors in the Haunted Castle to light matches or lighters to illuminate their way. Reportedly, the employees were constantly instructing guests to extinguish the matches or lighters. The investigators also determined that a strobe light was malfunctioning on the day of the fire and failed to operate for periods of 3 to 4 minutes, leaving the corridor in total darkness. The youth accidentally walked into the foam pad on the strobe-room wall, setting it on fire. The youth then attempted to beat out the fire, but was unsuccessful, and apparently continued through the Castle.

[The fire spread down the strobe room corridor, fueled by the plywood construction of the ceiling, floor, and walls. It then extended past the Phantom area and into other areas of the facility.]

Material identification tests and small-scale fire tests were performed on fire scene samples by the National Bureau of Standards/Center for Fire Research and the Consumer Products Safety Commission. Flexible foam samples [from the scene] were identified as polyurethane, and it was determined that the material did not show any of the elements normally used in flame retardants for foams of this type, suggesting that no such retardants were present. In addition, the foam was found to ignite readily with an approximately 1-second application of a small flame from a butane cigarette lighter. Because of the limited amount of foam available, no heat-release testing was possible.

[Testing was also performed on plywood samples from the scene.] The ¼-inch plywood was found to be typical of untreated plywoods with a flame spread index near 200 (Class D). The ½-inch plywood sample was typical of fire retardant treated plywoods with a flame spread index near 40 (Class B). Treated plywoods such as these generally contribute little to a fire until near flashover, at which time they will burn, but even then they release energy substantially slower than untreated plywood.

Investigators determined that the victims were traveling through the Haunted Castle in two groups. As the first group of five teenagers made its way through the darkened passages, it passed the hunchback display and then a view of the revolving barrel [which was visible from the adjacent passageway]. As the five visitors were nearing the Phantom of the Opera exhibit, they encountered smoke and heat. Investigators believe it was most likely at this point that they started to retreat back through the darkened passageways.

Meanwhile, a second group of four young adults was still advancing through the Haunted Castle and was approaching the revolving barrel display when it met the first group of teenagers in retreat. All nine visitors then attempted to reverse their path and exit through the main entrance of the Haunted Castle.

Two of the nine visitors were able to retreat as far as the coffin display when they were overcome by smoke and collapsed. A Great Adventure employee was able to rescue one of these two visitors. The other seven victims were found in a corridor near the hunchback display.

A review of employee actions during the early stages of the fire indicates there was a delay of approximately five minutes between the time the employee working in the Haunted Castle at the butcher display first smelled smoke (approximately 6:30 pm) and the time he telephoned the Great Adventure Fire Brigade at 6:35 pm. The fire by this point was well established, as the captain of the Fire Brigade reported observing heavy smoke when en route to the scene. By the time the two Fire Brigade members arrived at the front of the Haunted Castle and one of them advanced a 1 ½-inch handline through the entrance, the fire was already of such intensity that the captain was only able to progress approximately 20 feet into the structure before he was driven back by intense heat. [The first mutual aid unit arrived at 6:52, when the structure was fully on fire.]

Code Analysis

The following discussion is presented in order to compare life safety problems observed in this fire with the requirements of [applicable codes]. [The report then describes requirements for (1) means of egress lighting, (2) emergency lighting, (3) interior finish, and (4) exit marking.]

Life Safety Problems

Some evidence in this fire indicates special life-safety problems related to the darkened, haunted-house type of environment. Some of the visitors seemed to initially accept a smokey condition as part of the environment, and one group of youngsters apparently viewed the actual fire in its incipient stage and remarked how real the *illusion* seemed ... only to comprehend on closer examination that the fire was real. These facts would appear to support the necessity for both early detection and alarm systems in such a facility to: 1) establish that an emergency situation exists, and 2) activate emergency lighting to facilitate an orderly evacuation from an otherwise darkened environment.

This facility was designed with a darkened, convoluted series of passageways without a clear line of sight toward exits. This arrangement, typical of this type of amusement facility, may require special considerations in the design, arrangement, and marking of exits.

As exemplified by the fire growth and development in this facility, where combustible interior finishes and contents had been used to create passageways and displays, automatic sprinklers could have controlled the fire in the incipient stage, allowing time for safe evacuation.

Summary

The ignition scenario, involving synthetic foam at the point of fire origin, the combustibility of the interior finishes and contents, and the lack of detection and extinguishment of the fire in its incipient stages contributed to the loss of life in this fire. It's quite possible that even further loss of life could have occurred if both sections of the facility had been in operation at the time of the fire.

Special life safety problems exemplified in this fire may have contributed to the failure of some occupants to escape safely. These problems appear to be related to the haunted-house type of environment that utilizes a darkened, convoluted series of passageways. The application of code requirements and basic fire protection engineering principles would have greatly reduced the potential for fatalities in this fire.

The following are considered to be major factors contributing to loss of life in this fire:

- The failure to detect and extinguish the fire in its incipient stage by means of fixed fire detection and suppression systems;
- The ignition of synthetic foam material and subsequent fire and smoke spread involving combustible interior finishes and contents; [and]
- The difficulty of escape by occupants because of fire conditions in the haunted-house type of environment.

NOTES AND QUESTIONS

1. The Haunted Castle was inspected at the start of the season and met the building code's requirements. As noted in Chapter 6, it was considered a temporary attraction and therefore did not require a sprinkler system or various other things that would have been required of a permanent attraction. Reports indicate that the park intended to make the attraction permanent—with a stone structure—the next season. Joe Costal, *Fire at Haunted Castle*, HAUNTED ATTRACTION, https://costalwriting.blogspot.com/2016/08/fire-at-haunted-castle-originally.html.

   Do you think compliance with building codes should be sufficient to rebut potential criminal liability for incidents like this? What about civil liability?

2. While many particularly severe allegations (of chained doors and the like) were never substantiated, reports from employees indicate "deteriorating conditions" at the Castle, with an employee writing "forget it, too numerous to mention" on a safety report the year prior, and

employees evidently staging a walkout based on safety concerns (among other things). *Id.*

3. Civil litigation followed, of course, with the first settlement in the amount of $2.5 million (in a long-term structured settlement). Tom Torok, *Fire Victim's Family Gets $2.5 Million*, PHILADELPHIA INQUIRER, Dec. 21, 1985. Another five victims reached similar structured deals, and another one settled for a $750,000 payment immediately. *See Family Settles for $750,000 in Great Adventure Fire*, PHILADELPHIA INQUIRER B3, Feb. 7, 1987.

4. Grand juries charged two corporate defendants (Great Adventure, Inc., and Six Flags Corporation) with aggravated manslaughter, and two individuals, Larry Cochran (the park's former general manager) and David Paltzik (Cochran's successor), with manslaughter. Of particular note, the case was purportedly "the first in New Jersey and one of the first in the country" in which companies *in any industry* had been charged criminally with homicide. *See* Donald Janson, *Closing Statements to Jurors are Made in Park Fire Trial*, NEW YORK TIMES, B4, July 19, 1985. Additionally, the grand jury considered charges against, but ultimately did not indict, officials of Jackson Township, issuing a presentment criticizing the township for being "slipshod and ineffective" in enforcing the state's code. Donald Janson, *Great Adventure Juror Absolves Township in Fire*, NEW YORK TIMES, 129, July 28, 1985.

5. The criminal trial of the corporate defendants lasted for two months, including 83 witnesses and over 200 exhibits. In the jury charge, the judge permitted the jury to consider both aggravated manslaughter and the lesser included offense of simple manslaughter. In closings, the prosecutor described the park's management as "indifferent, reckless, greedy and callous" in their decisions not to install sprinklers or smoke alarms. The defense, on the other hand, conceded that the park was (plainly) wrong in believing that their efforts had been sufficient to prevent a fatal fire, but focused on the state's failure to meet its burden of proving conscious disregard of a known risk. In particular, the defense noted that the company had adopted some safety recommendations (human surveillance, for example, in place of smoke detectors after detectors had been vandalized).

The jury acquitted the corporate defendants in July 1985. Marc Duvoisin, *Jury Acquits Great Adventure*, Philadelphia Inquirer A1, July 21, 1985. Interviews with jurors indicated that the jurors concluded that the corporate defendants were blameless because they had relied on the inspectors. Donald Janson, *Great Adventure Juror Absolves Township in Fire*, New York Times 129, July 28, 1985.

6. The individual defendants entered a pretrial intervention program without a guilty plea; after completing that program, the indictments were dismissed. Neither individual admitted any wrongdoing in pursuing that program and performing community service. *Charges Dropped in Six Flags Case*, New York Times 130, March 8, 1986.
7. Based on what you know about the facts of this case—which is, of course, much less than the jury would have seen over the two-month trial—what do you think about the acquittals? Do you think these facts could have supported a jury finding of conscious disregard of a known risk (as necessary to convict)? What about the standards for punitive damages—would you have supported awarding punitive damages on these facts, if they had gone to trial? How might a modern jury have consider the charges differently than a 1980s jury?
8. We turn now to a much more recent incident that resulted in a death on a flat ride in Tennessee.

U.S. Consumer Products Safety Commission, Investigation Abbreviated Report Hawk Amusement Ride Incident

CPSC Technical Bulletin, July 2005

The victims involved in this incident were a 15-year-old male, a 54-year-old female, and a 50-year-old female. The 50-year-old female was the only fatality involved in the incident, with the other two victims escaping without injury. The physical characteristics of the two surviving victims were not known; however, the 50-year-old female victim was characterized as being "a heavy woman of short stature, 5'4" and approx. 230–250 lbs." The physical and mental health of the victims was not known and could not be determined. The 50-year-old female was the mother of the 15-year-old male, and the 54-year-old female was related to both, but whether she was an aunt, cousin, or in-law was not able to be determined. According to the Pigeon Forge Police Department, neither alcoholic beverages nor drugs, legal or illegal, were involved by either the victims or the operator of the ride involved in this incident.

On 3/14/04, at approximately 12:15 P.M. the three victims began riding an amusement ride at a local arcade/amusement park in Pigeon Forge, TN.... The three victims were the only ones on that ride and were placed in the first car of that ride, with the 50-year-old victim being placed in the third seat. All [were] supposedly locked into their respective seats by the [ride's] operator with an over-the-shoulder restraint system prior to the ride being started.

Shortly after the ride started, exact time not able to be determined; all three of the victims began to yell down to the ride's operator that the 50-year-old victim's safety harness was not locked. The operator of the ride began hitting buttons to try and stop the ride, but with no success. The ride, designed to go completely around/upside-down, finally reached a position of approximately 210 degrees and the 50-year-old female was ejected from her seat and fell approximately 60' to 65'.

As she fell the 60' to 65', the back of her head made contact with an air compressor on the back side of the ride and she then landed on her back on a concrete pad that supported the ride.

Shortly after the incident, 911 was notified, with the local police department getting the alarm at approximately 12:16 P.M. and an officer arrived on the scene at approximately 12:17 P.M. EMS personnel arrived a short time later, time not known, and the 50-year-old victim was pronounced dead at the scene. The scene was immediately sealed off, to include the ride, by the local police department and investigation into the cause began. Officers were placed at the incident site and remained on duty 24/7 during the investigation, keeping everyone away from the ride.

The following day, all interested parties met at the ride and began an examination. Pictures were taken of the electrical panel as well as various other aspects of the ride. It was noted during the investigation that alligator clips had been used inside the electrical panel to bypass the ride's safety systems and the local police department called in a P.E. from California to do an investigation. At that same time, the Lead Criminal Investigator of the local police department ascertained that the manager/maintenance manager of the facility was the only person that conducted maintenance on the rides at the facility and that that person had not maintained any type of maintenance log for that ride.

The aforementioned P.E. did an investigation and submitted his report to police department on 4/27/04. It was the opinion of the P.E. that the incident occurred because of the following reasons:

1. Intentional destruction of the ride safety systems
2. Ride operator inappropriately or inadequately trained
3. At a minimum, the following standards were violated: ASTM F 770-93 (Reapproved 2000) Standard Practice for Operation Procedures for Amusement Rides and Devices Sections 4.1 through 4.3; and ASTM F 353-98 Standard Practice for Maintenance Procedures for Amusement Ride and Devices Sections 6.1 through 6.4.3, and in particular, section 6.3.4.

INVESTIGATION OBSERVATIONS
[written by the investigator]

At 9:00 AM on March 24, 2004, I arrived at a small park … in Pigeon Forge, TN, the location of the incident. …

Within the main electrical panel, several wires had diagonal cuts into their insulation, exposing the conductor. These cuts were clearly intentional and were the type of cut typically made for "jumping out", or accessing the out wire. The wires noted with cuts were numbers 120, 126, 143, 144, 145, 146 and 175. A red jumper wire connected wires 142 and 143. A black jumper wire was shown to me and I was informed by Mr. Knight and Mr. Kendall that following the incident, the black jumper connected wires 144 and 145. Another un-numbered wire was found with a yellow jumper spliced into it, but the clips were not connected to any other wires.

State v. Martin

No. E2005-02155-CCA-R3-CD
(Ct. Crim. App. Tenn. Sept. 18, 2017)

The defendant, Charles Stan Martin, was convicted by a Sevier County jury of one count of reckless homicide, a Class D felony, and received a four-year sentence to be served on probation. On appeal, the defendant contends that: (1) the evidence was not sufficient to support his conviction, (2) the reckless homicide statute is unconstitutional as applied to him, (3) the trial court erred in admitting evidence of a prior incident, (4) the trial court erred in failing to instruct the jury on an alibi defense, and (5) the trial court abused its discretion in denying him judicial diversion. We affirm the judgment of the trial court.

On March 14, 2004, June Alexander fell to her death while riding the Hawk thrill ride at the Rockin Raceway amusement park in Pigeon Forge. The defendant was the general manager of Rockin Raceway and was responsible for maintenance of the Hawk. In September 2004, a Sevier County grand jury charged the defendant by presentment with second degree murder and reckless homicide. [] The state attempted to prove that the defendant attached a jumper wire to the electrical panel of the ride in order to bypass its safety restrictions.

[The opinion summarized most of the facts that appear in the report above as having been established through the testimony of Cody Alexander, the decedent's son, who was at the park with her.]

Cody testified that the ride began and moved backwards so far and high that they were facing the ground.... At a height of approximately sixty feet, the victim's harness opened completely and the victim fell out of her seat. At that point, the ride made a 360 degree turn. Cody said he began screaming at the attendant to stop the ride. The ride soon stopped, and he and his aunt came back down to the ground. He said he was stuck in his seat for approximately thirty minutes because his harness would not release. He estimated that his aunt was stuck in her seat for about forty-five minutes. He said that after he was released from his seat, he ran to see his mother and learned that she was dead. He said the defendant had never expressed condolences to his family.

[The court describes various aspects of the investigation.]

Officer Finney testified that he was present when the electrical cabinet on the back of the Hawk was opened. He said he could see electrical wiring in the box. He said two wires—one red and one black—that were attached to other wires with alligator clips caught his eye. He explained that he formerly inspected rides as the "chief safety security officer" for Silver Dollar City amusement park and that he never saw alligator clips used in the electrical panels of rides there. He said that if he had seen such wiring in a ride he would have "shut the ride down." The insulation of the wires to which the alligator clips were attached was peeled in order for the alligator clips to touch the copper wiring. He said he also saw in the electrical cabinet a cardboard box that contained, among other things, black wire and alligator clips. Officer Finney testified that he did not know how long the alligator clipped wires were in the electrical panel and did not know who put them there. He said that no fingerprints were taken from any wires. He said no one touched the inside of the electrical cabinet while he was there and that the cabinet was closed before he left the scene on March 15, 2004....

Bradley Burns testified that he was a seasonal employee of Rockin Raceway between March 1997 and August 2001 and that he was as an assistant manager there between August 2001 and September 2002. He was working at Rockin Raceway during the time that the Hawk arrived. He said that he sometimes operated the Hawk and that, at times, the lap bars came down but the ride did not move. At these times, an alarm on the ride would sound. Sometimes when this happened, people requested to get off the ride and demanded refunds....

Mr. Burns described the defendant as a "great employer" who was "more than fair to all of the employees." He said the defendant exhibited a great deal of concern for the safety of the Hawk and another ride, called the Rip Line, because those two rides involved more safety concerns than other rides at Rockin Raceway. He said that when there was a problem with a ride, the defendant would check the ride and instruct employees not to operate the ride or sell tickets for it until it was fixed. There were times when the Hawk was shut down for two to three days at a time. He said he never saw the defendant take "shortcuts" relating to the rides and that the only modification he was aware the defendant ever made to a ride was once removing the air filter from a go-cart. He said the defendant expressed concern when he noticed that one go-cart was significantly faster or slower than the others, as the defendant said this created a dangerous situation. He said that the defendant was very generous and that he had no reason to believe the defendant was more concerned with selling tickets than with the safety of the Hawk.

[A mechanical engineer retained as an expert witness by the prosecution, Ed Pribonic, said that he, too, had seen evidence that wires numbered 144 and 145 had been connected with a jumper wire. He further] testified that he was asked by the Pigeon Forge Police Department to determine the probable cause of the victim's fall. He said he determined that a connection between wires numbered 144 and 145 would bypass the "entire ride restraint system." He said that when a jumper wire connected those two circuits, the seventy-two lap bar safety switches—three on each of the twenty-four seats—became useless and no longer had any control over the operation of the ride. Thus, the ride would run even if one of the pins was not properly positioned and the switch did not send the appropriate signal to the computer. He said Mr. Burns' testimony that the ride sometimes would not operate while he was working at Rockin Raceway indicated that the safety system was not bypassed at that time. He also said that, after speaking with Ken Mace, who nearly fell out of his seat on the Hawk in July 2003, he thought that the restraint safety system was bypassed at that time. He said he "firmly believed" this because if the safety system were functioning properly, two things would have prevented the incident: (1) the "ride would never have left the station" if Mr. Mace was not secured in his seat; and (2) if some kind of force pulled the pins out of their secured position, the ride would have shut down immediately. Mr. Pribonic testified that it was "absolutely not" standard for a ride to have a jumper wire with alligator clips in its electric panel and that he was of the opinion that the black jumper wire was purposefully placed on wires 144 and 145.

On cross-examination, Mr. Pribonic testified that he did not know who put the jumper wire on the ride. He acknowledged that he was a member of the Amusement Industries Manufacturers and Suppliers International and that Zamperla, the Hawk's manufacturer, was also a member of that organization. He said he never saw the black jumper wire on the electrical panel because it was removed by the time he arrived at the scene. He also acknowledged that he did not turn on the ride during his inspection of it. Although he said he did not initially intend to power the ride, he admitted that he tried but was unable to do so. He said that the ride was the only Hawk 24 trailer-mounted ride in existence and that he was not able to look at any other ride that operated in the same fashion. He said he reached his conclusions by reviewing drawings, the ride's manual, other documents provided by the manufacturer, and witness statements relayed to him by Detective Kendall. He said he believed the ride's manual to be well-written and reliable. He said he was not an electrical engineer but consulted with one to confirm his conclusions....

Jerry Lindsey, the owner of Rockin Raceway and the defendant's brother-in-law, testified that, as manager, the defendant was responsible for overseeing outside operations at Rockin Raceway, including rides and go-carts. He said the defendant was probably the person who would handle any electrical problems on the rides or make necessary repairs to the rides. He said he experienced problems with the Hawk when it was first purchased. Mr. Lindsey said the defendant was a salaried employee whose pay was not tied to the profitability of the business but who received a bonus at the end of the year, which depended, in part, on how well the business did that year. He said that about a year before the victim's death, the defendant expressed a desire to resign his position at Rockin Raceway. The defendant agreed to continue as manager after Mr. Lindsey told him he would no longer be responsible for maintenance. Mr. Lindsey acknowledged, however, that the defendant continued after this time to oversee some maintenance on the rides and that, when interviewed by Detective Kendall, he never said the defendant had stopped doing maintenance on the rides. He said that other employees may have performed maintenance on the Hawk but that any "major problems" probably would have been handled by the defendant. Mr. Lindsey agreed that he was a "hands off" owner who was not involved in the daily operations of Rockin Raceway. He acknowledged that the business made more money when the Hawk was in operation, but he said he would never prioritize money ahead of safety.

[The defendant testified at length.] He said that about a year before the victim's death, he stopped doing maintenance work on the rides because it was too much for him to handle, although he later said he did work in the Hawk's electrical cabinet six weeks before the victim died. He said he saw Mr. Castellano or another Zamperla associate do the following work in the Hawk's electrical panel: replace a converter, add two wires related to the platform system, add jumper wires when the gate safety switches were taken out, and turn on the alarm bypass switch during set up. He said that neither the cardboard box that was found in the electrical cabinet nor the items that were inside it belonged to him.

The defendant testified that on July 22, 2003, when Ken Mace rode the Hawk, he was in West Tennessee, due to his father's death that morning. He said that his wife informed him that someone's lap bar had come forward while riding the Hawk and that the passenger was very upset. He said he was not told that someone almost fell out of the ride. He said that when he arrived back to Pigeon Forge, he and Joey Dickson checked all the safety devices of the ride and that they all appeared to work. He said he determined that an anomaly had occurred due to Mr. Mace's large size, and he made the decision to put the ride back in operation. He said it appeared to him that the safety device in the back of Mr. Mace's seat kept him from falling out of the seat, and this was consistent with what Mr. Castellano had told him....

[On cross-examination, he] agreed that the Hawk was the most dangerous ride at Rockin Raceway and that it could be deadly without the lap bars. He was aware that all three safety pins on the lap bar and seat of the Hawk were supposed to be secured before the ride could run. He said he did not call Zamperla after the Ken Mace incident, even though he previously had called Zamperla about other problems with the ride, such as those with the platform, fuses, and the lap bars not opening or closing. He said he did not call Zamperla because his own tests did not indicate that anything was wrong and convinced him that the ride was safe to operate....

He said he never saw the red and black jumper wires on the electrical panel, including when he worked on the ride six weeks before the victim's death. He said he did not see them until after the ride was released back to him following the victim's death. He agreed that the wires looked very unusual....

[Experts for the defense testified that they thought the ride was defectively designed and that, in fact, it would not have run at all without the jumper cables—and that they thought those had been there for all of the ride's operation, effectively bypassing the safety system for its entire existence. In rebuttal, fact witnesses testified that in prior years, the ride would not operate unless all restraints were in place, suggesting that the jumper cables were not required for the ride to operate.]

Based on this evidence, the jury found the defendant guilty of reckless homicide as a lesser-included offense of second degree murder. After a sentencing hearing, the defendant received a sentence of four years to be served on probation....

A. *Circumstantial Evidence*

The defendant contends that the state's circumstantial evidence did not prove that he placed on the Hawk the jumper wires that bypassed the ride's safety restraint system. He argues that, in fact, the evidence proves his alternate theory: that the ride could not operate without the jumper wires and that, thus, the wires were on the Hawk since it was first assembled and operated, before arriving at Rockin Raceway....

If the jury accredited the testimony of Mr. Castellano, Mr. Pribonic, and the various Rockin Raceway employees, it could reject the defendant's theory that the jumper wires were on the Hawk before it arrived at Rockin Raceway and accept the state's theory that the defendant had placed the wires on the ride. As such, the evidence was sufficient to prove that the defendant was responsible for placing on the ride the jumper wire that bypassed the safety restraint mechanisms.

[The court concluded that there was adequate evidence from which a jury could conclude that the defendant had acted recklessly—being aware of but consciously disregarding a substantial and unjustifiable risk. The court also concluded that there was adequate evidence of causation, despite there being supposed other intervening causes—defendant asserted that the ticket seller should not have sold a ticket to an obese patron, the ride operator should have done more to check the restraints, and the ride operator should have allowed her to get off when she asked.]

[The court also rejected a challenge that the reckless homicide statute was unconstitutionally vague, and rejected an argument that the Ken Mace incident should not have been admitted under Rule 404 of the rules of evidence relating to prior crimes, wrongs, or acts. Finally, the court rejected, on a state-specific basis, defendant's argument that he should have been given diversion rather than probation.]

NOTES AND QUESTIONS

1. No criminal charges were filed in the Glenwood Caverns case discussed in Chapter 9. Assuming the standards for charges are the same in Colorado as described in this case, do you think that is an appropriate outcome? If you were a prosecutor in Colorado, why or why not you have sought an indictment?
2. If you were a juror in the *Martin* case, would the circumstantial evidence presented here be adequate to get you to vote to convict?

Alexander v. Zamperla

No. E2009-01049-COA-R3-CV
(Ct. App. Tenn. Aug. 27, 2010)

[Plaintiffs] filed this products liability suit against Antonio Zamperla, S.p.A. and Zamperla, Inc. ("Defendants"), as a result of June Alexander's death that occurred while riding an amusement park ride manufactured by Defendants. Defendants moved for summary judgment. After a hearing, the trial court entered an order granting Defendants summary judgment, finding the act of a third party constituted both a superseding cause of the death and an alteration of the product which relieved Defendants of liability. Plaintiffs appeal. We affirm.

[BACKGROUND]

Rockin' Raceway ("Raceway"), an amusement park in Pigeon Forge, Tennessee, purchased an amusement ride called the "Hawk 24" ("the Hawk") manufactured by [Zamperla]. The Hawk was delivered to Raceway's Pigeon Forge site in March 1998. The Hawk consists of 24 seats attached to the bottom of a pendulum.

Zamperla, Inc.'s Field Service Manager, Phil Castellano, was at Raceway from March 4, 1998, to March 6, 1998, to oversee the ride's set up, assembly, testing and operation training. Raceway's General Manager, Stan Martin, participated in the instruction and training conducted by Mr. Castellano. Mr. Martin, who had previously worked on missiles for the United States Air Force and on nuclear reactors for the Tennessee Valley Authority, would be responsible for the regular maintenance of the Hawk.

The Hawk's safety system utilized a harness that lowers over each passenger's torso. Once the harness is lowered over the passenger, steel rods engage to lock the harness to the seat frame in three locations: behind the passenger's head, above the passenger's right hip, and above the passenger's left hip. Once locked into place, any one of the three rods is strong enough to hold a rider in place by itself. The safety system prevented the ride from operating unless all of the passenger restraints were secure and all steel rods were engaged.

After March 6, 1998, Raceway and its staff, including Mr. Martin, were in exclusive custody and control of the Hawk. At Raceway's request, Mr. Castellano returned in October 1998 to address issues relating to the

Hawk's loading platform and again in July 2000, to replace a coupler on the motor. Mr. Castellano did not place or observe any jumper wires in the Hawk's electrical cabinet at any time during his three visits to Raceway. Various Raceway employees confirmed that between 1998 and 2002, the Hawk would only run if all of the seat restraints were engaged; if all of the restraints were not secure, the Hawk would not operate because of safety devices in the ride.

Mr. Martin was the only person at Raceway who was "competent enough to work on the [Hawk]" and performed the regular maintenance. At some time between July 2000 and July 23, 2003, Mr. Martin intentionally and purposefully re-wired the Hawk's control panel to bypass the safety devices in the ride which are designed and intended to prevent it from operating unless the passenger restraints were secure.

On July 23, 2003, nearly five years post sale and three years after Zamperla Inc.'s last contact with the Hawk, a Raceway guest, Ken Mace, was riding on the Hawk when his harness opened while he was upside down.... Raceway employees told the Maces "the ride would not be used again until it was inspected by someone from Italy." Mr. Mace also contacted the Pigeon Forge Police Department to report his incident with the Hawk. When he learned of Mr. Mace's incident, and despite the life-threatening nature of it, Mr. Martin did not notify [Zamperla] of the occurrence and did not ask [Zamperla] to inspect the Hawk as promised to both Mr. Mace and the police. Instead, the ride continued to be operated by Mr. Martin and Raceway after Mr. Mace's close call.

On March 14, 2004, eight months after Mr. Mace's incident, June Alexander, her son R.C.A., and her sisters Judy Sprinkles and Gail Young, traveled to Pigeon Forge.... After the ride started, Mrs. Alexander became aware that the restraining device which was supposed to secure her in her seat was not functioning properly. She called out that she was not secure, but there was no response. When the ride was about 60 to 70 feet in the air, Mrs. Alexander was ejected and fell to her death. Unlike Mr. Mace, Mrs. Alexander was not able to hang on....

[The court summarized the evidence about the wiring as described above.]

At his criminal trial, it was established that Mr. Martin: 1) had a technical background; 2) was the only person maintaining the Hawk; 3) knew of at least one incident of the Hawk operating when a passenger's restraint was not engaged; and 4) the Hawk's safety system was intentionally destroyed. At the conclusion of a jury trial, Mr. Martin was found guilty of reckless homicide. On appeal, the Court of Criminal Appeals affirmed the trial court's verdict and held that Mr. Martin "was responsible for placing on the ride the jumper wire that bypassed the safety restraint mechanism."

In March 2005, Plaintiffs filed a complaint against Defendants, as well as against Hamlinco, Inc. d/b/a Rockin' Raceway and Mr. Martin, as the owner and general manager respectively of the amusement park at the time Mrs. Alexander was killed. The owner of Raceway and Mr. Martin were voluntarily nonsuited by Plaintiffs and were dismissed from the action without prejudice. Thereafter, Plaintiffs filed a First Amended Complaint against only these Defendants. Following discovery, Defendants moved for summary judgment, and on April 14, 2009, the trial court conducted a hearing on the dispositive motion. After argument by counsel, the court stated that it was granting Defendants' motion on the basis 1) that a third party's placement of a jumper wire in the electrical control panel of the ride was not foreseeable and was a criminal act constituting a superseding cause of the decedent's death, and 2) that the safety system of the Hawk had been significantly altered. On June 3, 2009, the trial court entered its order granting Defendants' motion for summary judgment on the above grounds. Plaintiffs filed this timely appeal.

[ISSUES]

Plaintiffs argue that the intervening act of a third party in placing a jumper wire in the ride's electrical control panel was reasonably foreseeable to Defendants and thus does not absolve them of liability. In support of this contention, Plaintiffs correctly assert that an act cannot be a superseding cause that relieves the original wrongdoer of liability unless the intervening act could not reasonably have been foreseen and unless the act was a substantial factor in bringing about the harm....

Even viewing the evidence in favor of Plaintiffs as the nonmoving party and drawing all reasonable inferences in favor of them, we are unable to say a genuine issue of material fact exists as to the foreseeability of the park manager's act in placing the jumper wire in the ride's electrical control panel. Plaintiffs contend that one of their experts, Mr. Timothy Rickard, testified to the foreseeability of the intentional bypassing of the ride's safety system. We find, however, that Mr. Rickard's proffered testimony, the same sparse and limited evidence which Plaintiffs primarily rely on throughout their case to demonstrate the existence of material factual issues, makes no reference to the foreseeability of the park manager's intentional conduct at issue. Instead, Mr. Rickard describes in his testimony his "preferred" design for safety systems in general. Specifically, he opines to his preference for safety systems that "have three layers," that Plaintiffs ostensibly contrast with the Hawk's safety system which the park manager was able to bypass "by a single act, namely, a jumper wire." Yet Mr. Rickard concedes that even with this preferred design, "someone with an electrical background and the desire to jump this out ... could do that and get the ride to run." [W]e disagree that this testimony even impliedly addresses the foreseeability of the intentional bypassing of the ride's safety system sufficient to raise a genuine issue of material fact, whether by an individual as technically knowledgeable as Mr. Martin or otherwise.

Furthermore, as Defendants correctly assert, the record reveals no reason to suspect that the park manager would intentionally bypass the safety system on the Hawk ride....

Similarly, Plaintiffs have failed to offer any proof to suggest that the Hawk deviated in any significant way from industry standards as to amusement park ride safety systems, either at the time the ride was sold to Raceway or at present. Moreover, as Defendants have shown, the Hawk complied not only with industry practice, but also applicable federal and state standards governing amusement ride safety systems. The Consumer Product Safety Commission ("CPSC"), who investigated and reported on this incident, did not order a recall for this ride; did not issue any public warnings; and did not take any action against Defendants as a result of the incident. In other words, despite knowing that there was a fatality on a device the CPSC is charged with safely maintaining, the CPSC allowed and continues to allow all such Zamperla rides to remain in operation today. We find the fact that major amusement parks, including Six Flags, at present continue to operate rides with identical or similar safety systems as the Hawk to be particularly revealing in terms of Defendants' culpability under the prudent manufacturer test. Furthermore, Defendants have shown that the Hawk was designed and manufactured in full compliance with the American Society of Testing Materials ("A.S.T.M.") standards applicable to Defendants when the ride was manufactured in 1997. Therefore, we are convinced of the ride's compliance with all applicable federal and state statutes, administrative

regulations and industry standards, and further of Plaintiff's lack of proof to establish Defendants' liability under the prudent manufacturer test, or to otherwise effectively demonstrate a defective/unreasonably unsafe design that caused the death....
[Affirmed.]

NOTES AND QUESTIONS

1. Why do you think the plaintiffs dismissed Mr. Martin as an individual defendant? If a jury heard a civil case against him, do you think negligence *per se* would apply, based on his conviction? Would plaintiffs have a strong argument for punitive damages against him?
2. One challenge, referenced in an earlier chapter, is ride operators getting distracted or bored and failing to attend to their obligations. In the summer of 2010, that happened at Extreme World in Wisconsin Dells, Wisconsin, on a ride called Terminal Velocity.

   Terminal Velocity was a free-fall ride, where patrons were lifted in a basket up over 100 feet and then dropped—attached to nothing—into a net below. (Videos are readily findable on YouTube.) Twelve-year-old Teagan Marti, visiting from Florida, went up in the basket, and the ride operator, Charles A. Carnell, released her without confirming that the net had been lifted into place (and the ride had no mechanical or other safeguard to prevent the release without the net in place). Carnell told investigators that he "blanked out" and had not seen the "all-clear" signal before releasing Marti. Marti, who was estimated to be going roughly 40 miles per hour upon landing, was very seriously injured but survived, in part because her father, a physician, was there to help. *See Mother Sees 'Miracle' in Girl Surviving 100-Foot Fall From Ride, as Worker Faces Charges*, FoxNews.com, Aug. 20, 2010.

   Carnell was charged with first-degree-reckless injury under Wisconsin law. He ultimately reached a plea agreement where he was found guilty of felony second-degree reckless injury and received no time in prison. Marti's family settled a lawsuit with Extreme World and, as of the time of Carnell's guilty plea, had a pending lawsuit against the manufacturer, a German company called Montic. Andy Steinke, *Thrill ride operator accepts plea deal*, Wisconsin State

JOURNAL, Mar. 2, 2011. As far as I can tell, that lawsuit has not publicly been addressed again, but I assume it has been settled. Marti, who is able to walk again, received a service dog in 2013, somehow as a gift from Charlie Sheen.

Do you think those facts reasonably support a criminal charge against Carnell? If you were bringing a civil case based on these facts, how would you articulate a claim for design defect as to the manufacturer of the ride?

The coverage notes that Ms. Marti's parents were with her and witnessed her fall—indeed, her father likely saved her life. Consider what intentional tort claims, if any, her parents might have. Consider also what negligence claims they might have.

Seven years earlier, when a very similar ride made by the same manufacturer was being shown at a trade conference, approximately the same thing happened: a 13-year-old boy was released without the net in place and fell. He, too, survived. How, if at all, would that fact affect your views of any civil or criminal claims against any of the people or entities involved?

3. There have been relatively few criminal charges against individuals or companies related to ride accidents.

   When a patron on a Himalaya ride at the Travis County Rodeo was ejected and died, the ride owner and ride inspector companies, as well as individuals, were charged, alleging that required modifications to the lap bar cotter pins were not made and that resulted in the death. Both pleaded guilty to various charges, insisting that doing so was strictly for practical reasons. *Man Sentenced for Girl's Death on Carnival Ride*, HOUSTON CHRONICLE A40, December 8, 2000; Tom Powell, *Gill Pleads to Misdemeanor*, AMUSEMENT BUSINESS 32, May 21, 2001.

   We earlier learned about the "Scooters" ride in Ohio, where eight-year-old Greyson Yoe was electrocuted. The electrician, ride owner, and inspectors were all prosecuted. A jury convicted the electrician of reckless homicide and involuntary manslaughter, and a judge sentenced him to thirty days in jail. The ride owner pleaded guilty to attempted involuntary manslaughter and was sentenced to six months in jail. Prosecutors charged the inspectors with various forms of homicide, and they eventually pleaded no contest to dereliction of duty. The various defendants did not contest most of the key facts alleged by the prosecution but focused instead on whether those facts supported criminal liability. The inspectors, for their part, argued that they were insufficiently trained to test the grounding and that the form was flawed by including the items in the first place, but conceded that they had not attempted to test the grounding of the ride.

4. Do you think criminal charges were appropriate in all of those cases?

Index